03

ART BY **HIROKI MIYASHITA**
STORY BY **TAKESHI NATSUHARA**

CONTENTS

CHAPTER 9:
THE KING OF DANIEMI

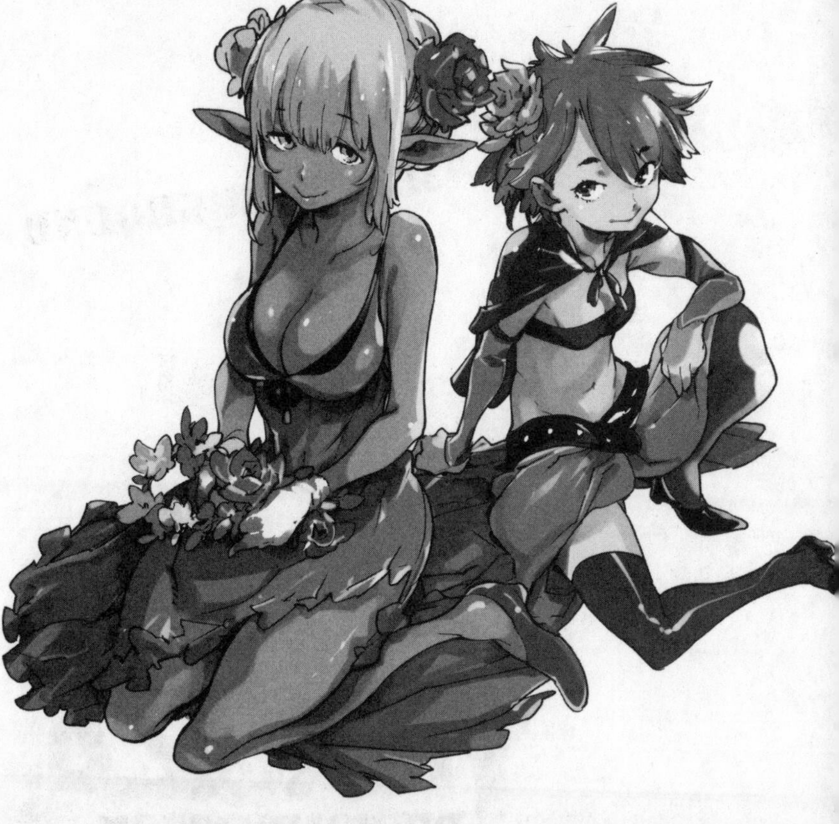

YAKUZA
REINCARNATION

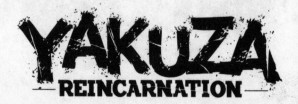

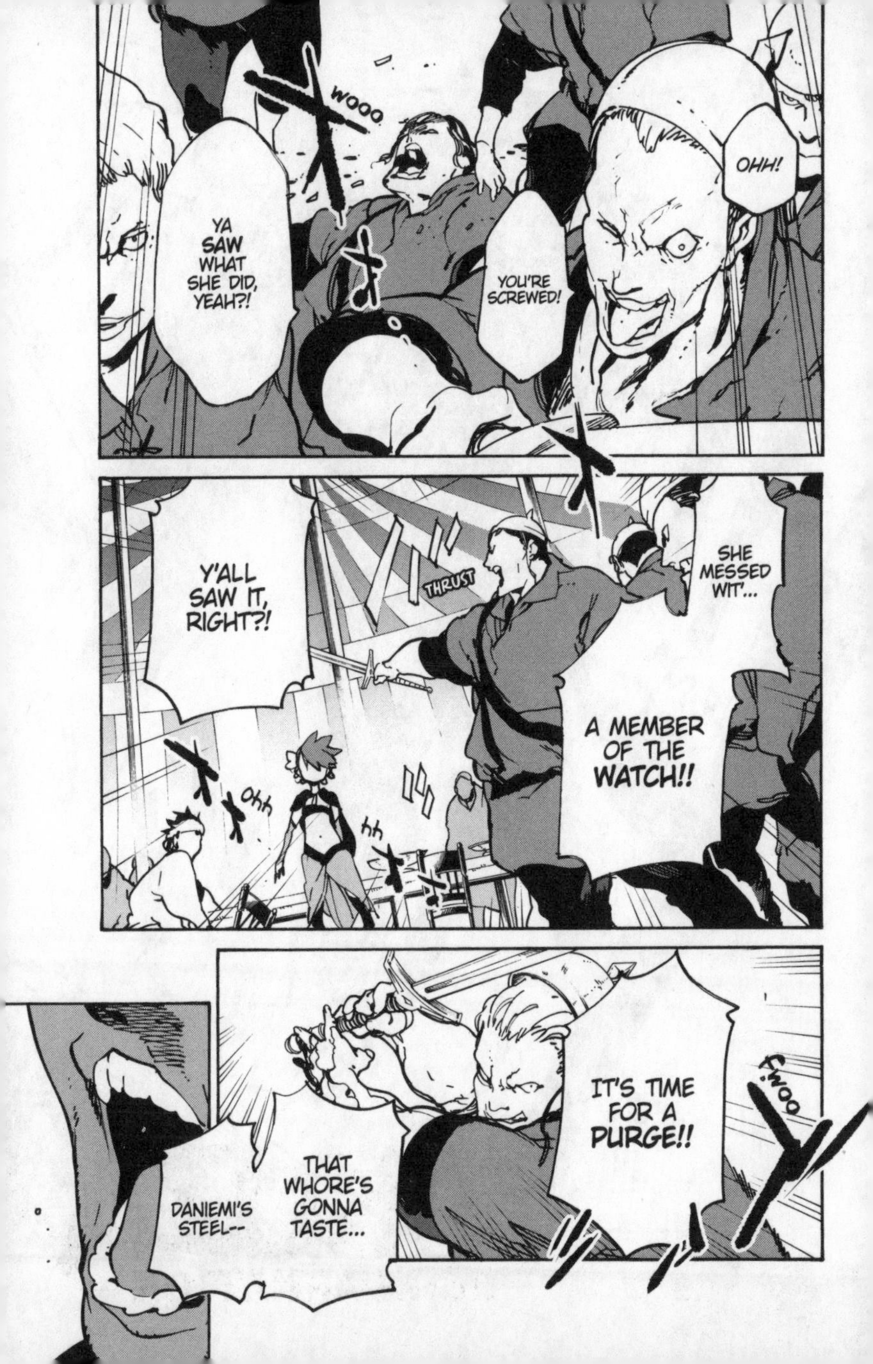
OHH!
YOU'RE SCREWED!
WOOO
YA SAW WHAT SHE DID, YEAH?!
SHE MESSED WIT'...
A MEMBER OF THE WATCH!!
THRUST
Y'ALL SAW IT, RIGHT?!
ohh
hh
FWOO
IT'S TIME FOR A PURGE!!
THAT WHORE'S GONNA TASTE...
DANIEMI'S STEEL--

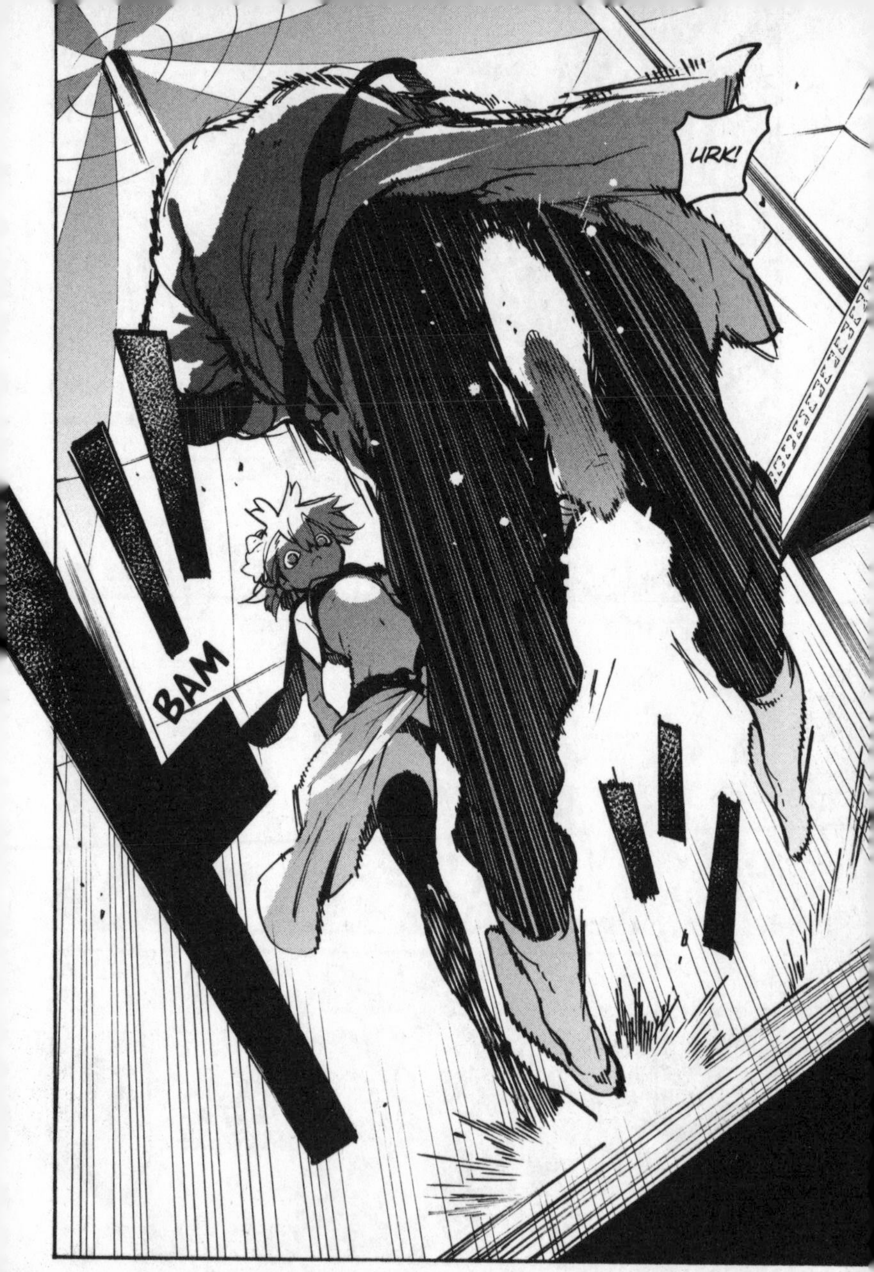
URK!
BAM

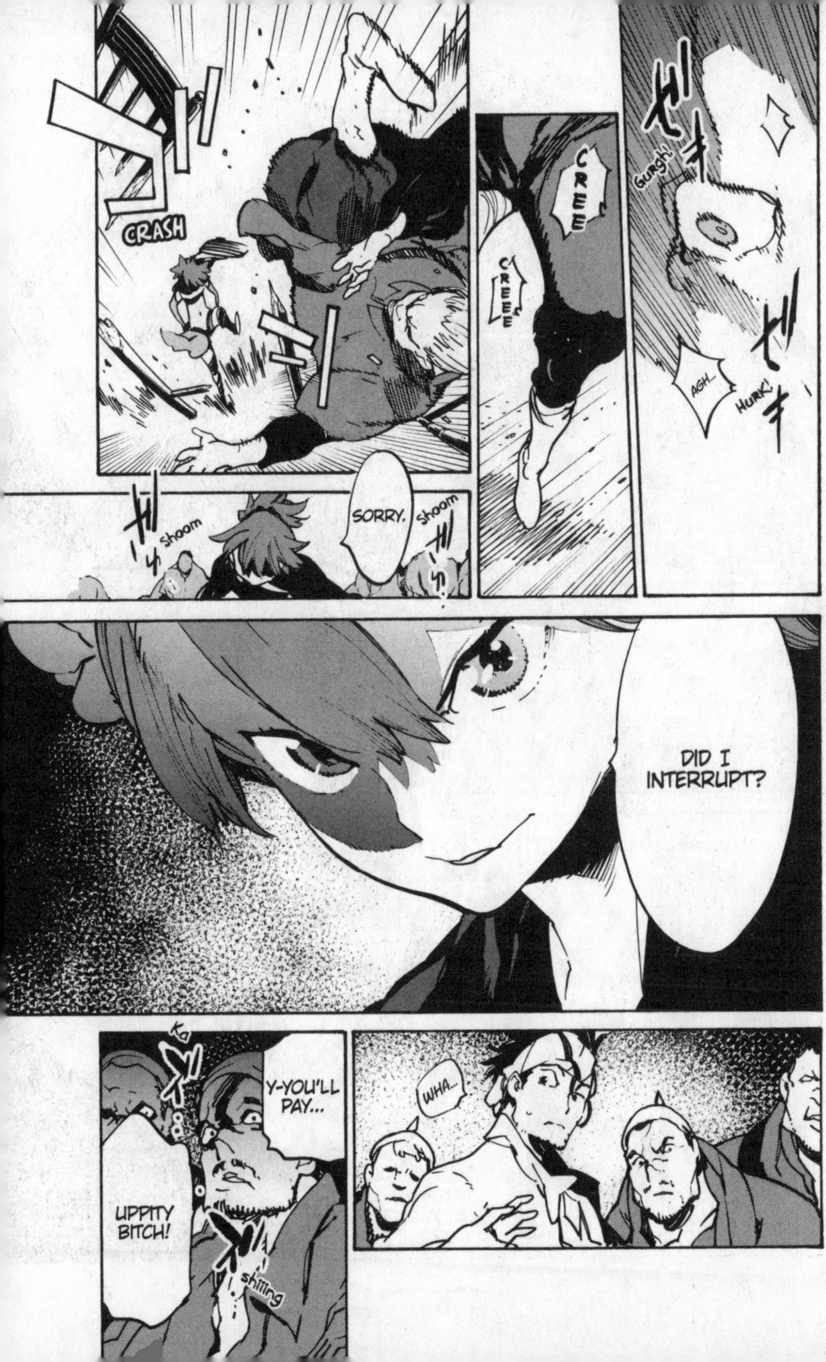

Gurgh
Agh...
Hurk!
CREEE
CREEEE
CRASH
shoom
SORRY.
shoom
DID I INTERRUPT?
WHA...
Ka
Y-YOU'LL PAY...
UPPITY BITCH!
shiiing

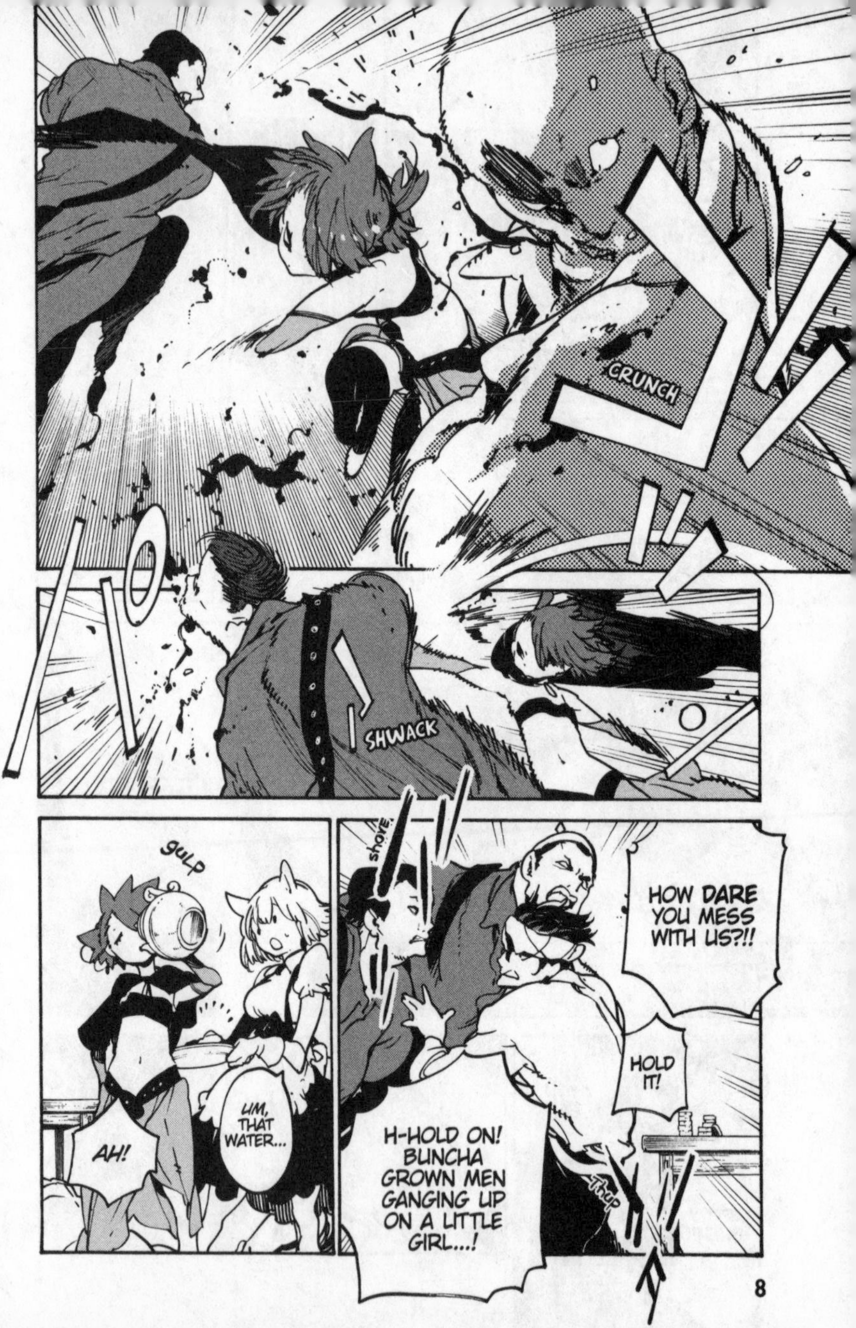
CRUNCH
SHWACK
HOW DARE YOU MESS WITH US?!!
shove
HOLD IT!
Thup
H-HOLD ON! BUNCHA GROWN MEN GANGING UP ON A LITTLE GIRL...!
gulp
UM, THAT WATER...
AH!

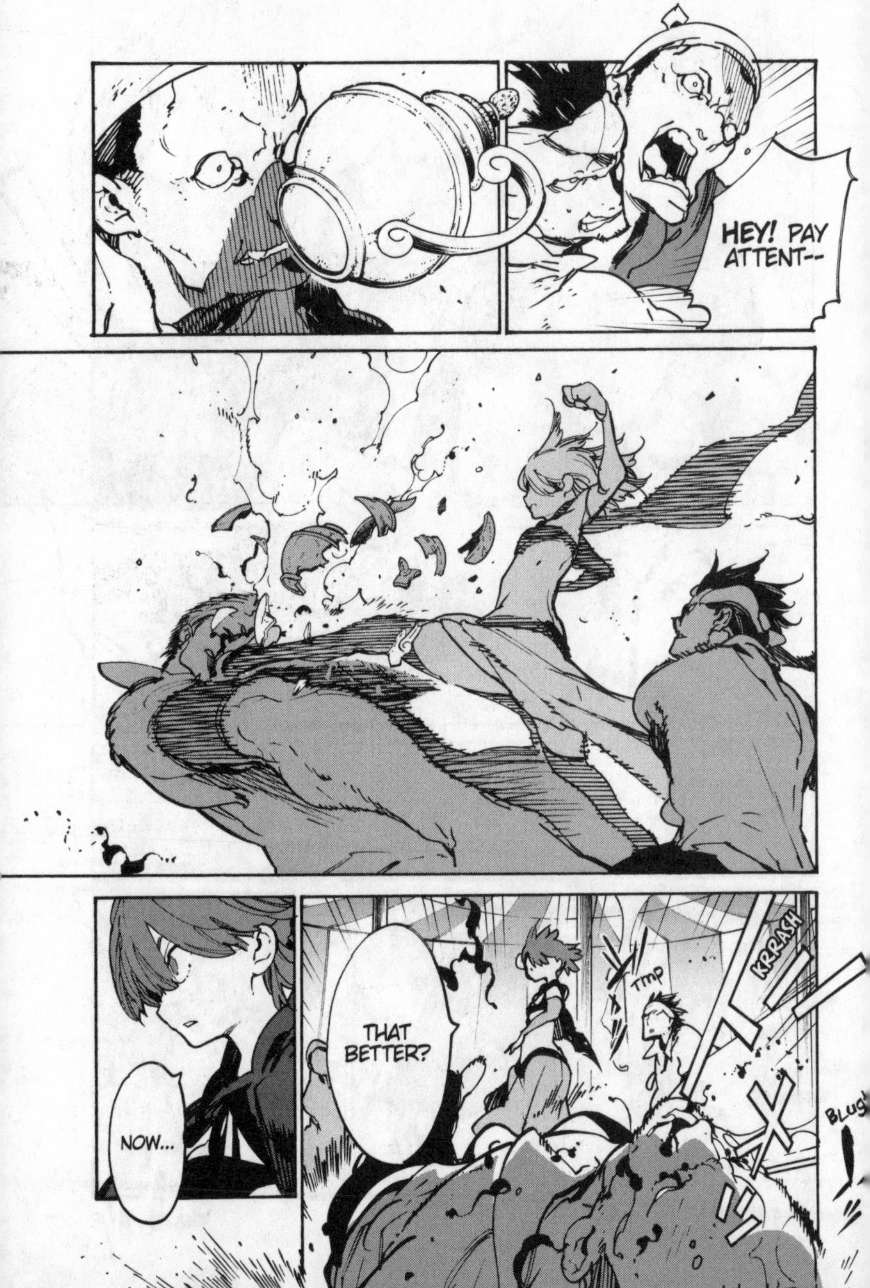
HEY! PAY ATTENT--
KRRASH
Tmp
THAT BETTER?
Blug
NOW...

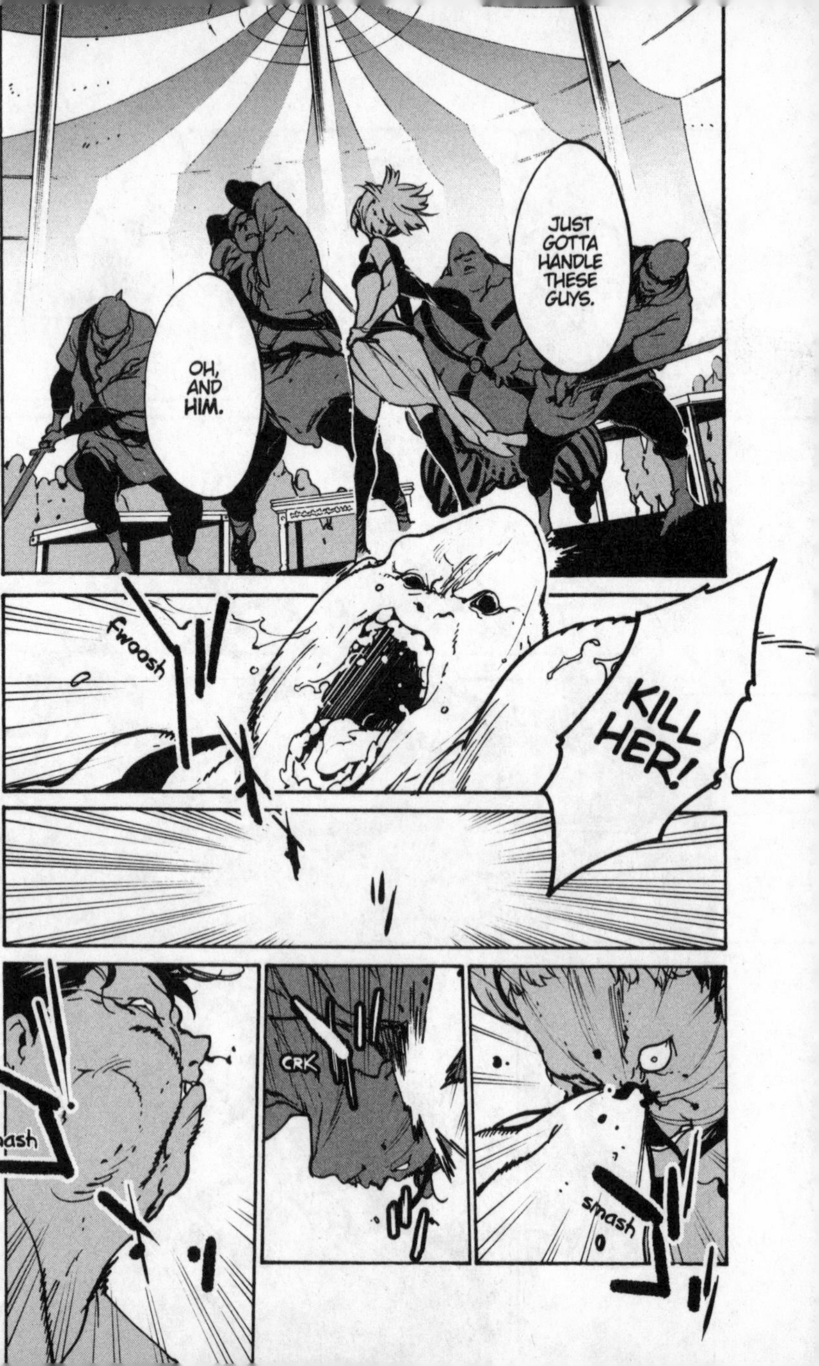
JUST GOTTA HANDLE THESE GUYS.
OH, AND HIM.
KILL HER!
fwoosh
smash
CRK
smash

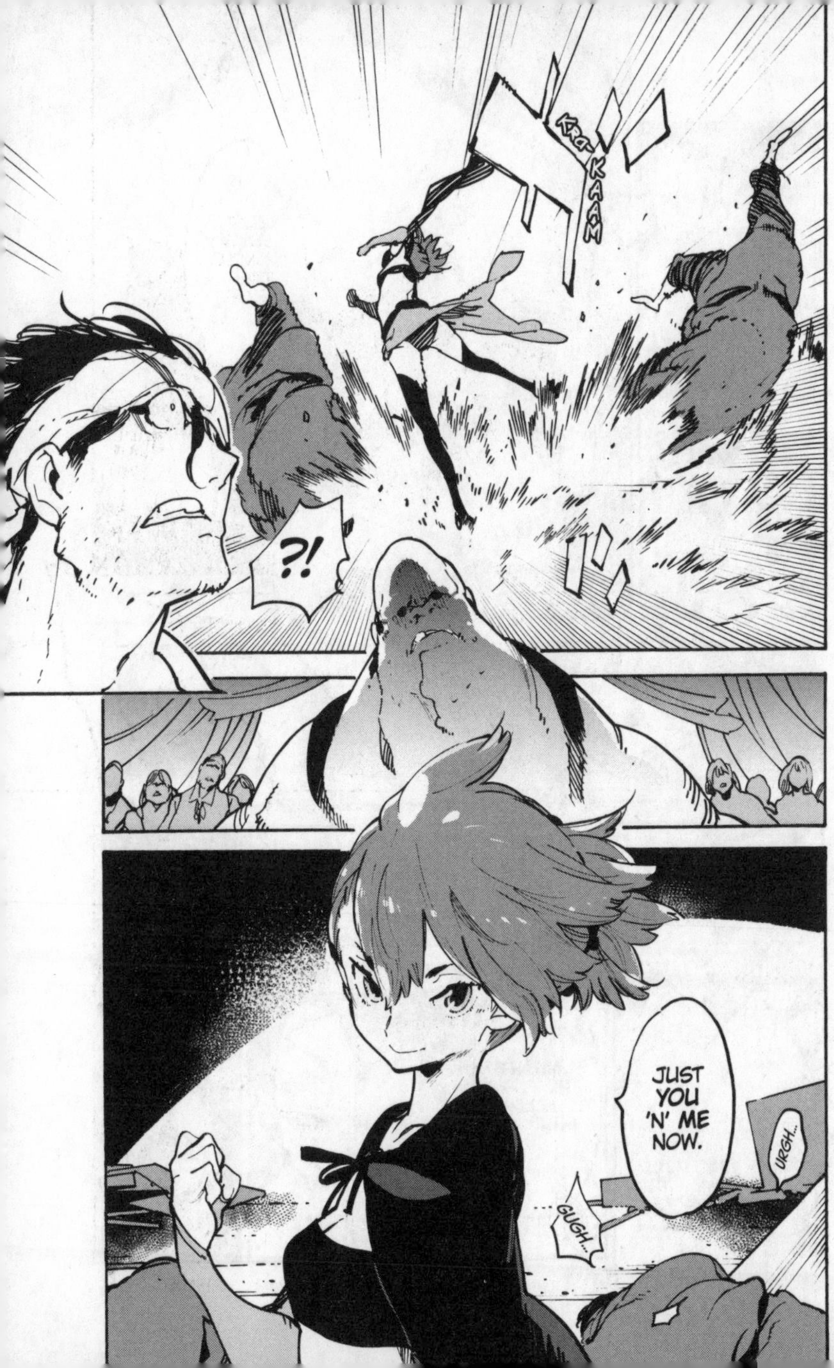
KRA-KAAM
?!
URGH...
JUST YOU 'N' ME NOW.
GUGH...

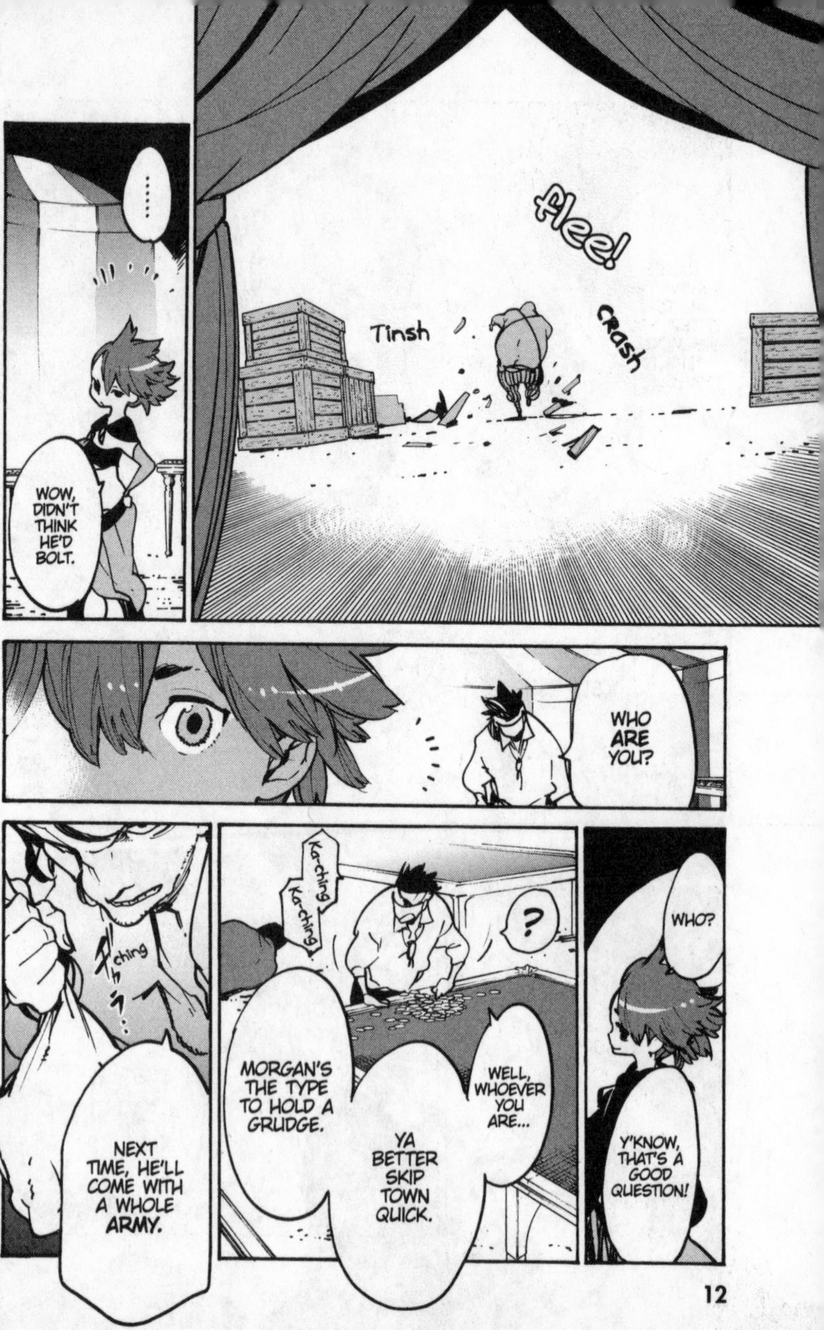
flee!
CRASH
Tinsh
......
WOW, DIDN'T THINK HE'D BOLT.
WHO ARE YOU?
WHO?
Y'KNOW, THAT'S A GOOD QUESTION!
Ka-ching
Ka-ching
?
WELL, WHOEVER YOU ARE...
YA BETTER SKIP TOWN QUICK.
MORGAN'S THE TYPE TO HOLD A GRUDGE.
ching
NEXT TIME, HE'LL COME WITH A WHOLE ARMY.

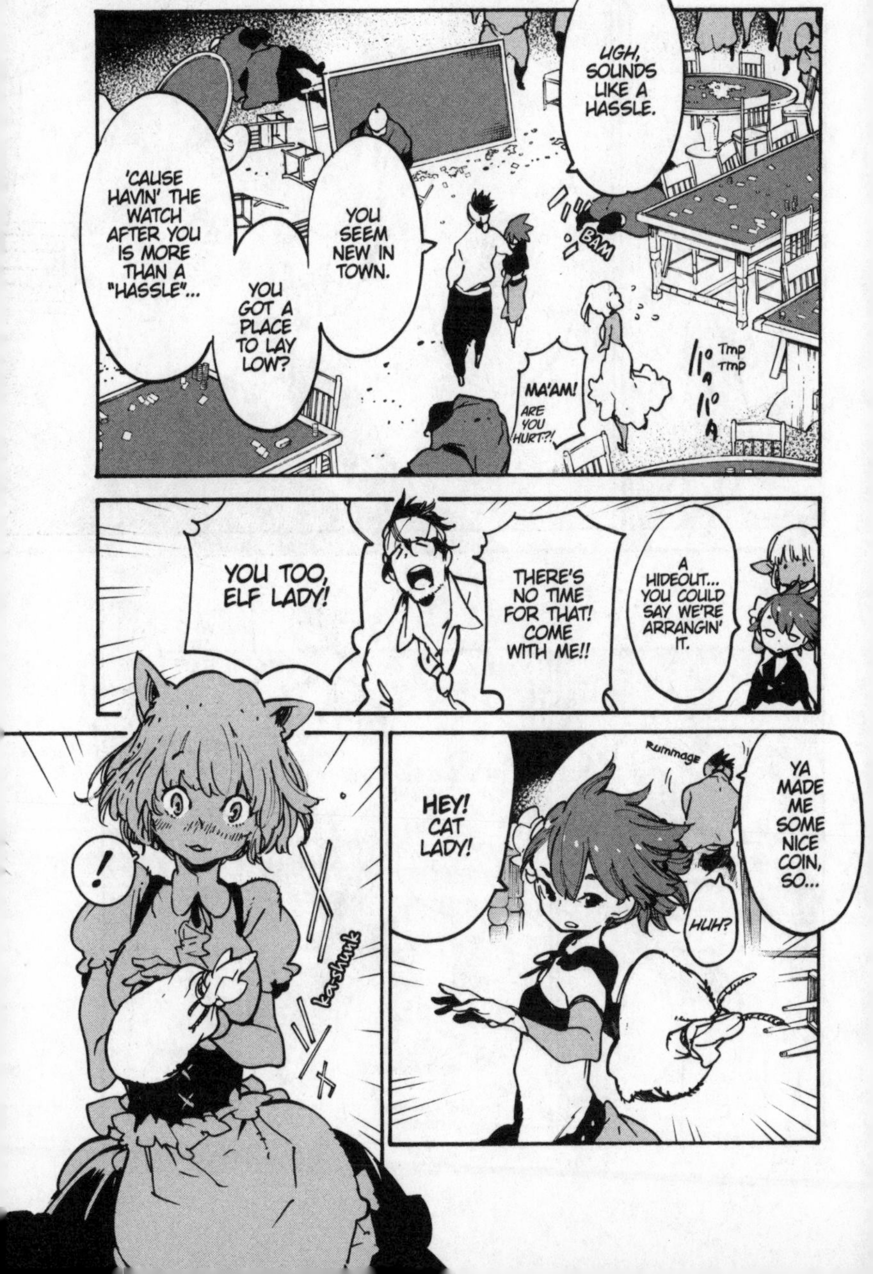
UGH, SOUNDS LIKE A HASSLE.
BAM
'CAUSE HAVIN' THE WATCH AFTER YOU IS MORE THAN A "HASSLE"...
YOU SEEM NEW IN TOWN.
YOU GOT A PLACE TO LAY LOW?
Tmp Tmp
MA'AM!
ARE YOU HURT?!
A HIDEOUT... YOU COULD SAY WE'RE ARRANGIN' IT.
THERE'S NO TIME FOR THAT! COME WITH ME!!
YOU TOO, ELF LADY!
YA MADE ME SOME NICE COIN, SO...
Rummage
HUH?
HEY! CAT LADY!
!
ka-shunk

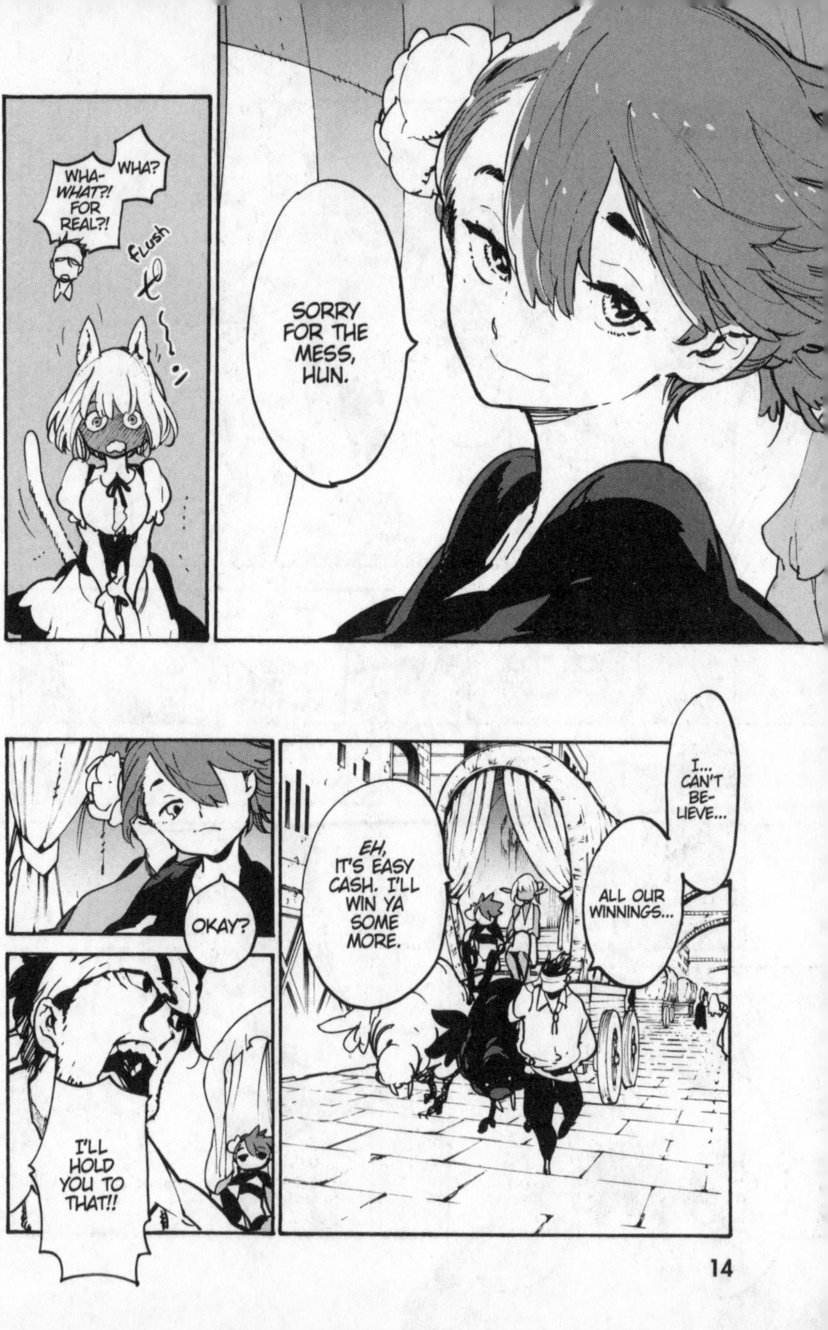
SORRY FOR THE MESS, HUN.
WHA?
WHA- WHAT?! FOR REAL?!
flush
I... CAN'T BE- LIEVE...
ALL OUR WINNINGS...
EH, IT'S EASY CASH. I'LL WIN YA SOME MORE.
OKAY?
I'LL HOLD YOU TO THAT!!

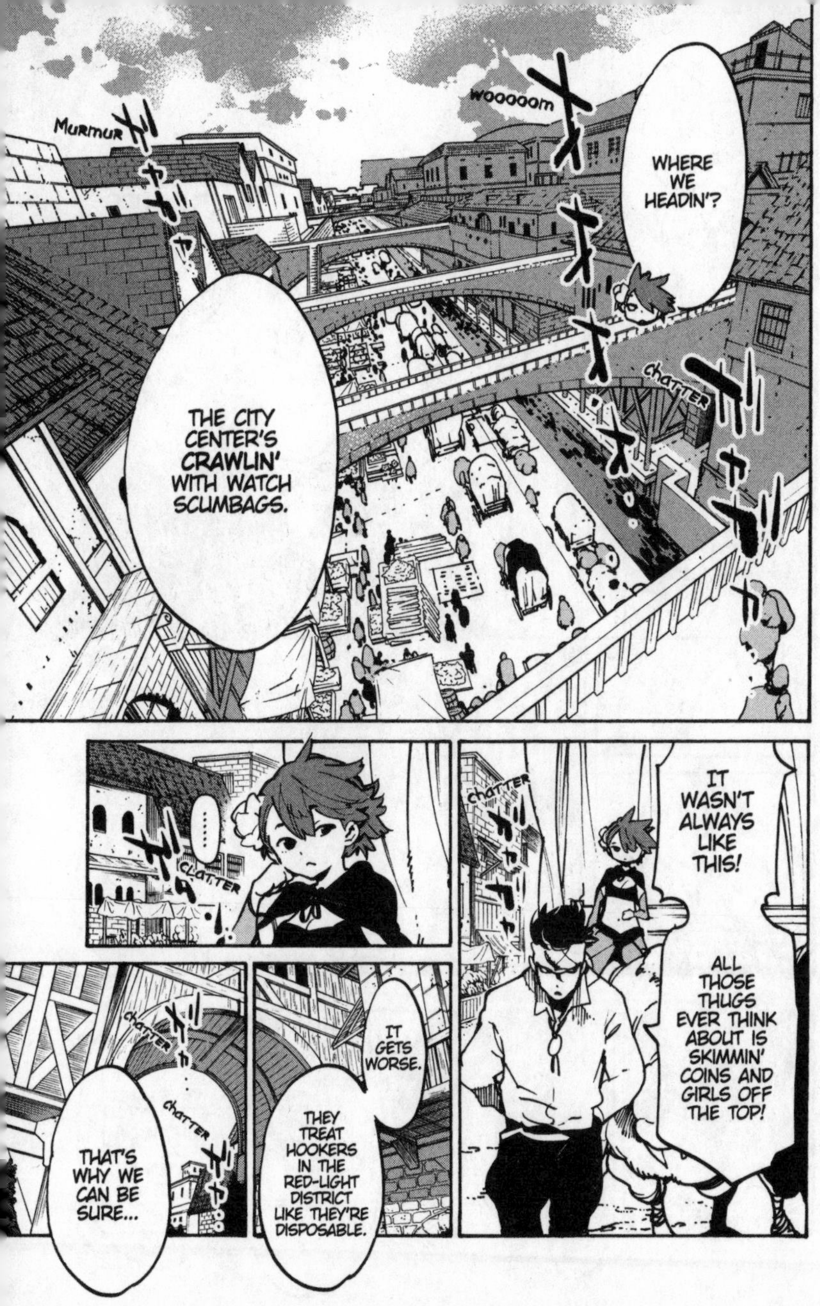
WHERE WE HEADIN'?
wooooom
THE CITY CENTER'S CRAWLIN' WITH WATCH SCUMBAGS.
Murmur
chatter
IT WASN'T ALWAYS LIKE THIS!
ALL THOSE THUGS EVER THINK ABOUT IS SKIMMIN' COINS AND GIRLS OFF THE TOP!
chatter
......
clatter
IT GETS WORSE.
THEY TREAT HOOKERS IN THE RED-LIGHT DISTRICT LIKE THEY'RE DISPOSABLE.
chatter
chatter
THAT'S WHY WE CAN BE SURE...

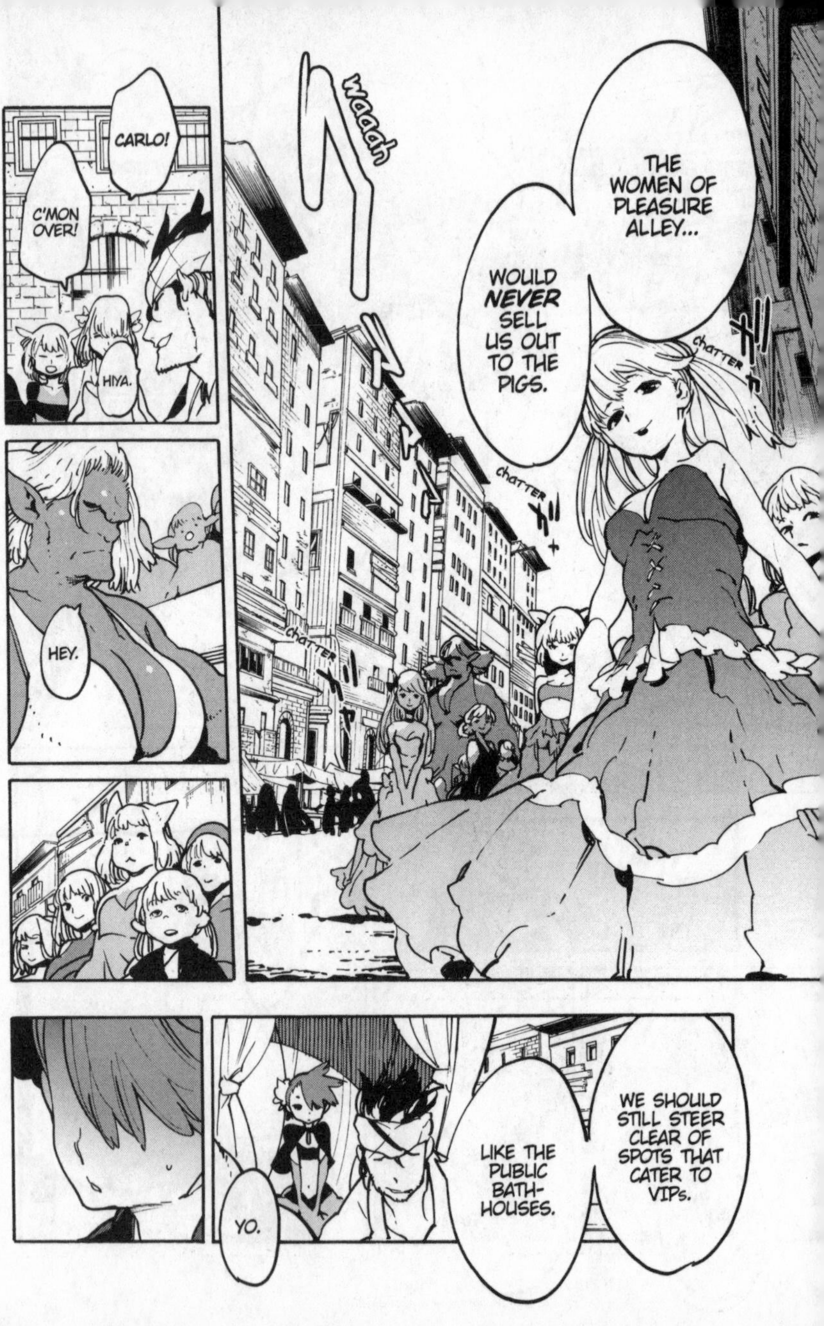
THE WOMEN OF PLEASURE ALLEY...
WOULD NEVER SELL US OUT TO THE PIGS.
waaah
chatter
chatter
chatter
CARLO!
C'MON OVER!
HIYA.
HEY.
WE SHOULD STILL STEER CLEAR OF SPOTS THAT CATER TO VIPs.
LIKE THE PUBLIC BATH-HOUSES.
YO.

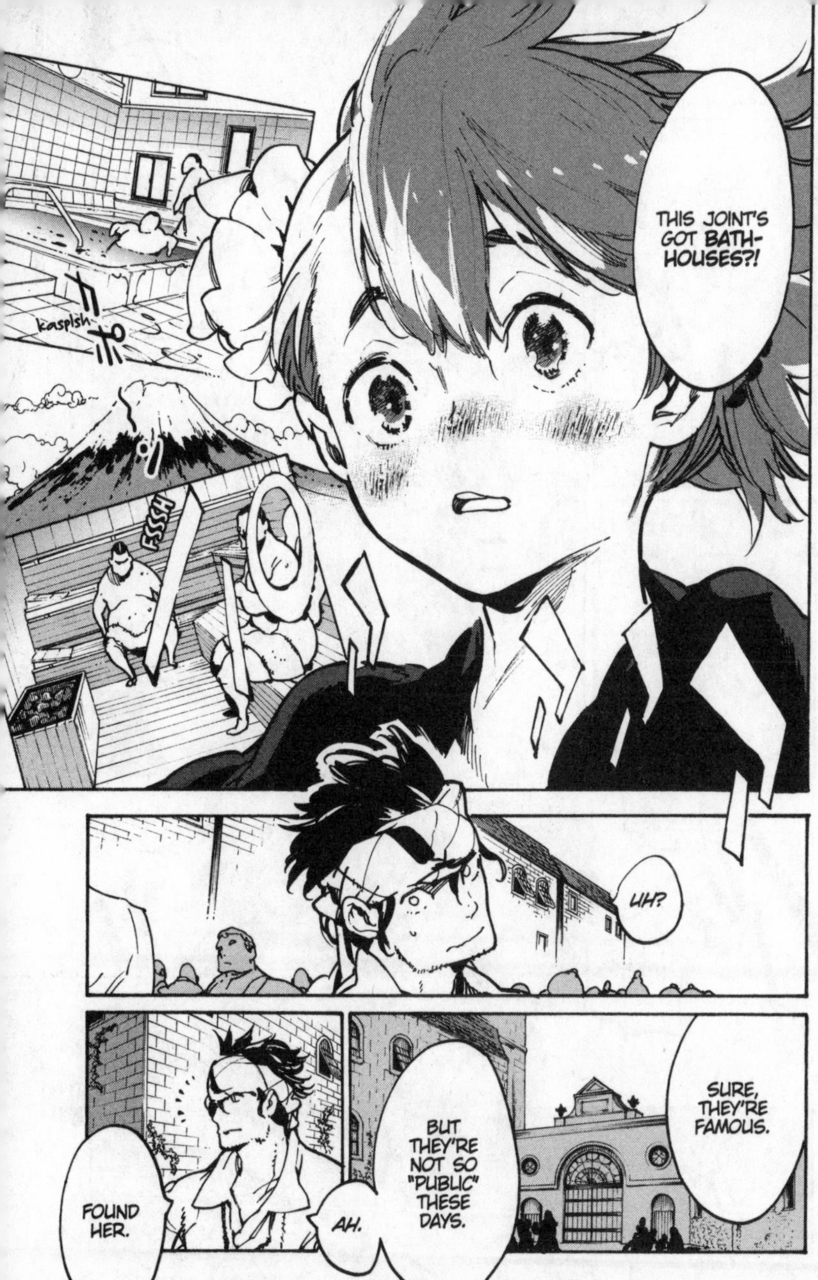
THIS JOINT'S GOT BATH-HOUSES?!
kasplsh
FSSSH
UH?
SURE, THEY'RE FAMOUS.
BUT THEY'RE NOT SO "PUBLIC" THESE DAYS.
AH.
FOUND HER.

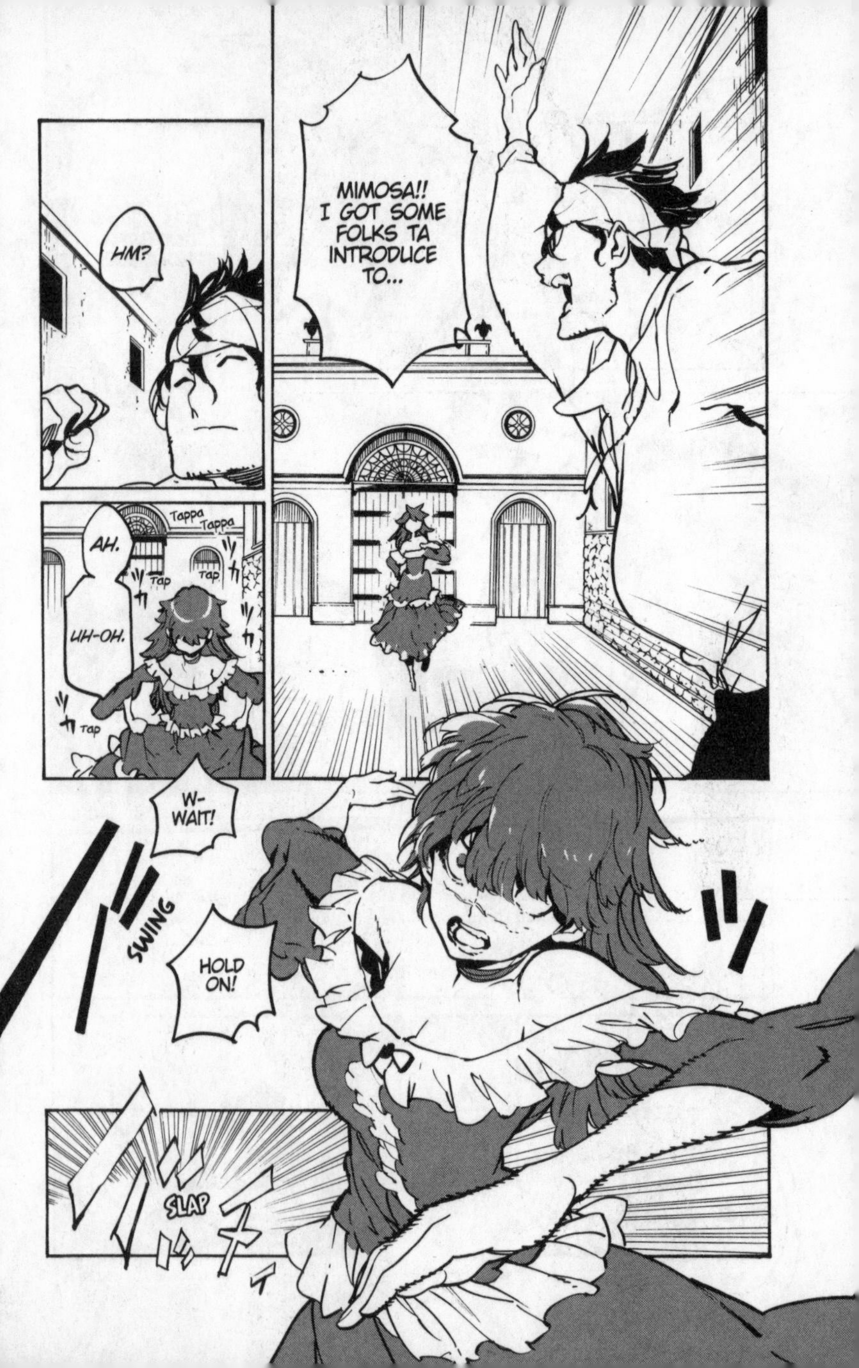
MIMOSA!! I GOT SOME FOLKS TA INTRODUCE TO...
HM?
AH.
Tappa Tappa
Tap
Tap
UH-OH.
Tap
W-WAIT!
SWING
HOLD ON!
SLAP

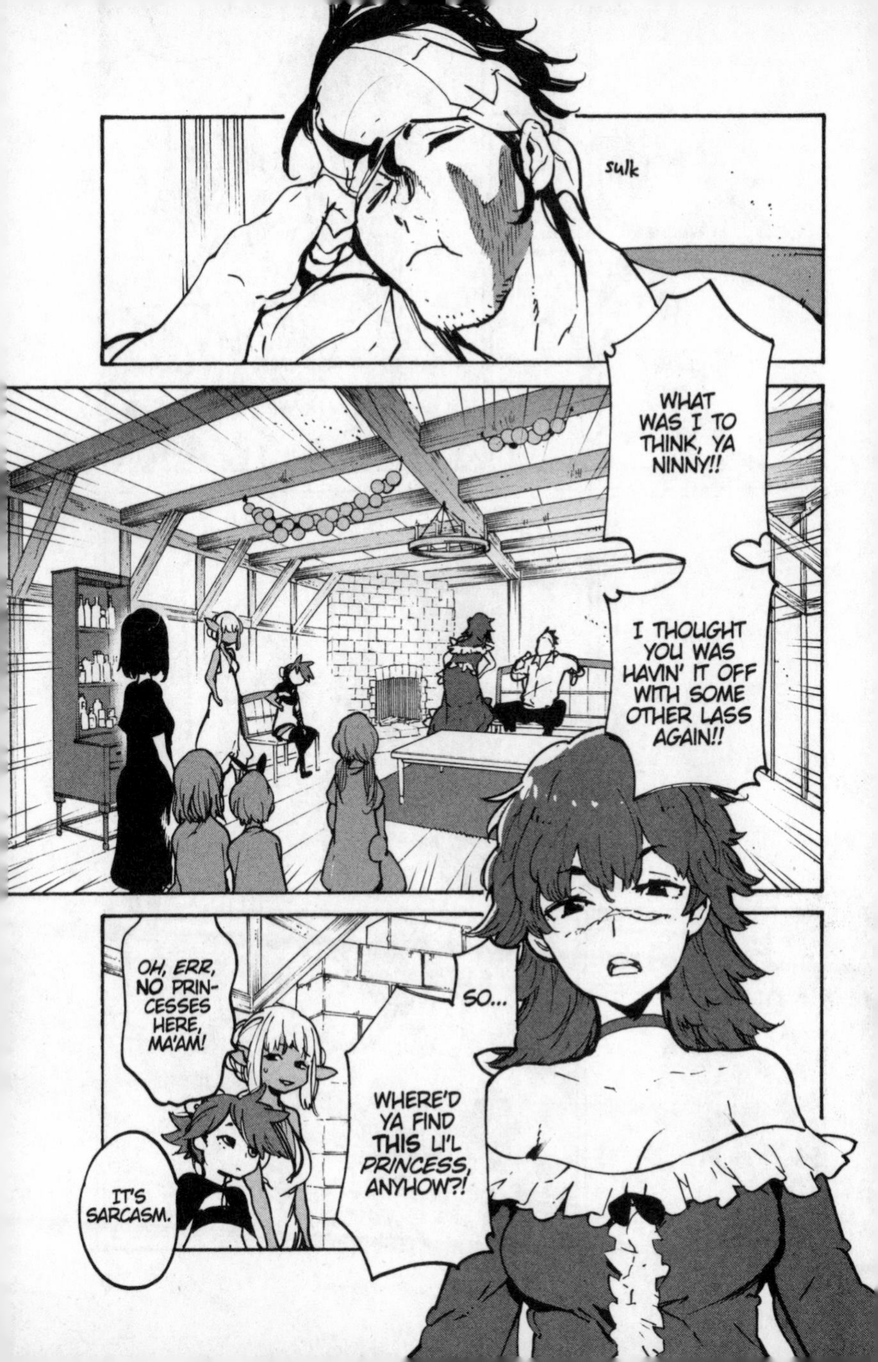
sulk
WHAT WAS I TO THINK, YA NINNY!!
I THOUGHT YOU WAS HAVIN' IT OFF WITH SOME OTHER LASS AGAIN!!
SO...
WHERE'D YA FIND THIS LI'L PRINCESS, ANYHOW?!
OH, ERR, NO PRIN-CESSES HERE, MA'AM!
IT'S SARCASM.

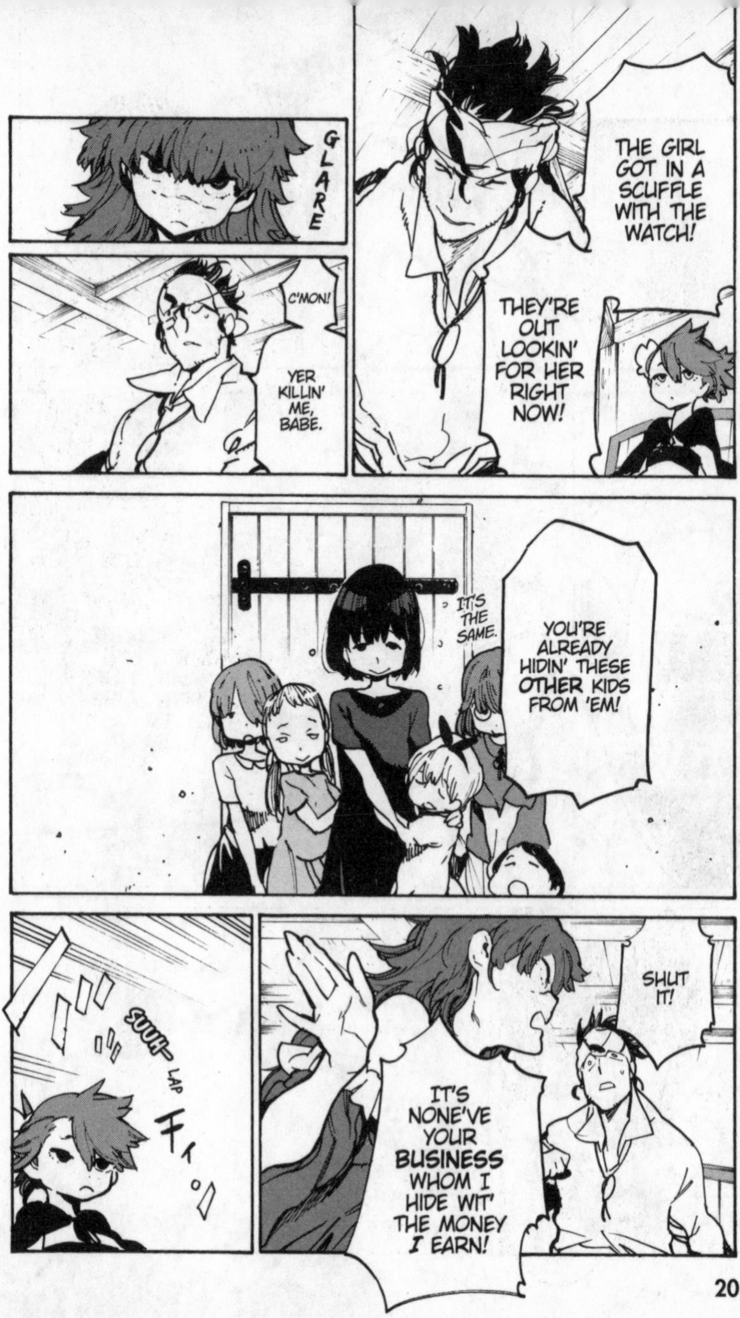
THE GIRL GOT IN A SCUFFLE WITH THE WATCH!
THEY'RE OUT LOOKIN' FOR HER RIGHT NOW!
GLARE
C'MON!
YER KILLIN' ME, BABE.
YOU'RE ALREADY HIDIN' THESE OTHER KIDS FROM 'EM!
IT'S THE SAME.
SHUT IT!
IT'S NONE'VE YOUR BUSINESS WHOM I HIDE WIT' THE MONEY I EARN!
SUUH-LAP
チィ

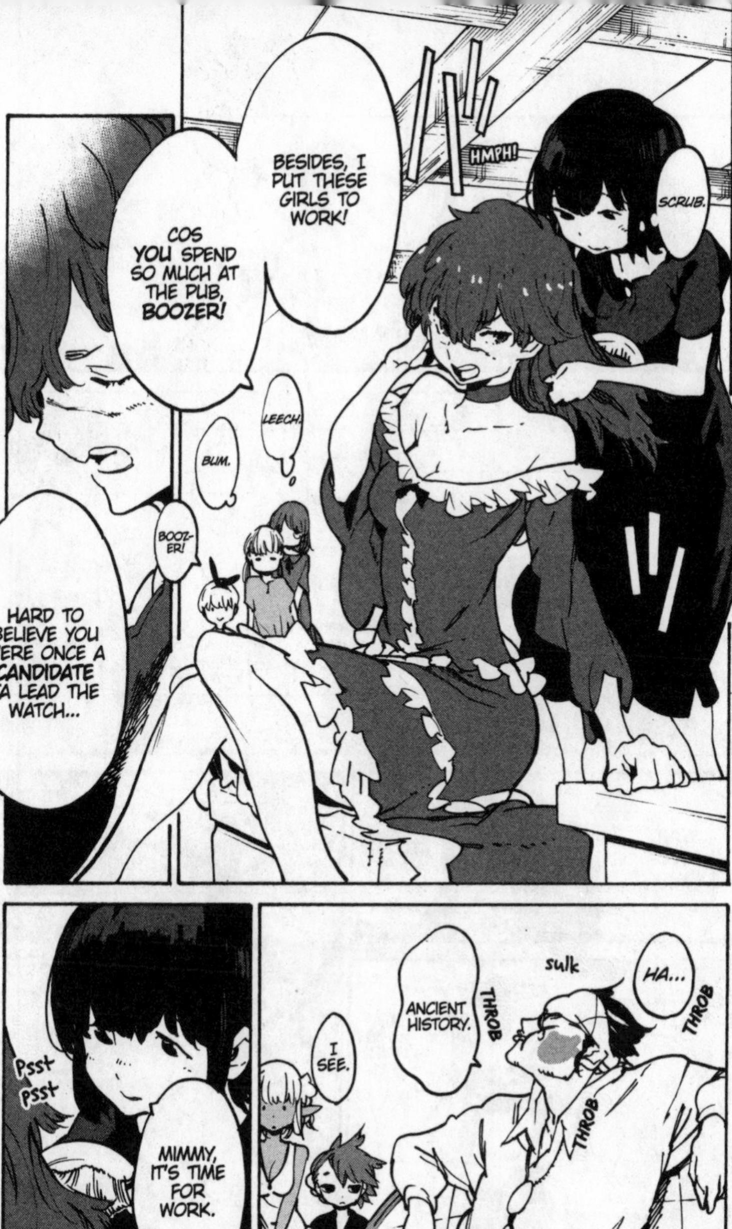
HMPH!
SCRUB.
BESIDES, I PUT THESE GIRLS TO WORK!
COS YOU SPEND SO MUCH AT THE PUB, BOOZER!
LEECH!
BUM.
BOOZ-ER!
HARD TO BELIEVE YOU WERE ONCE A CANDIDATE TA LEAD THE WATCH...
HA...
sulk
THROB
ANCIENT HISTORY.
THROB
THROB
I SEE.
Psst
psst
MIMMY, IT'S TIME FOR WORK.

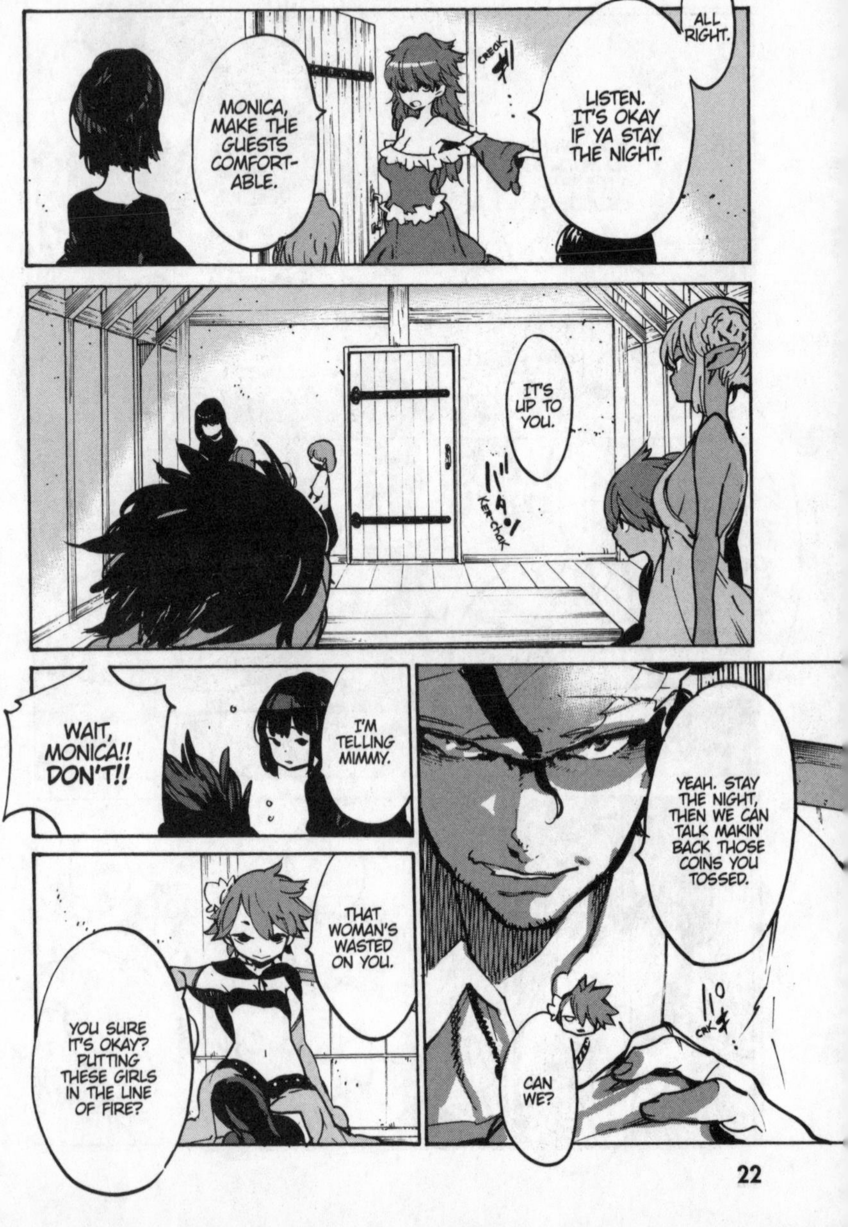
ALL RIGHT.
CREAK
LISTEN. IT'S OKAY IF YA STAY THE NIGHT.
MONICA, MAKE THE GUESTS COMFORT-ABLE.
IT'S UP TO YOU.
KER-CHAK
YEAH. STAY THE NIGHT, THEN WE CAN TALK MAKIN' BACK THOSE COINS YOU TOSSED.
CRK
CAN WE?
I'M TELLING MIMMY.
WAIT, MONICA!! DON'T!!
THAT WOMAN'S WASTED ON YOU.
YOU SURE IT'S OKAY? PUTTING THESE GIRLS IN THE LINE OF FIRE?

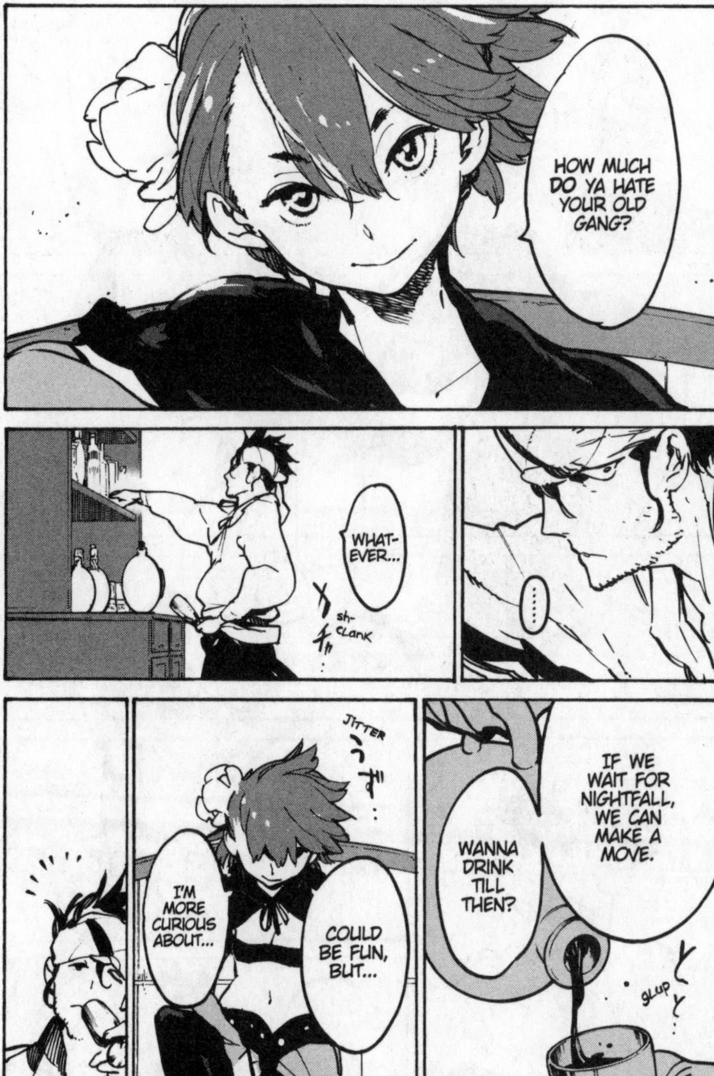

HOW MUCH DO YA HATE YOUR OLD GANG?
......
WHAT-EVER...
sh-CLANK
IF WE WAIT FOR NIGHTFALL, WE CAN MAKE A MOVE.
WANNA DRINK TILL THEN?
glup
JITTER
COULD BE FUN, BUT...
I'M MORE CURIOUS ABOUT...

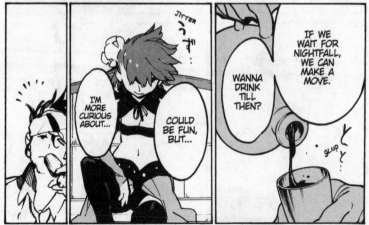

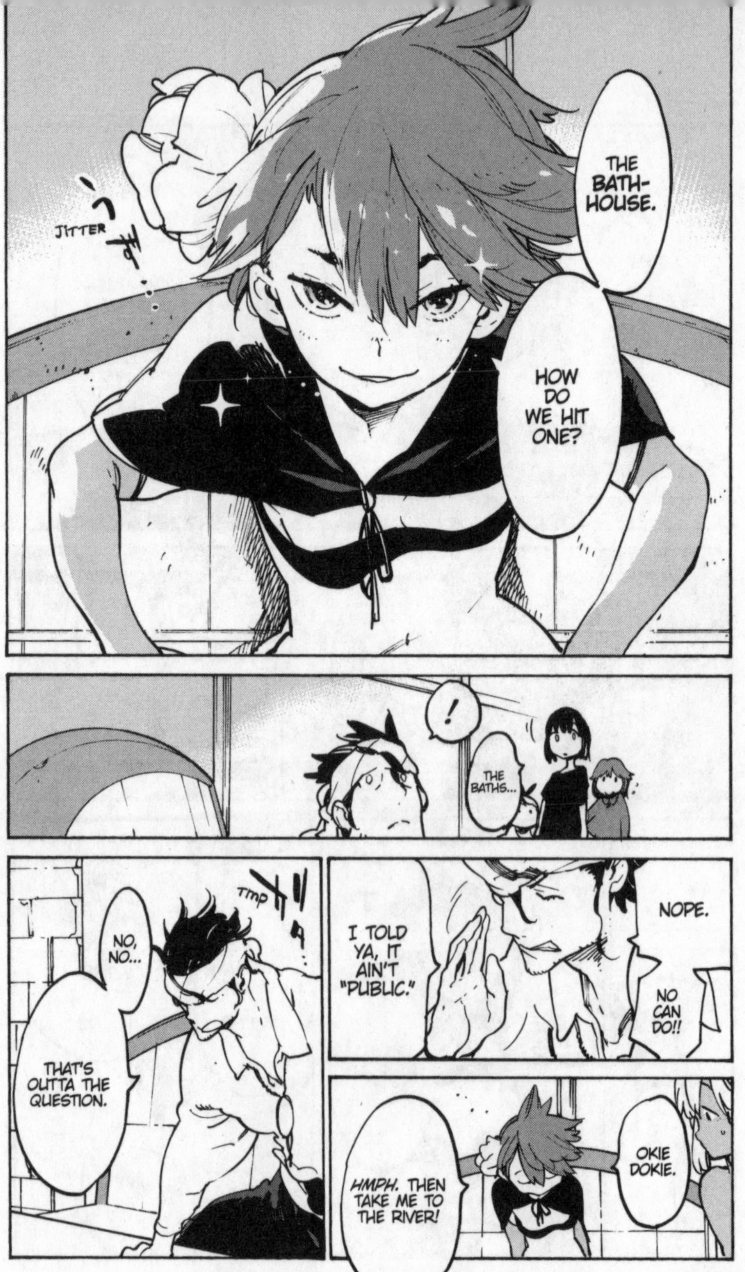
THE BATH-HOUSE.
HOW DO WE HIT ONE?
JITTER
!
THE BATHS...
NOPE.
I TOLD YA, IT AIN'T "PUBLIC."
NO CAN DO!!
OKIE DOKIE.
HMPH. THEN TAKE ME TO THE RIVER!
TMP
NO, NO...
THAT'S OUTTA THE QUESTION.

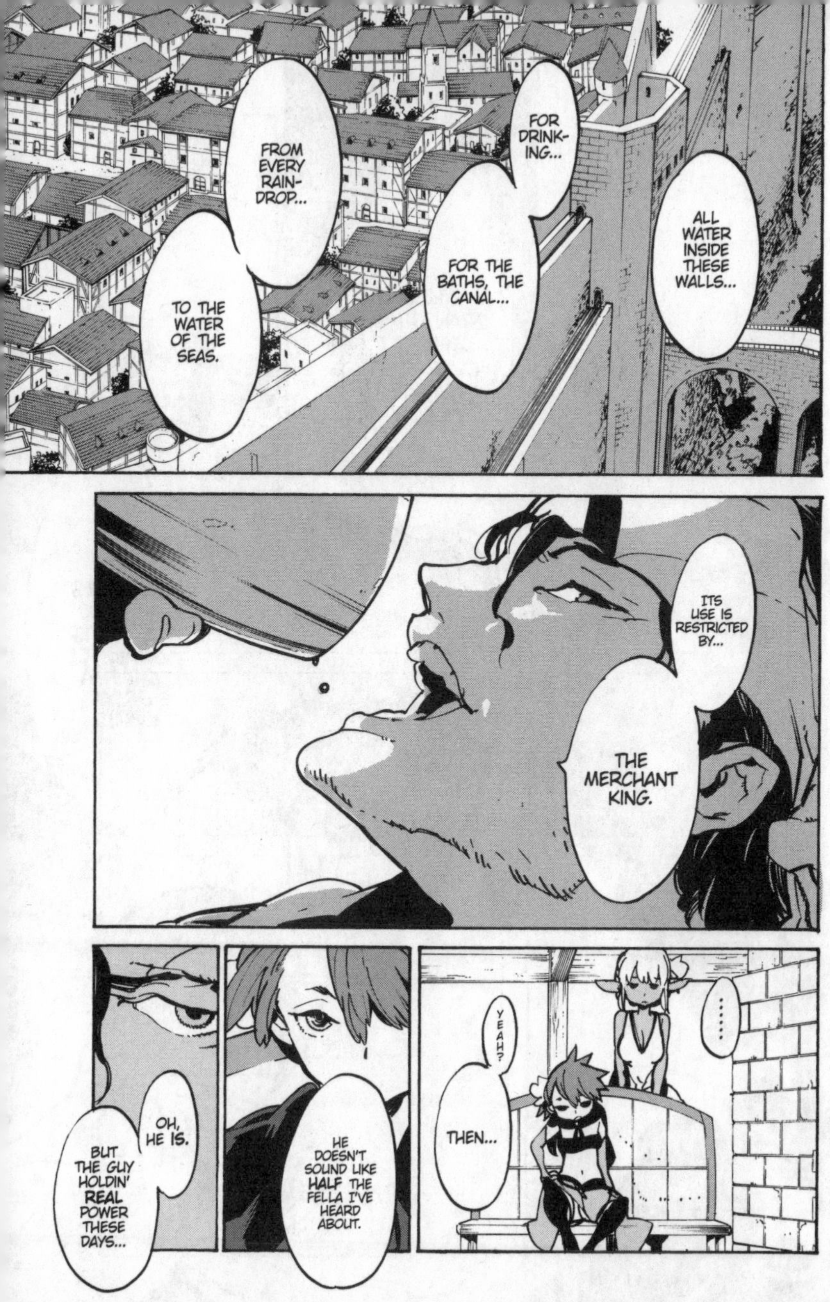
ALL WATER INSIDE THESE WALLS...
FOR DRINKING...
FOR THE BATHS, THE CANAL...
FROM EVERY RAINDROP...
TO THE WATER OF THE SEAS.
ITS USE IS RESTRICTED BY...
THE MERCHANT KING.
......
YEAH?
THEN...
HE DOESN'T SOUND LIKE HALF THE FELLA I'VE HEARD ABOUT.
OH, HE IS.
BUT THE GUY HOLDIN' REAL POWER THESE DAYS...

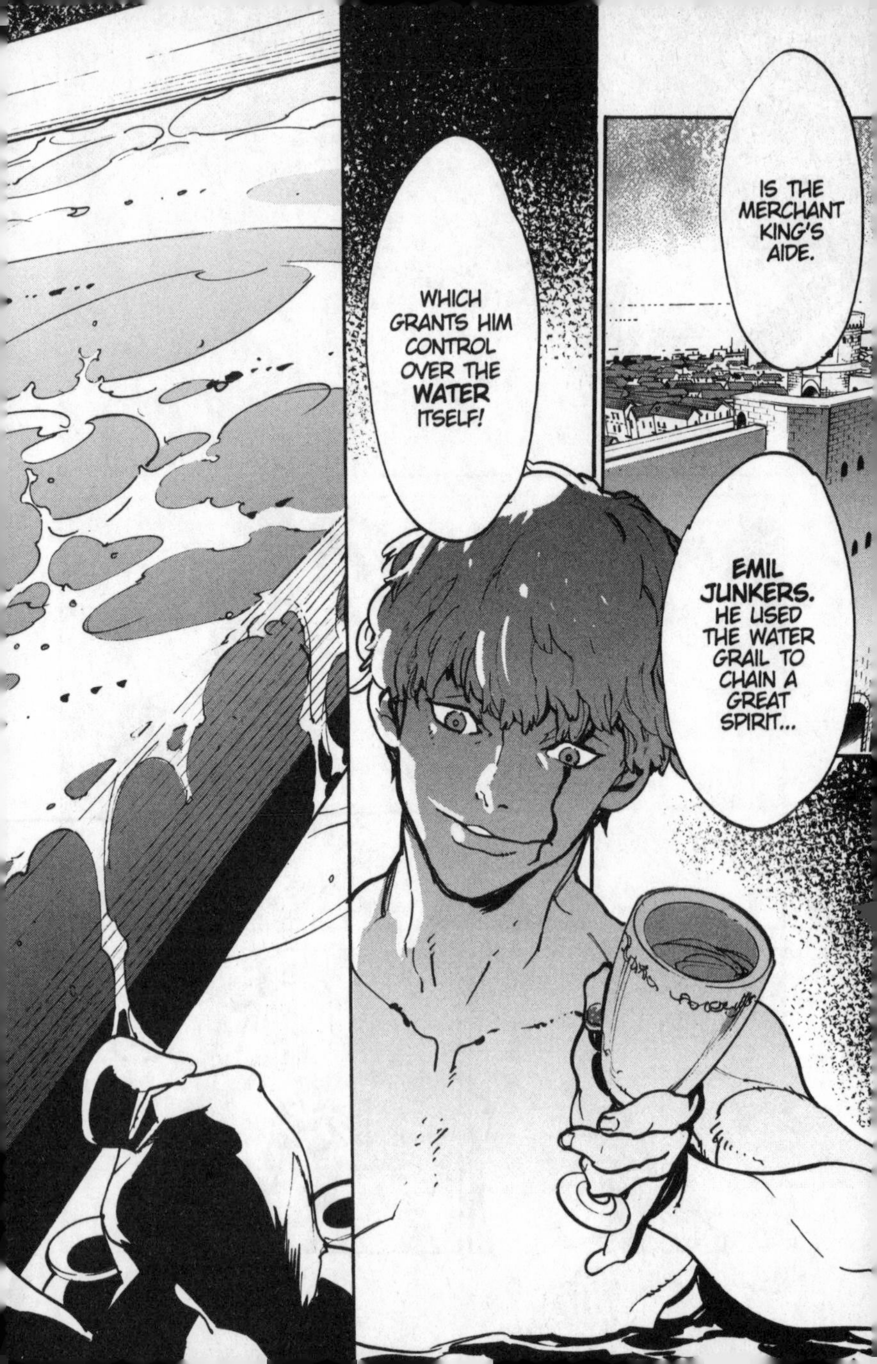
IS THE MERCHANT KING'S AIDE.
EMIL JUNKERS. HE USED THE WATER GRAIL TO CHAIN A GREAT SPIRIT...
WHICH GRANTS HIM CONTROL OVER THE WATER ITSELF!

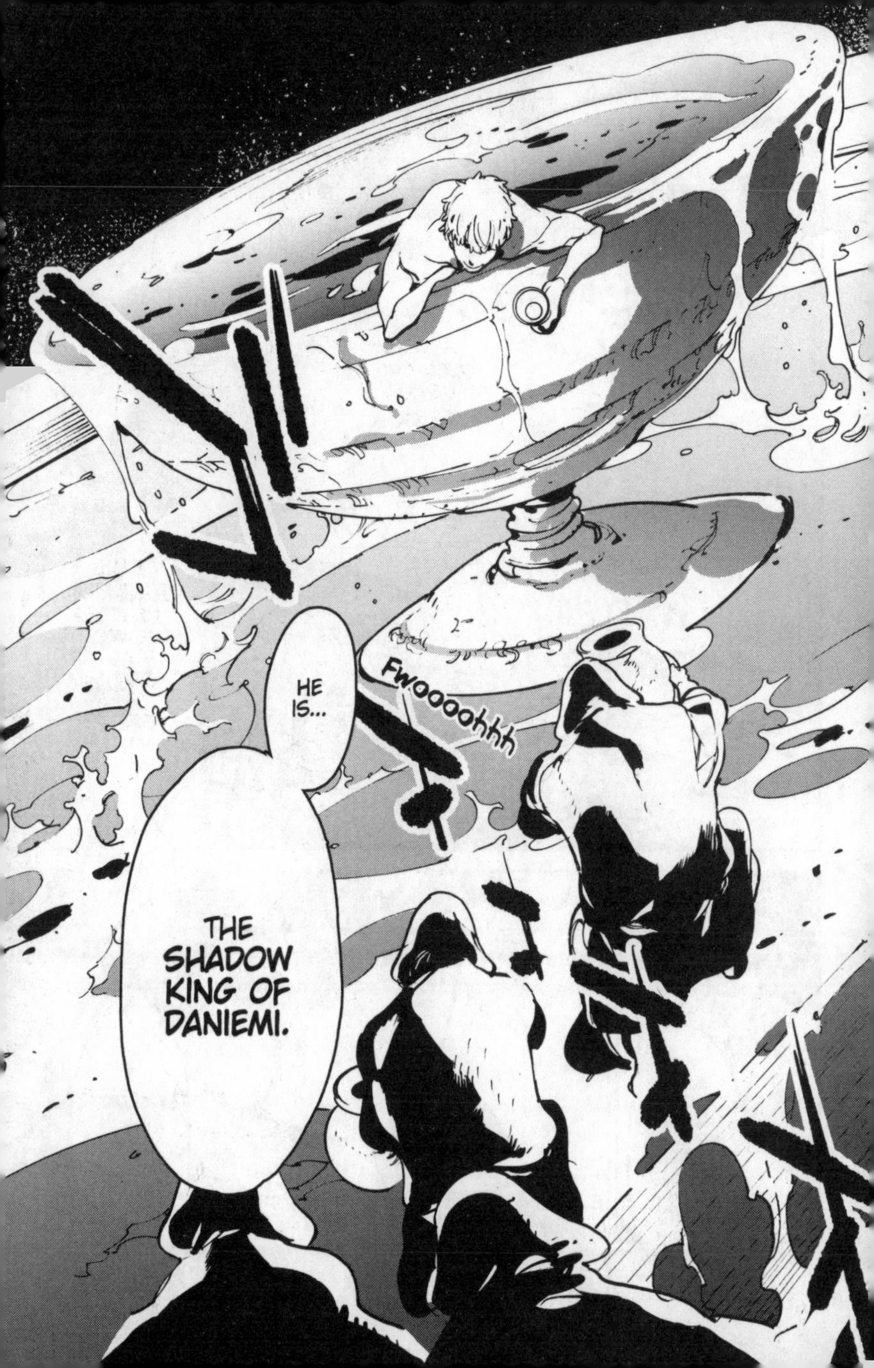
Fwooooohhh
HE IS...
THE SHADOW KING OF DANIEMI.

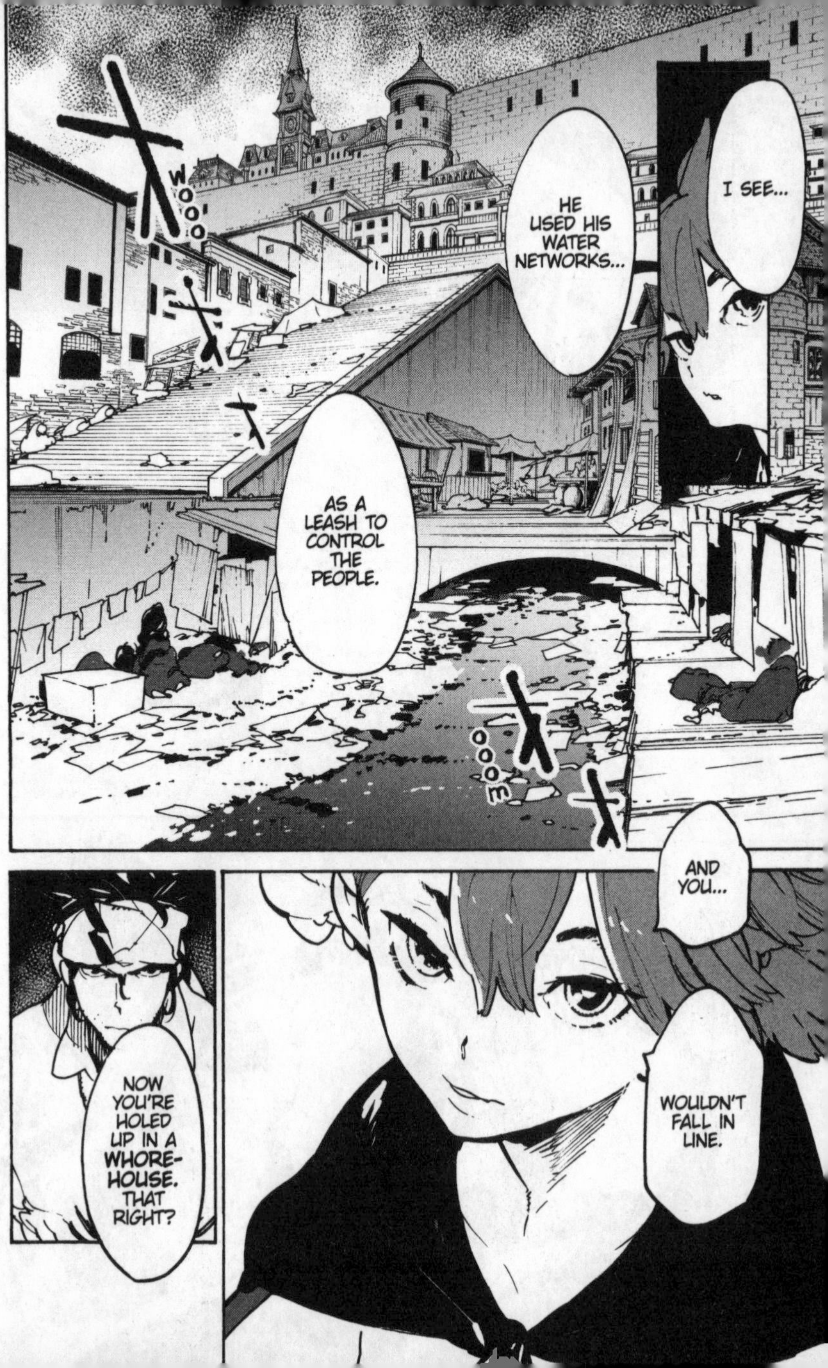
I SEE...
HE USED HIS WATER NETWORKS...
AS A LEASH TO CONTROL THE PEOPLE.
WOOOO
OOOM
AND YOU...
WOULDN'T FALL IN LINE.
NOW YOU'RE HOLED UP IN A WHORE-HOUSE. THAT RIGHT?

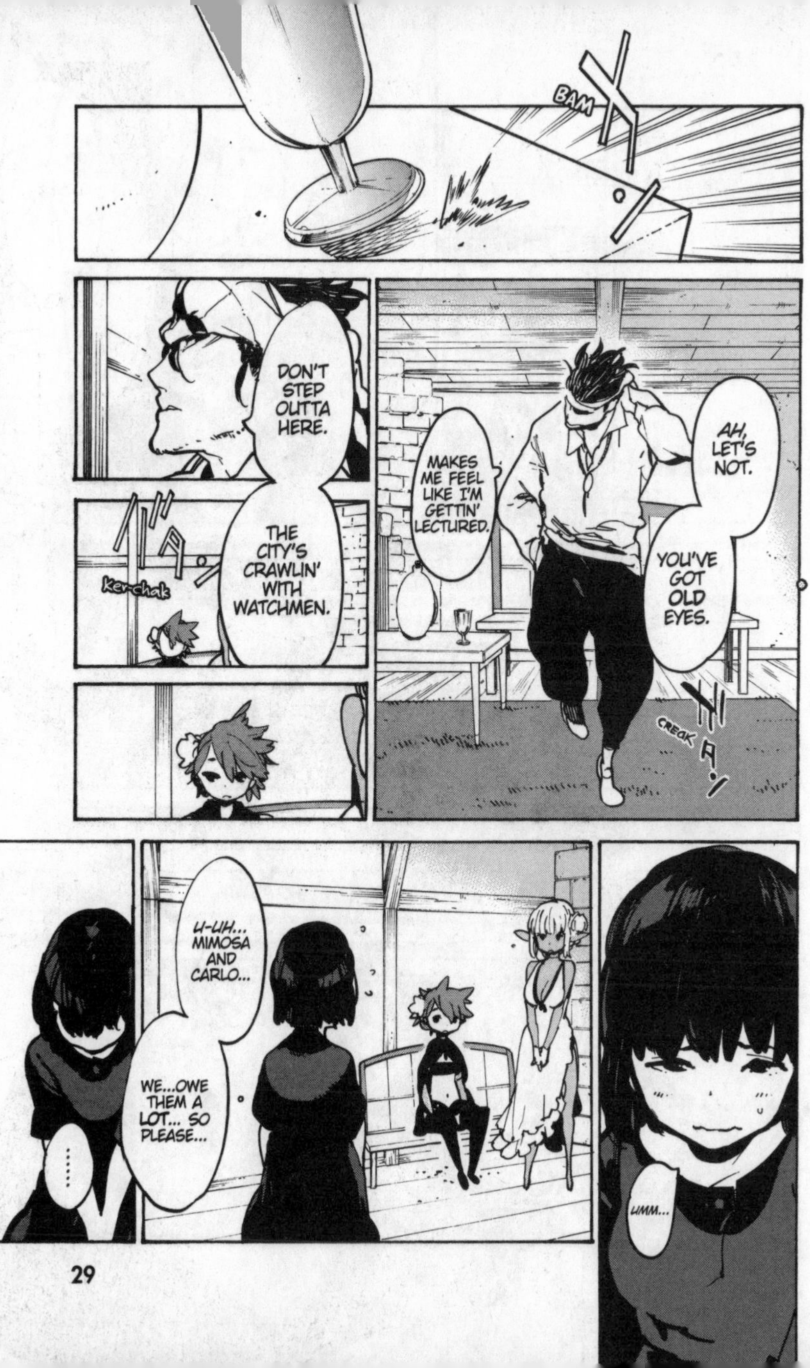
BAM
AH, LET'S NOT.
YOU'VE GOT OLD EYES.
MAKES ME FEEL LIKE I'M GETTIN' LECTURED.
CREAK
DON'T STEP OUTTA HERE.
THE CITY'S CRAWLIN' WITH WATCHMEN.
Ker-chak
UMM...
U-UH... MIMOSA AND CARLO...
WE...OWE THEM A LOT... SO PLEASE...
......

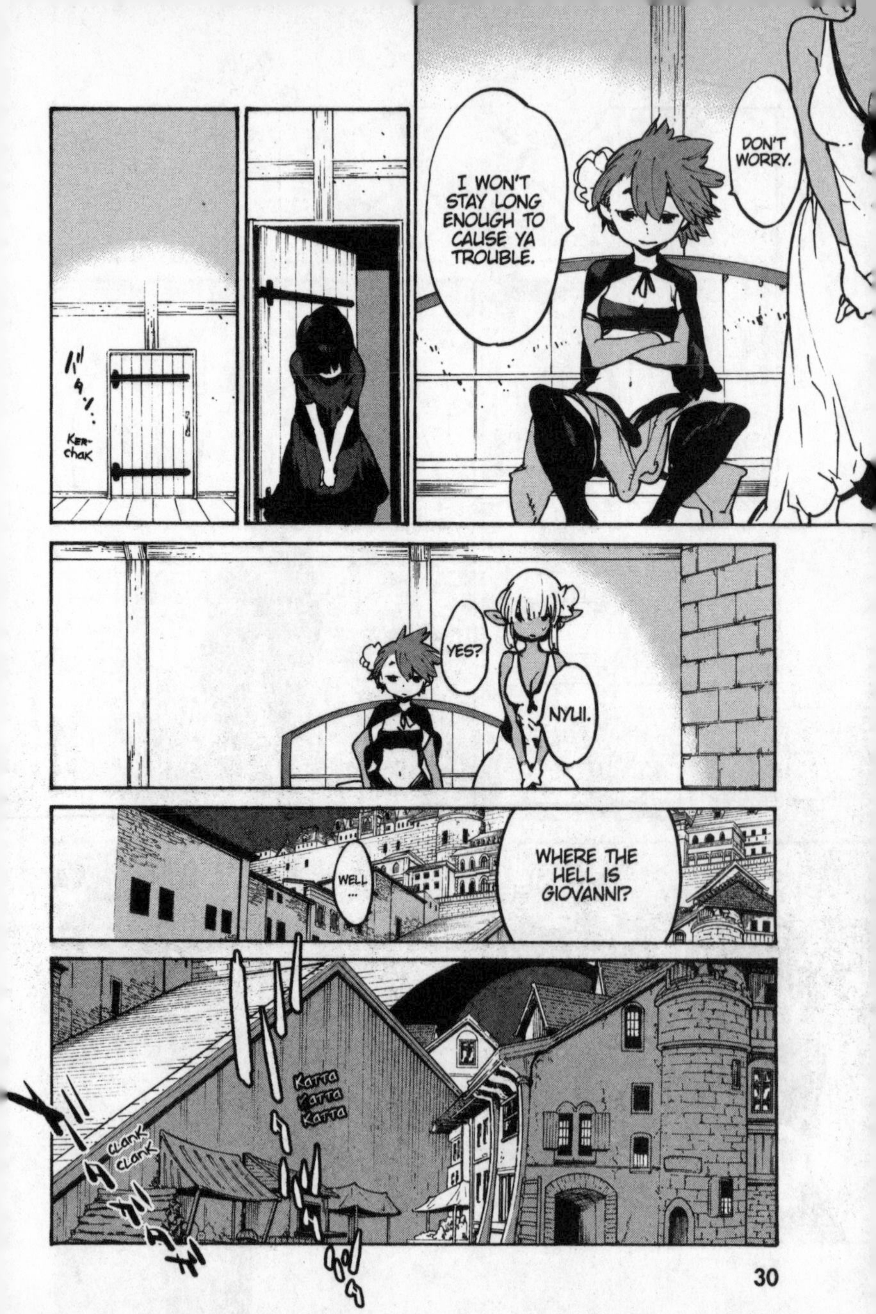
DON'T WORRY.
I WON'T STAY LONG ENOUGH TO CAUSE YA TROUBLE.
KER-CHAK
NYUI.
YES?
WHERE THE HELL IS GIOVANNI?
WELL ...
Karta Karta Karta
Clank Clank

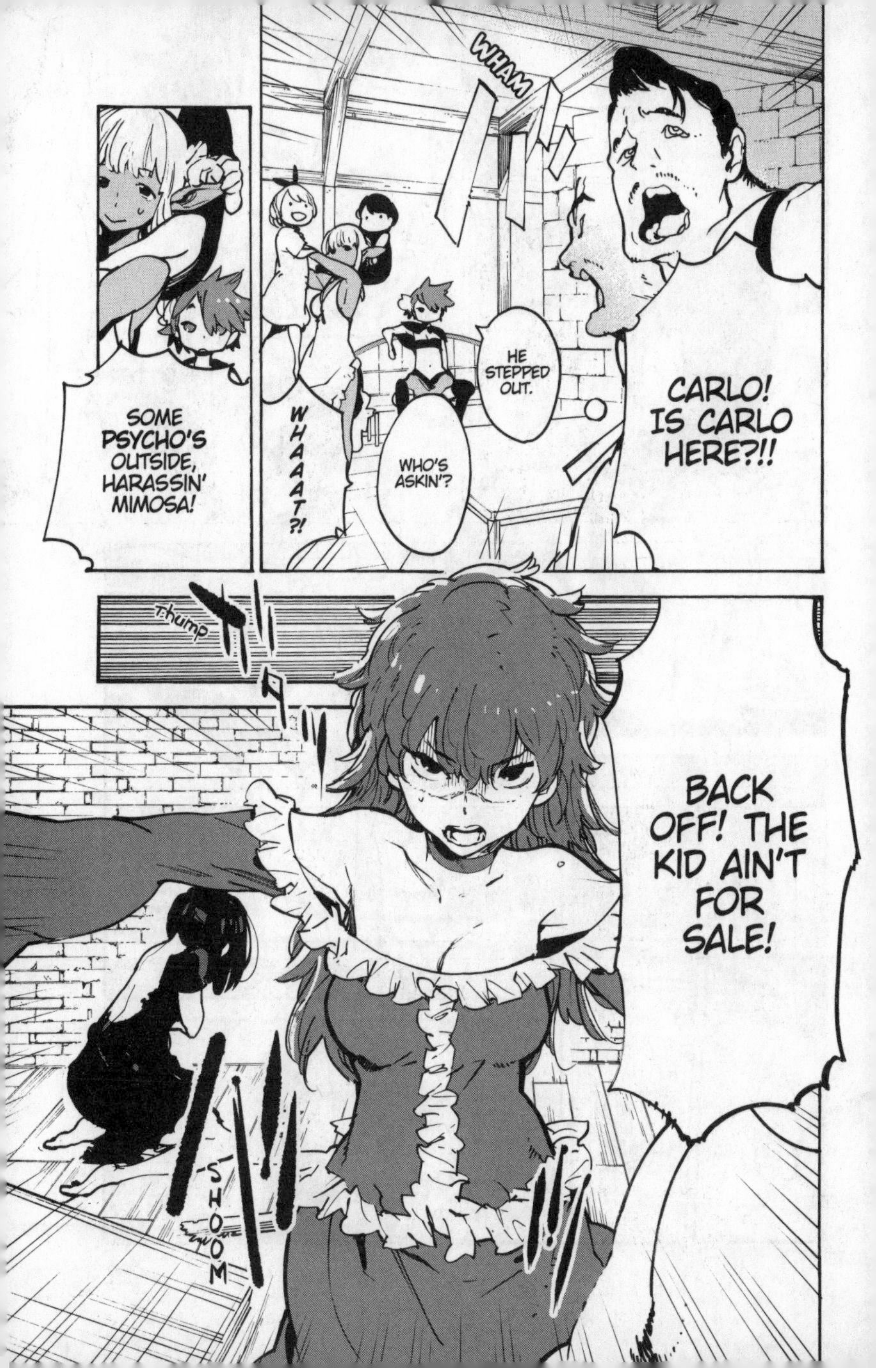
WHAM
CARLO! IS CARLO HERE?!!
HE STEPPED OUT.
WHO'S ASKIN'?
WHAAAAT?!
SOME PSYCHO'S OUTSIDE, HARASSIN' MIMOSA!
BACK OFF! THE KID AIN'T FOR SALE!
Thump
SHOOM

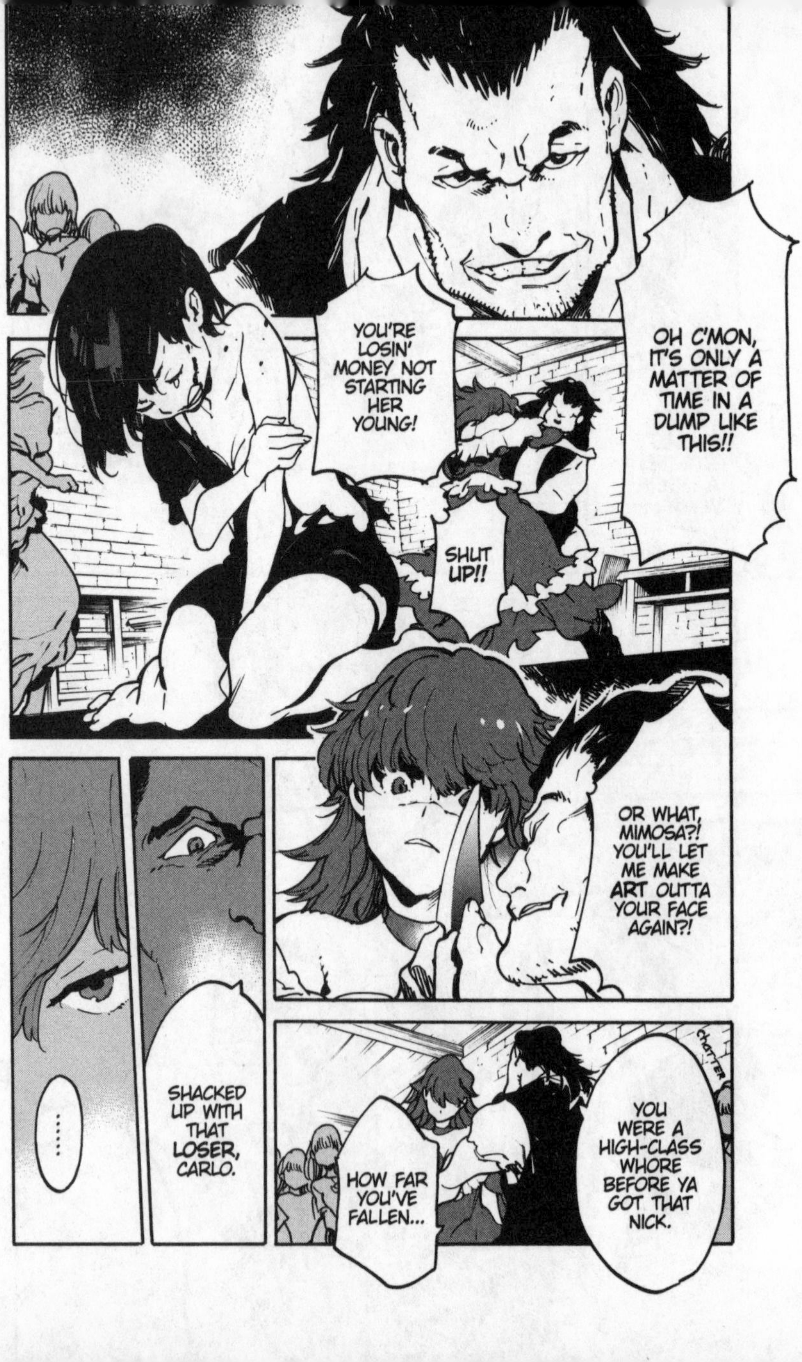
OH C'MON, IT'S ONLY A MATTER OF TIME IN A DUMP LIKE THIS!!
YOU'RE LOSIN' MONEY NOT STARTING HER YOUNG!
SHUT UP!!
OR WHAT, MIMOSA?! YOU'LL LET ME MAKE ART OUTTA YOUR FACE AGAIN?!
CHATTER
YOU WERE A HIGH-CLASS WHORE BEFORE YA GOT THAT NICK.
HOW FAR YOU'VE FALLEN...
SHACKED UP WITH THAT LOSER, CARLO.
......

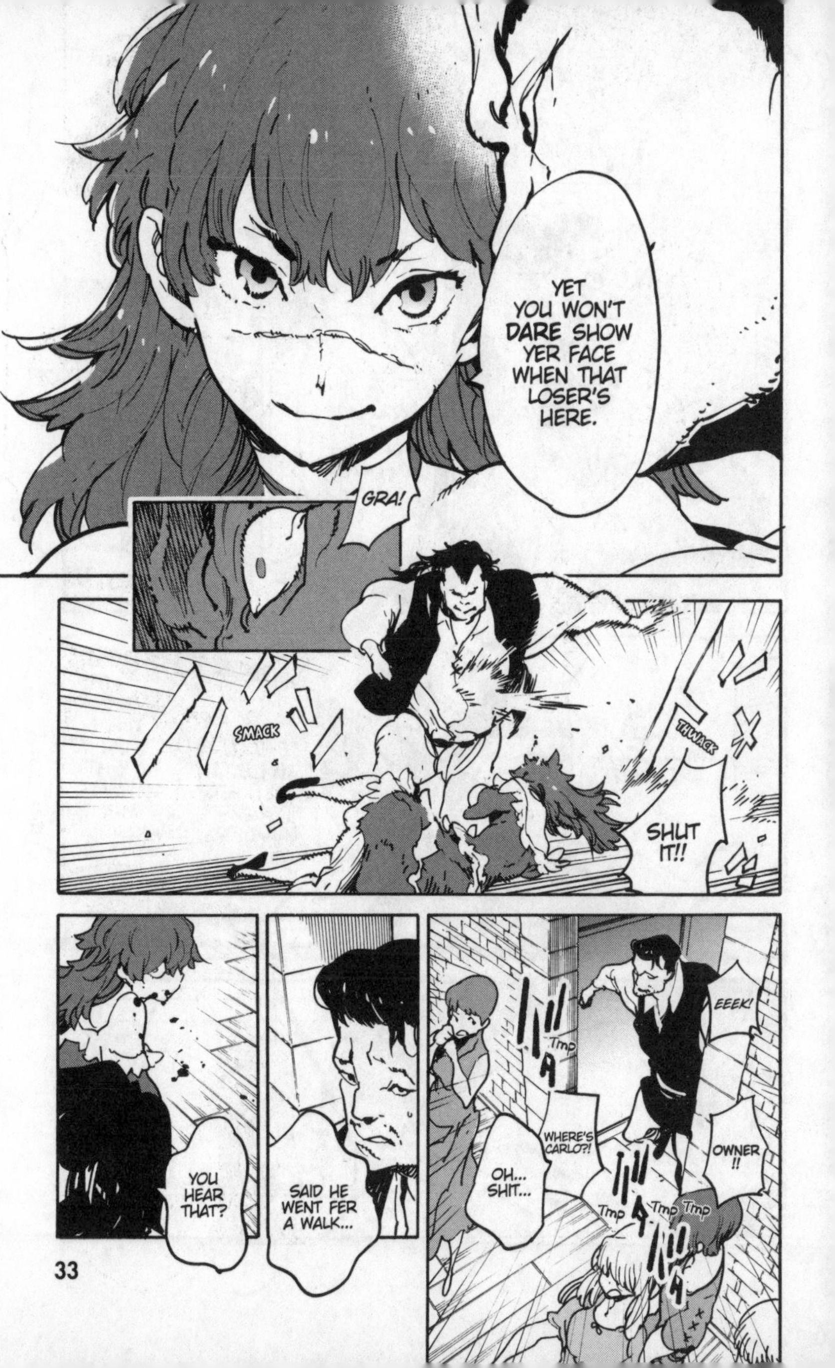
YET YOU WON'T DARE SHOW YER FACE WHEN THAT LOSER'S HERE.
GRA!
THWACK
SHUT IT!!
SMACK
EEEK!
OWNER!!
WHERE'S CARLO?!
Tmp
Tmp Tmp Tmp
OH... SHIT...
SAID HE WENT FER A WALK...
YOU HEAR THAT?

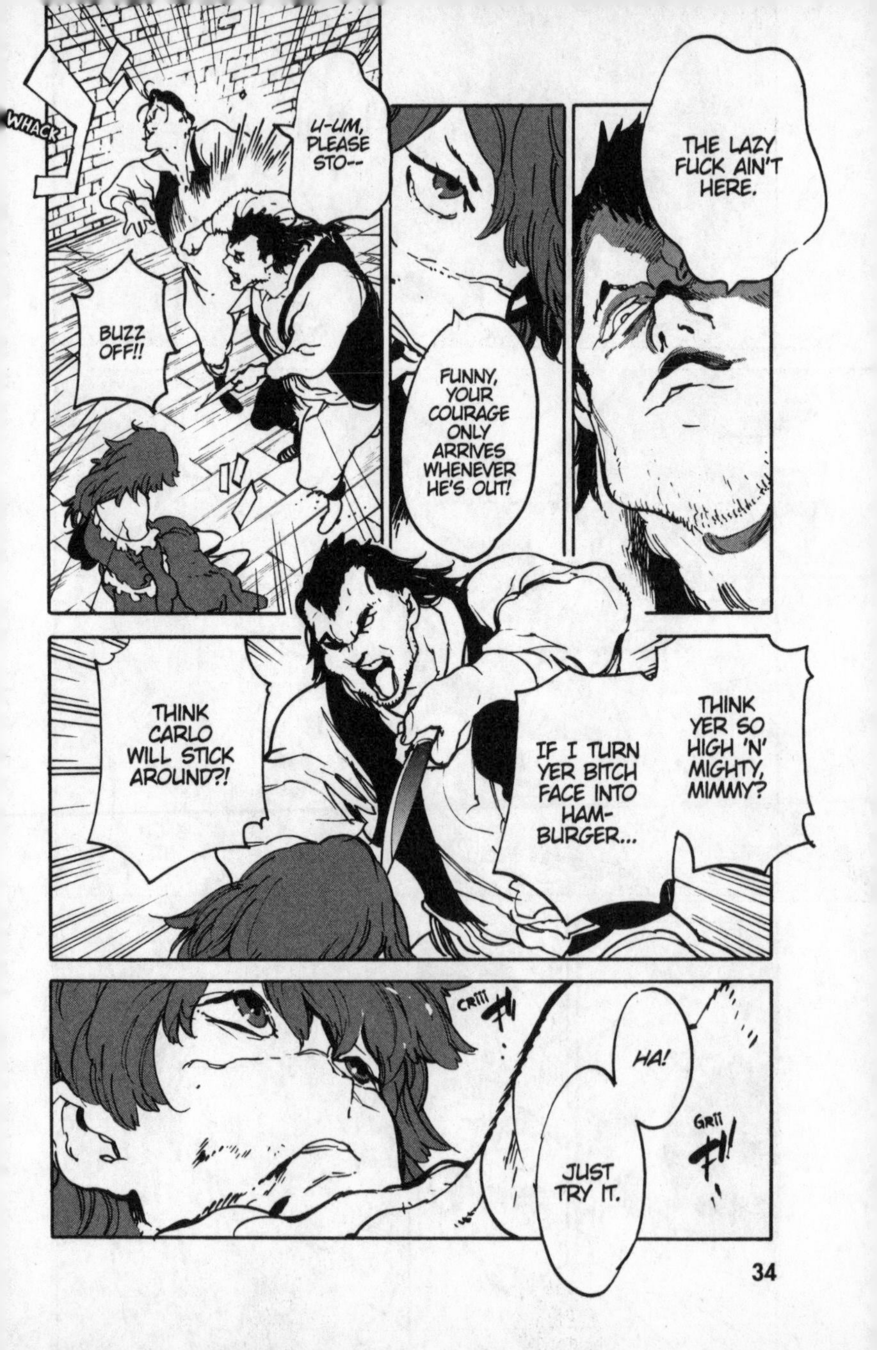
THE LAZY FUCK AIN'T HERE.
FUNNY, YOUR COURAGE ONLY ARRIVES WHENEVER HE'S OUT!
U-UM, PLEASE STO--
WHACK
BUZZ OFF!!
THINK YER SO HIGH 'N' MIGHTY, MIMMY?
IF I TURN YER BITCH FACE INTO HAM-BURGER...
THINK CARLO WILL STICK AROUND?!
CRIII
HA!
GRII
JUST TRY IT.

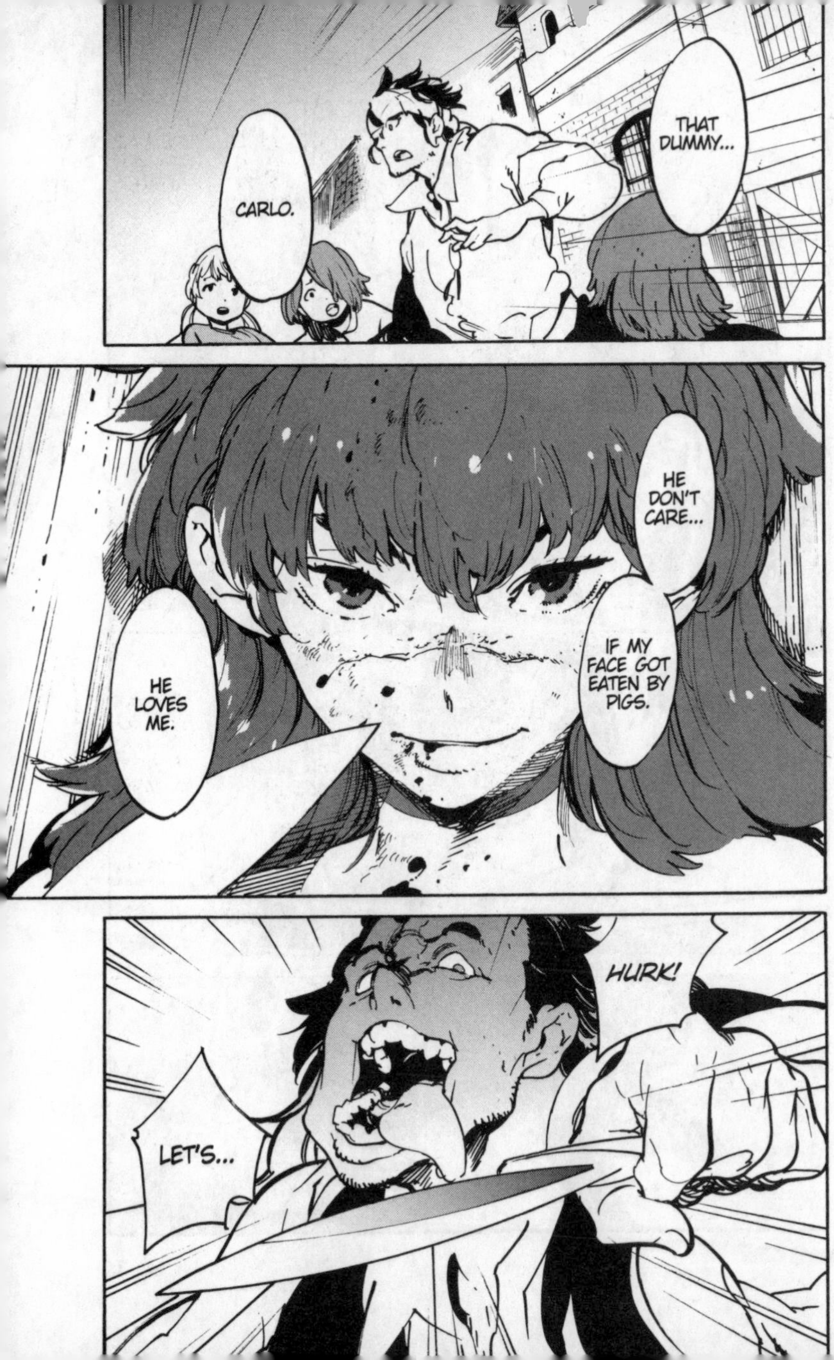
THAT DUMMY...
CARLO.
HE DON'T CARE...
IF MY FACE GOT EATEN BY PIGS.
HE LOVES ME.
HURK!
LET'S...

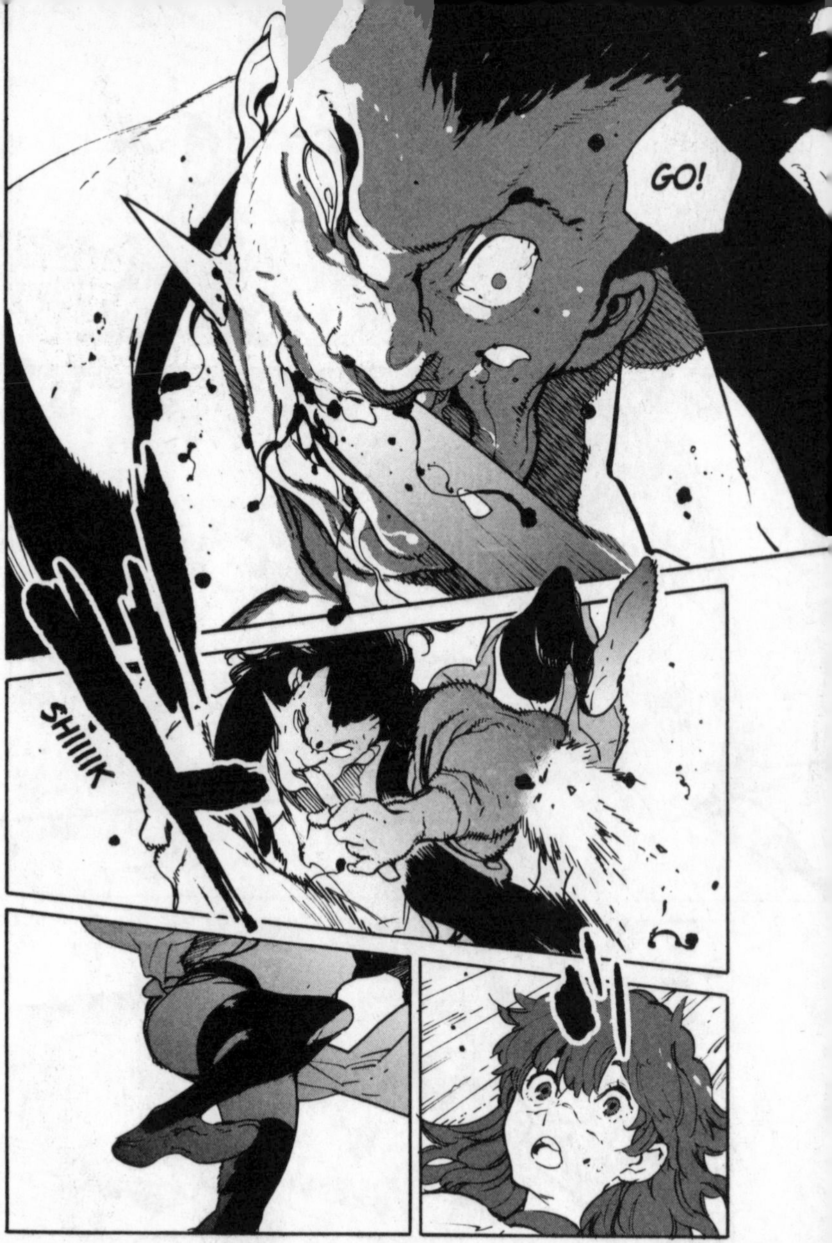
GO!
SHIIIIK

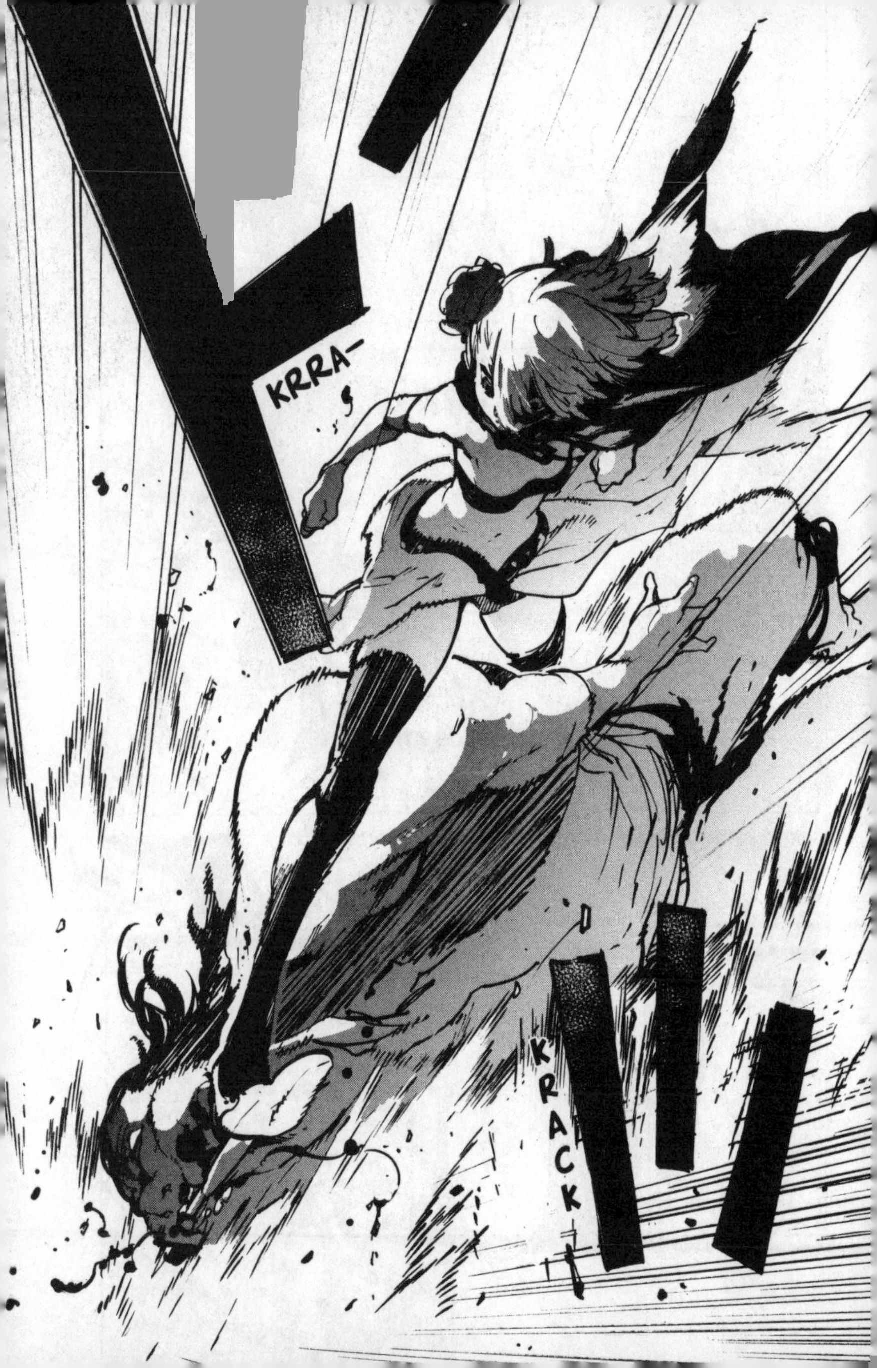
KRRA-
KRACK

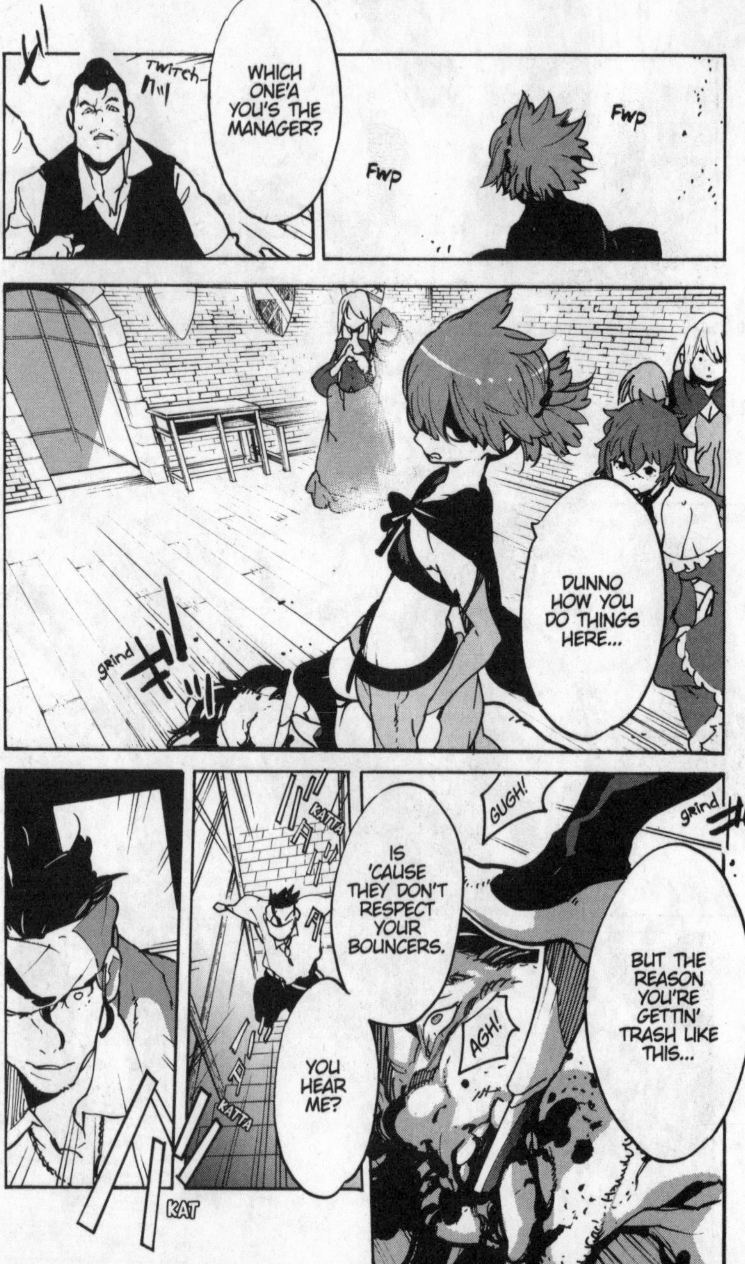
Fwp
Fwp
WHICH ONE'A YOU'S THE MANAGER?
Twitch
DUNNO HOW YOU DO THINGS HERE...
grind
grind
BUT THE REASON YOU'RE GETTIN' TRASH LIKE THIS...
GUGH!
AGH!
IS 'CAUSE THEY DON'T RESPECT YOUR BOUNCERS.
YOU HEAR ME?
KATTA
KATTA
KAT

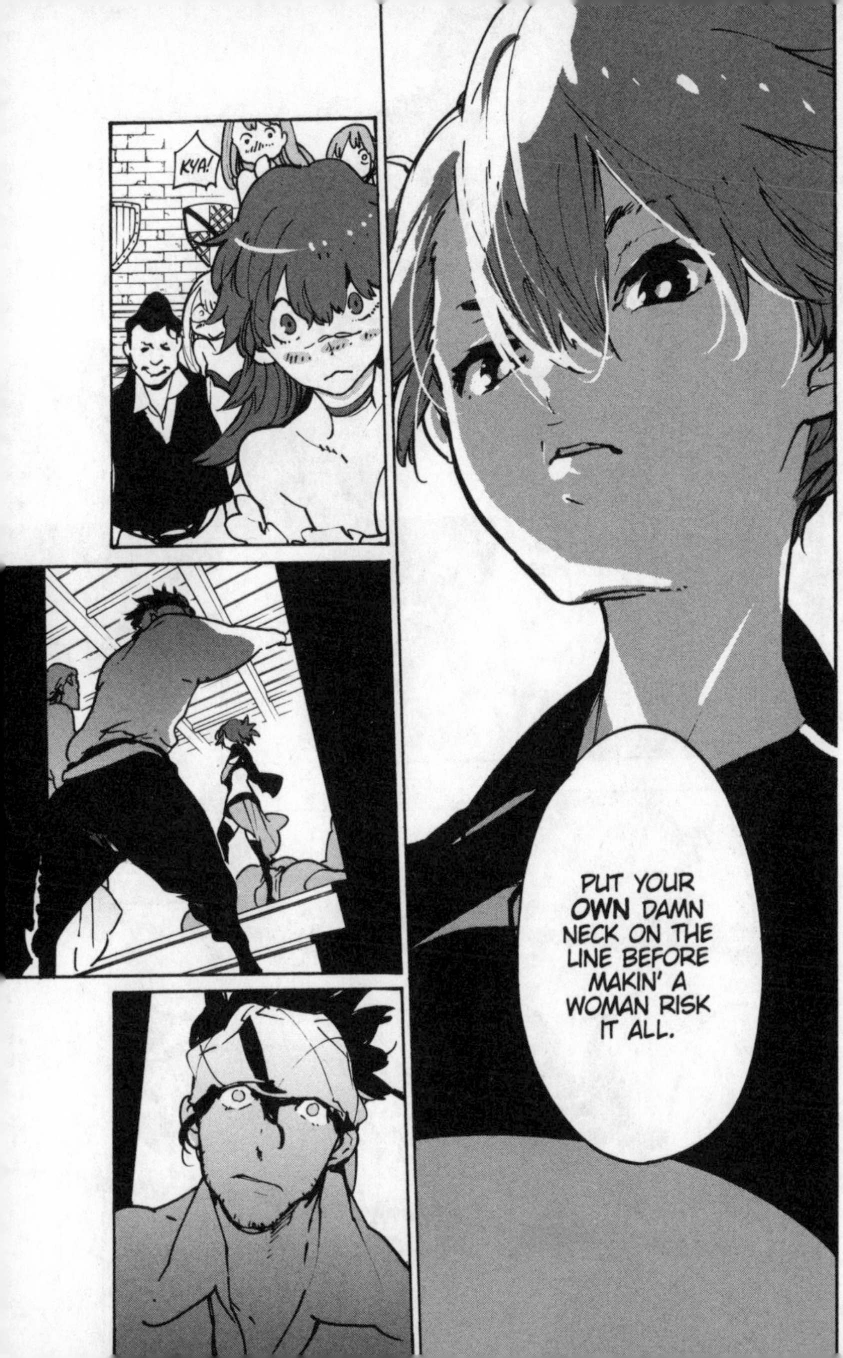
PUT YOUR OWN DAMN NECK ON THE LINE BEFORE MAKIN' A WOMAN RISK IT ALL.
KYA!

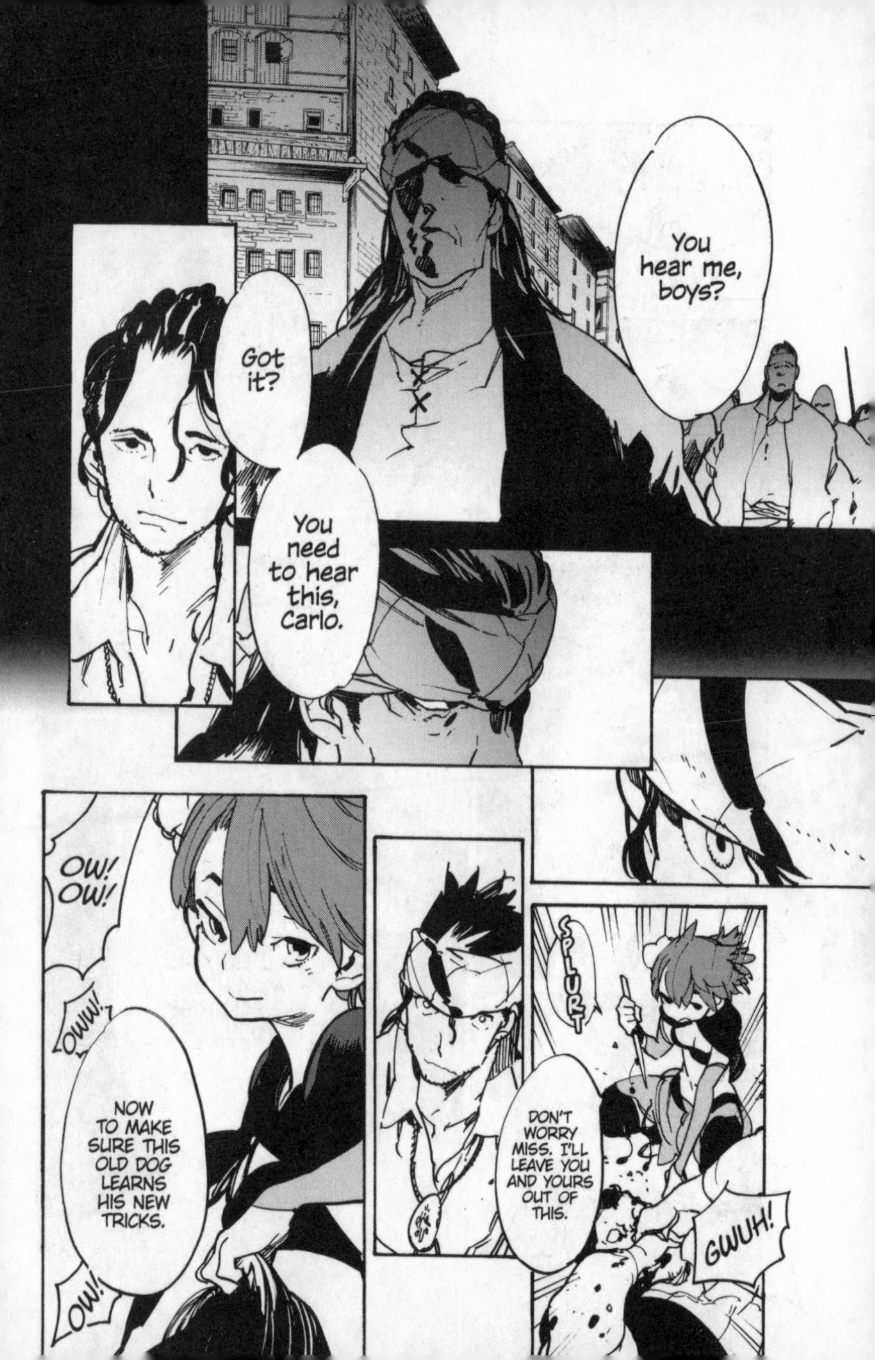
You hear me, boys?
Got it?
You need to hear this, Carlo.
SPLURT
GWUH!
DON'T WORRY MISS. I'LL LEAVE YOU AND YOURS OUT OF THIS.
OW! OW!
OWW!
NOW TO MAKE SURE THIS OLD DOG LEARNS HIS NEW TRICKS.
OW!

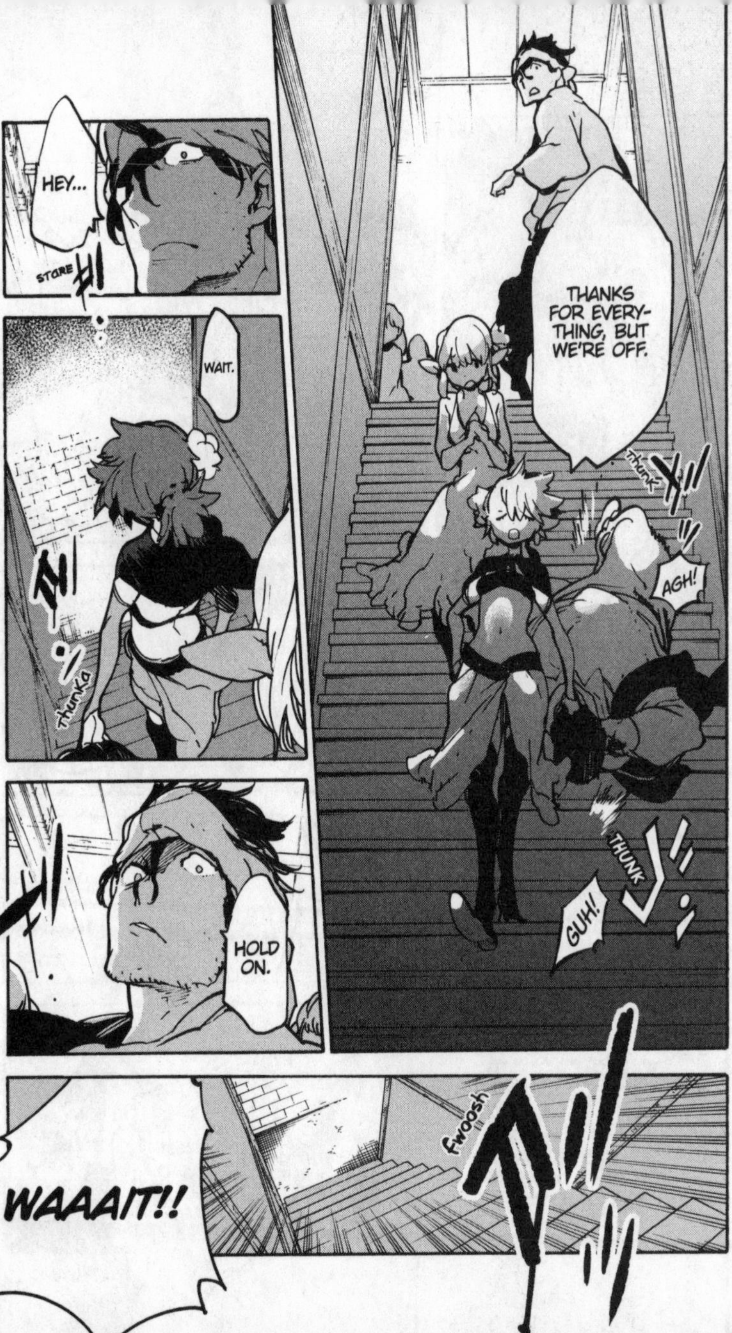
THANKS FOR EVERY-THING, BUT WE'RE OFF.
thunk
AGH!
THUNK
GUH!
HEY...
STARE
WAIT.
thunka
STARE
HOLD ON.
fwoosh
WAAAIT!!

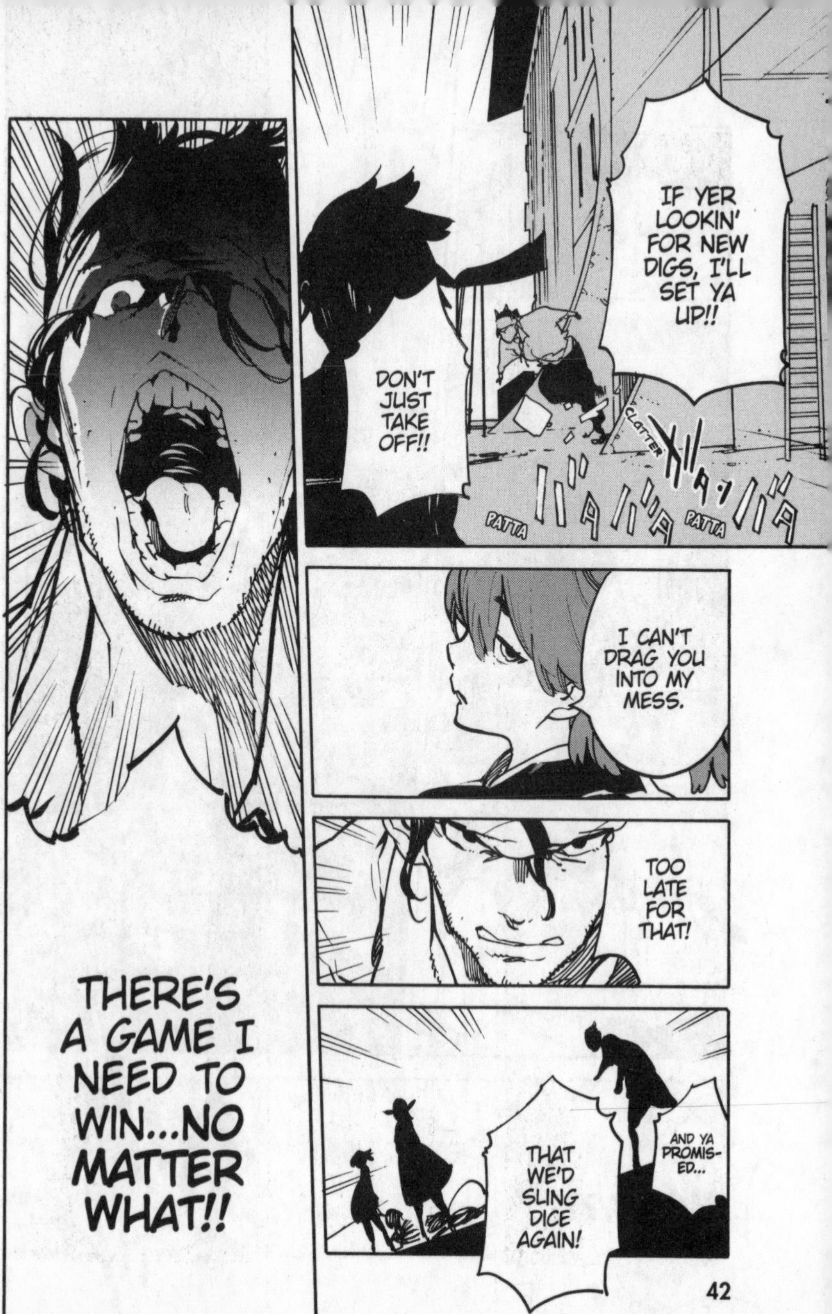
IF YER LOOKIN' FOR NEW DIGS, I'LL SET YA UP!!
DON'T JUST TAKE OFF!!
CLATTER
PATTA
PATTA
I CAN'T DRAG YOU INTO MY MESS.
TOO LATE FOR THAT!
AND YA PROMIS-ED...
THAT WE'D SLING DICE AGAIN!
THERE'S A GAME I NEED TO WIN...NO MATTER WHAT!!

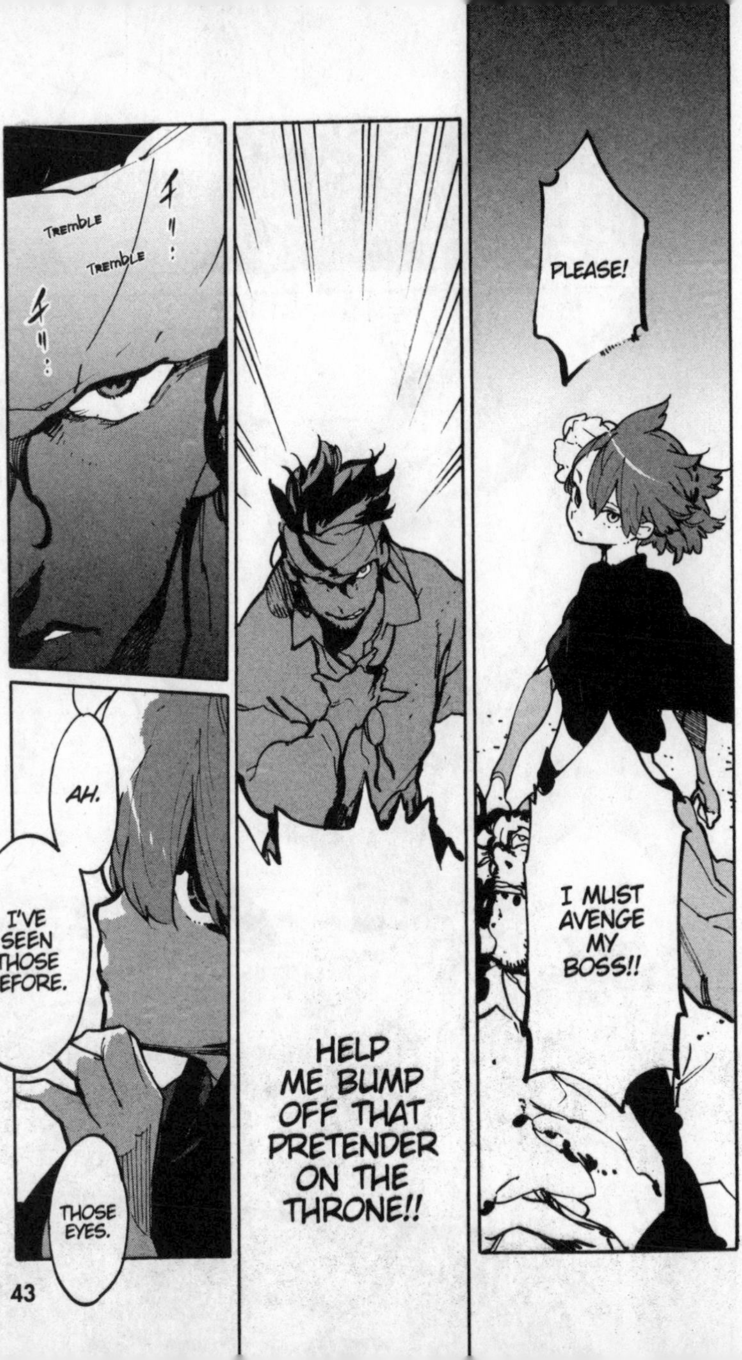
PLEASE!
I MUST AVENGE MY BOSS!!
HELP ME BUMP OFF THAT PRETENDER ON THE THRONE!!
TREMBLE
TREMBLE
チリ…
チリ…
AH.
I'VE SEEN THOSE BEFORE.
THOSE EYES.

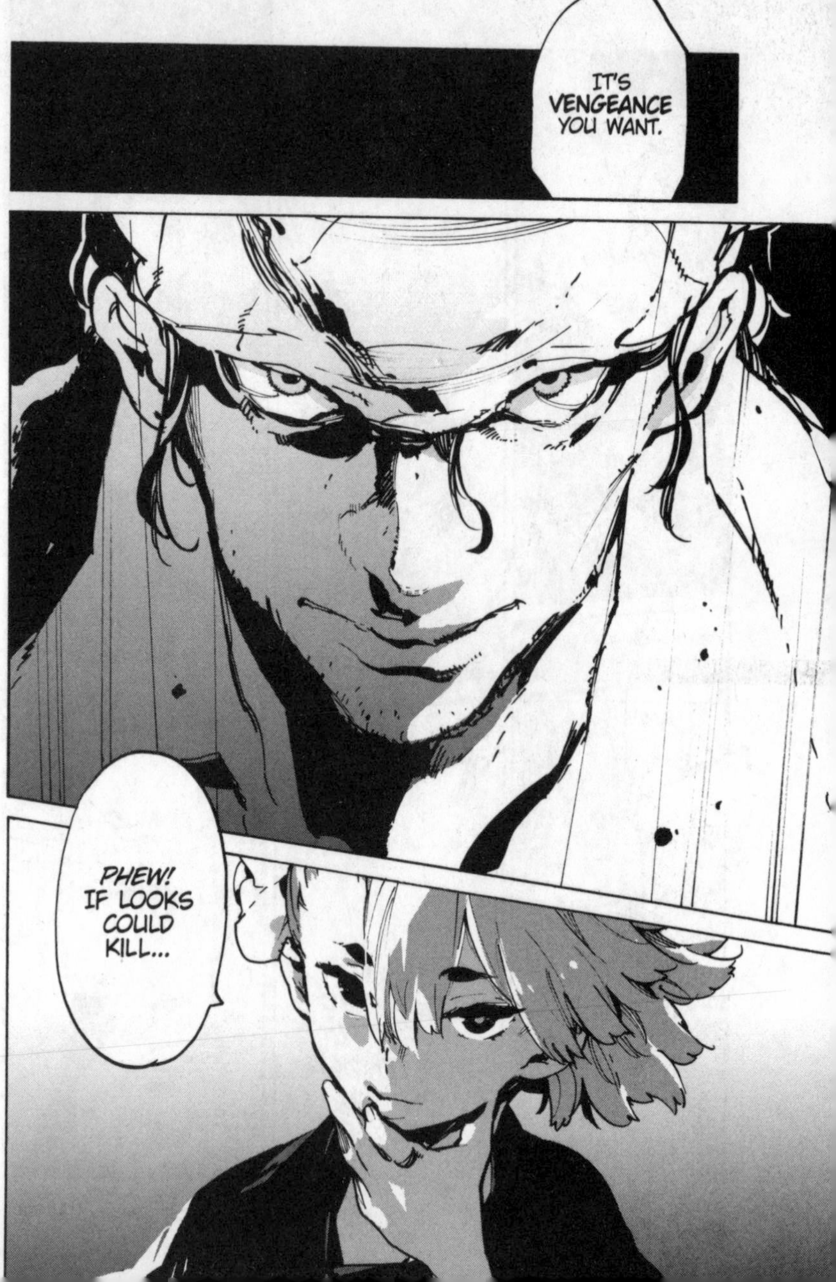
IT'S VENGEANCE YOU WANT.
PHEW! IF LOOKS COULD KILL...

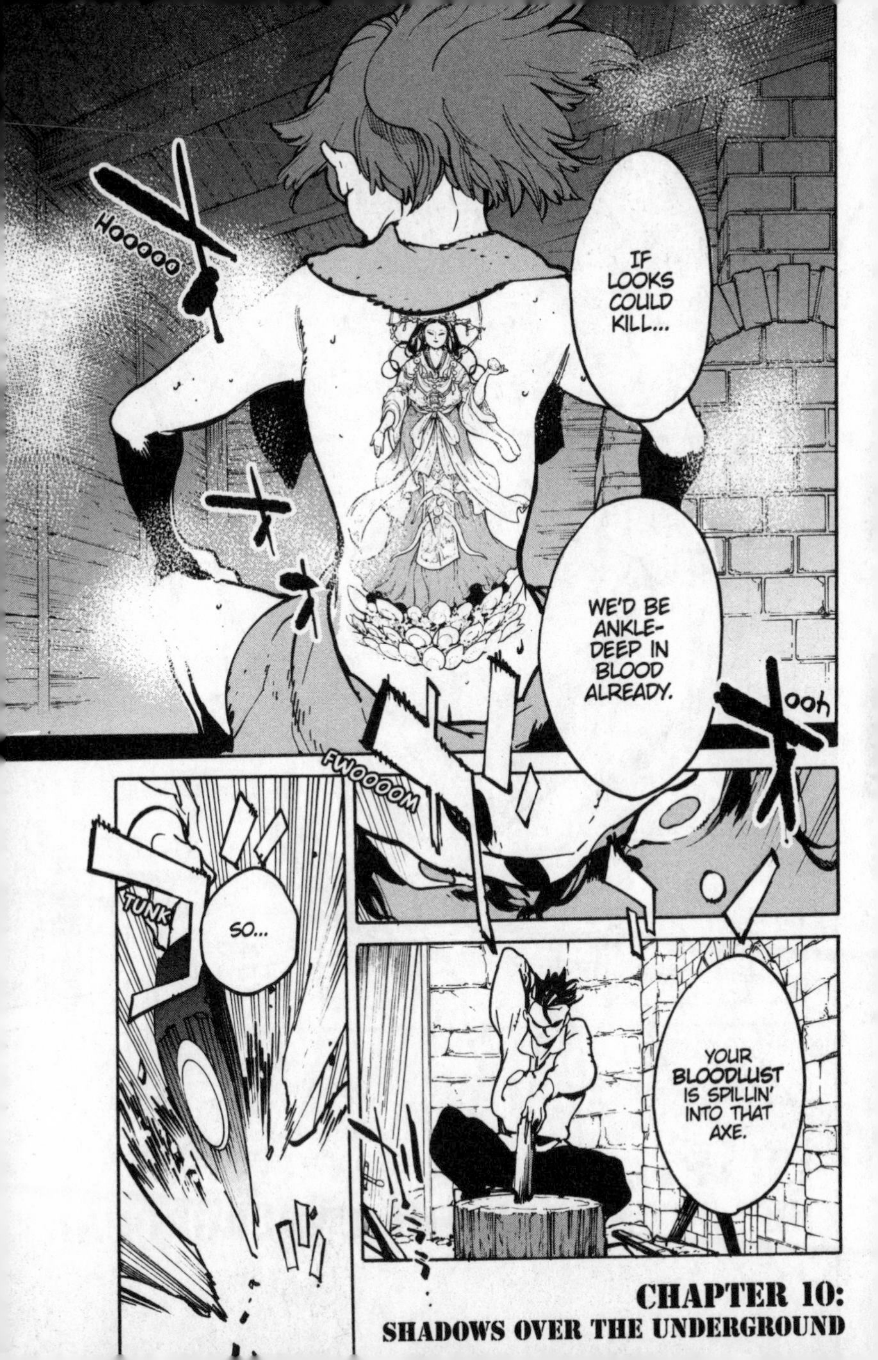
IF LOOKS COULD KILL...
WE'D BE ANKLE-DEEP IN BLOOD ALREADY.
HOOOOOO
ooh
FWOOOOM
YOUR BLOODLUST IS SPILLIN' INTO THAT AXE.
TUNK
SO...

CHAPTER 10: SHADOWS OVER THE UNDERGROUND

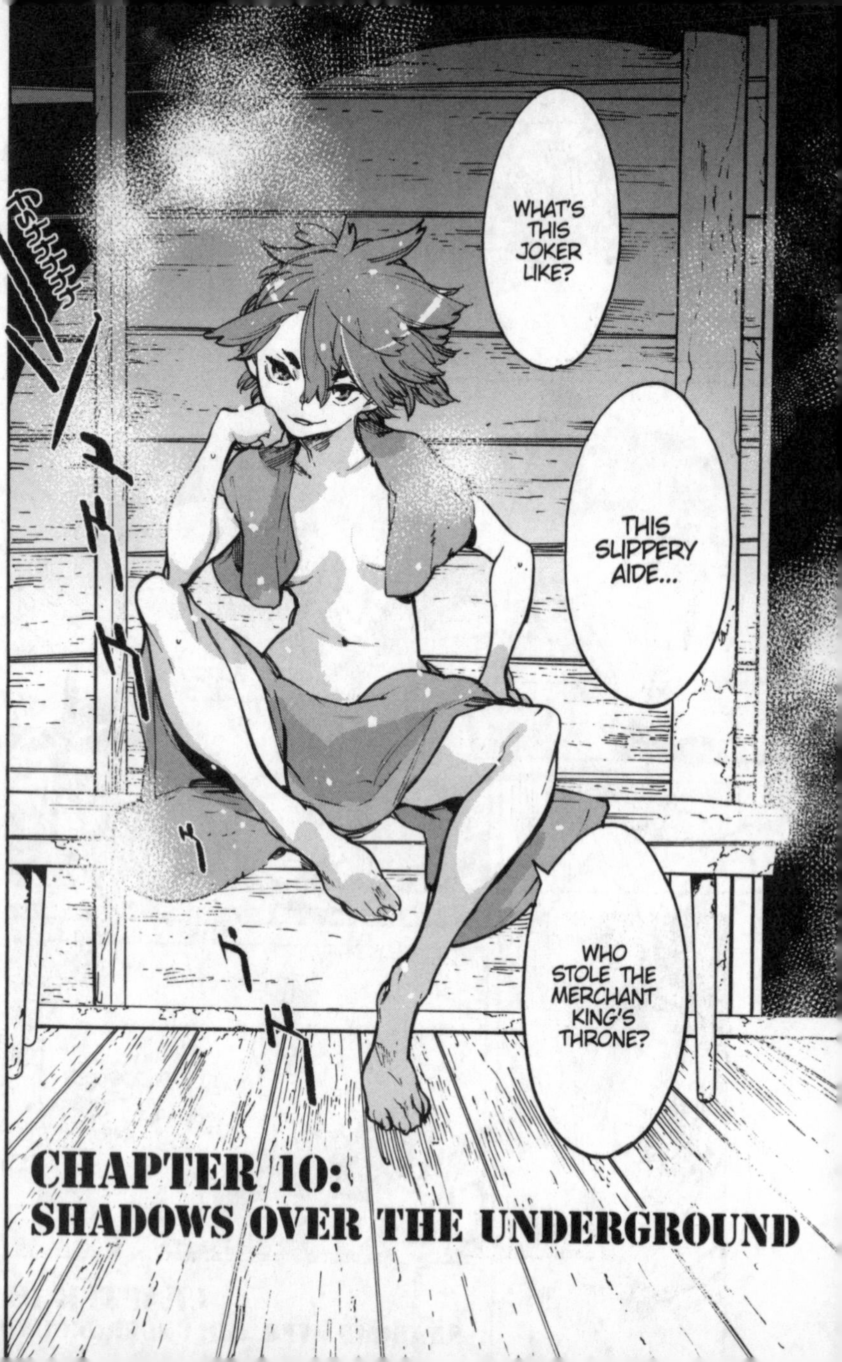
WHAT'S THIS JOKER LIKE?
THIS SLIPPERY AIDE...
WHO STOLE THE MERCHANT KING'S THRONE?

CHAPTER 10: SHADOWS OVER THE UNDERGROUND

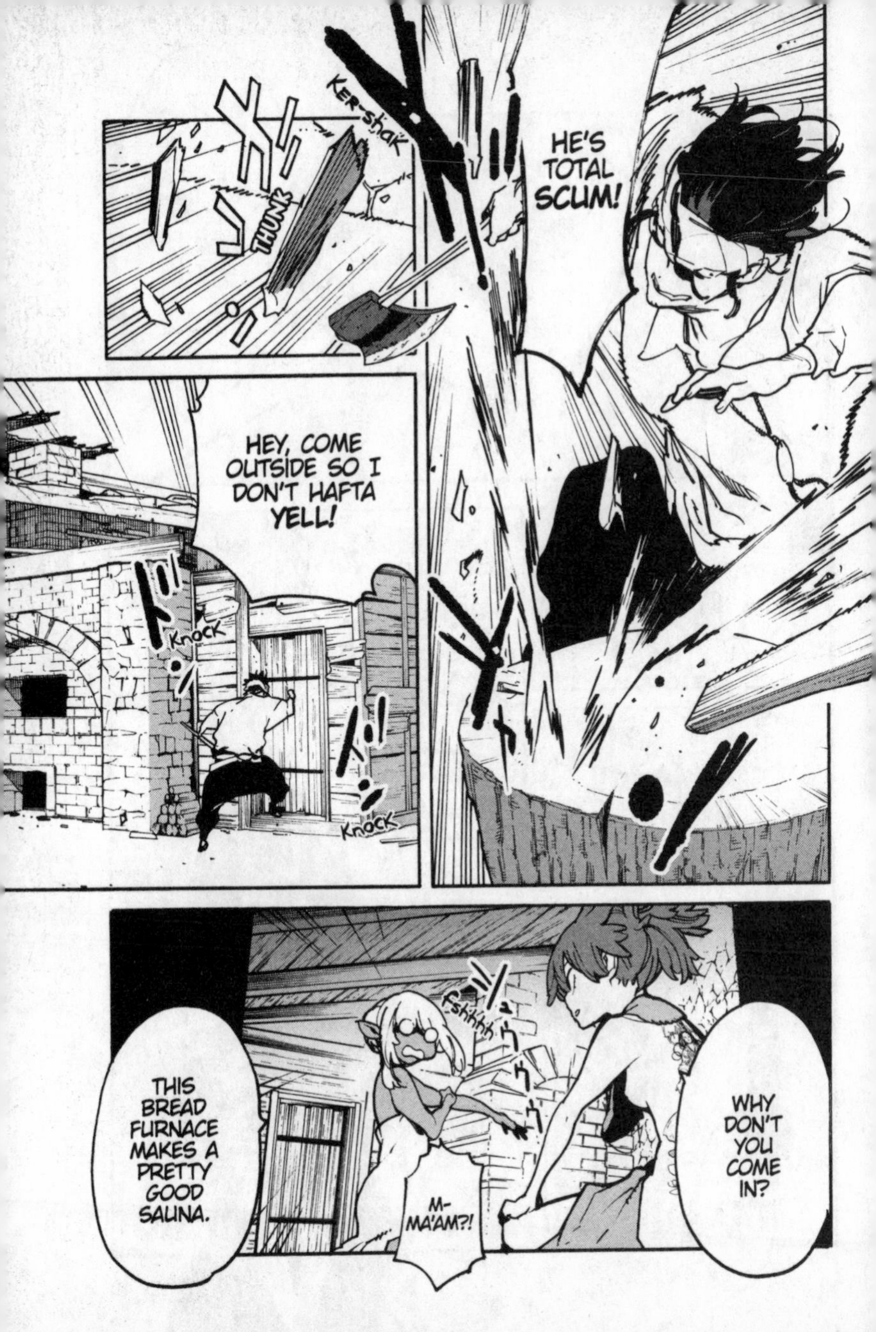
HE'S TOTAL SCUM!
KER-shak
THUNK
HEY, COME OUTSIDE SO I DON'T HAFTA YELL!
Knock
Knock
WHY DON'T YOU COME IN?
fshhhh
M-MA'AM?!
THIS BREAD FURNACE MAKES A PRETTY GOOD SAUNA.

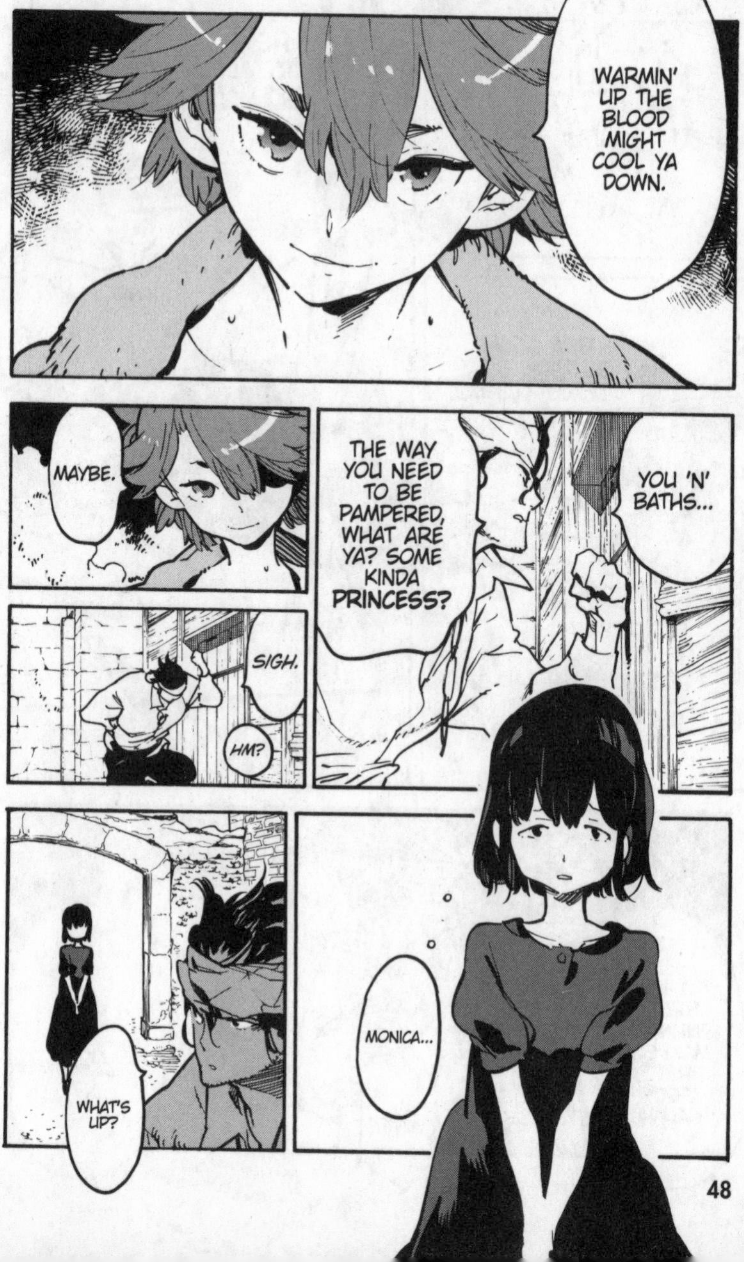
WARMIN' UP THE BLOOD MIGHT COOL YA DOWN.
YOU 'N' BATHS...
THE WAY YOU NEED TO BE PAMPERED, WHAT ARE YA? SOME KINDA PRINCESS?
MAYBE.
SIGH.
HM?
MONICA...
WHAT'S UP?

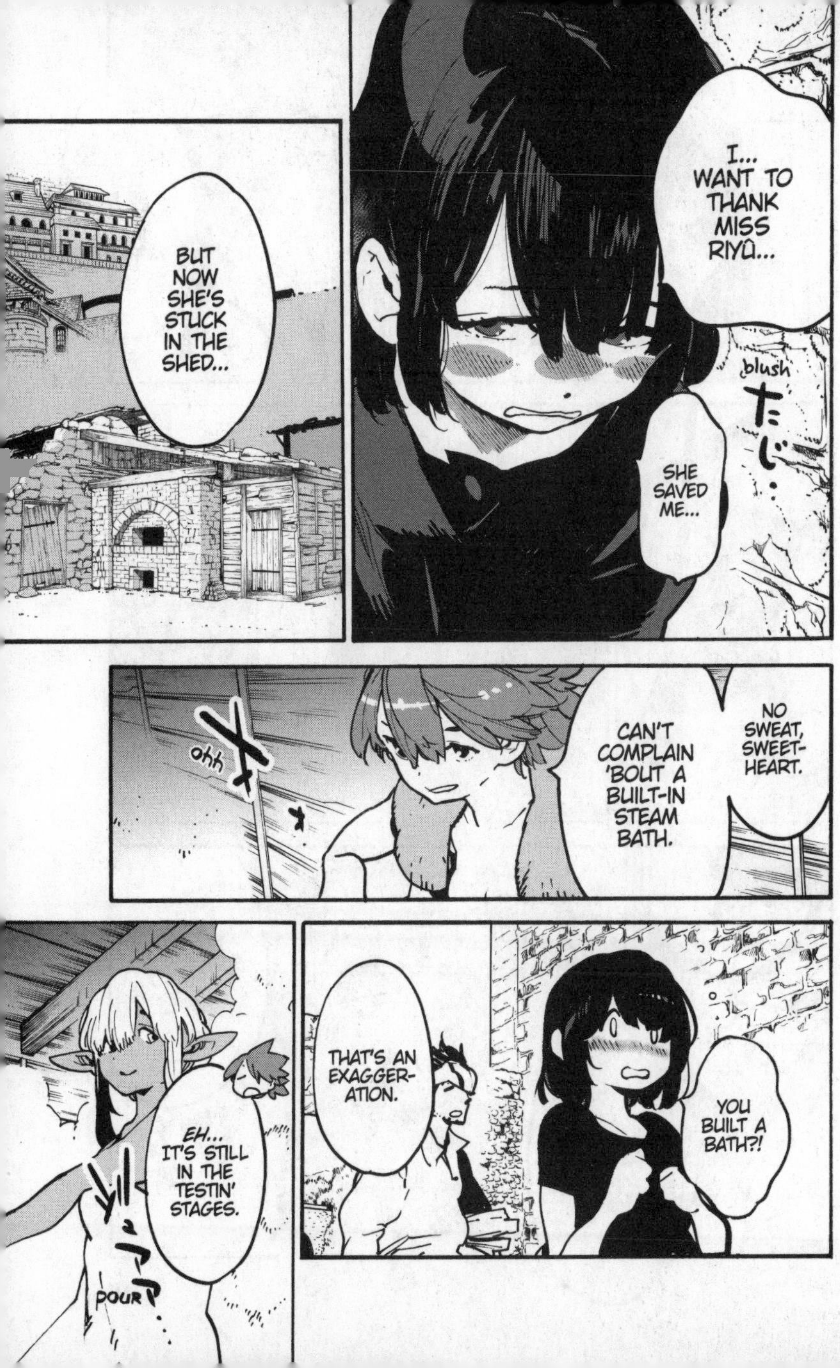
I... WANT TO THANK MISS RIYÛ...
blush
SHE SAVED ME...
BUT NOW SHE'S STUCK IN THE SHED...
NO SWEAT, SWEET-HEART.
CAN'T COMPLAIN 'BOUT A BUILT-IN STEAM BATH.
ohh
YOU BUILT A BATH?!
THAT'S AN EXAGGER-ATION.
EH... IT'S STILL IN THE TESTIN' STAGES.
POUR

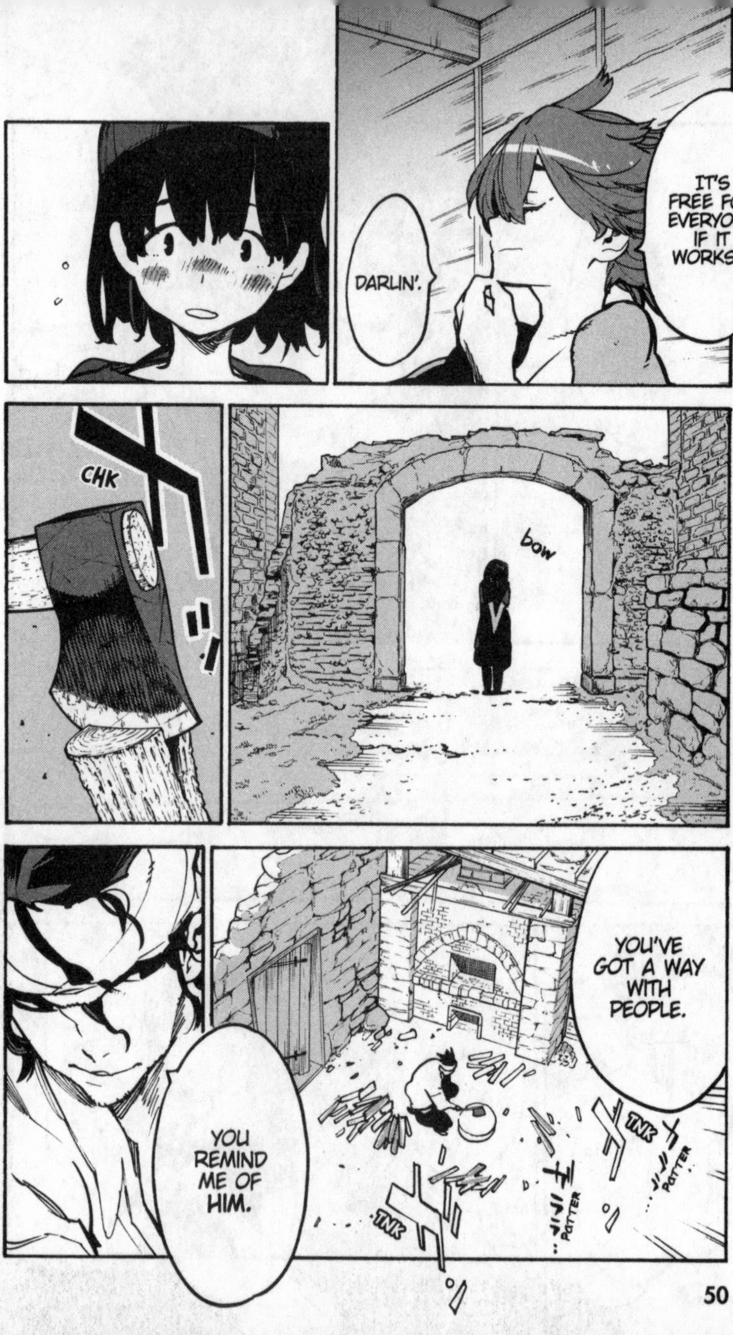
IT'S FREE FOR EVERYONE IF IT WORKS...
DARLIN'.
bow
CHK
YOU'VE GOT A WAY WITH PEOPLE.
TNK
PATTER
PATTER
TNK
YOU REMIND ME OF HIM.

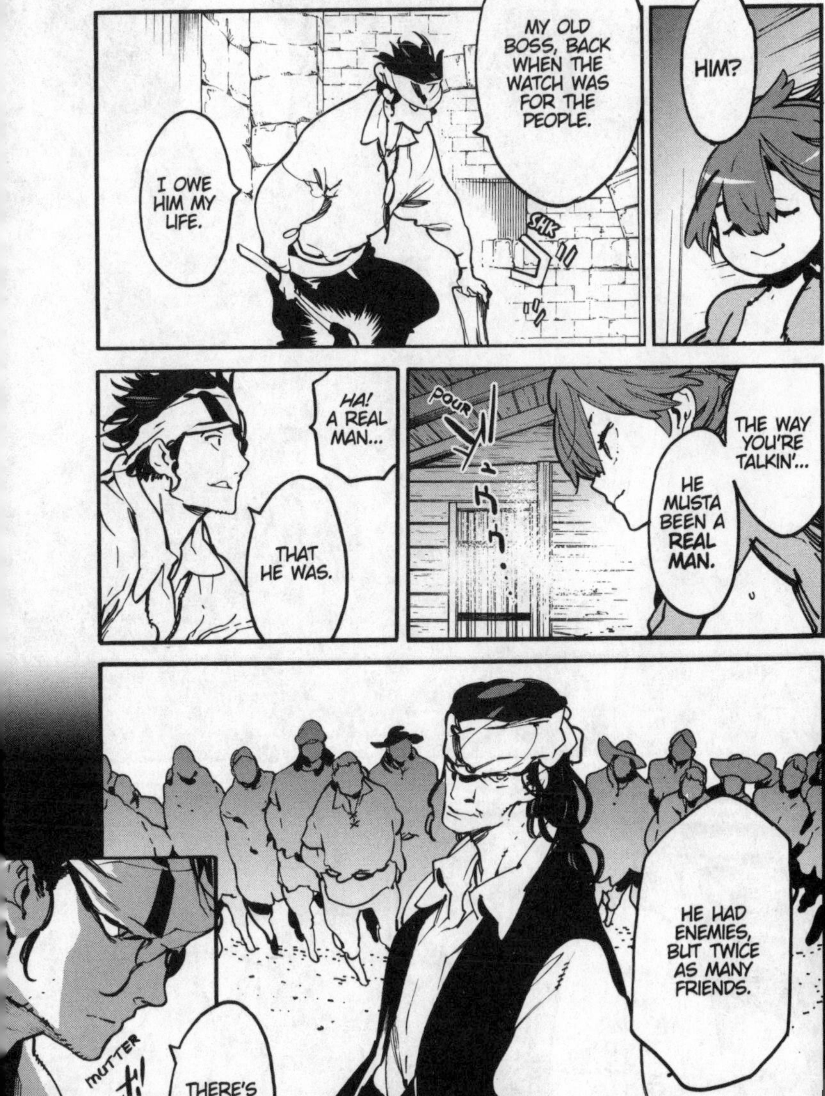
HIM?
MY OLD BOSS, BACK WHEN THE WATCH WAS FOR THE PEOPLE.
SHK
I OWE HIM MY LIFE.
THE WAY YOU'RE TALKIN'...
POUR
HE MUSTA BEEN A REAL MAN.
HA! A REAL MAN...
THAT HE WAS.
HE HAD ENEMIES, BUT TWICE AS MANY FRIENDS.
MUTTER
THERE'S NO WAY...

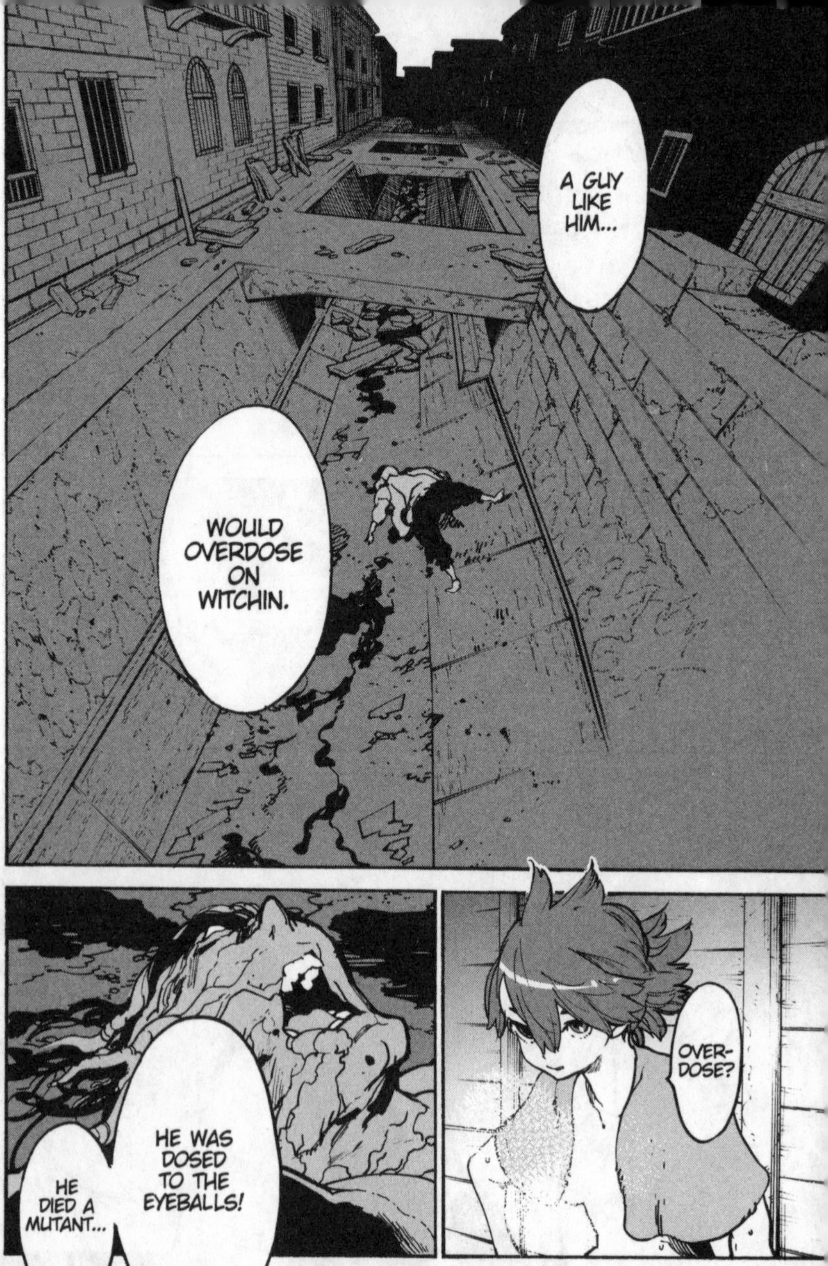
A GUY LIKE HIM...
WOULD OVERDOSE ON WITCHIN.
OVER-DOSE?
HE WAS DOSED TO THE EYEBALLS!
HE DIED A MUTANT...

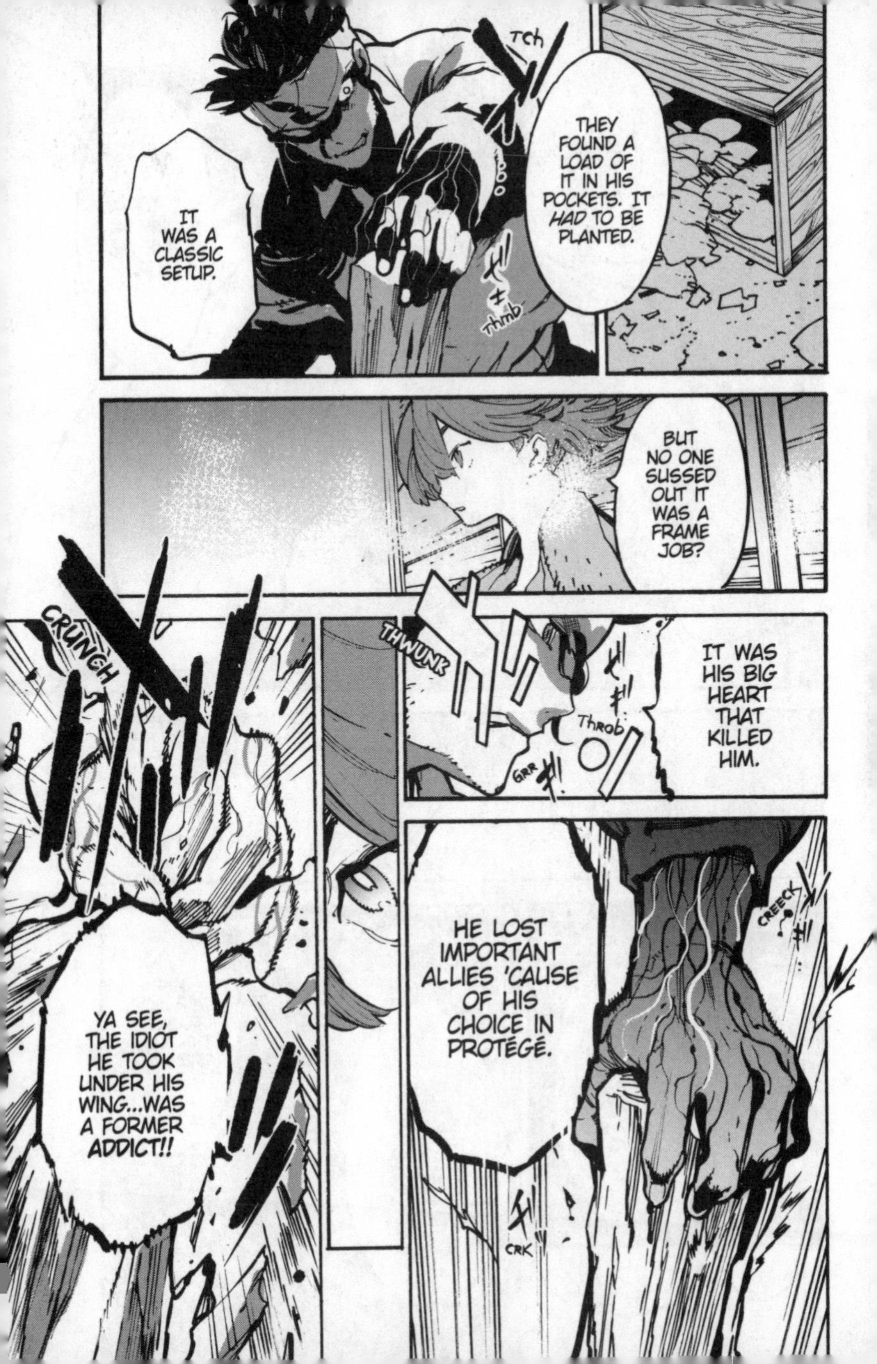
Tch
THEY FOUND A LOAD OF IT IN HIS POCKETS. IT *HAD* TO BE PLANTED.
thmb
IT WAS A CLASSIC SETUP.
BUT NO ONE SUSSED OUT IT WAS A FRAME JOB?
THWUNK
Throb
GRR
IT WAS HIS BIG HEART THAT KILLED HIM.
CREECK
HE LOST IMPORTANT ALLIES 'CAUSE OF HIS CHOICE IN PROTÉGÉ.
CRK
CRUNCH
YA SEE, THE IDIOT HE TOOK UNDER HIS WING...WAS A FORMER ADDICT!!

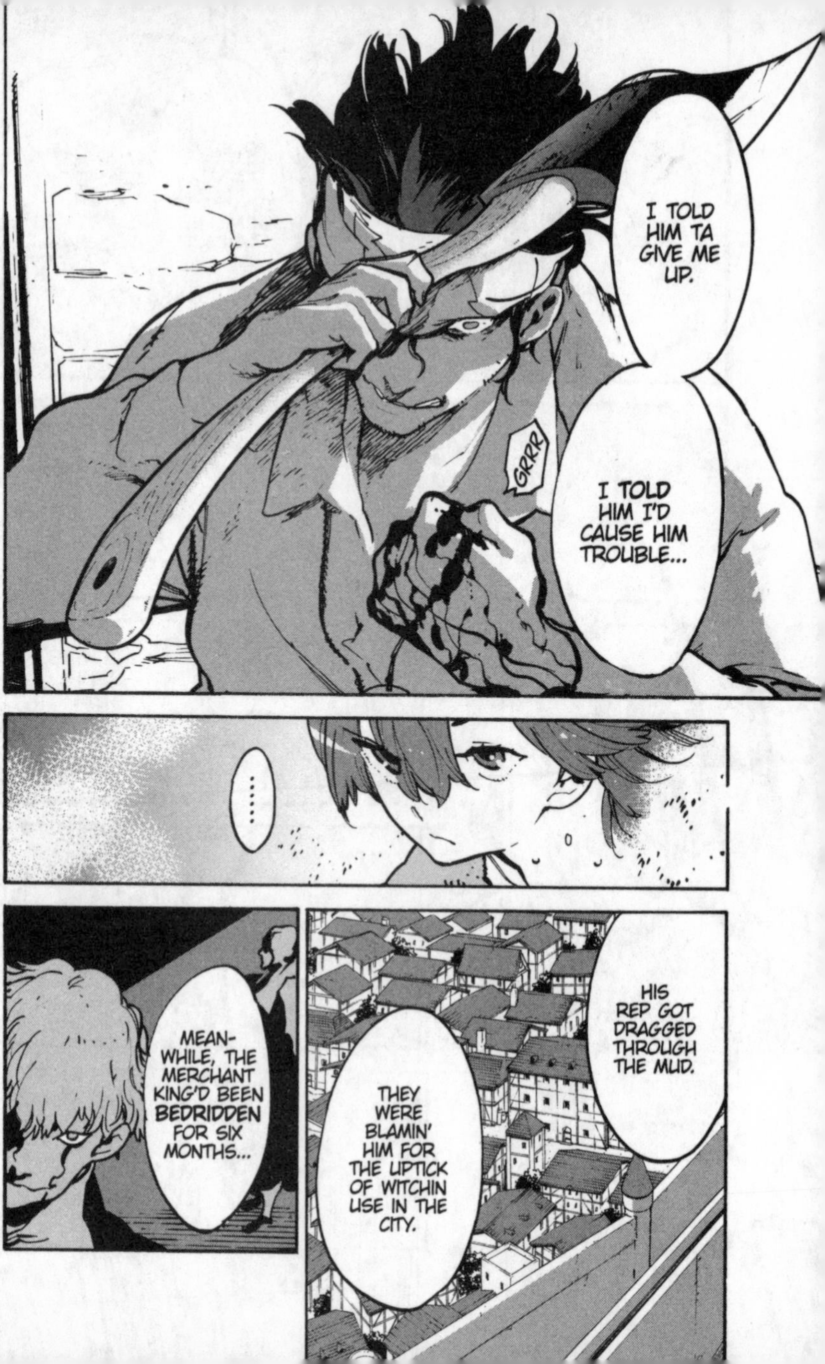
I TOLD HIM TA GIVE ME UP.
GRRR
I TOLD HIM I'D CAUSE HIM TROUBLE...
......
HIS REP GOT DRAGGED THROUGH THE MUD.
THEY WERE BLAMIN' HIM FOR THE UPTICK OF WITCHIN USE IN THE CITY.
MEAN-WHILE, THE MERCHANT KING'D BEEN BEDRIDDEN FOR SIX MONTHS...

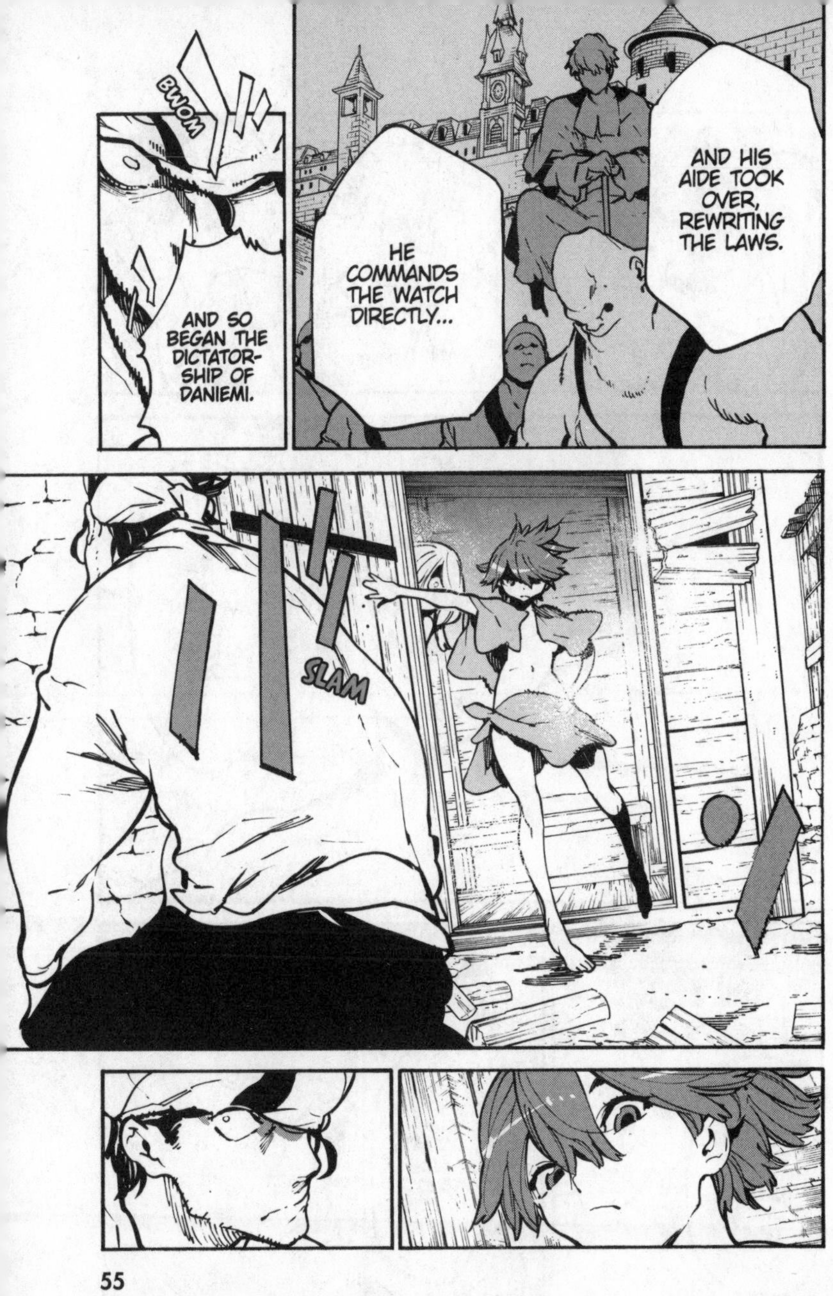
AND HIS AIDE TOOK OVER, REWRITING THE LAWS.
HE COMMANDS THE WATCH DIRECTLY...
BWOM
AND SO BEGAN THE DICTATOR-SHIP OF DANIEMI.
SLAM

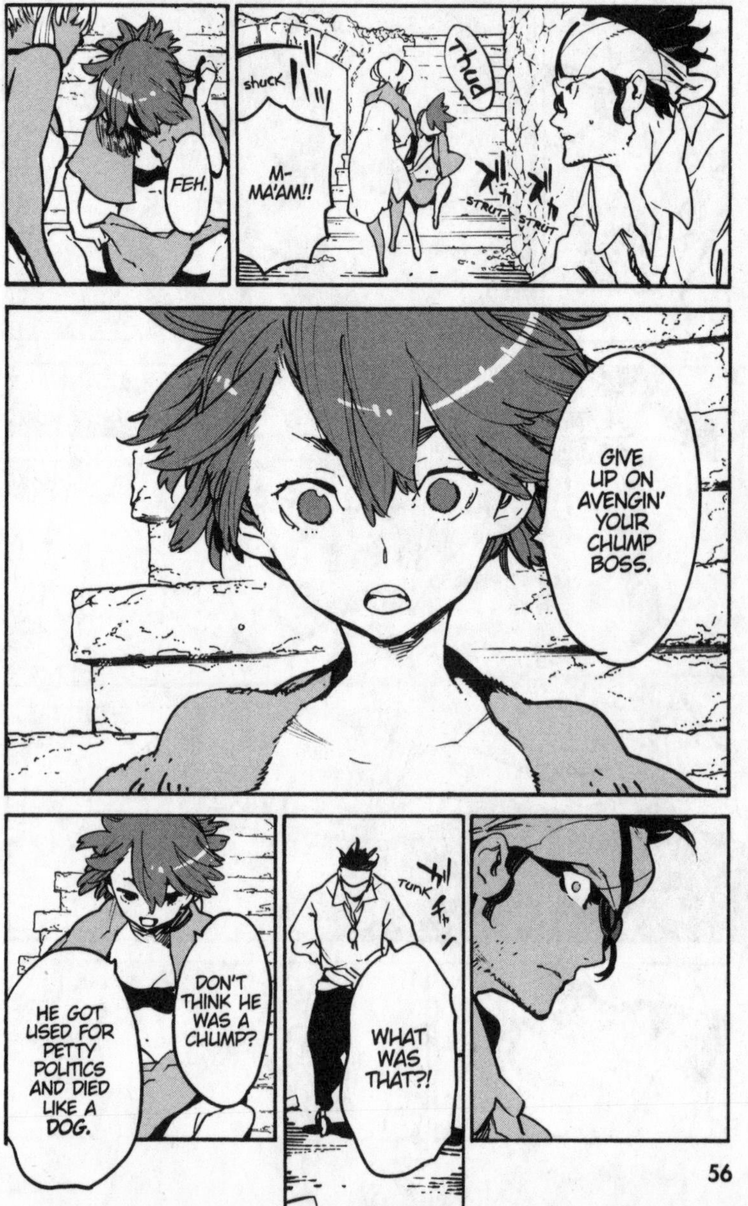
Thud
shuck
M-MA'AM!!
STRUT
STRUT
FEH.
GIVE UP ON AVENGIN' YOUR CHUMP BOSS.
Tunk
WHAT WAS THAT?!
DON'T THINK HE WAS A CHUMP?
HE GOT USED FOR PETTY POLITICS AND DIED LIKE A DOG.

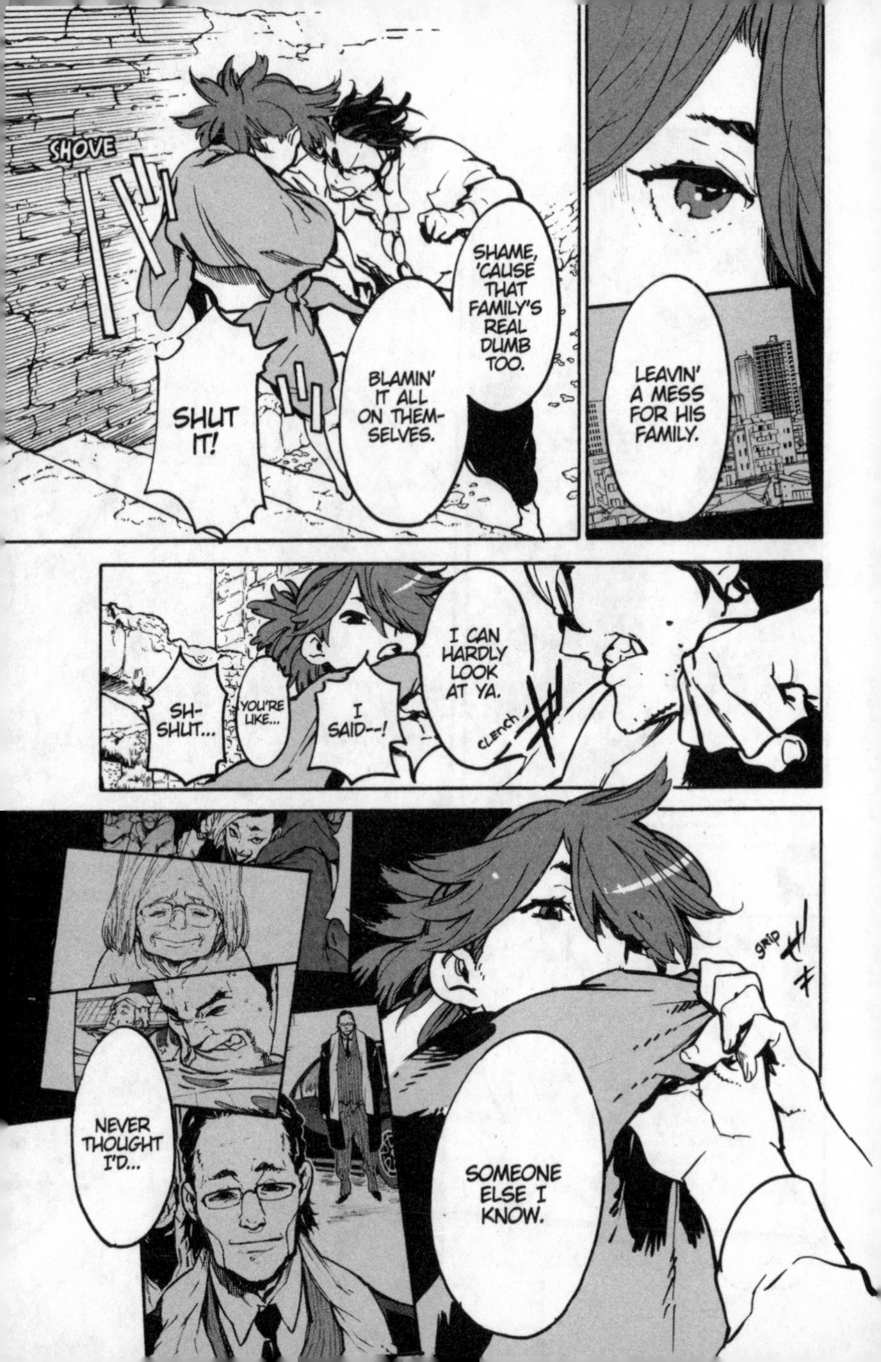
LEAVIN' A MESS FOR HIS FAMILY.
SHAME, 'CAUSE THAT FAMILY'S REAL DUMB TOO.
BLAMIN' IT ALL ON THEM-SELVES.
SHOVE
SHUT IT!
I CAN HARDLY LOOK AT YA.
CLENCH
I SAID--!
YOU'RE LIKE...
SH-SHUT...
GRIP
SOMEONE ELSE I KNOW.
NEVER THOUGHT I'D...

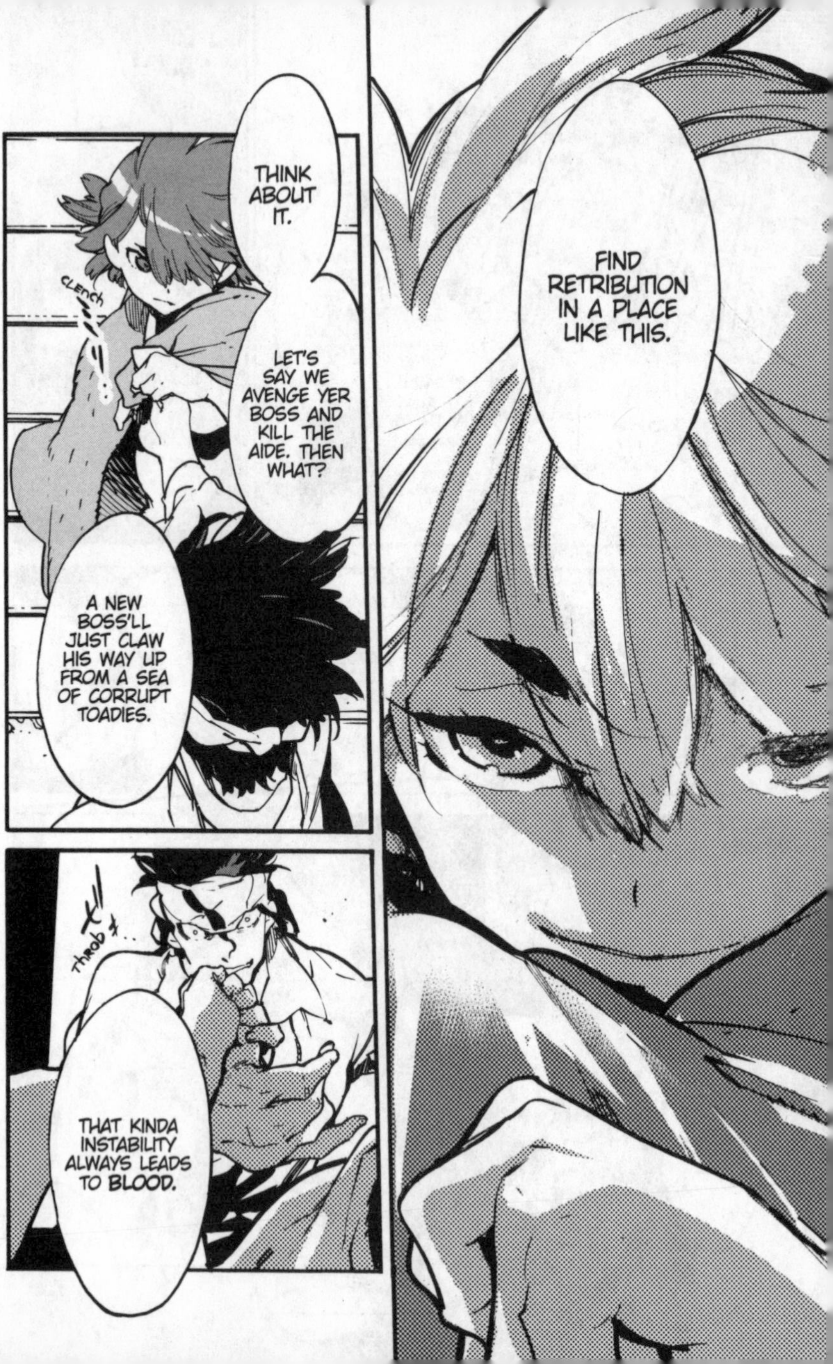
FIND RETRIBUTION IN A PLACE LIKE THIS.
THINK ABOUT IT.
CLENCH
LET'S SAY WE AVENGE YER BOSS AND KILL THE AIDE. THEN WHAT?
A NEW BOSS'LL JUST CLAW HIS WAY UP FROM A SEA OF CORRUPT TOADIES.
throb
THAT KINDA INSTABILITY ALWAYS LEADS TO **BLOOD.**

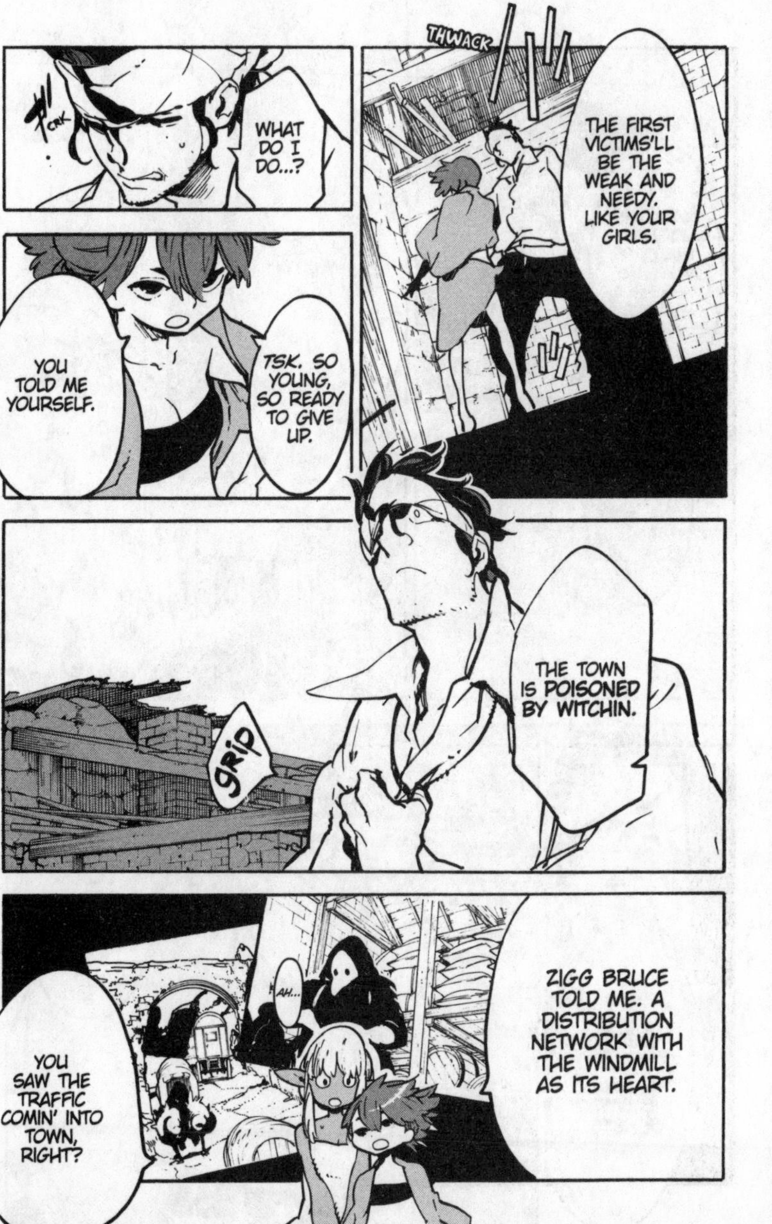
THWACK
THE FIRST VICTIMS'LL BE THE WEAK AND NEEDY. LIKE YOUR GIRLS.
CRK
WHAT DO I DO...?
TSK. SO YOUNG, SO READY TO GIVE UP.
YOU TOLD ME YOURSELF.
THE TOWN IS POISONED BY WITCHIN.
grip
ZIGG BRUCE TOLD ME. A DISTRIBUTION NETWORK WITH THE WINDMILL AS ITS HEART.
AH...
YOU SAW THE TRAFFIC COMIN' INTO TOWN, RIGHT?

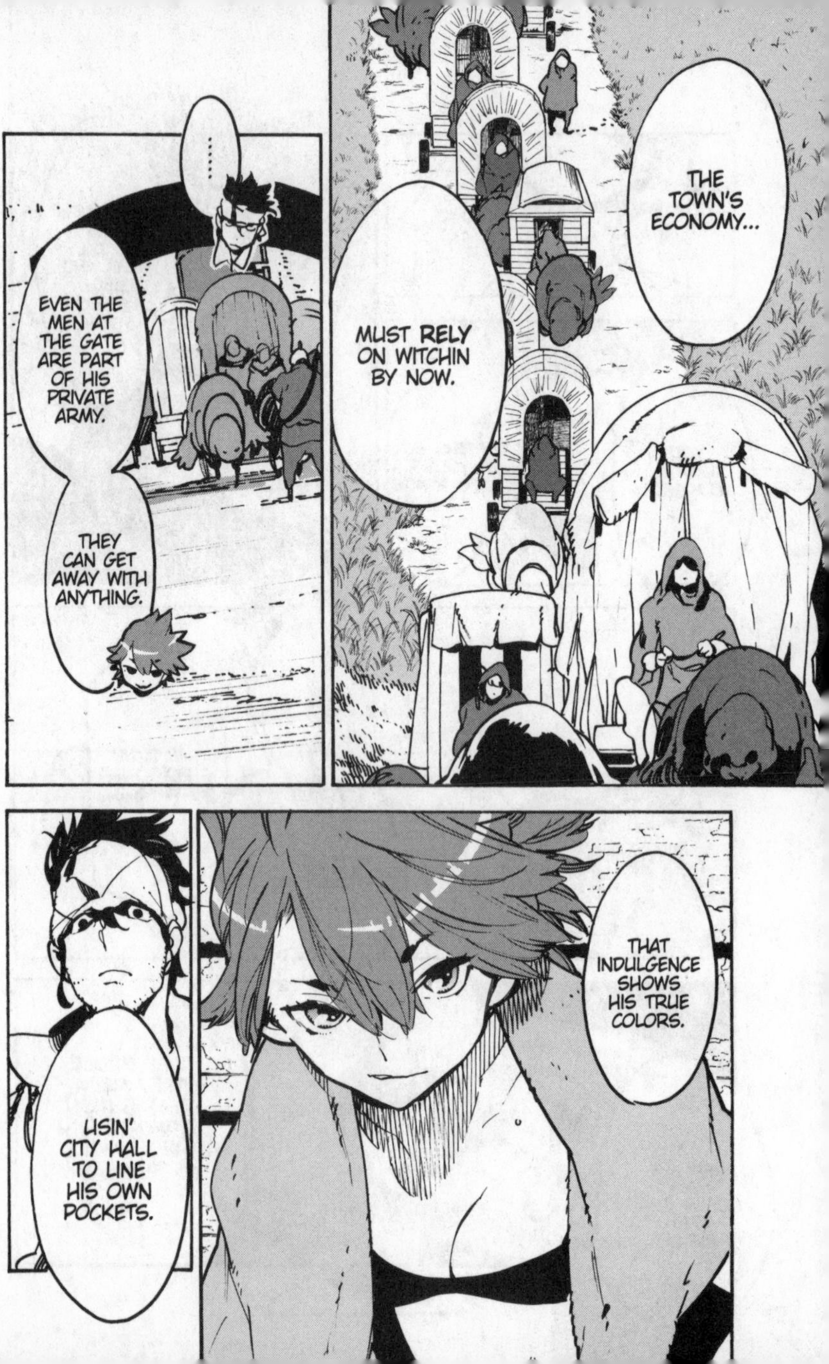
THE TOWN'S ECONOMY...
MUST RELY ON WITCHIN BY NOW.
...
EVEN THE MEN AT THE GATE ARE PART OF HIS PRIVATE ARMY.
THEY CAN GET AWAY WITH ANYTHING.
THAT INDULGENCE SHOWS HIS TRUE COLORS.
USIN' CITY HALL TO LINE HIS OWN POCKETS.

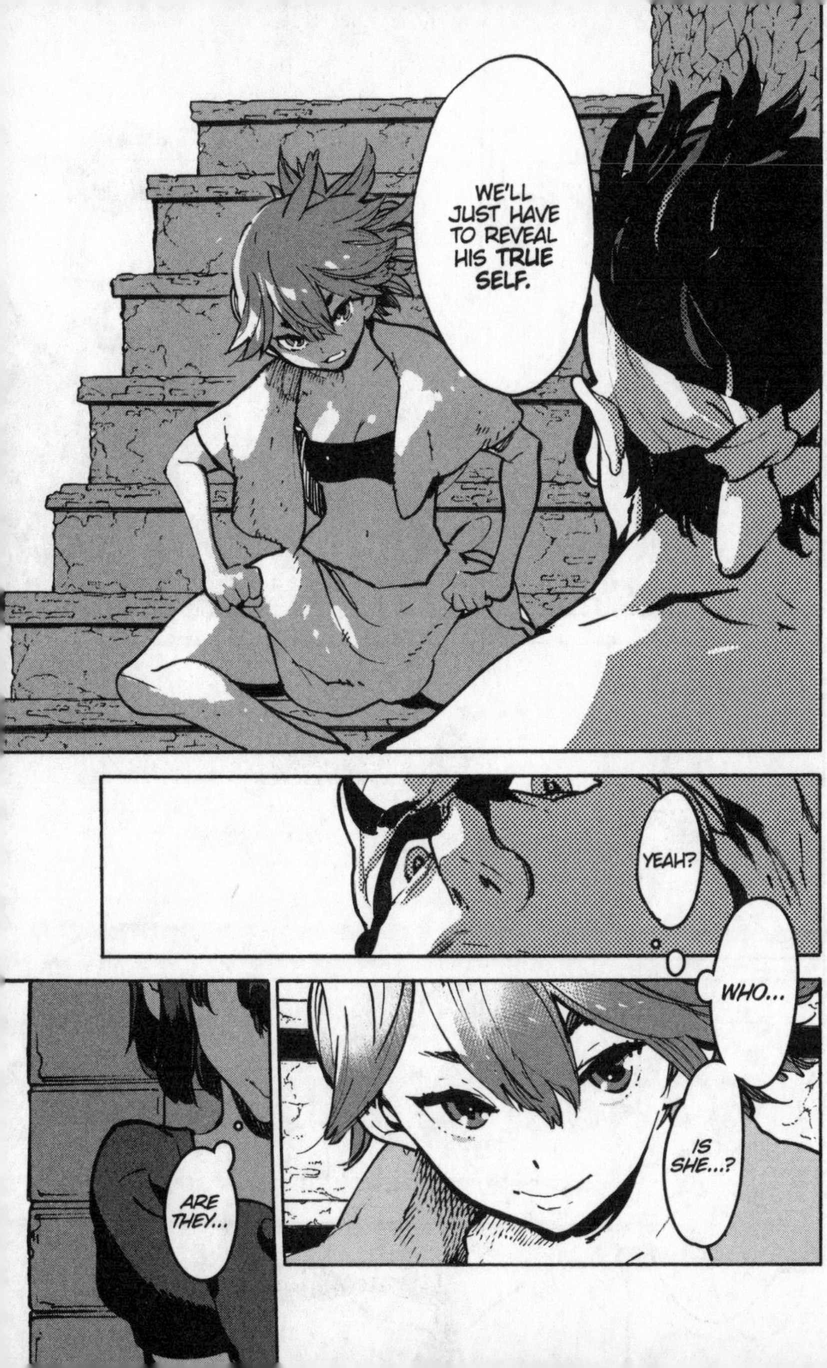
WE'LL JUST HAVE TO REVEAL HIS TRUE SELF.
YEAH?
WHO...
IS SHE...?
ARE THEY...

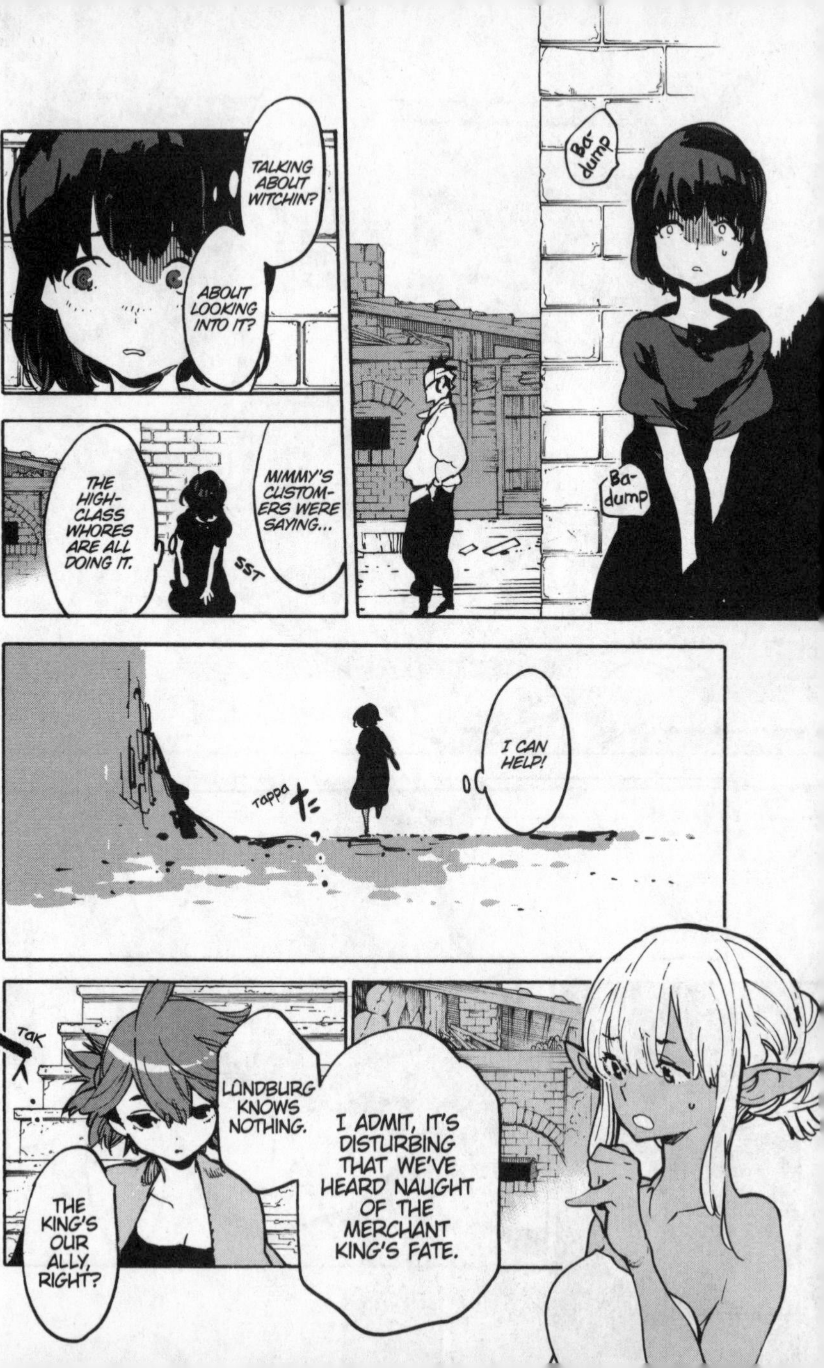
Ba-dump
Ba-dump
TALKING ABOUT WITCHIN?
ABOUT LOOKING INTO IT?
MIMMY'S CUSTOMERS WERE SAYING...
SST
THE HIGH-CLASS WHORES ARE ALL DOING IT.
I CAN HELP!
Tappa
I ADMIT, IT'S DISTURBING THAT WE'VE HEARD NAUGHT OF THE MERCHANT KING'S FATE.
LUNDBURG KNOWS NOTHING.
TAK
THE KING'S OUR ALLY, RIGHT?

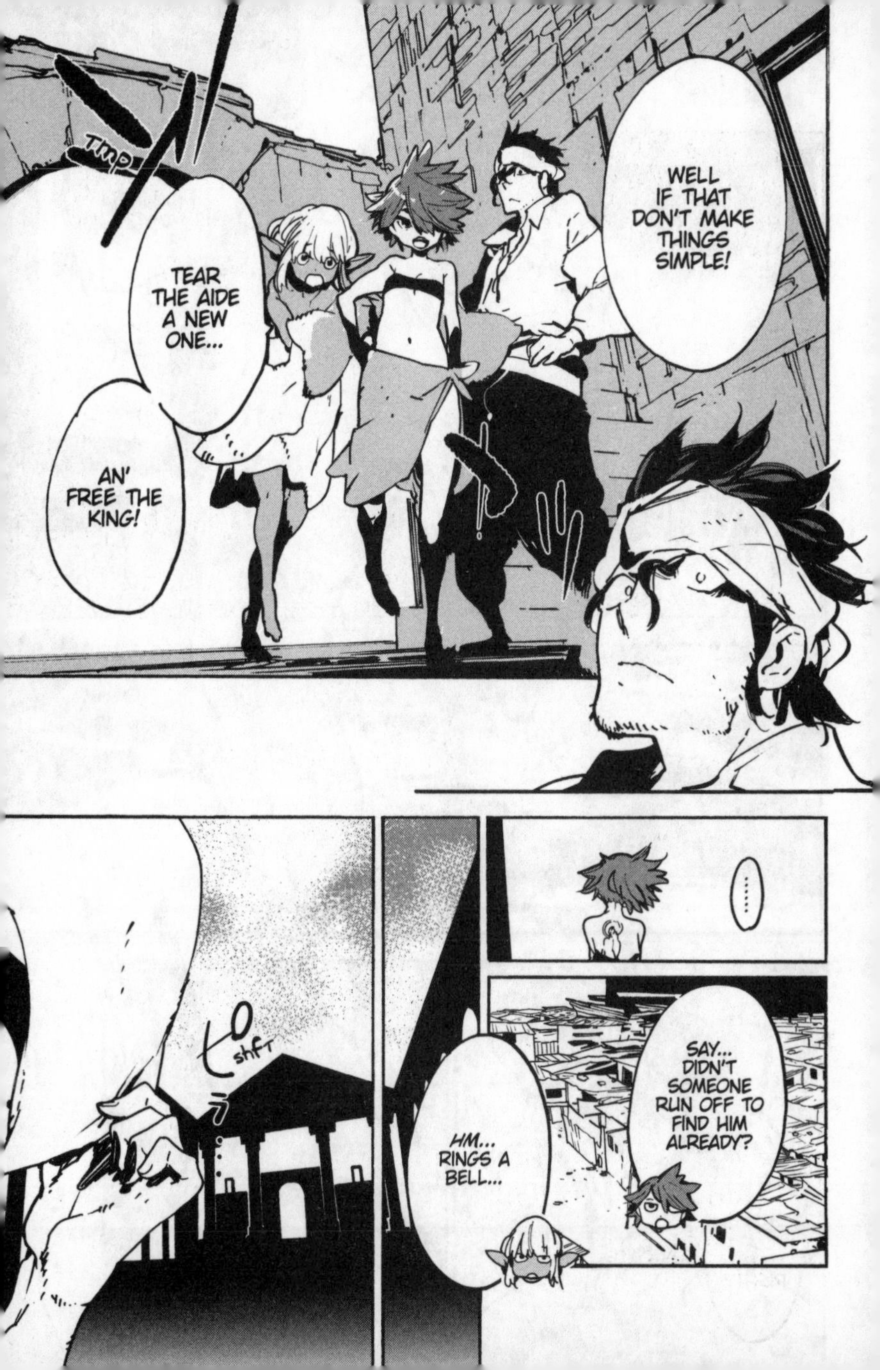
WELL IF THAT DON'T MAKE THINGS SIMPLE!
TMP
TEAR THE AIDE A NEW ONE...
AN' FREE THE KING!
......
SAY... DIDN'T SOMEONE RUN OFF TO FIND HIM ALREADY?
HM... RINGS A BELL...
shft

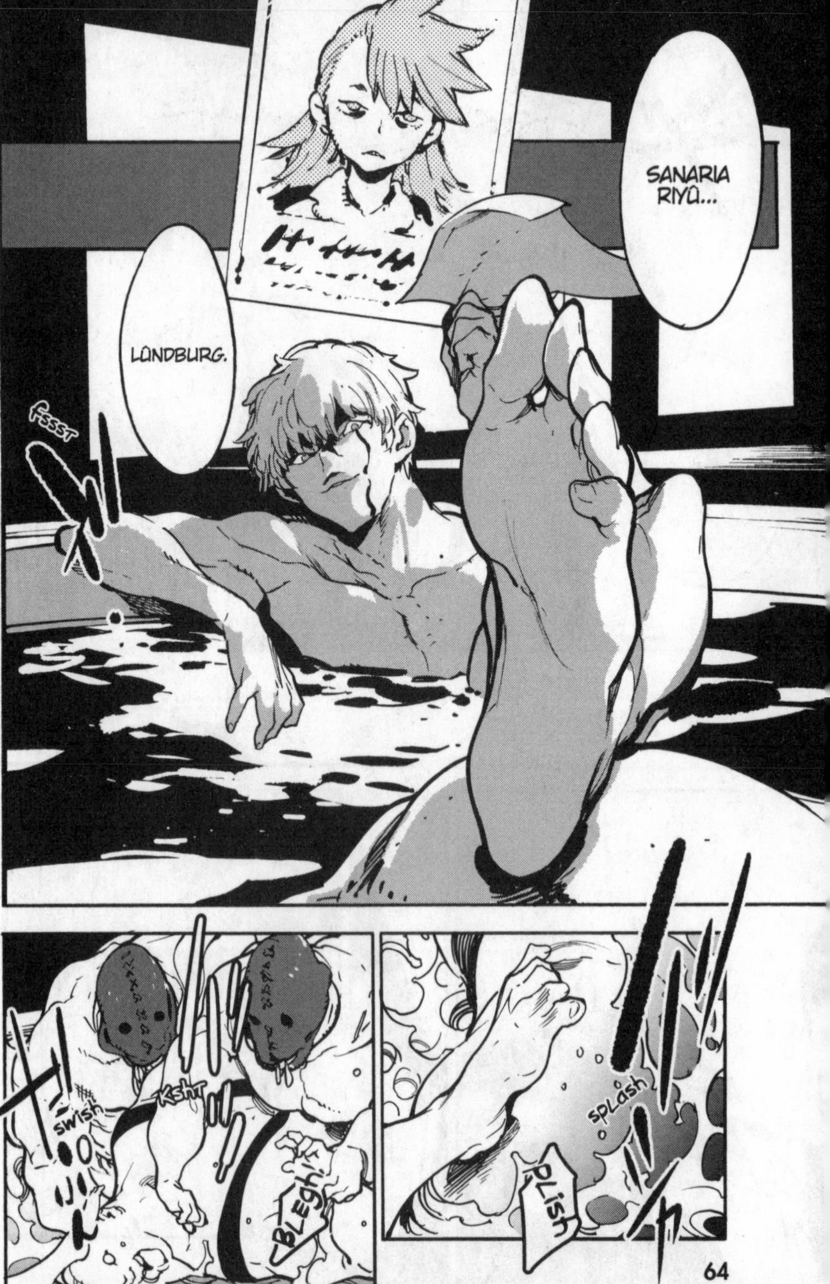
SANARIA RIYÛ...
LÛNDBURG.
fssst
splash
PLish
KshT
swish
Blegh!

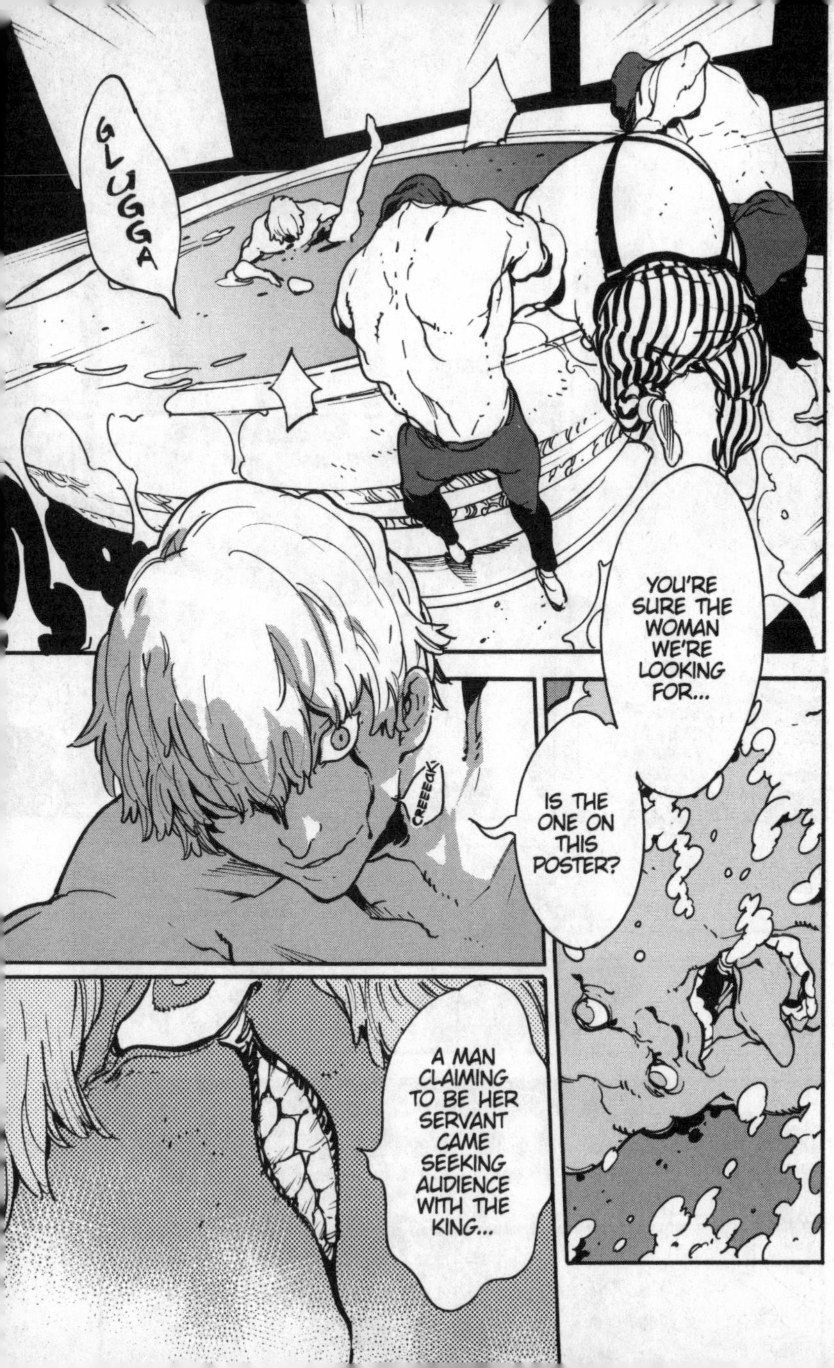
GLUGGA
YOU'RE SURE THE WOMAN WE'RE LOOKING FOR...
IS THE ONE ON THIS POSTER?
CREEEAK
A MAN CLAIMING TO BE HER SERVANT CAME SEEKING AUDIENCE WITH THE KING...

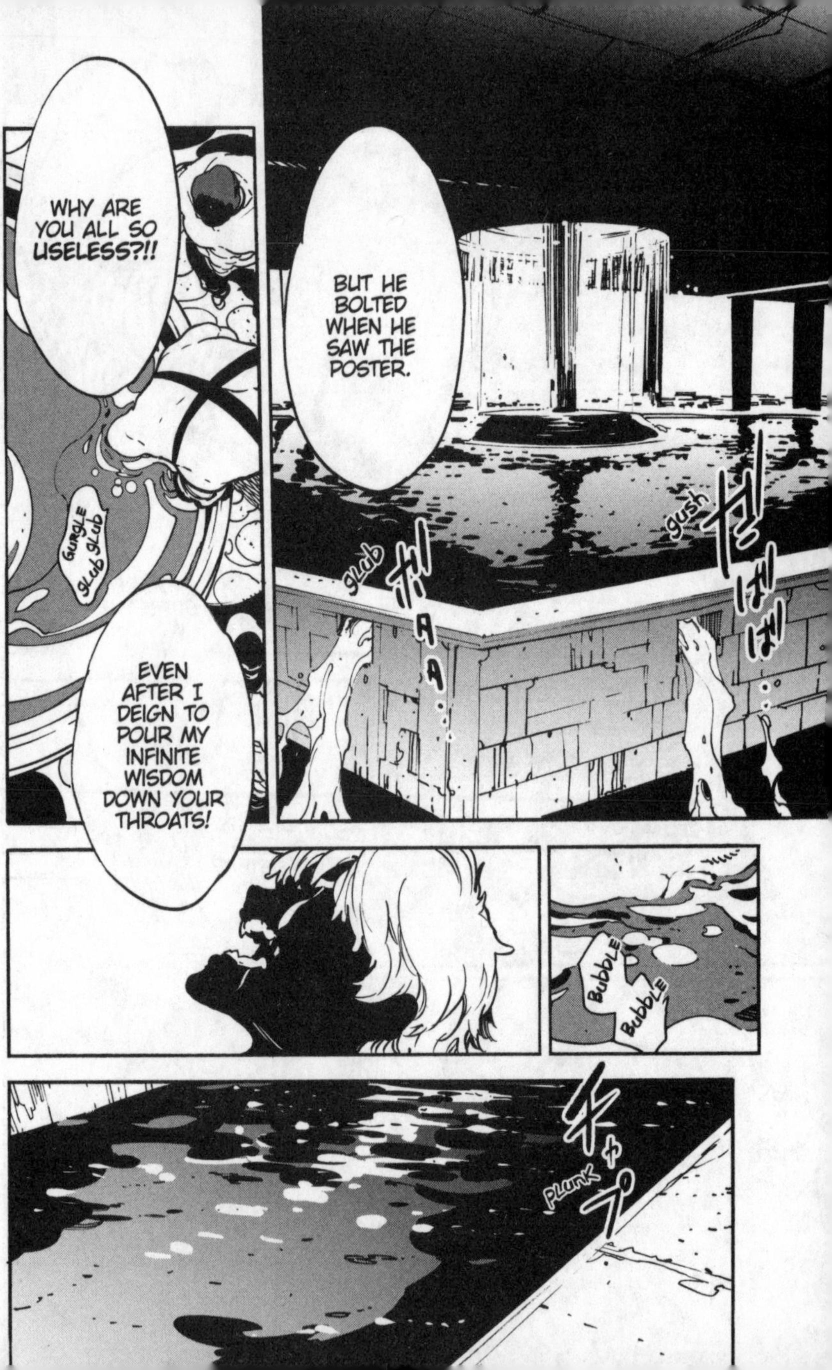
BUT HE BOLTED WHEN HE SAW THE POSTER.
gush
glub
WHY ARE YOU ALL SO USELESS?!!
GURGLE GLUB GLUB
EVEN AFTER I DEIGN TO POUR MY INFINITE WISDOM DOWN YOUR THROATS!
BUBBLE BUBBLE
PLUNK

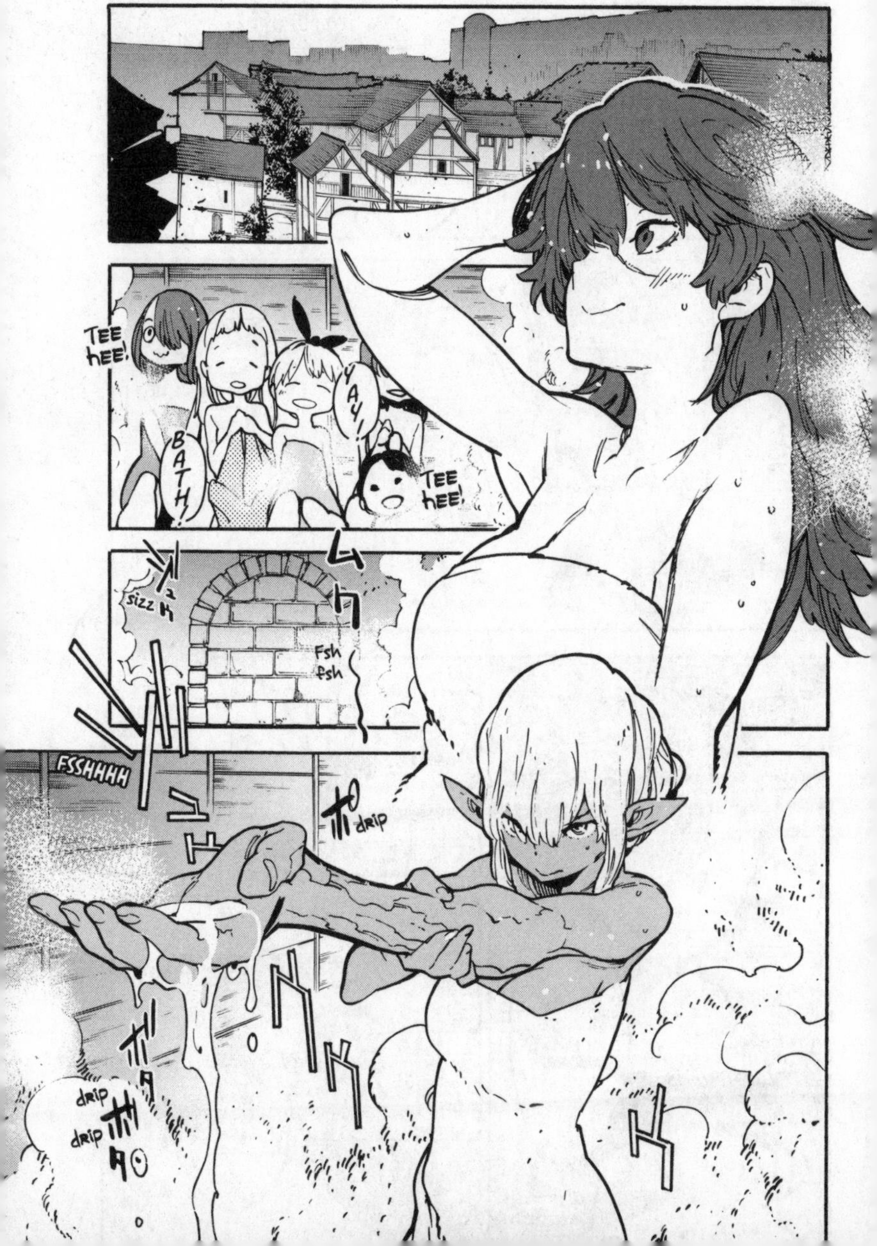
YAY!
TEE hee!
TEE hee!
BATH!
Fsh fsh
sizz
FSSHHHH
drip
drip
drip

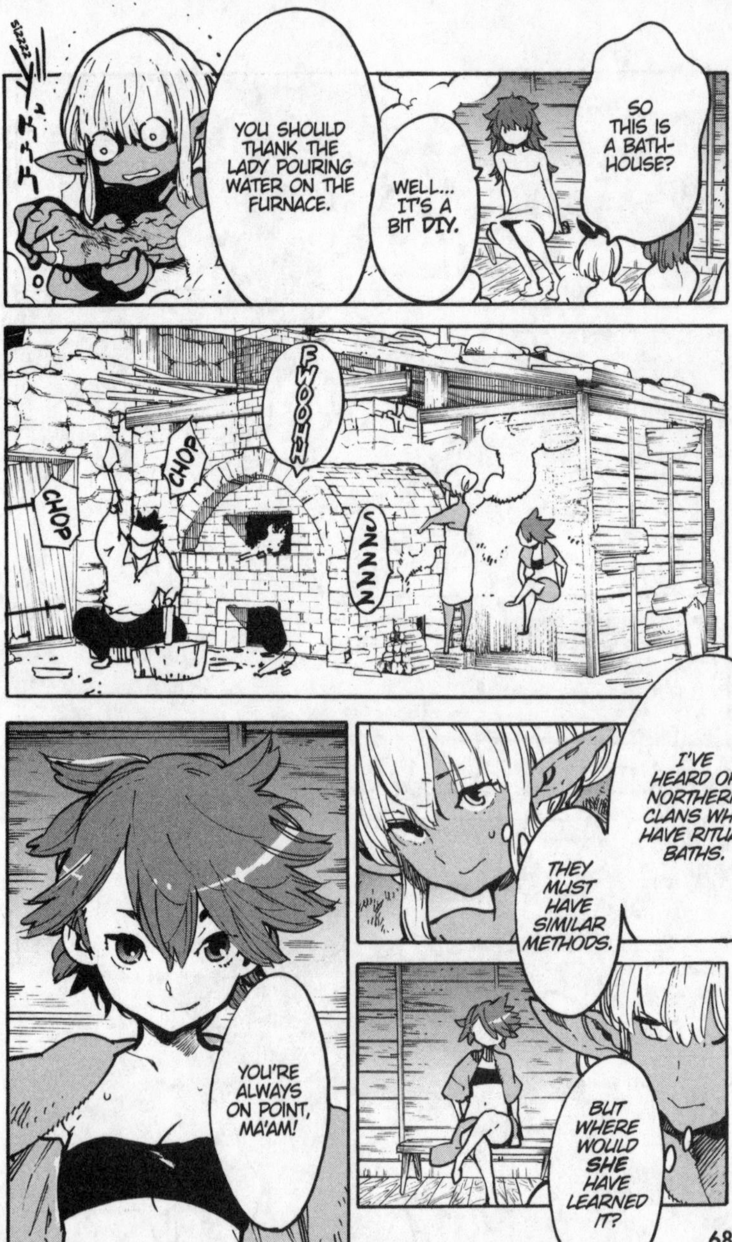
SO THIS IS A BATH-HOUSE?
WELL... IT'S A BIT DIY.
YOU SHOULD THANK THE LADY POURING WATER ON THE FURNACE.
SIZZZZ
FWOOOHH
NNNNN
CHOP
CHOP
I'VE HEARD OF NORTHERN CLANS WHO HAVE RITUAL BATHS.
THEY MUST HAVE SIMILAR METHODS.
BUT WHERE WOULD SHE HAVE LEARNED IT?
YOU'RE ALWAYS ON POINT, MA'AM!

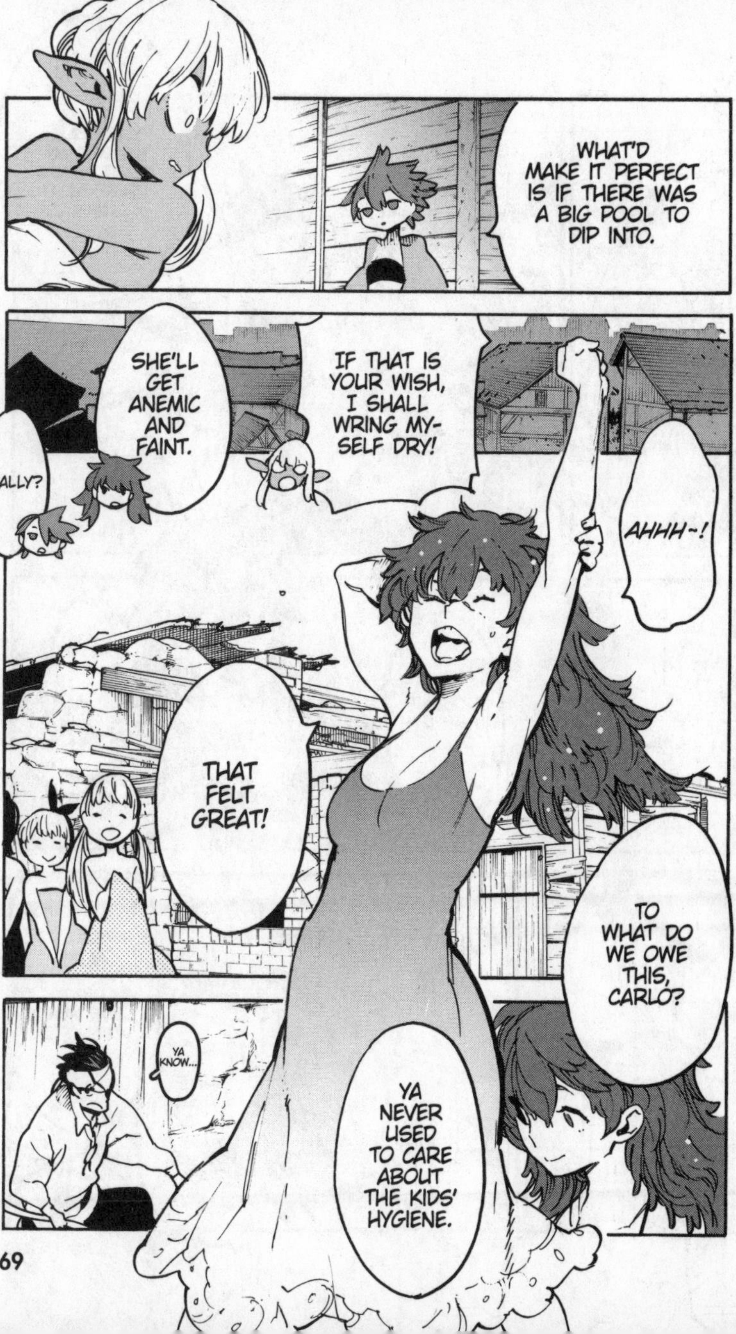
WHAT'D MAKE IT PERFECT IS IF THERE WAS A BIG POOL TO DIP INTO.
IF THAT IS YOUR WISH, I SHALL WRING MY-SELF DRY!
SHE'LL GET ANEMIC AND FAINT.
REALLY?
AHHH~!
THAT FELT GREAT!
TO WHAT DO WE OWE THIS, CARLO?
YA NEVER USED TO CARE ABOUT THE KIDS' HYGIENE.
YA KNOW...

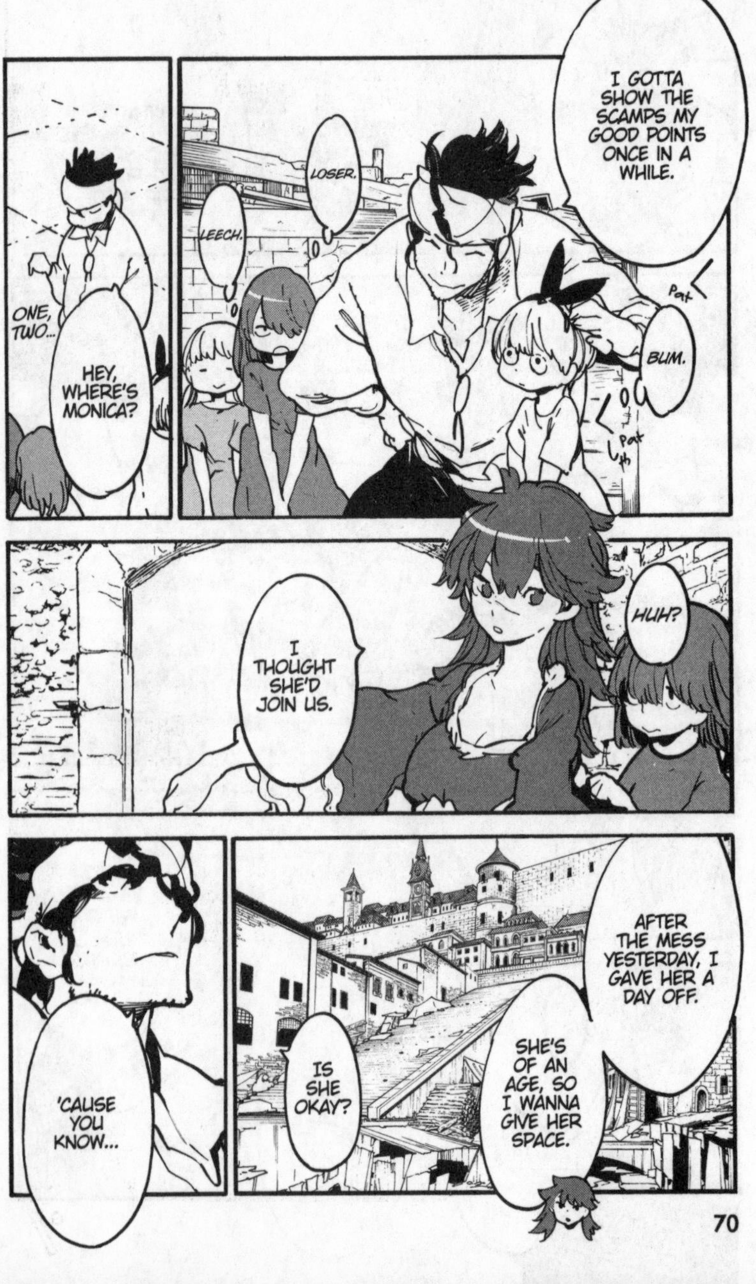
I GOTTA SHOW THE SCAMPS MY GOOD POINTS ONCE IN A WHILE.
Pat
BUM.
Pat
LOSER.
LEECH.
ONE, TWO...
HEY, WHERE'S MONICA?
HUH?
I THOUGHT SHE'D JOIN US.
AFTER THE MESS YESTERDAY, I GAVE HER A DAY OFF.
SHE'S OF AN AGE, SO I WANNA GIVE HER SPACE.
IS SHE OKAY?
'CAUSE YOU KNOW...

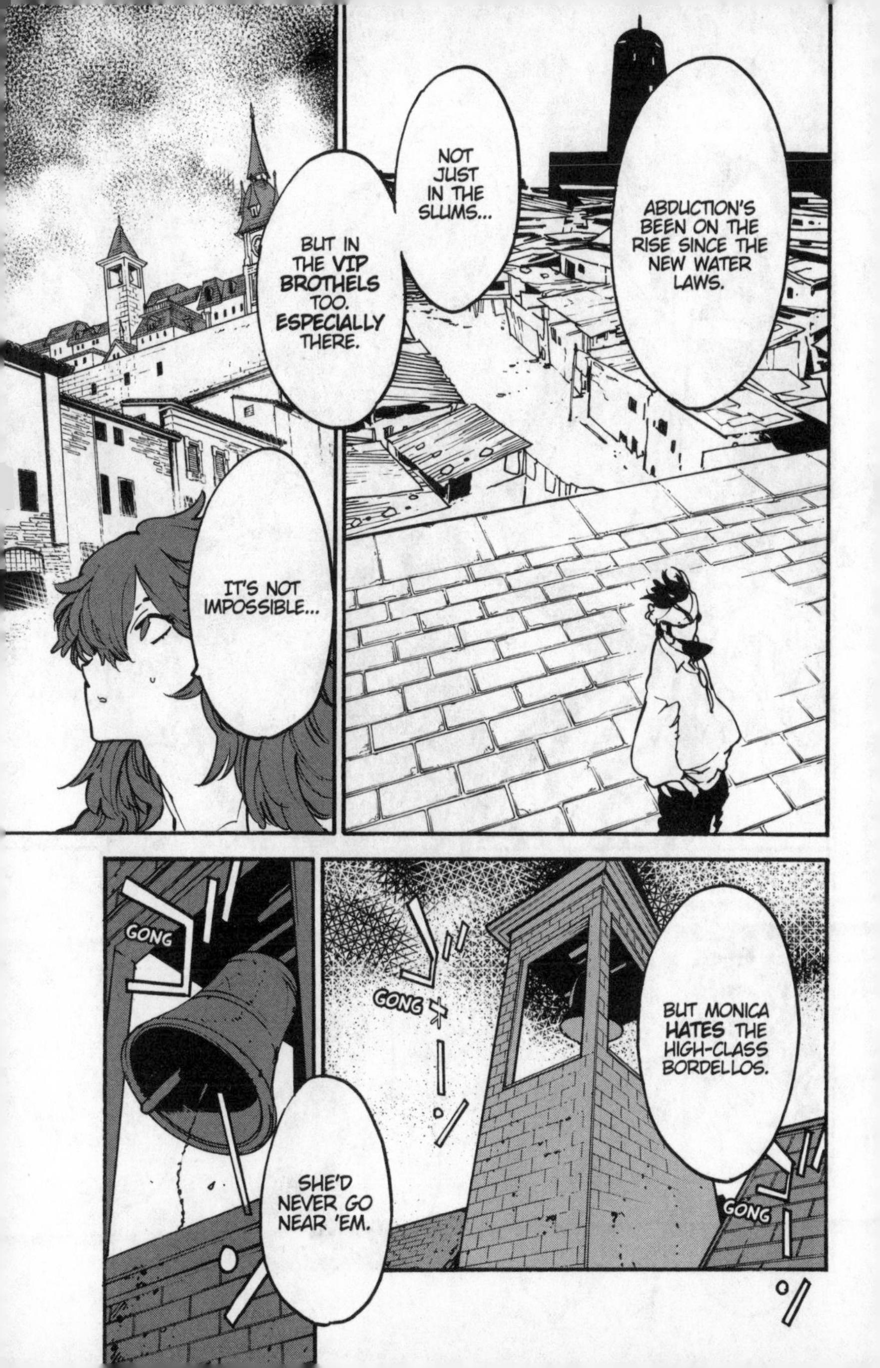
ABDUCTION'S BEEN ON THE RISE SINCE THE NEW WATER LAWS.
NOT JUST IN THE SLUMS...
BUT IN THE VIP BROTHELS TOO. ESPECIALLY THERE.
IT'S NOT IMPOSSIBLE...
GONG
BUT MONICA HATES THE HIGH-CLASS BORDELLOS.
GONG
GONG
SHE'D NEVER GO NEAR 'EM.

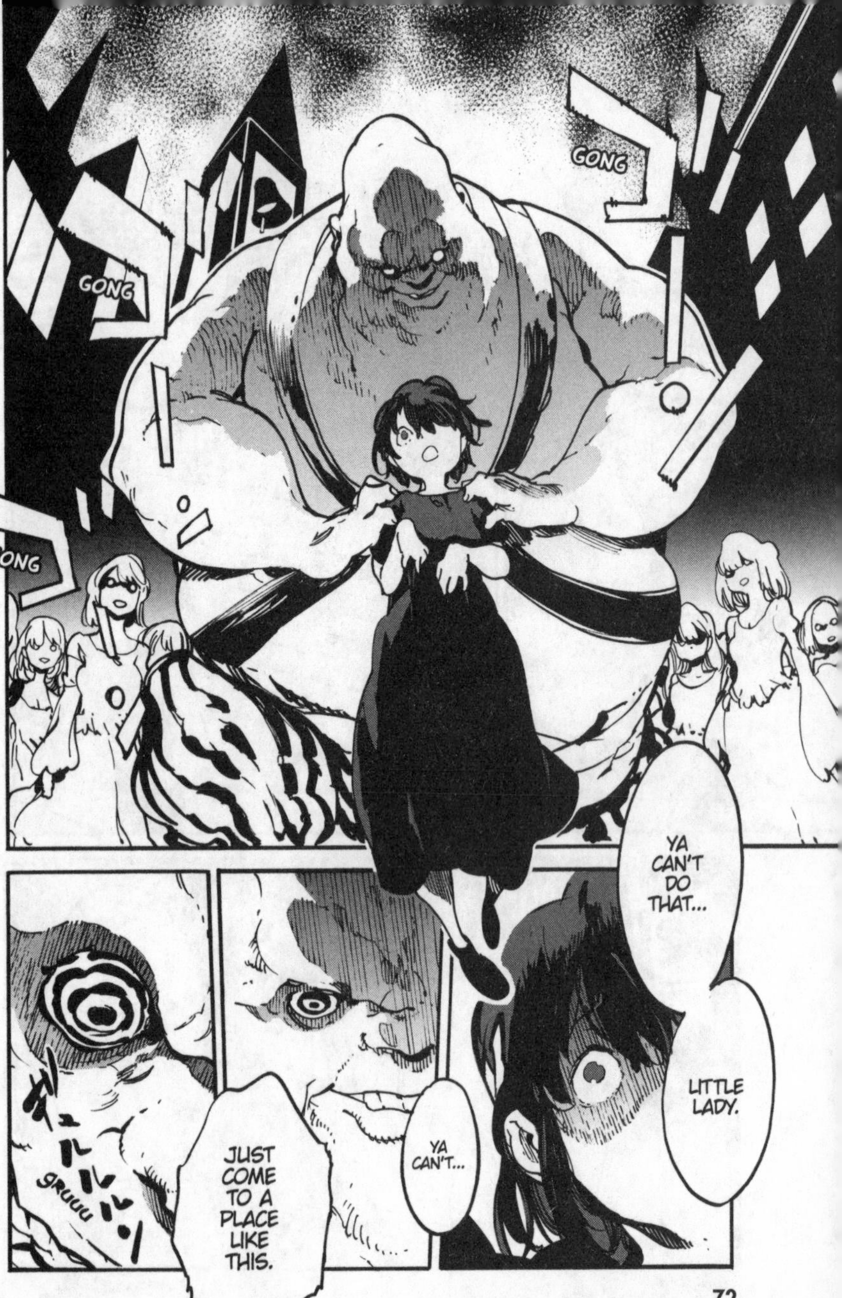
GONG
GONG
GONG
YA CAN'T DO THAT...
LITTLE LADY.
YA CAN'T...
JUST COME TO A PLACE LIKE THIS.
gruuu

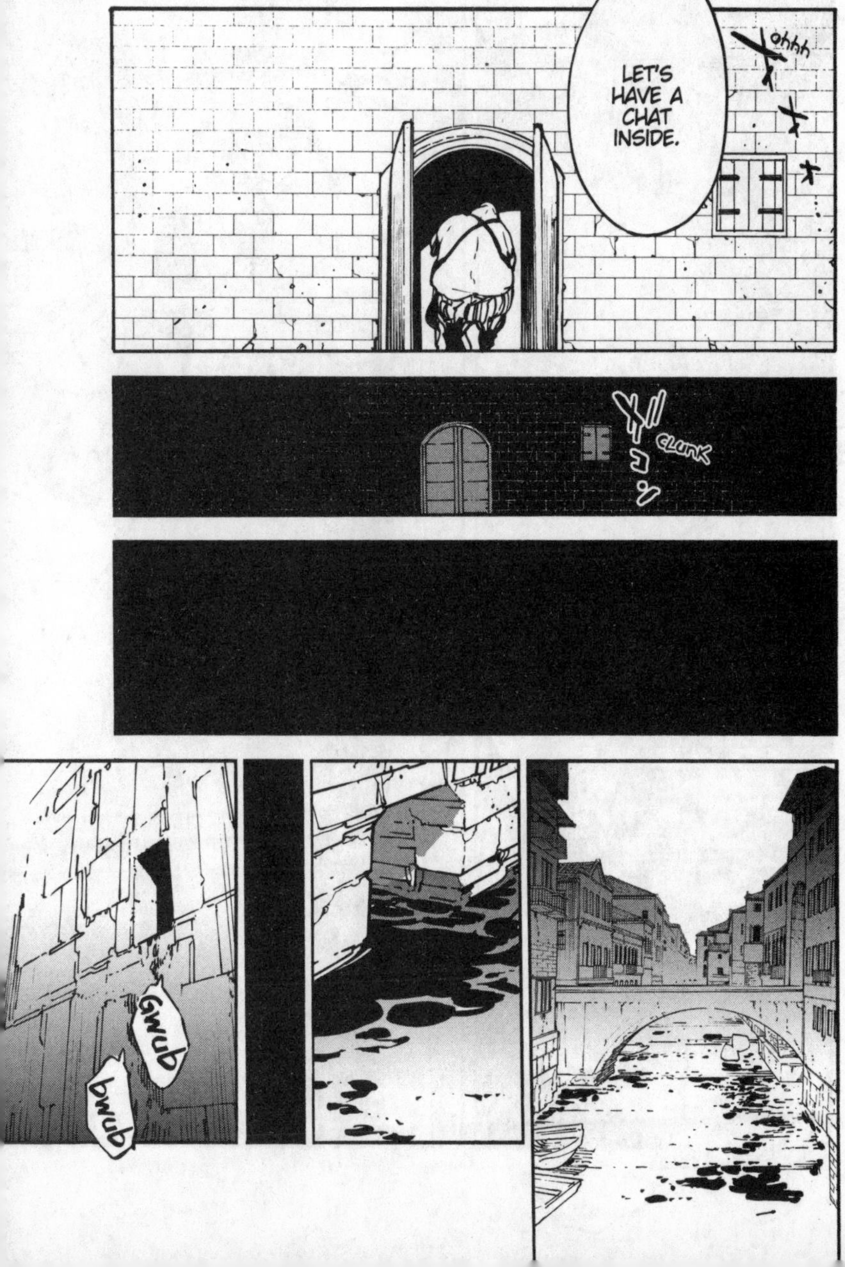
LET'S HAVE A CHAT INSIDE.
ohhh
CLUNK
Gwub
bwub

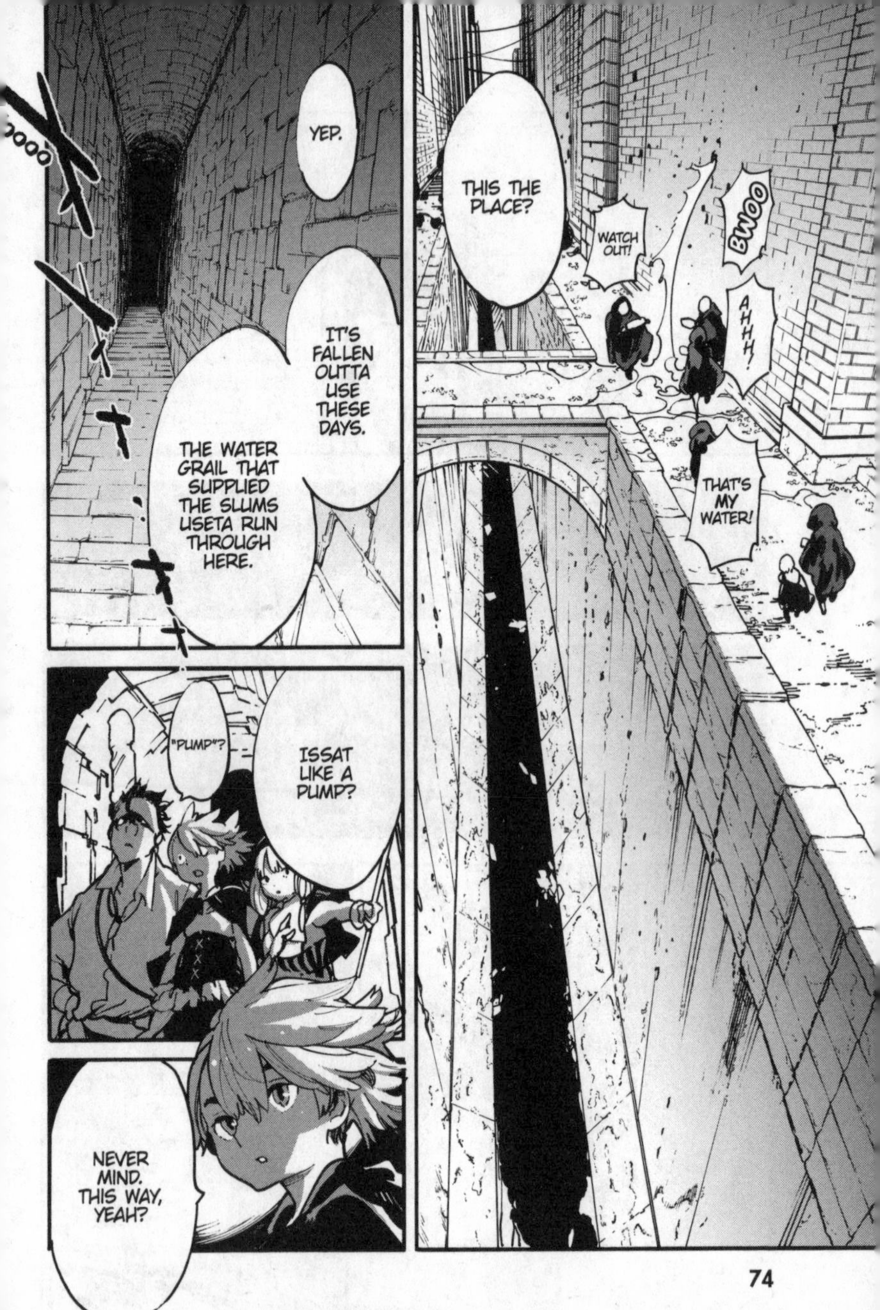
THIS THE PLACE?
WATCH OUT!
BWOO
AHHH!
THAT'S MY WATER!
YEP.
IT'S FALLEN OUTTA USE THESE DAYS.
THE WATER GRAIL THAT SUPPLIED THE SLUMS USETA RUN THROUGH HERE.
ISSAT LIKE A PUMP?
"PUMP"?
NEVER MIND. THIS WAY, YEAH?

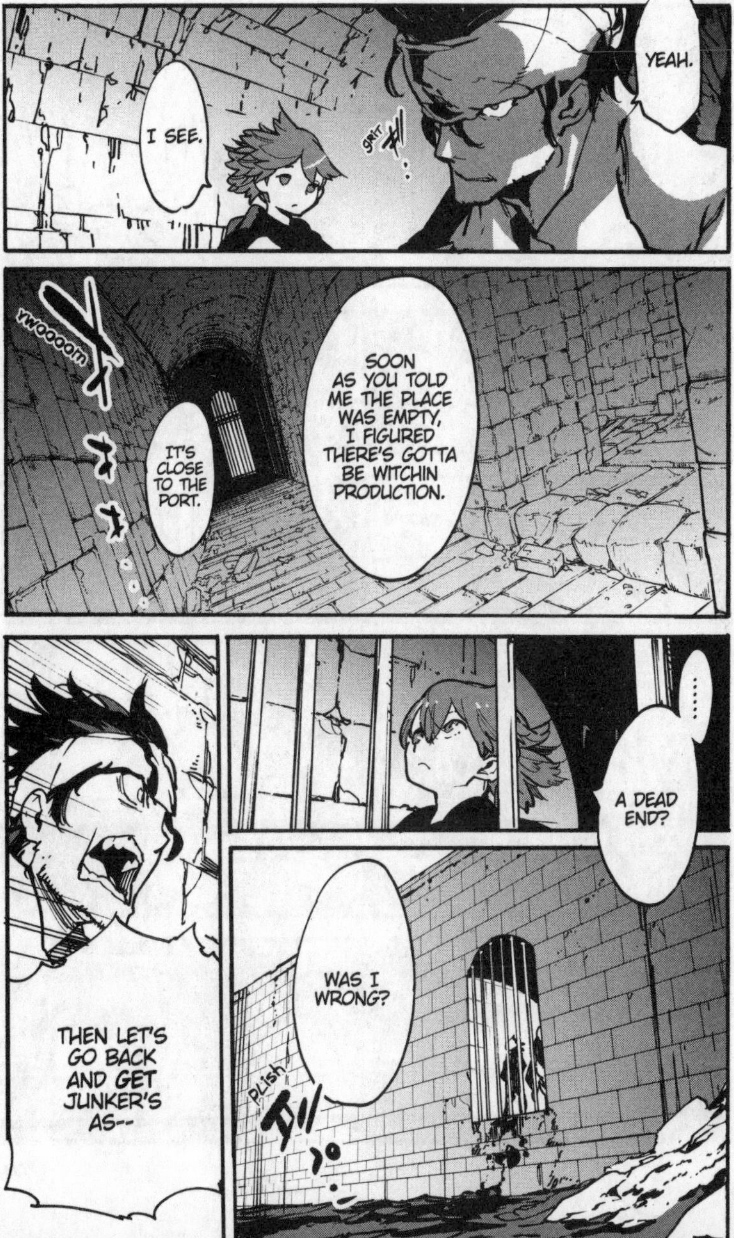
YEAH.
GRIT
I SEE.
SOON AS YOU TOLD ME THE PLACE WAS EMPTY, I FIGURED THERE'S GOTTA BE WITCHIN PRODUCTION.
IT'S CLOSE TO THE PORT.
ywoooom
......
A DEAD END?
WAS I WRONG?
PLISH
THEN LET'S GO BACK AND GET JUNKER'S AS--

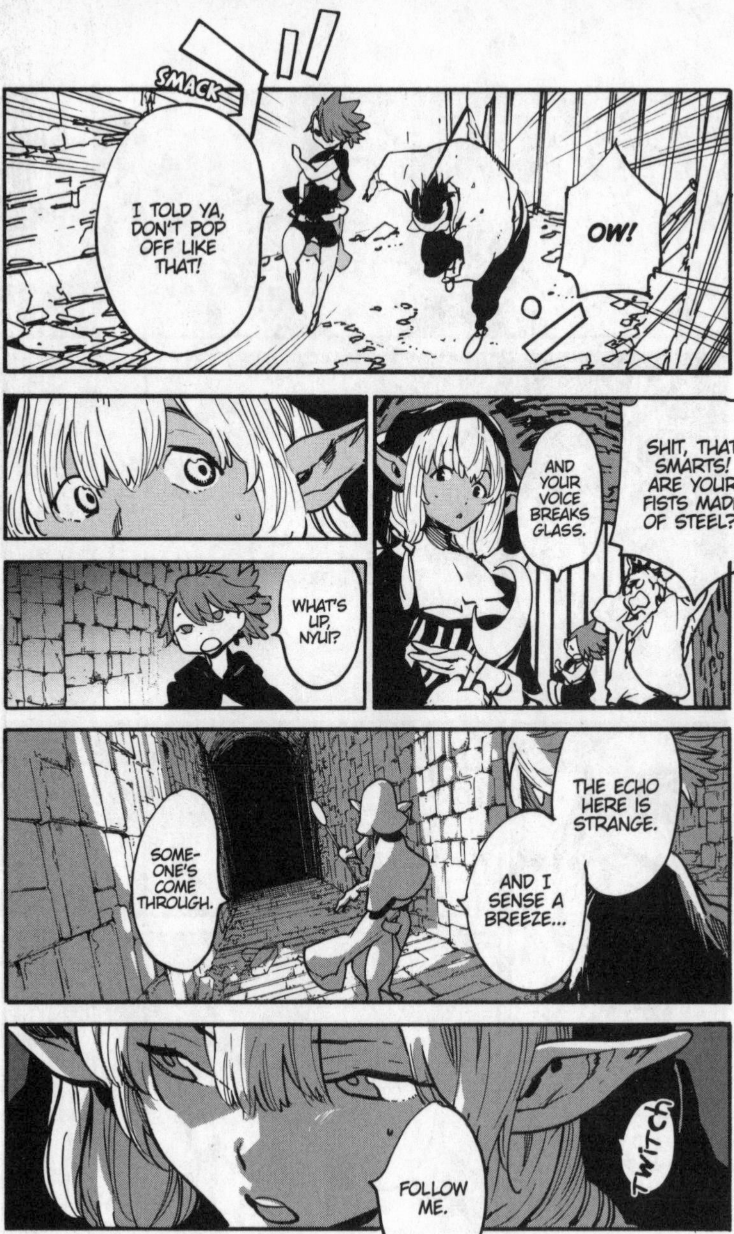
SMACK
OW!
I TOLD YA, DON'T POP OFF LIKE THAT!
SHIT, THAT SMARTS! ARE YOUR FISTS MADE OF STEEL?!
AND YOUR VOICE BREAKS GLASS.
WHAT'S UP, NYUI?
THE ECHO HERE IS STRANGE.
AND I SENSE A BREEZE...
SOME-ONE'S COME THROUGH.
TWITCH
FOLLOW ME.

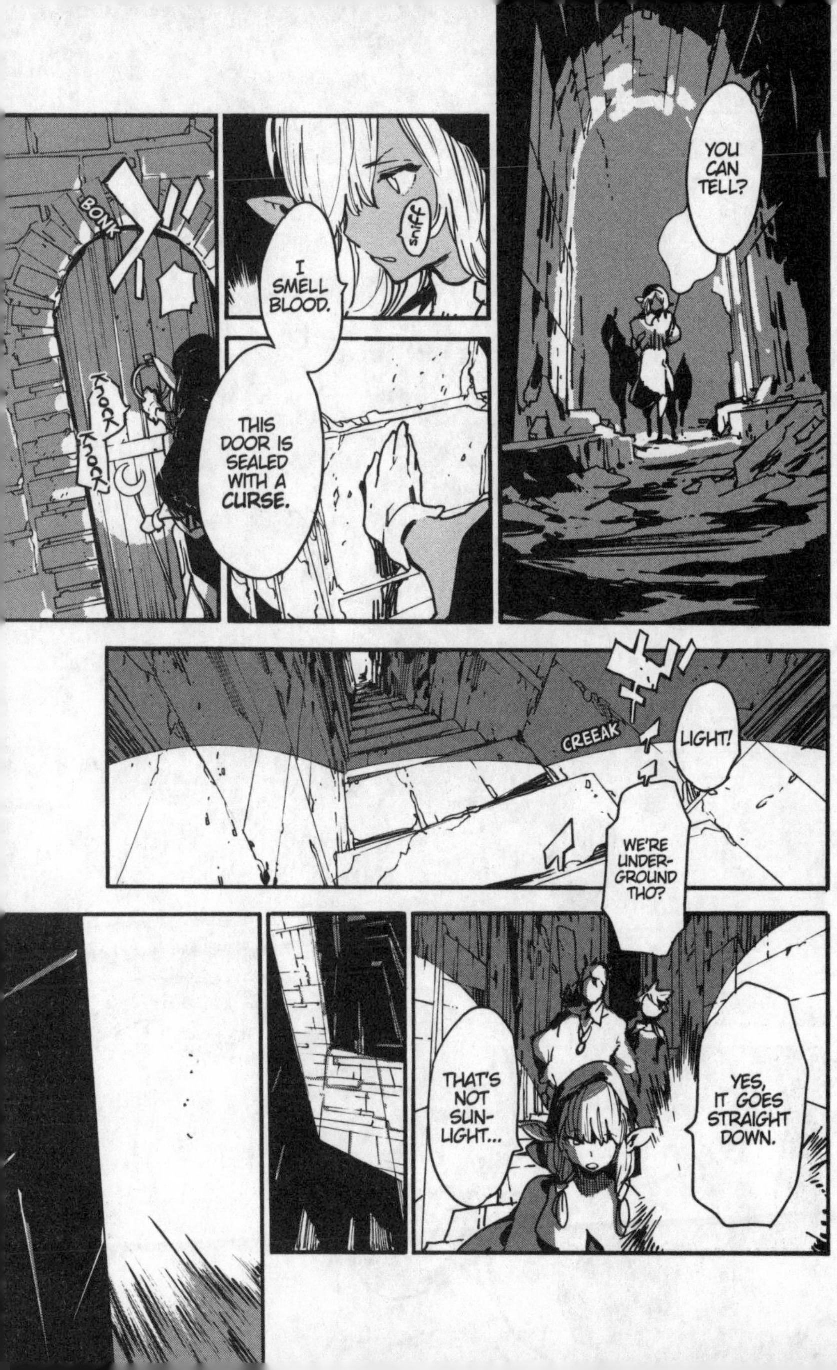
YOU CAN TELL?
sniff
I SMELL BLOOD.
THIS DOOR IS SEALED WITH A CURSE.
BONK
KNOCK KNOCK
CREEAK
LIGHT!
WE'RE UNDER-GROUND THO?
YES, IT GOES STRAIGHT DOWN.
THAT'S NOT SUN-LIGHT...

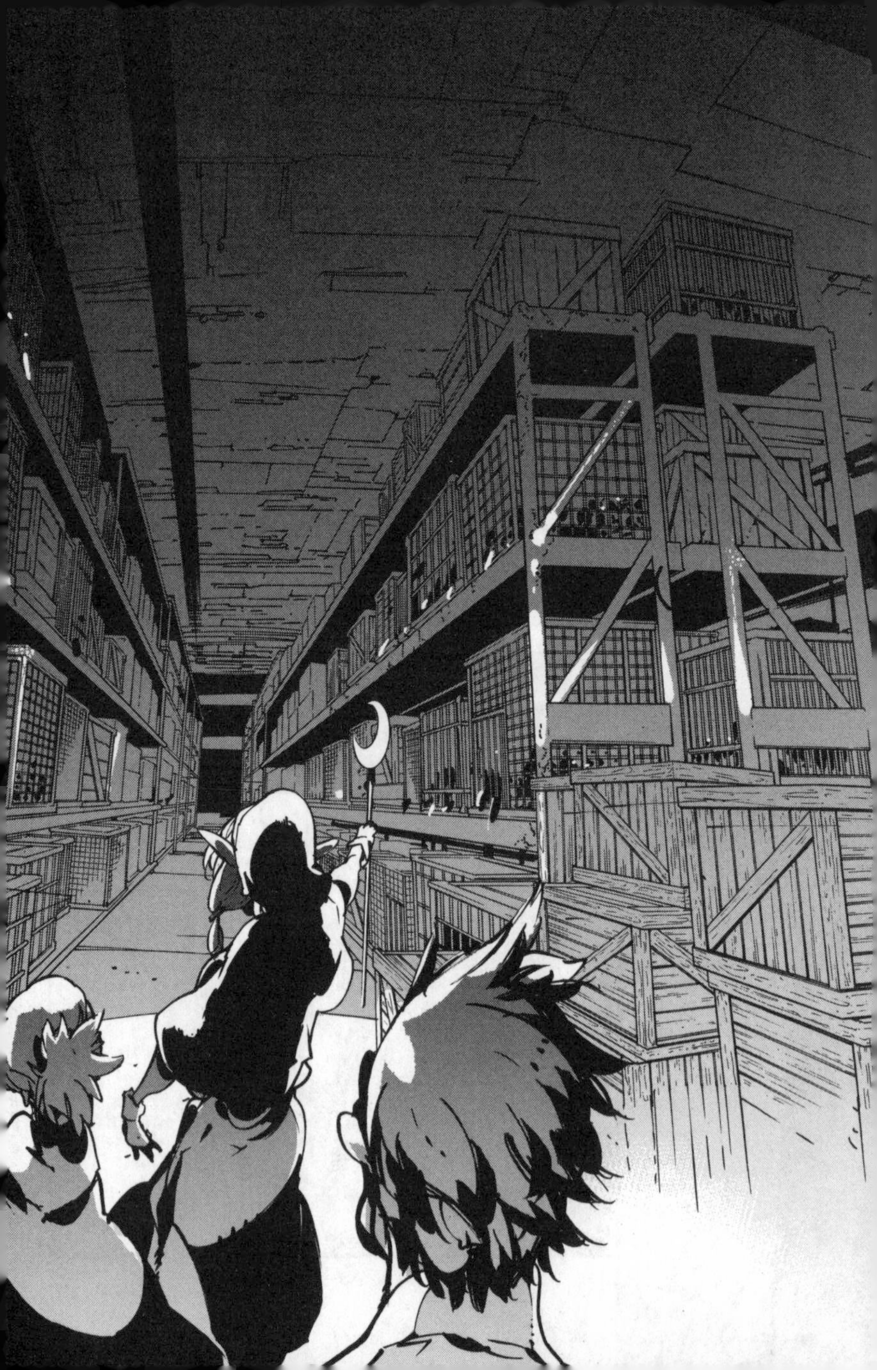

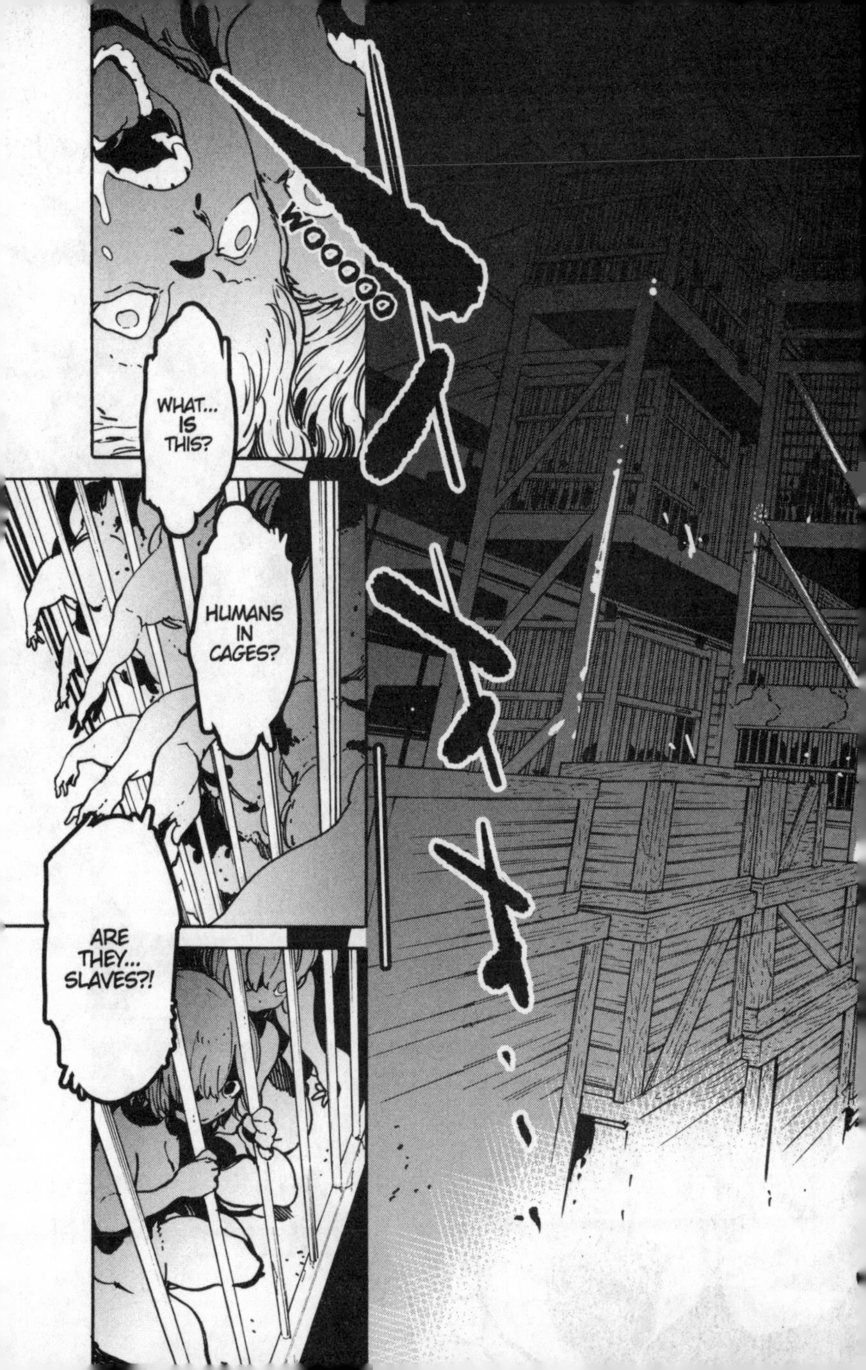
WOOOOOO
WHAT... IS THIS?
HUMANS IN CAGES?
ARE THEY... SLAVES?!

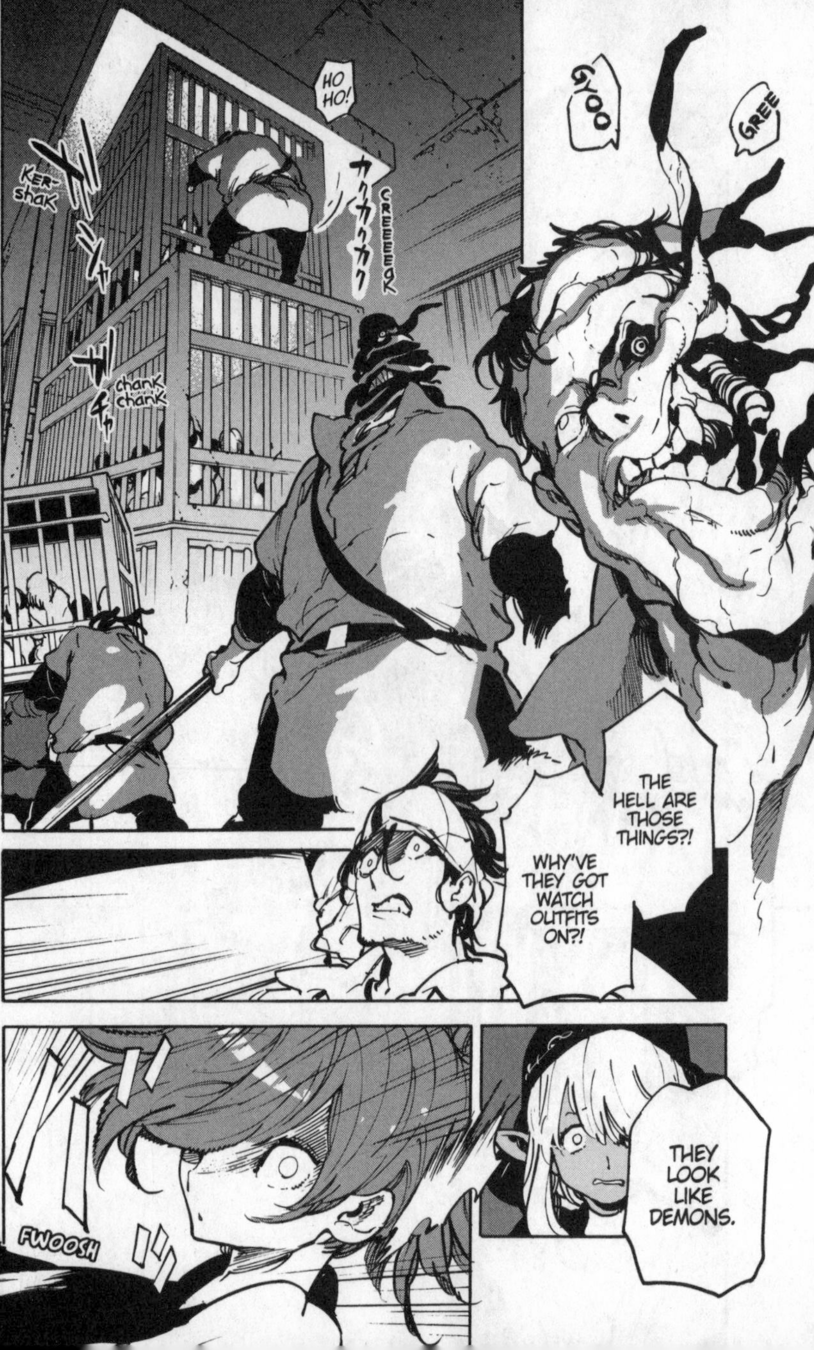
GREE
GYOO
HO HO!
カクカクカク
CREEEEK
KER-SHAK
chank chank
THE HELL ARE THOSE THINGS?!
WHY'VE THEY GOT WATCH OUTFITS ON?!
THEY LOOK LIKE DEMONS.
FWOOSH

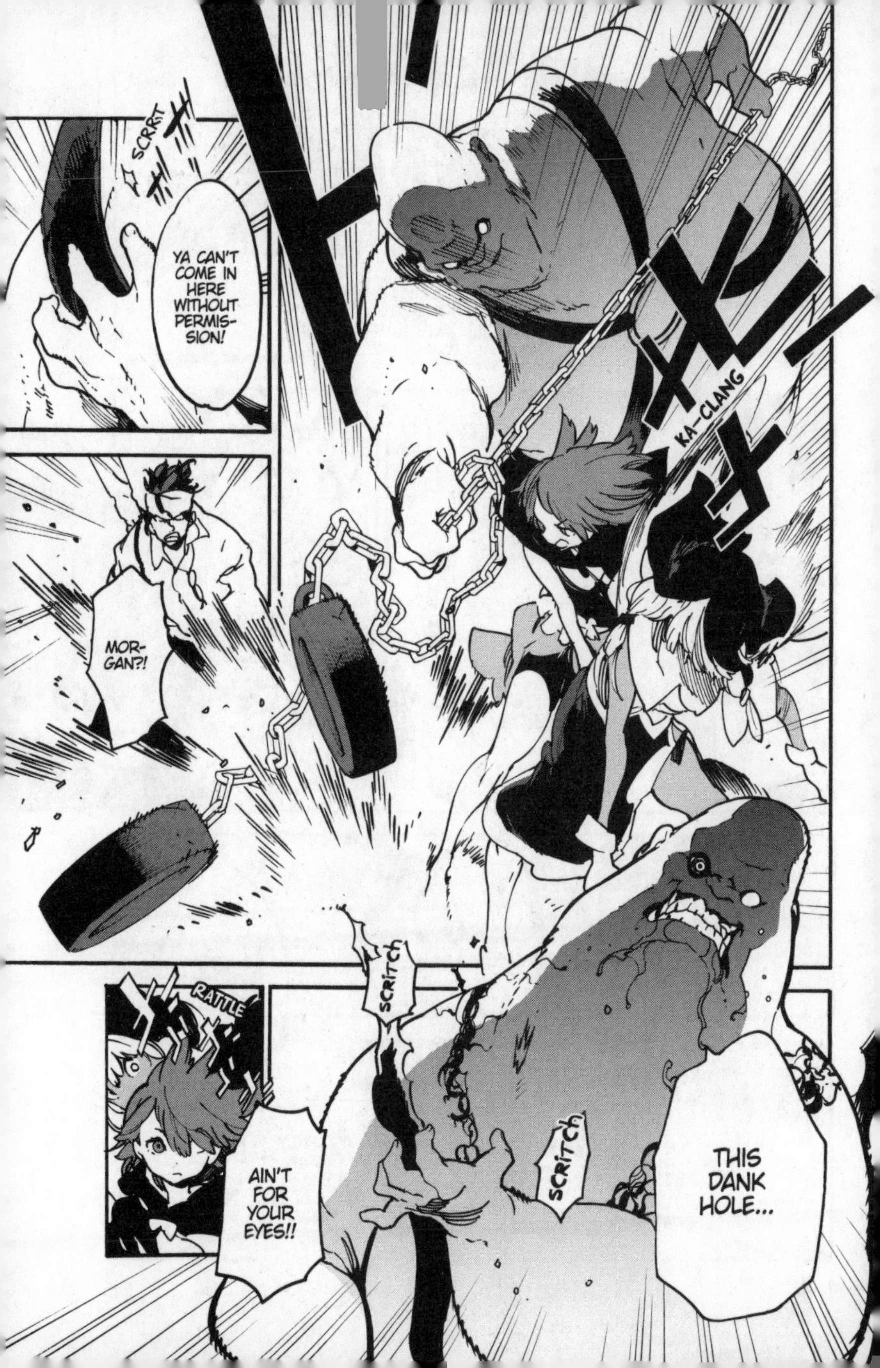
KA-CLANG
SCRRT
YA CAN'T COME IN HERE WITHOUT PERMISSION!
MOR-GAN?!
SCRITCH
THIS DANK HOLE...
SCRITCH
AIN'T FOR YOUR EYES!!
RATTLE

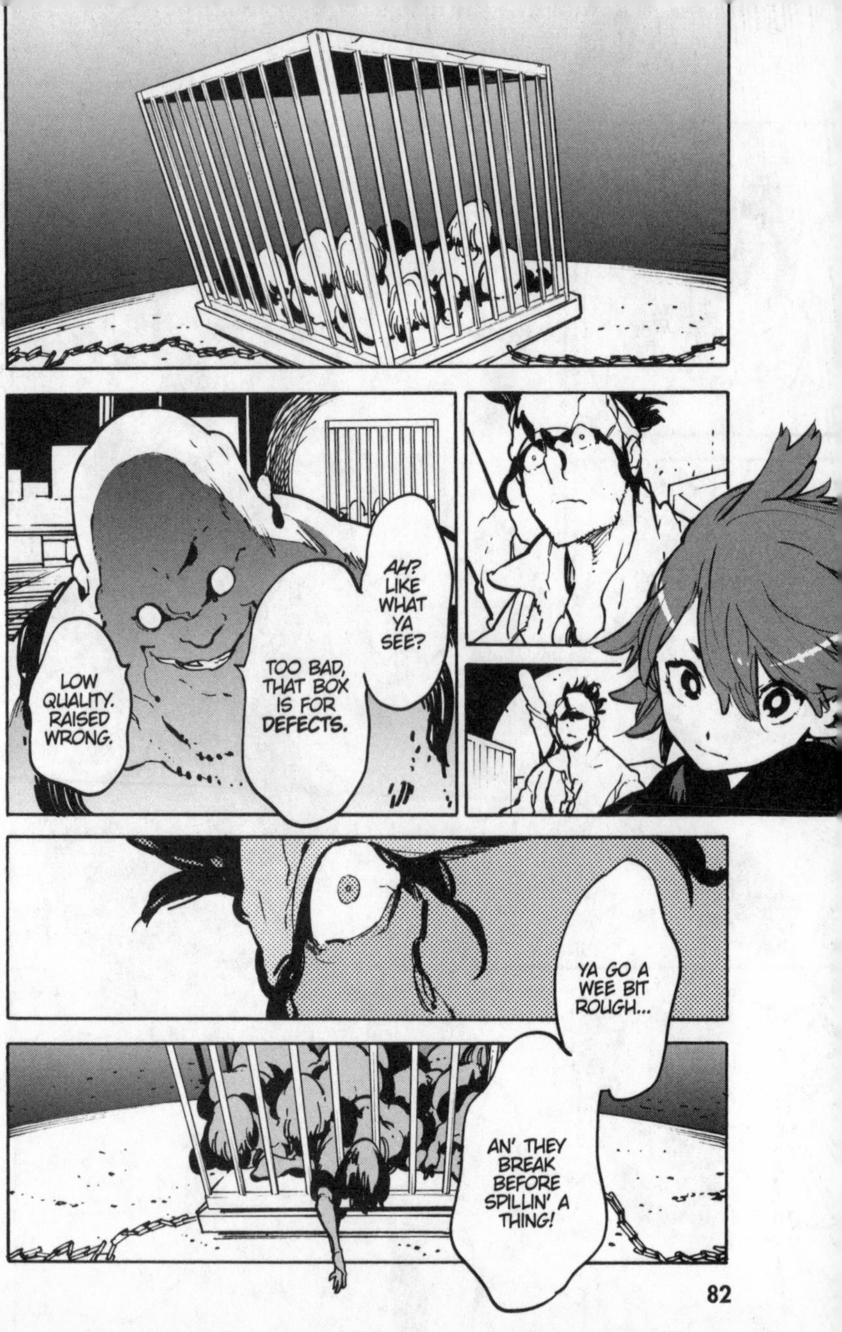
AH? LIKE WHAT YA SEE?
TOO BAD, THAT BOX IS FOR DEFECTS.
LOW QUALITY. RAISED WRONG.
YA GO A WEE BIT ROUGH...
AN' THEY BREAK BEFORE SPILLIN' A THING!

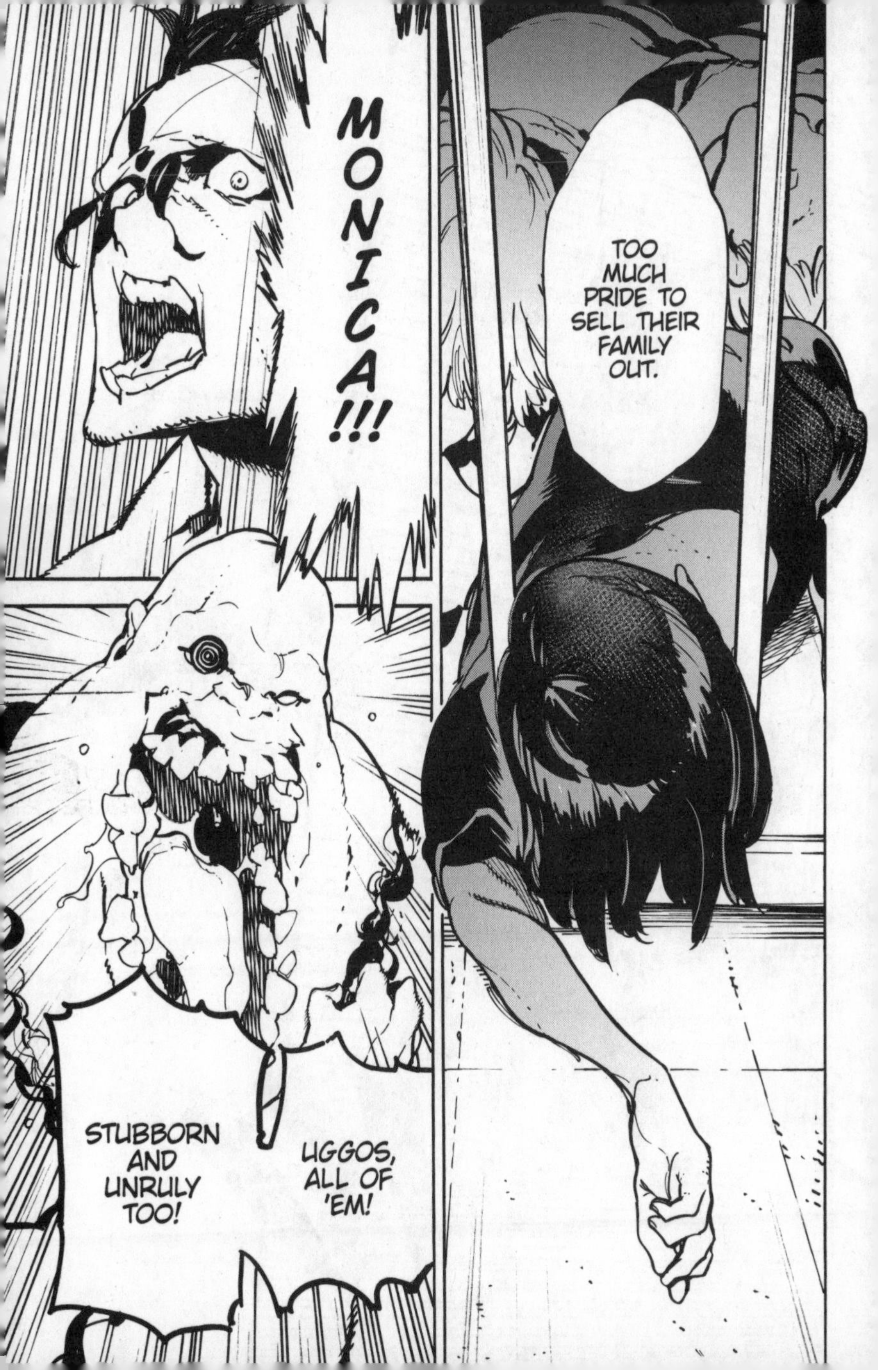
TOO MUCH PRIDE TO SELL THEIR FAMILY OUT.
MONICA!!!
UGGOS, ALL OF 'EM!
STUBBORN AND UNRULY TOO!

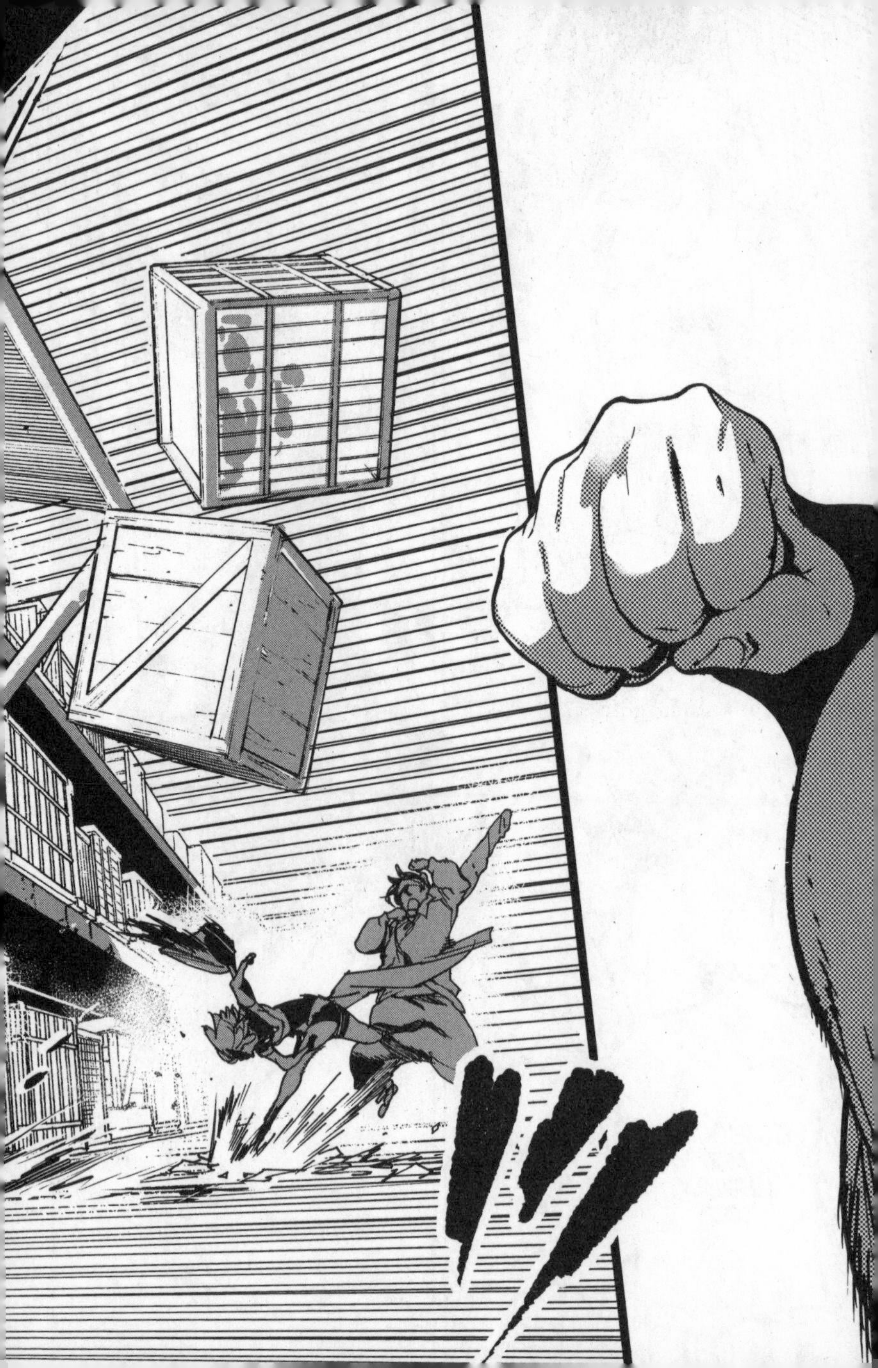

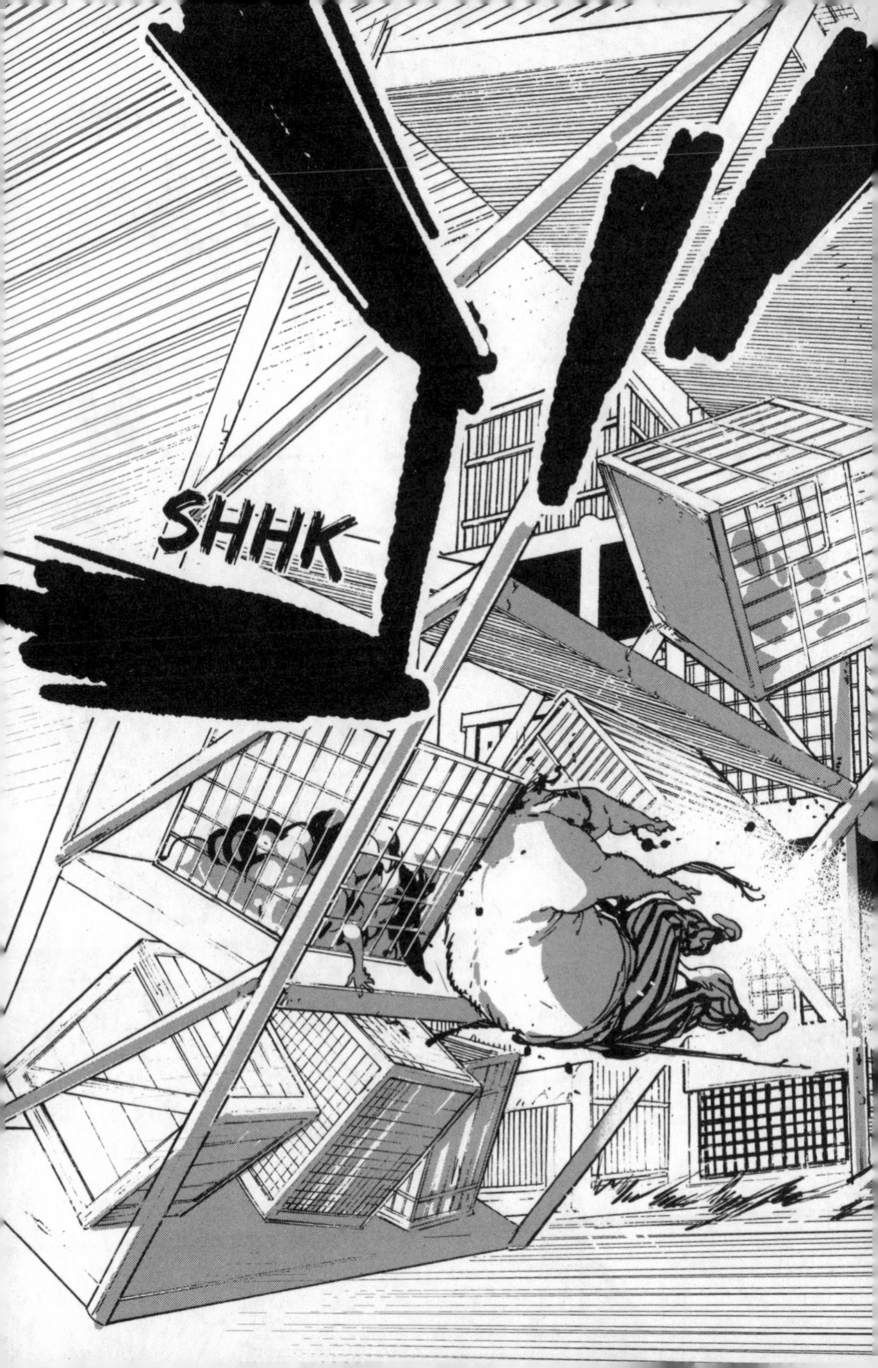
SHHK

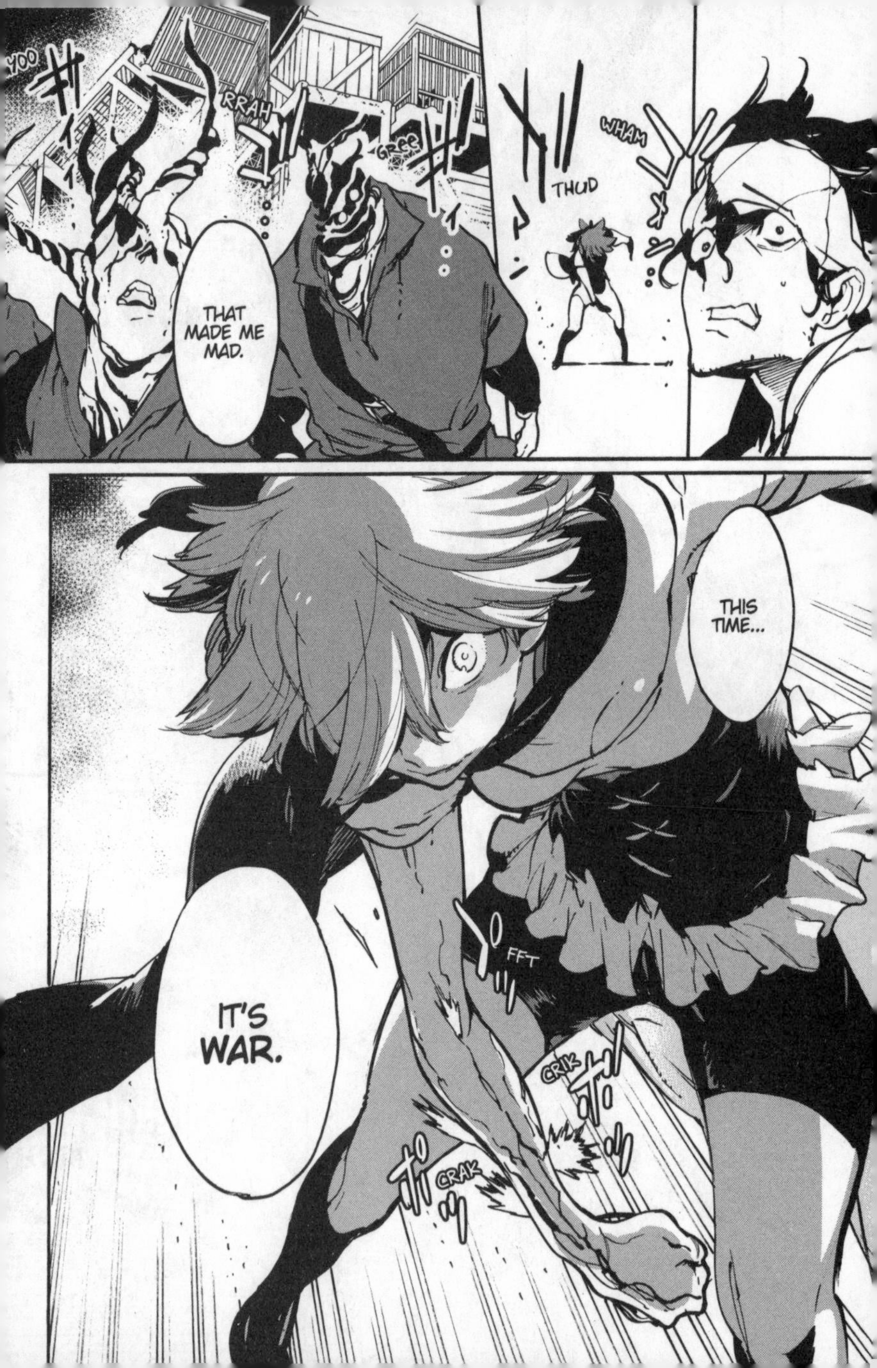
WHAM
THUD
YOO
RRAH
GREE
THAT MADE ME MAD.
THIS TIME...
FFT
CRIK
CRAK
IT'S WAR.

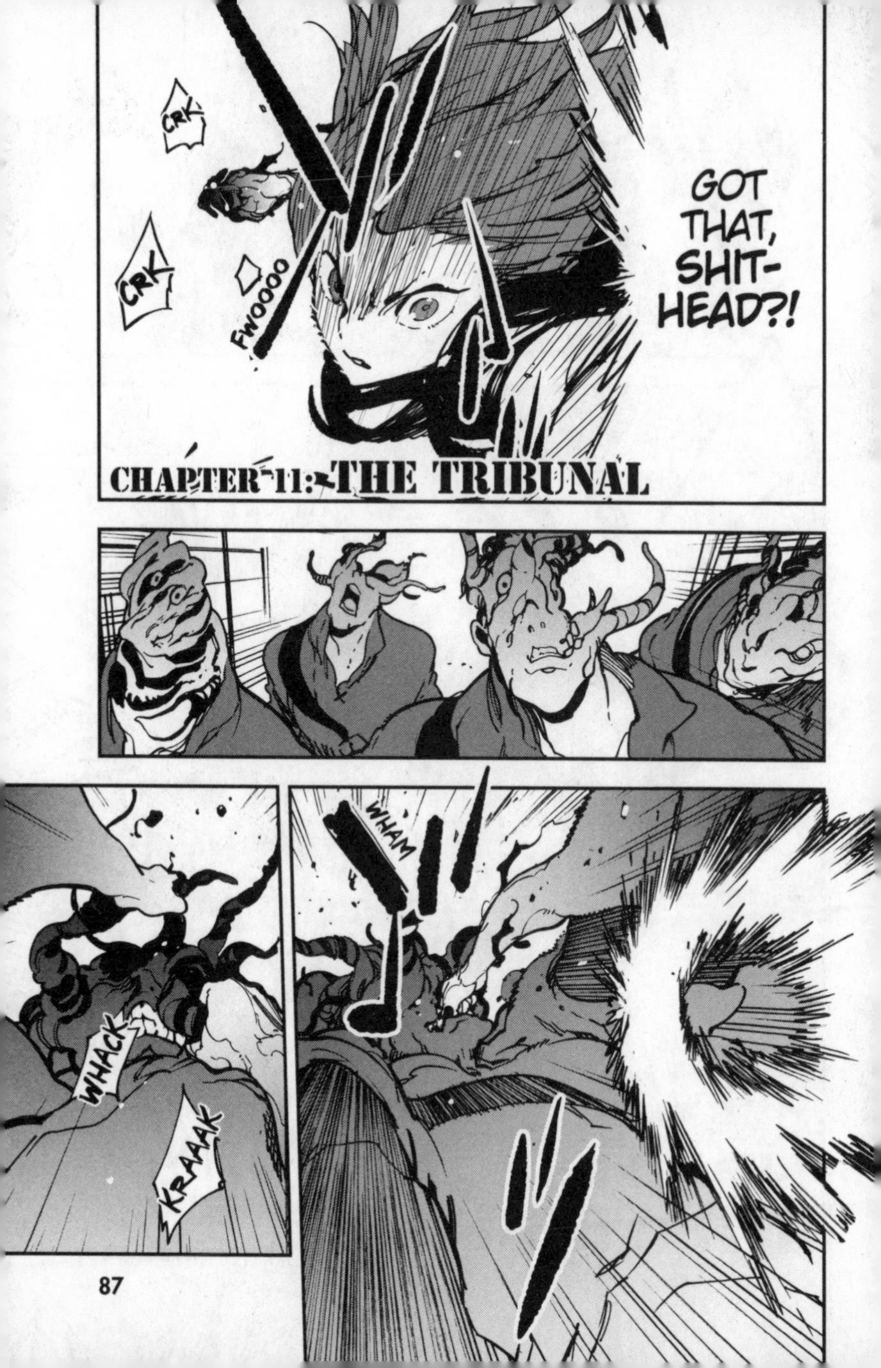
GOT THAT, SHIT-HEAD?!
CRK
CRK
FWOOOO
CHAPTER 11: THE TRIBUNAL
WHAM
WHACK
KRAAAK

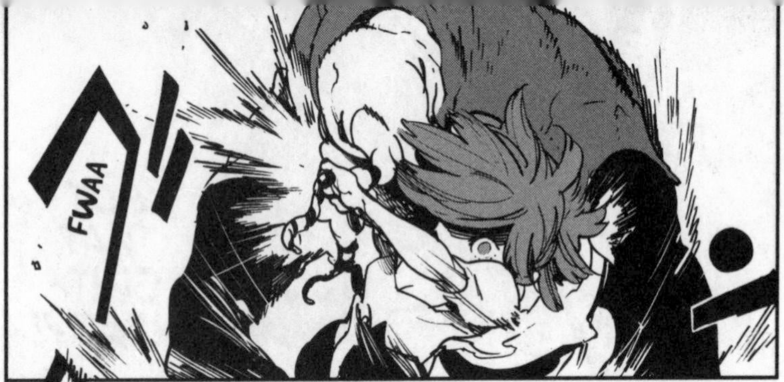
FWAA
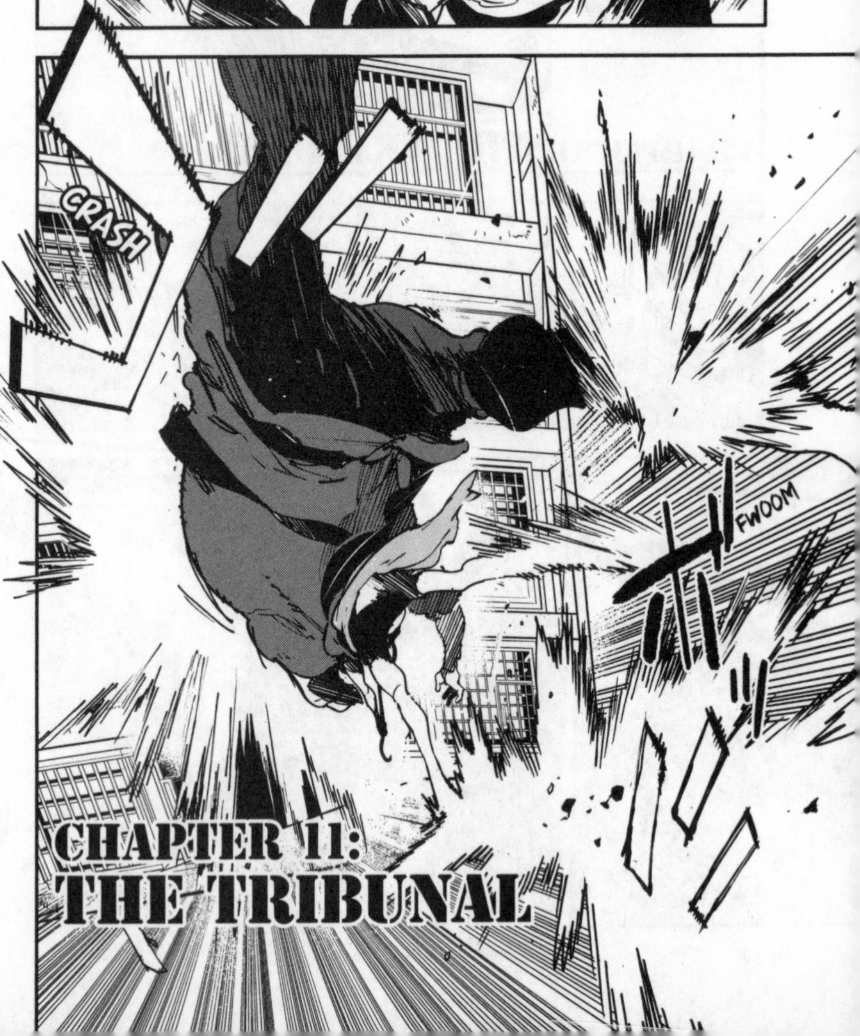
FWOOM
CRASH
CHAPTER 11:
THE TRIBUNAL

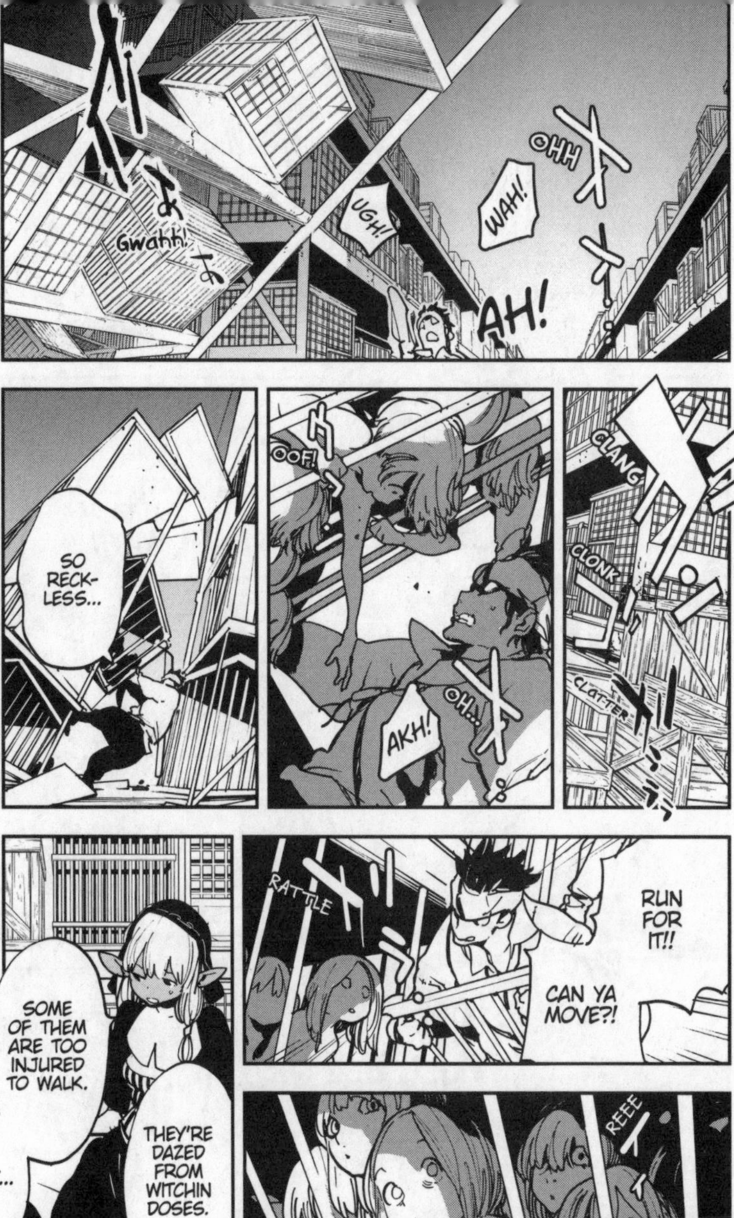
OHH
WAH!
UGH!
AH!
Gwahh!
CLANG
CLONK
CLATTER
OOF!
OH...
AKH!
SO RECK-LESS...
RUN FOR IT!!
CAN YA MOVE?!
RATTLE
REEE
SOME OF THEM ARE TOO INJURED TO WALK.
THEY'RE DAZED FROM WITCHIN DOSES.
BUT...

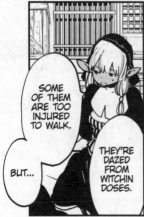

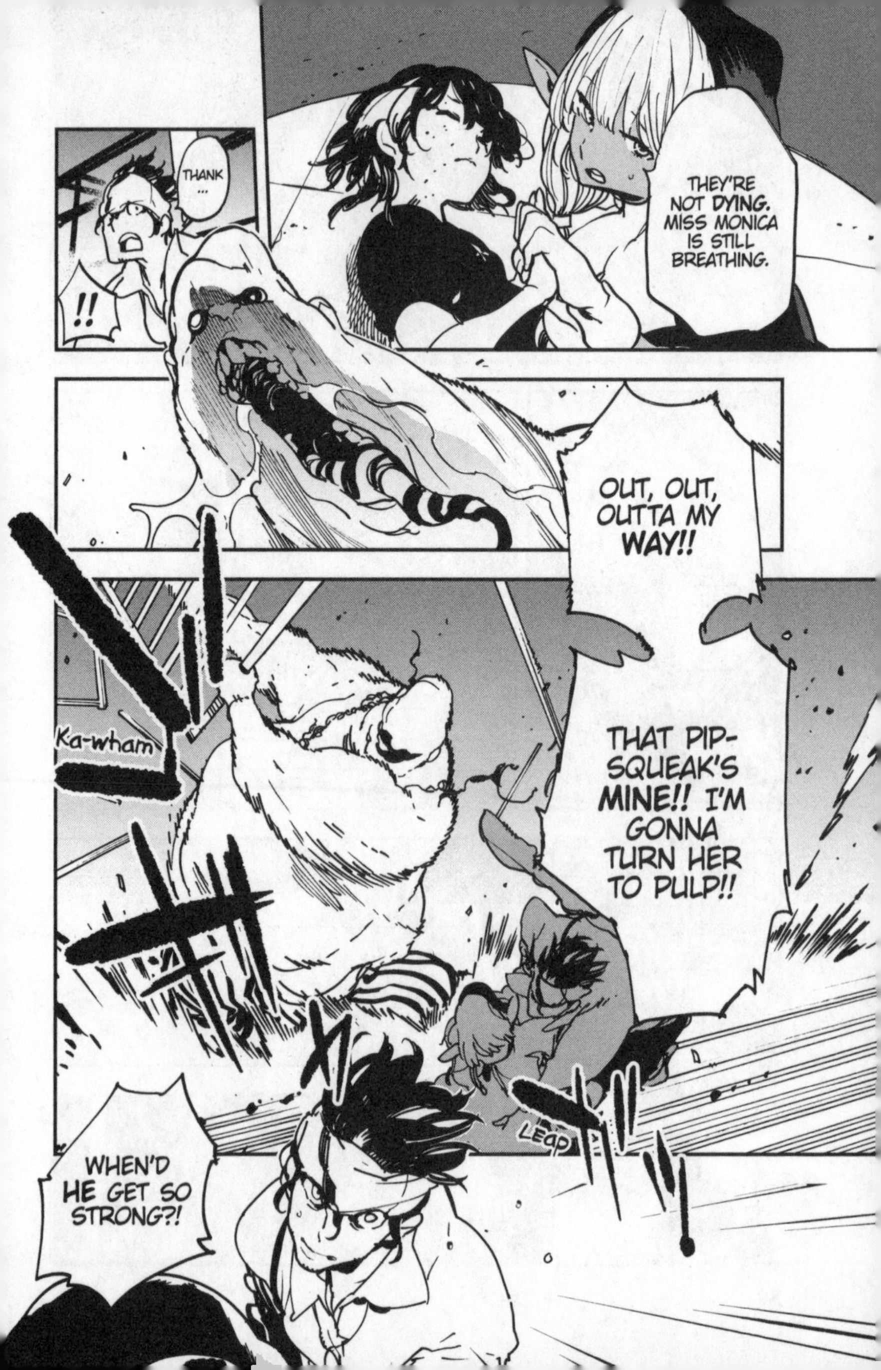
THEY'RE NOT DYING. MISS MONICA IS STILL BREATHING.
THANK ...
!!
OUT, OUT, OUTTA MY WAY!!
THAT PIP-SQUEAK'S MINE!! I'M GONNA TURN HER TO PULP!!
Ka-wham
Leap
WHEN'D HE GET SO STRONG?!

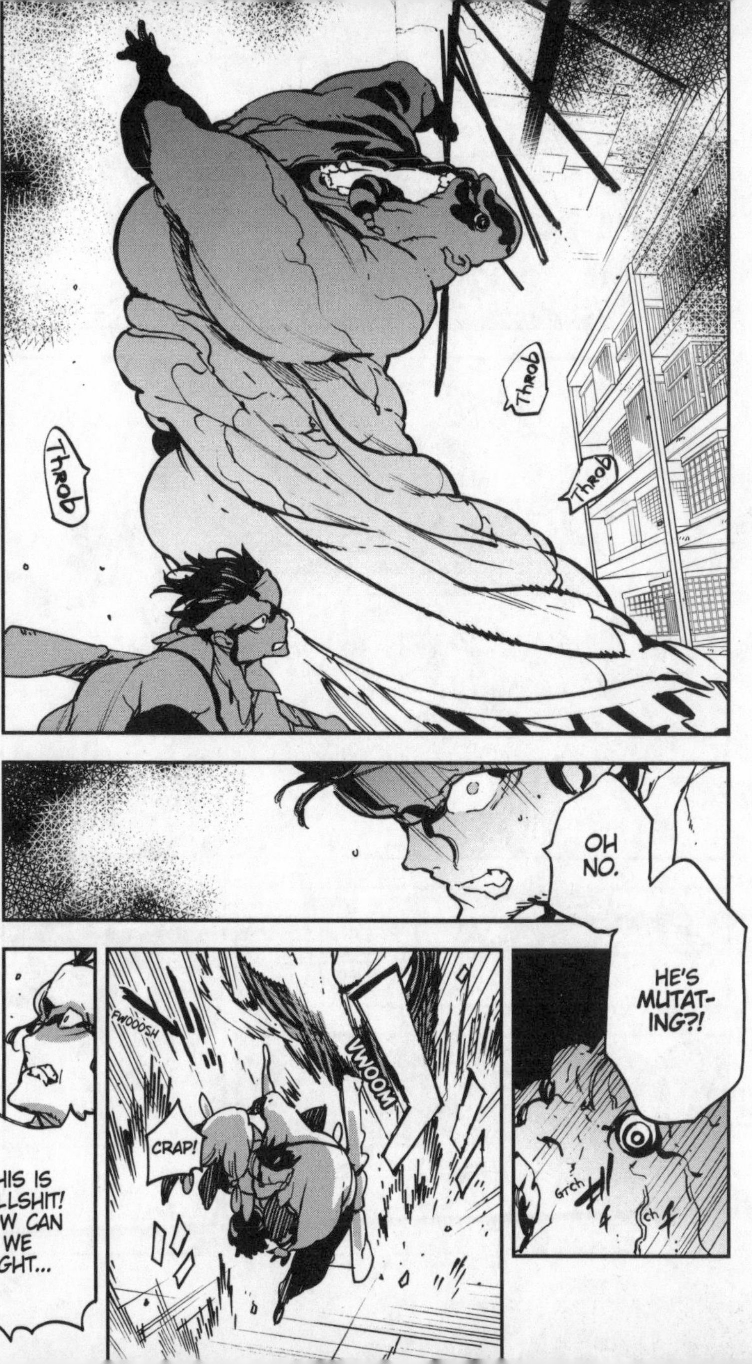
Throb
Throb
Throb
OH NO.
HE'S MUTAT-ING?!
Grch
ch
FWOOOSH
VWOOM
CRAP!
THIS IS BULLSHIT! HOW CAN WE FIGHT...

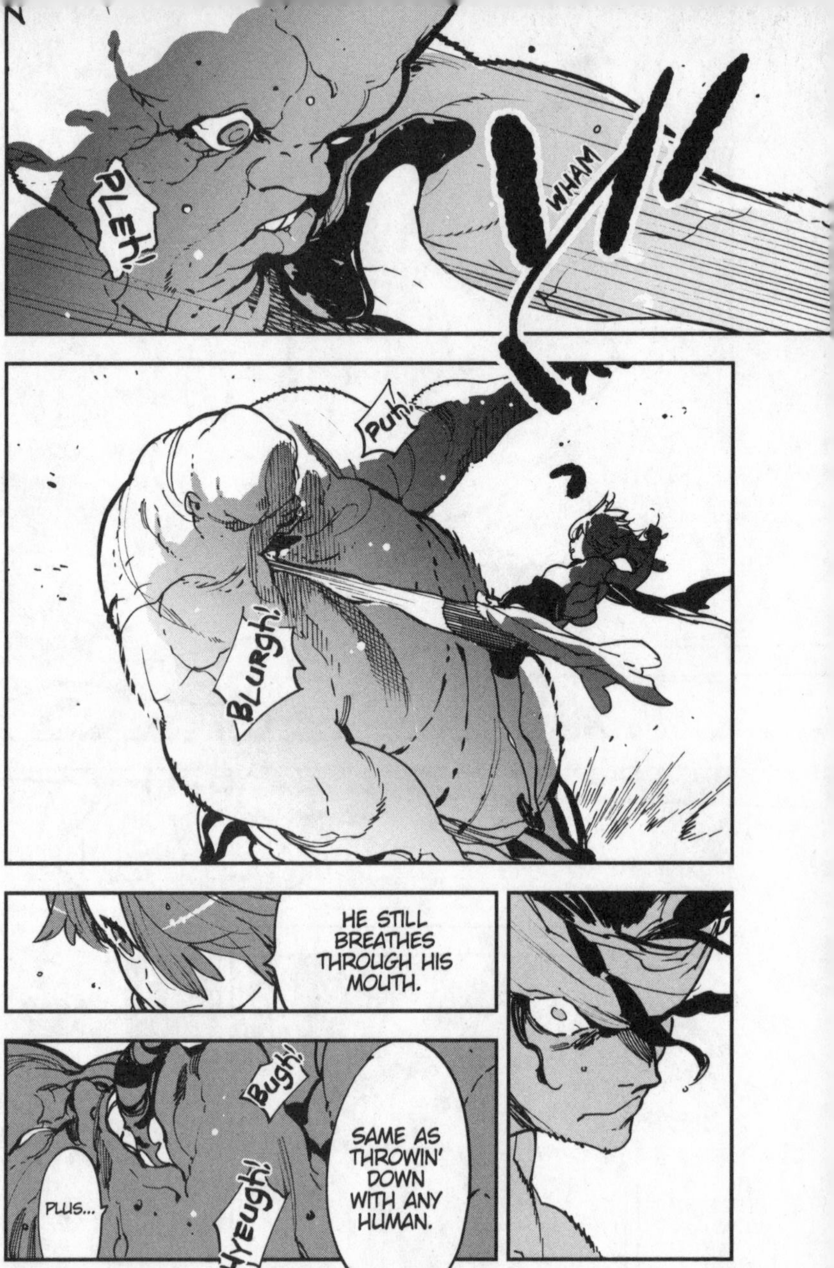
WHAM
PLEH!
PUH!
BLURGH!
HE STILL BREATHES THROUGH HIS MOUTH.
BUGH!
SAME AS THROWIN' DOWN WITH ANY HUMAN.
HYEUGH!
PLUS...

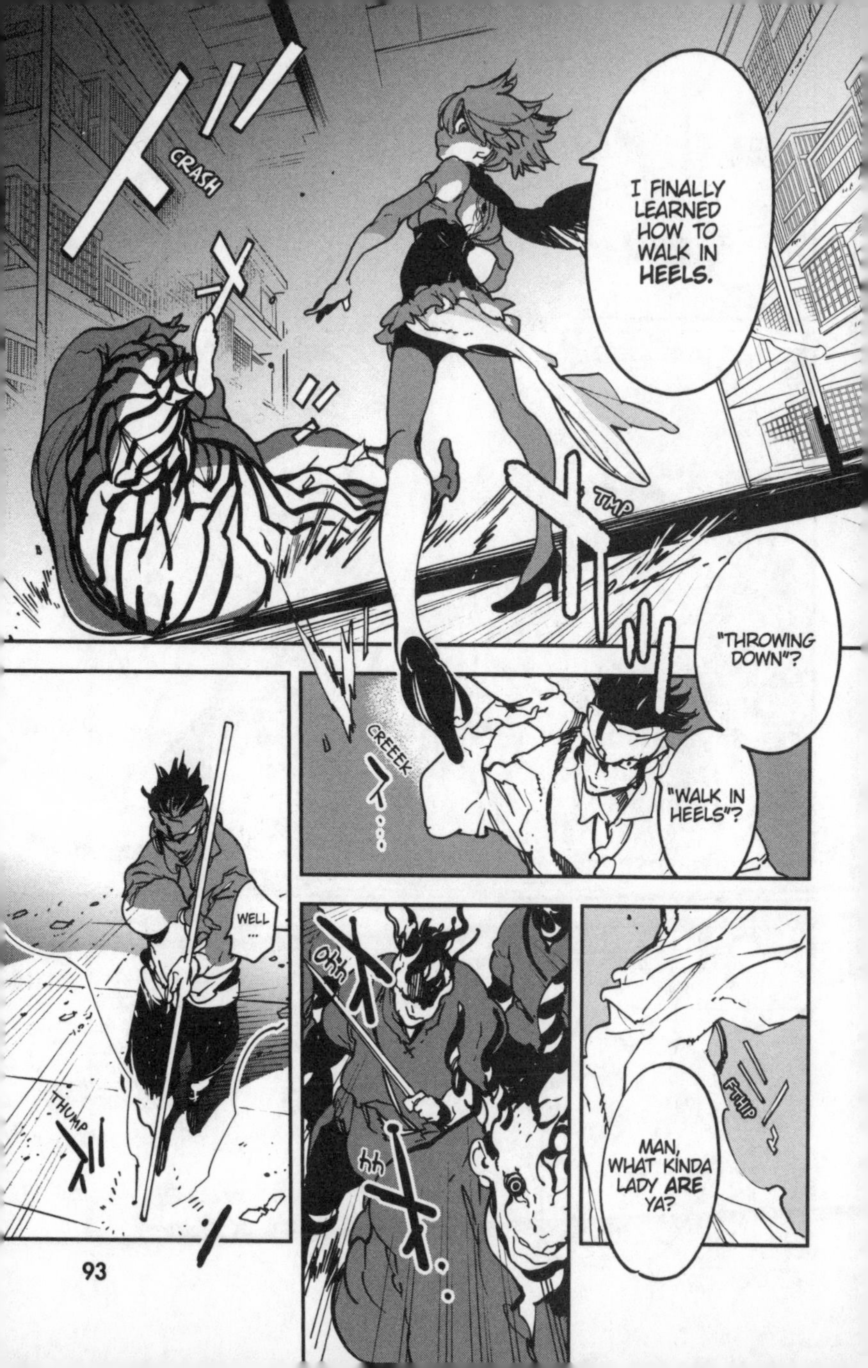
I FINALLY LEARNED HOW TO WALK IN HEELS.
CRASH
TMP
"THROWING DOWN"?
"WALK IN HEELS"?
CREEEK
FWHIP
MAN, WHAT KINDA LADY ARE YA?
Ohh
hh
WELL ...
THUMP

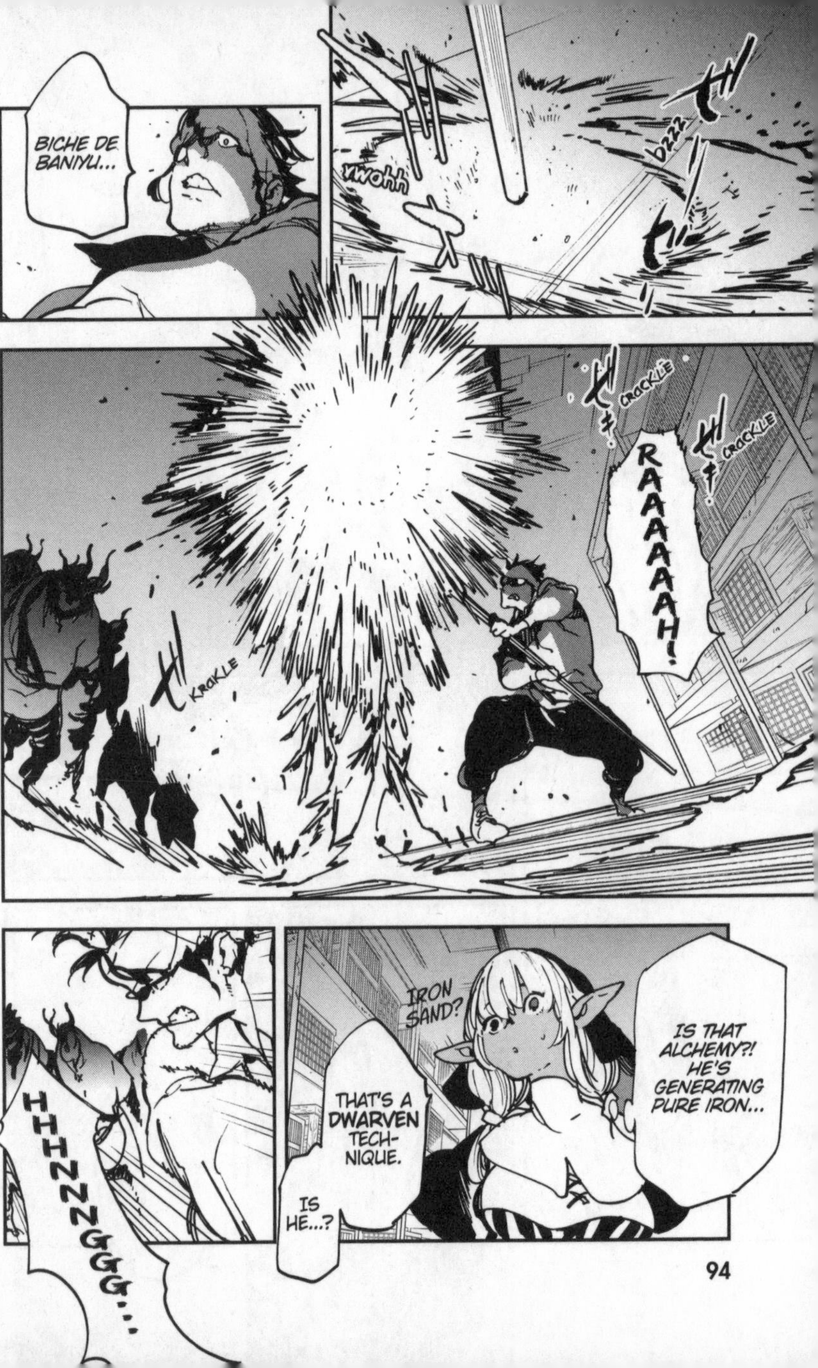
bzzz
vwohh
BICHE DE BANIYU...
CRACKLE
CRACKLE
RAAAAAAAH!
KRAKLE
IS THAT ALCHEMY?! HE'S GENERATING PURE IRON...
IRON SAND?
THAT'S A DWARVEN TECHNIQUE.
IS HE...?
HHHNNNGGG...

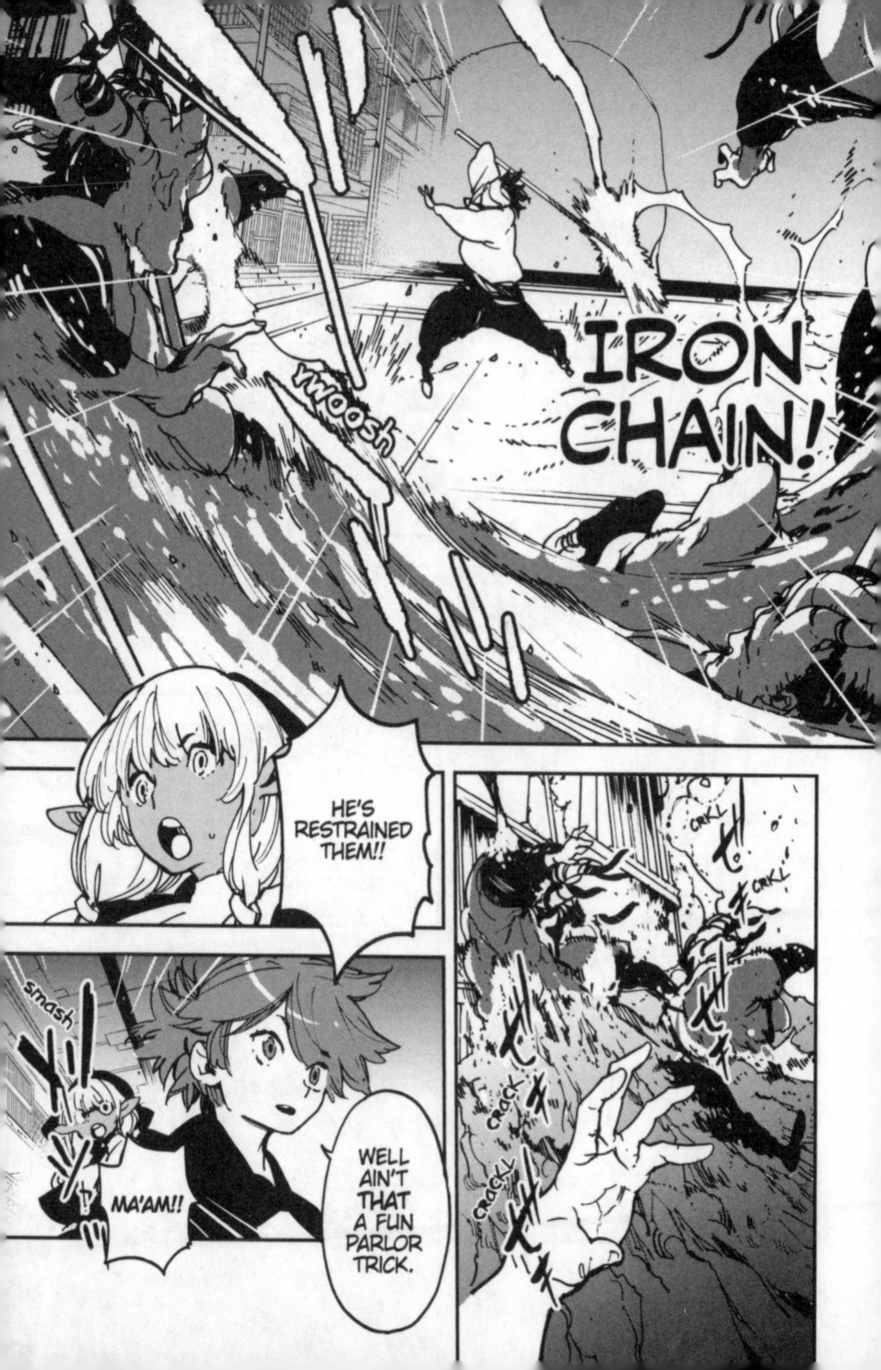
IRON CHAIN!
ywoosh
CRKL
CRKL
crack
crackl
HE'S RESTRAINED THEM!!
WELL AIN'T THAT A FUN PARLOR TRICK.
smash
MA'AM!!

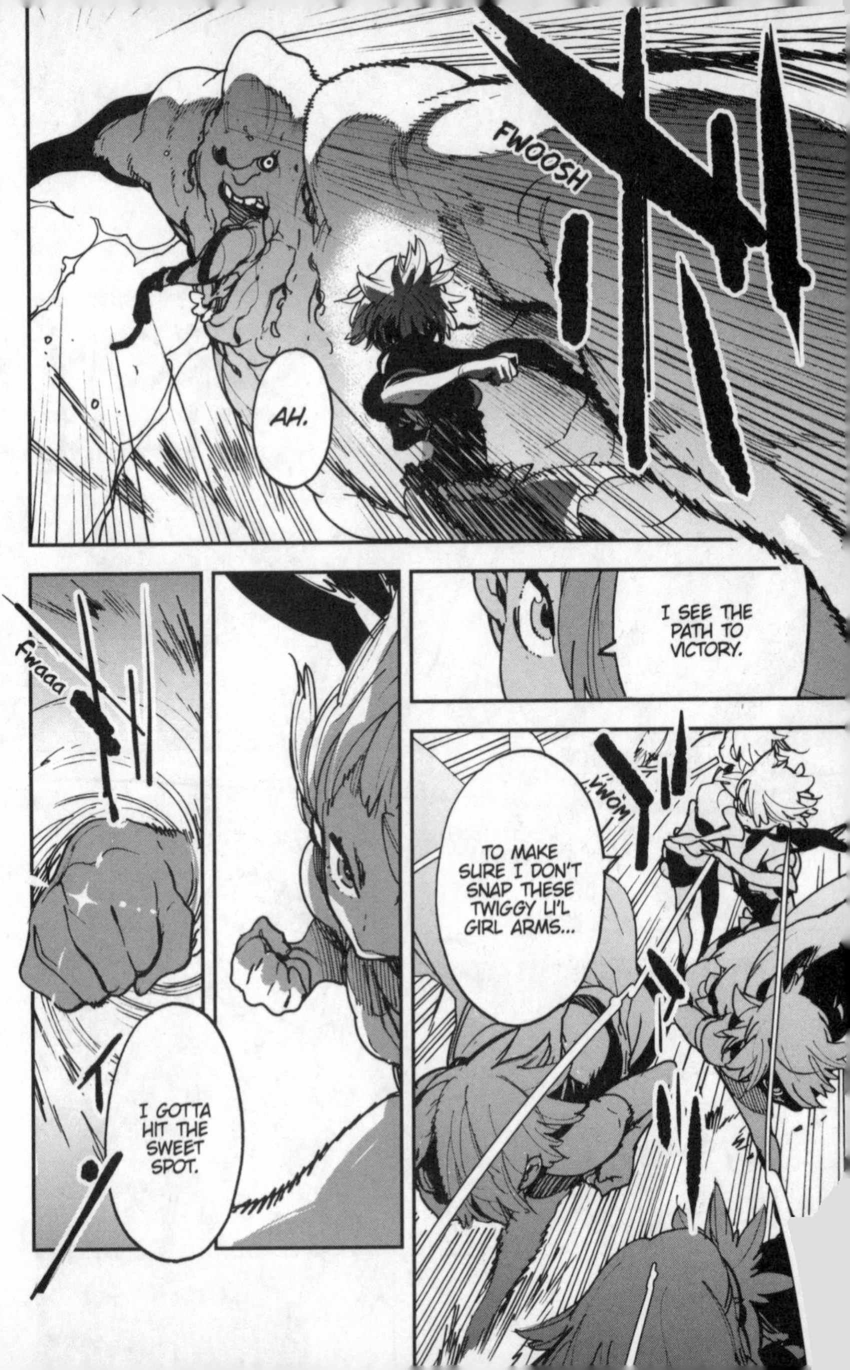
FWOOSH
AH.
I SEE THE PATH TO VICTORY.
VWOM
TO MAKE SURE I DON'T SNAP THESE TWIGGY LI'L GIRL ARMS...
fwaaa
I GOTTA HIT THE SWEET SPOT.

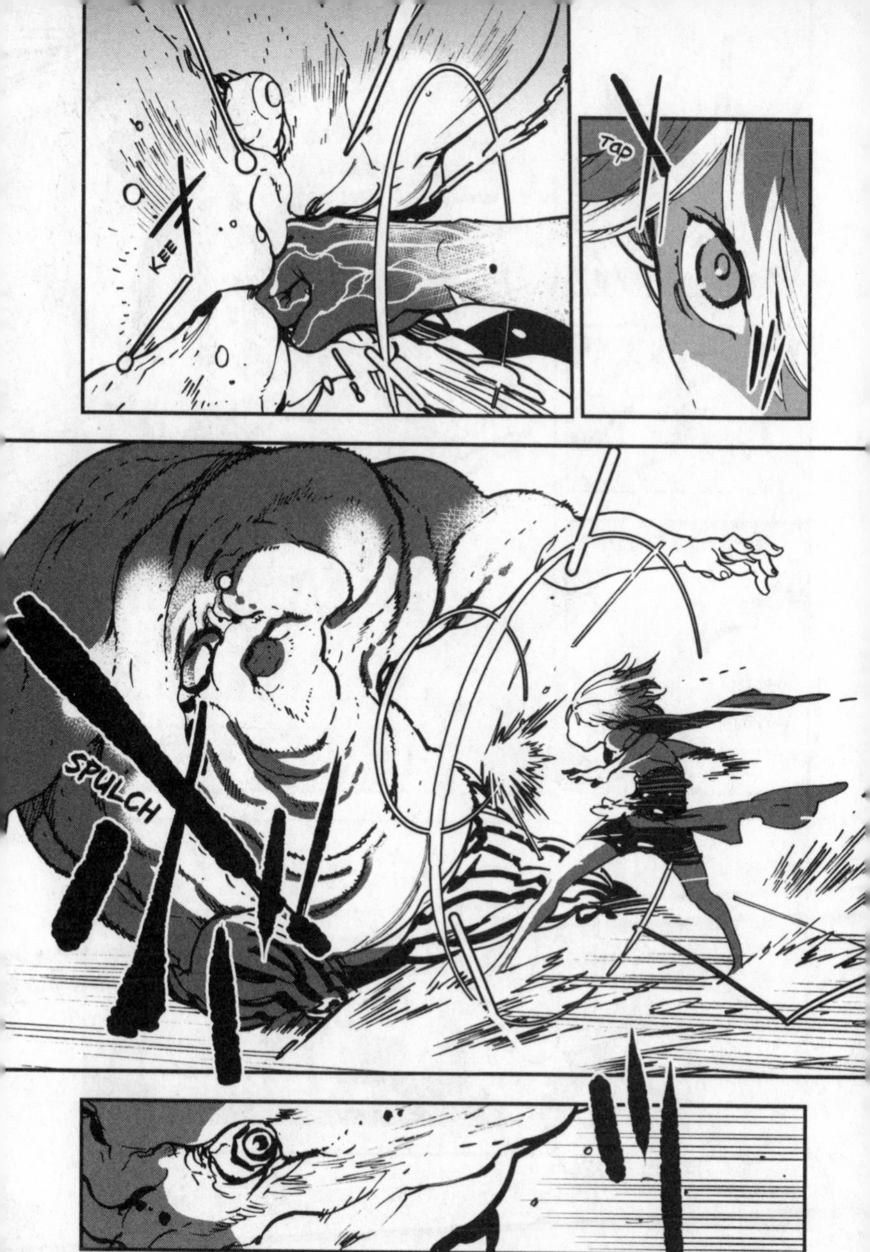
TAP
KEE
SPULCH

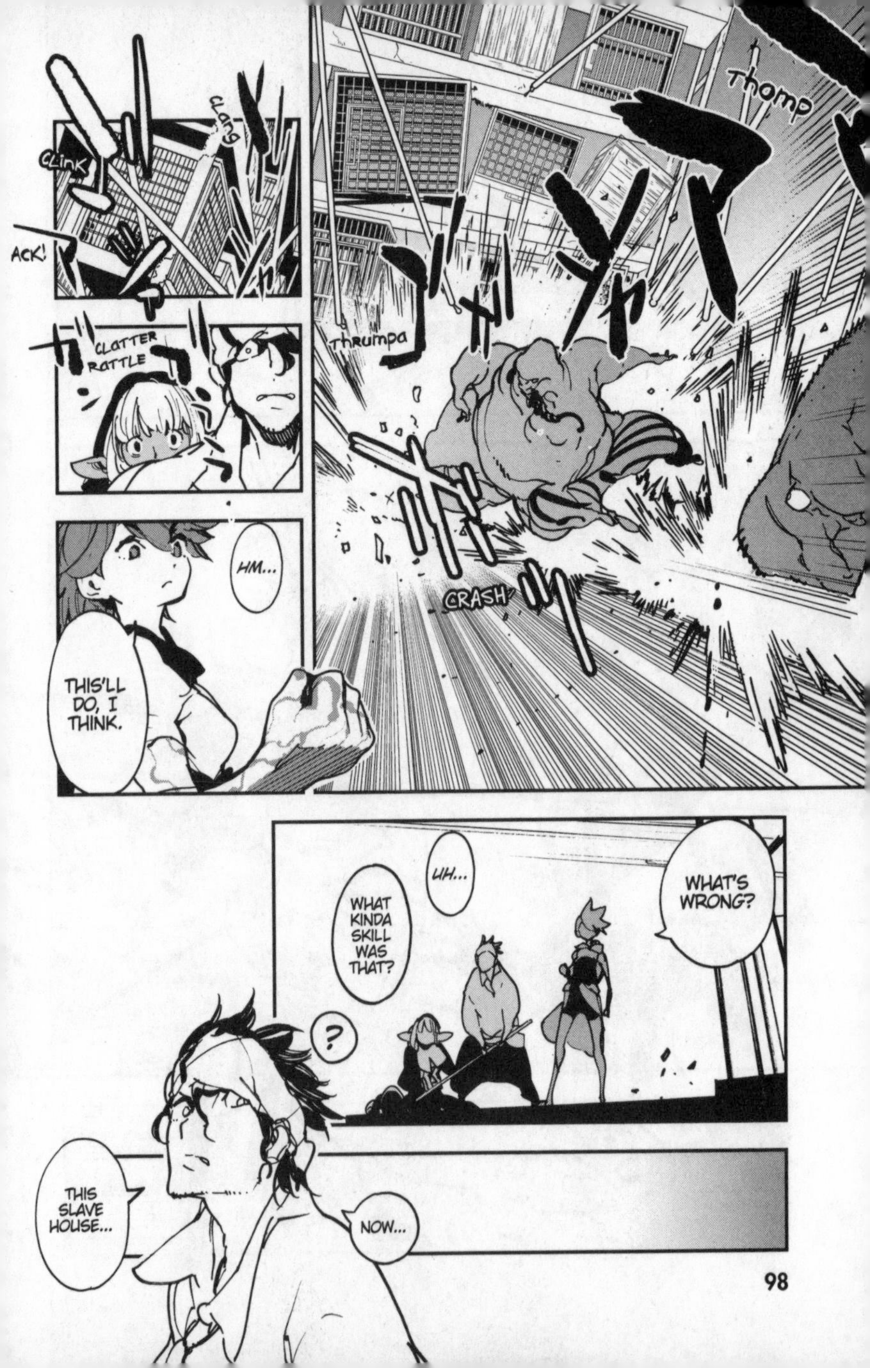
Thomp
Thrumpa
CRASH
Clang
Clink
ACK!
CLATTER
RATTLE
HM...
THIS'LL DO, I THINK.
WHAT'S WRONG?
UH...
WHAT KINDA SKILL WAS THAT?
?
NOW...
THIS SLAVE HOUSE...

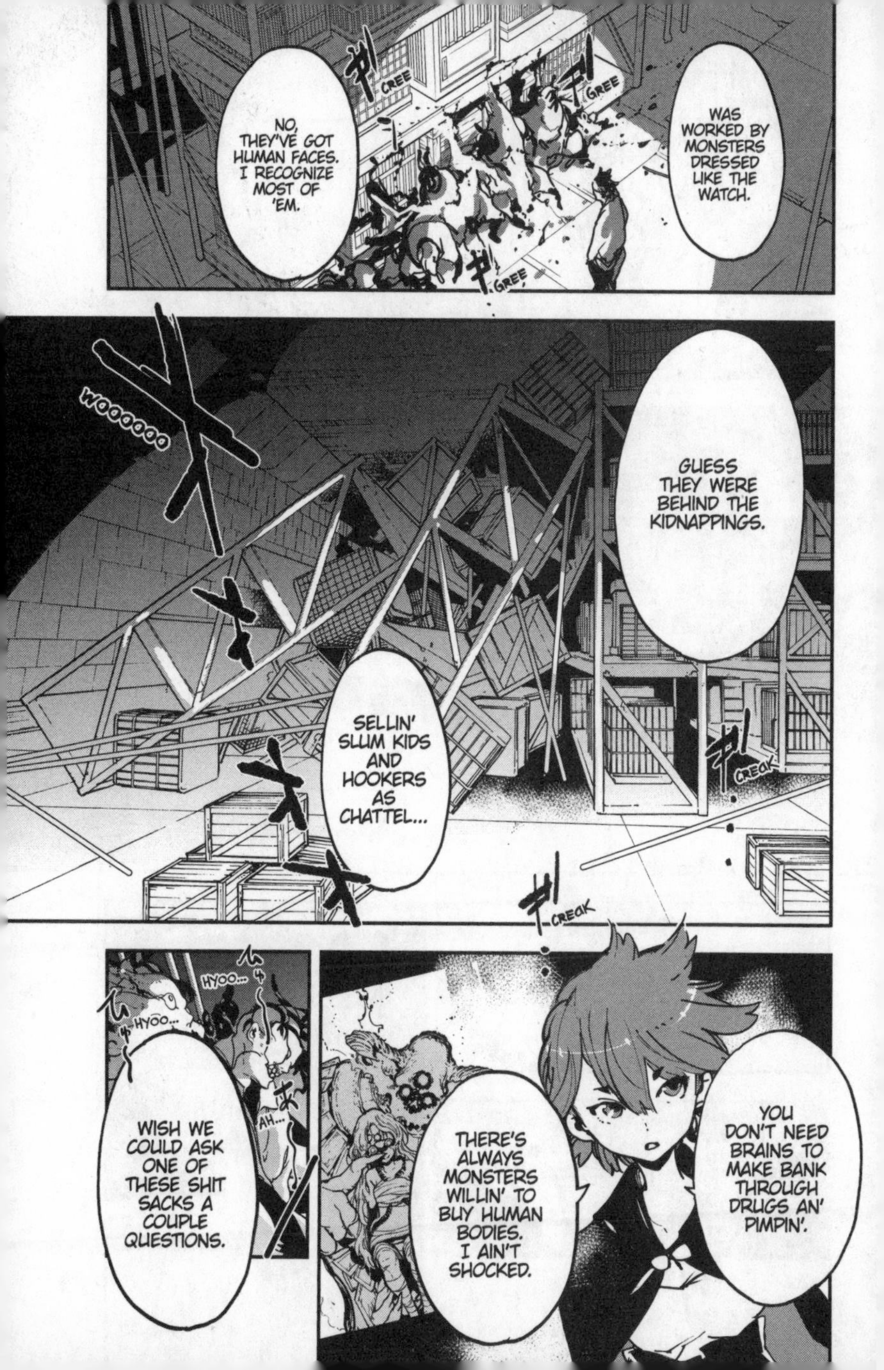
WAS WORKED BY MONSTERS DRESSED LIKE THE WATCH.
GREE
GREE
NO, THEY'VE GOT HUMAN FACES. I RECOGNIZE MOST OF 'EM.
GREE
GUESS THEY WERE BEHIND THE KIDNAPPINGS.
WOOOOOO
CREAK
SELLIN' SLUM KIDS AND HOOKERS AS CHATTEL...
CREAK
YOU DON'T NEED BRAINS TO MAKE BANK THROUGH DRUGS AN' PIMPIN'.
THERE'S ALWAYS MONSTERS WILLIN' TO BUY HUMAN BODIES. I AIN'T SHOCKED.
HYOO...
HYOO...
AH...
WISH WE COULD ASK ONE OF THESE SHIT SACKS A COUPLE QUESTIONS.

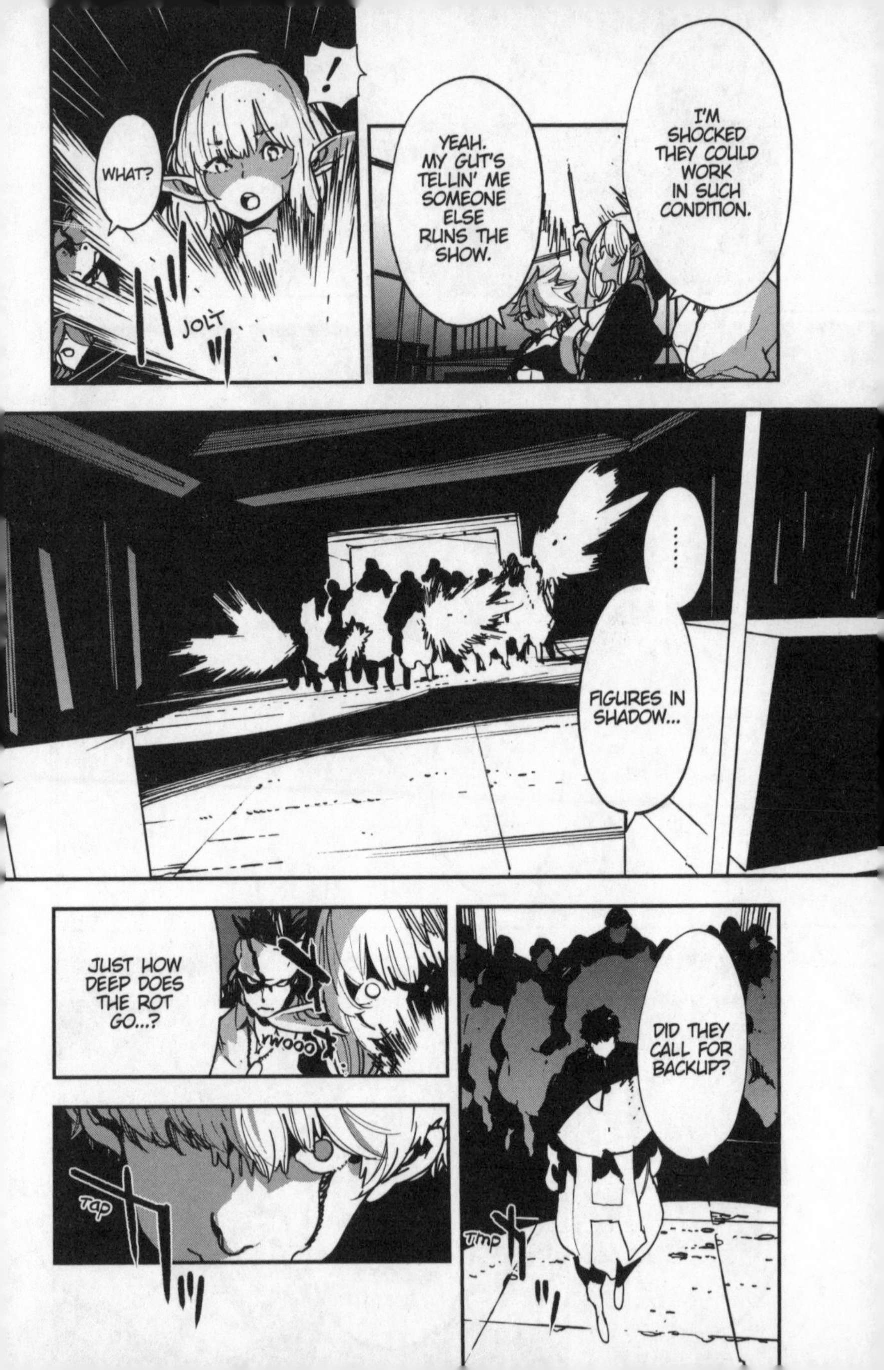
I'M SHOCKED THEY COULD WORK IN SUCH CONDITION.
YEAH. MY GUT'S TELLIN' ME SOMEONE ELSE RUNS THE SHOW.
!
WHAT?
JOLT
......
FIGURES IN SHADOW...
DID THEY CALL FOR BACKUP?
TIMP
JUST HOW DEEP DOES THE ROT GO...?
VWOOO
TAP

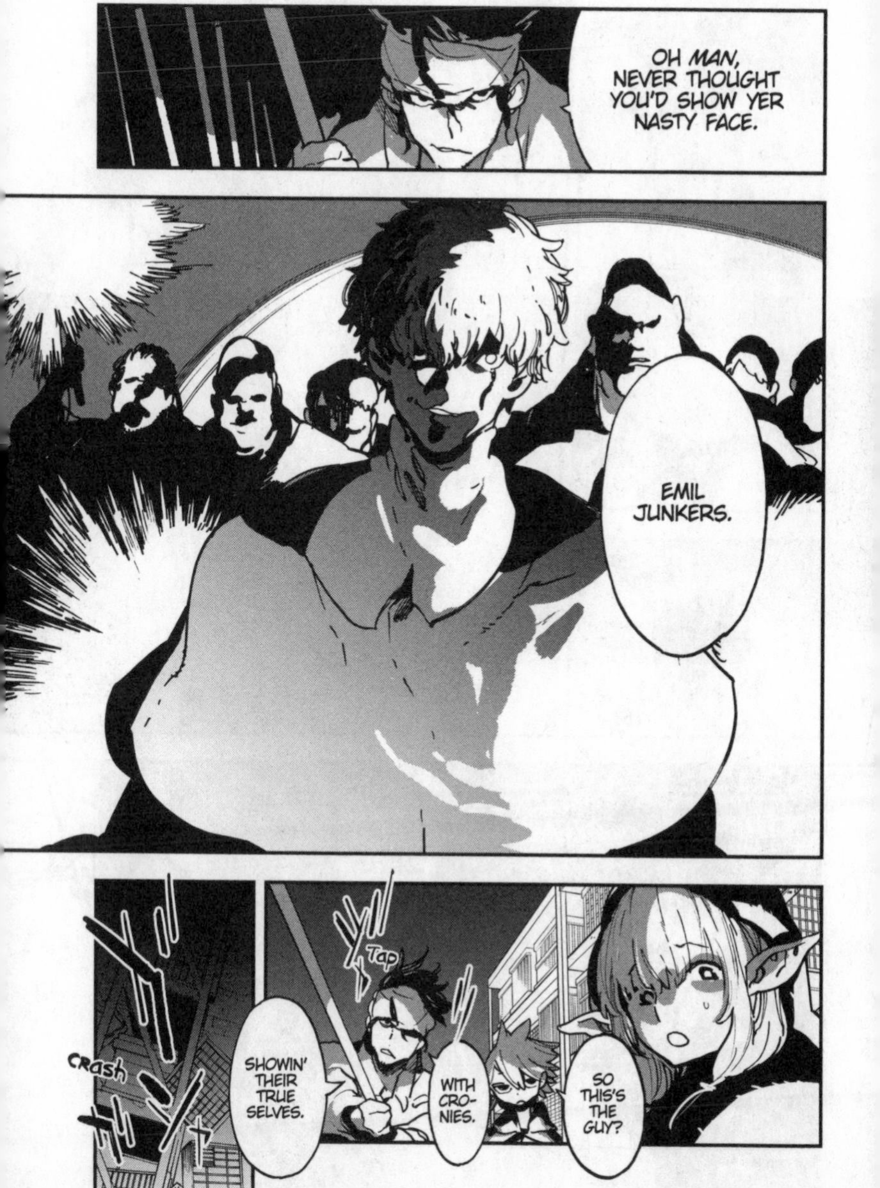
OH *MAN*, NEVER THOUGHT YOU'D SHOW YER NASTY FACE.
EMIL JUNKERS.
SO THIS'S THE GUY?
WITH CRO-NIES.
Tap
SHOWIN' THEIR TRUE SELVES.
Crash

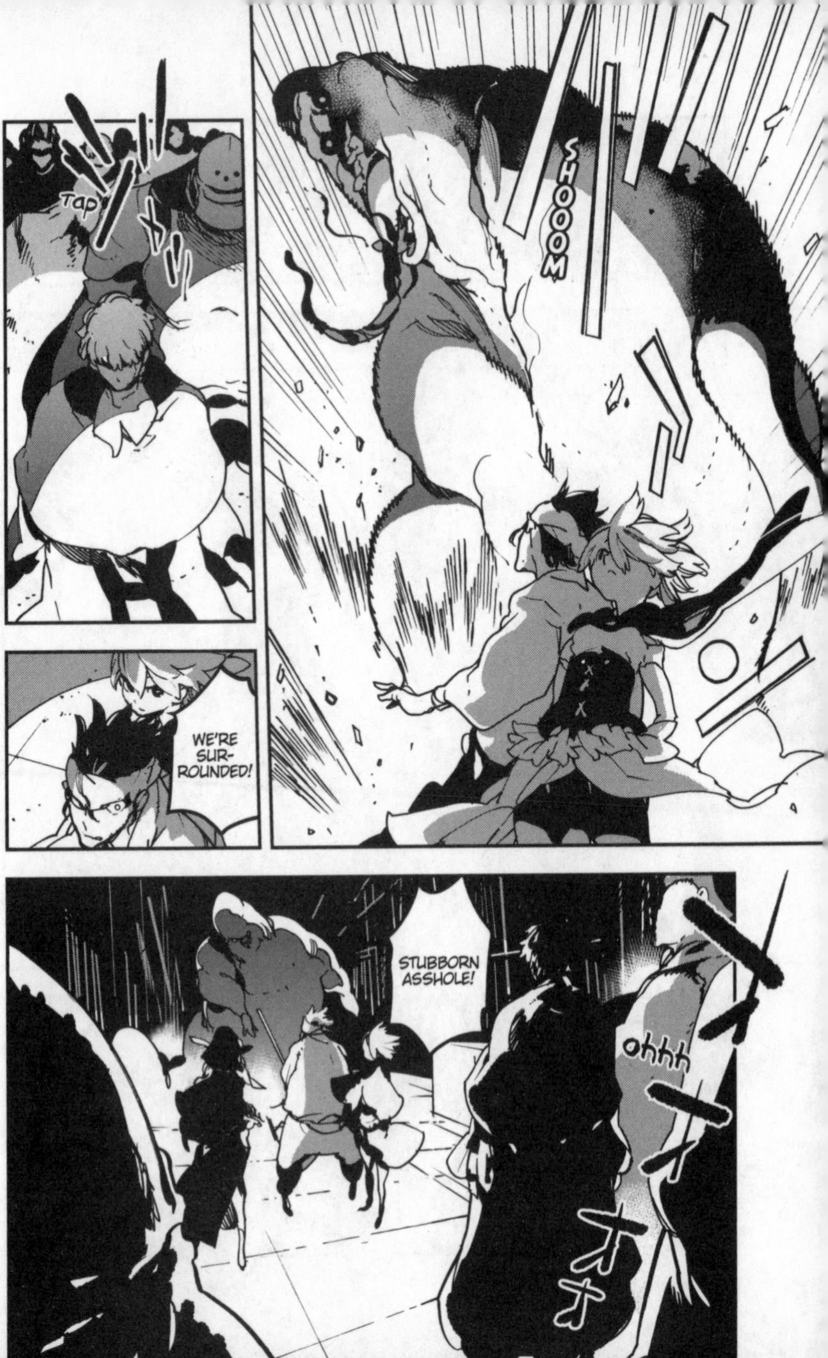
SHOOOM
tap
WE'RE SUR-ROUNDED!
STUBBORN ASSHOLE!
ohhh

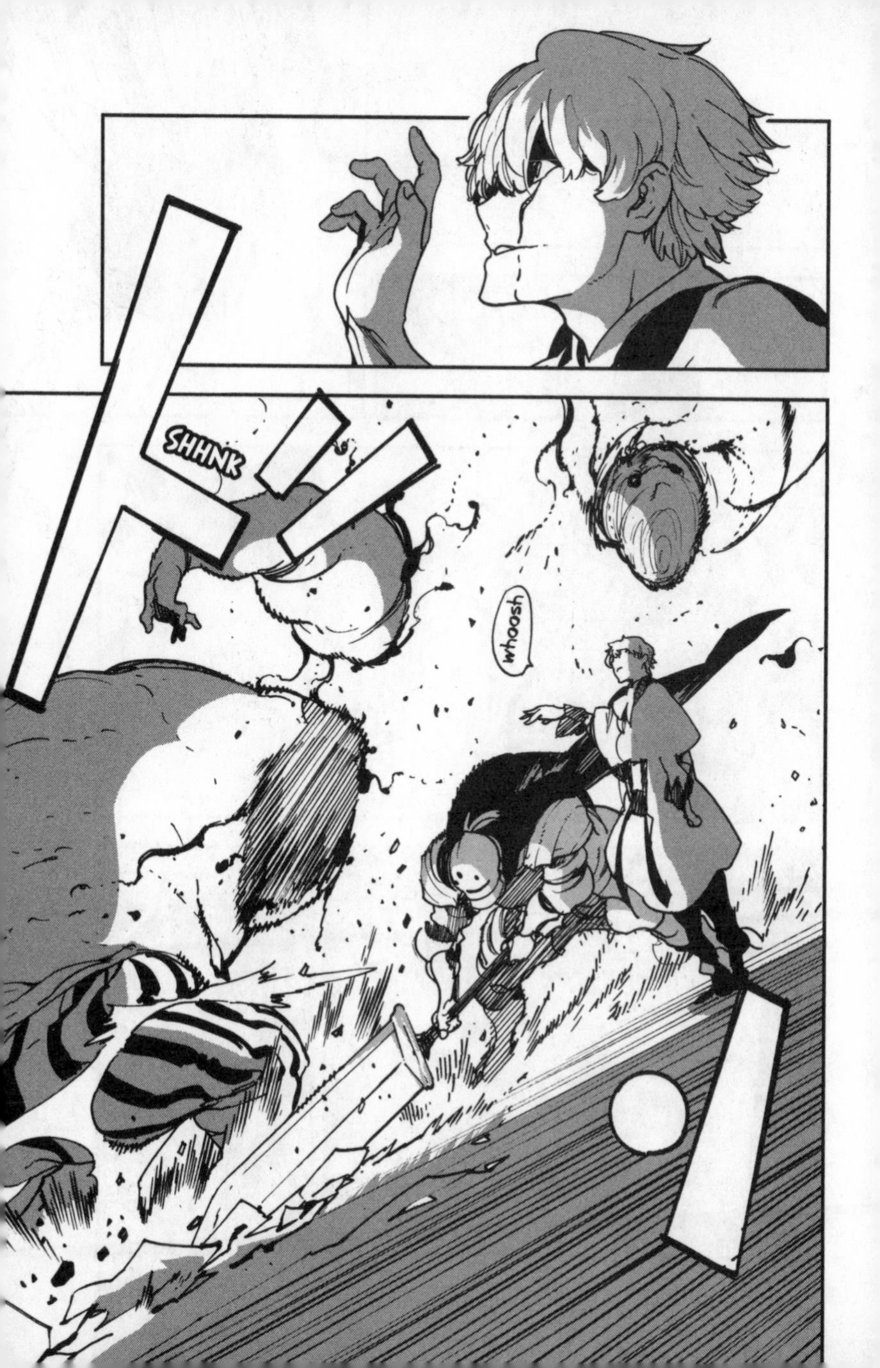
SHHNK
whoosh

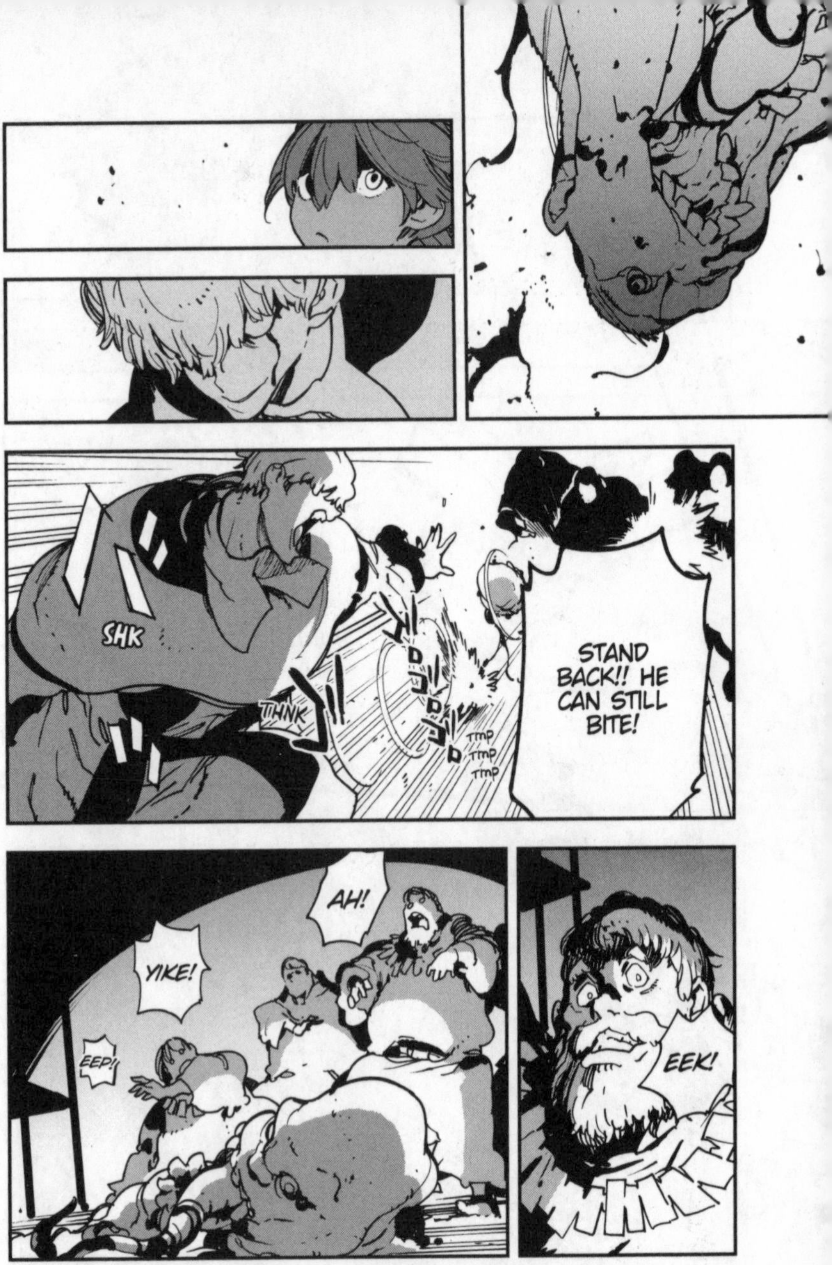

STAND BACK!! HE CAN STILL BITE!
TMP TMP TMP
THNK
SHK
EEK!
AH!
YIKE!
EEP!!

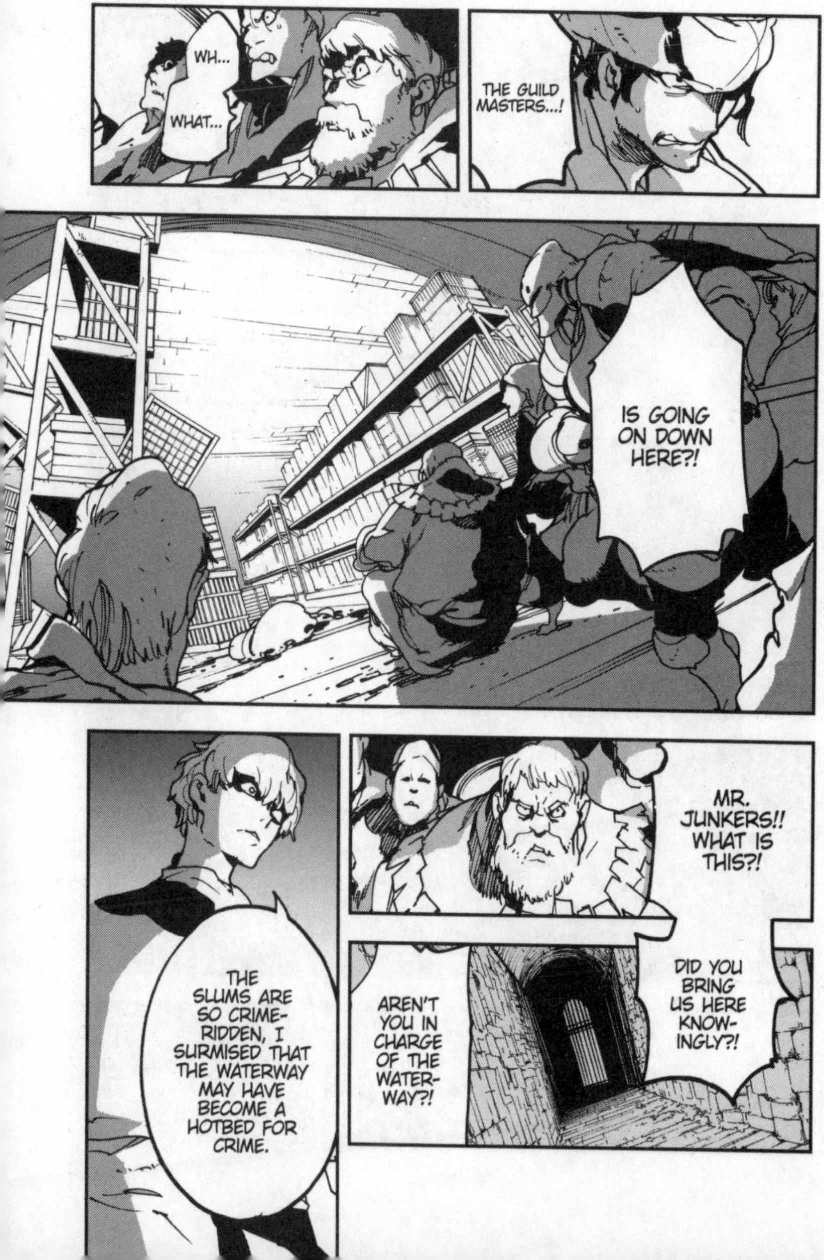
THE GUILD MASTERS...!
WH...
WHAT...
IS GOING ON DOWN HERE?!
MR. JUNKERS!! WHAT IS THIS?!
DID YOU BRING US HERE KNOWINGLY?!
AREN'T YOU IN CHARGE OF THE WATERWAY?!
THE SLUMS ARE SO CRIME-RIDDEN, I SURMISED THAT THE WATERWAY MAY HAVE BECOME A HOTBED FOR CRIME.

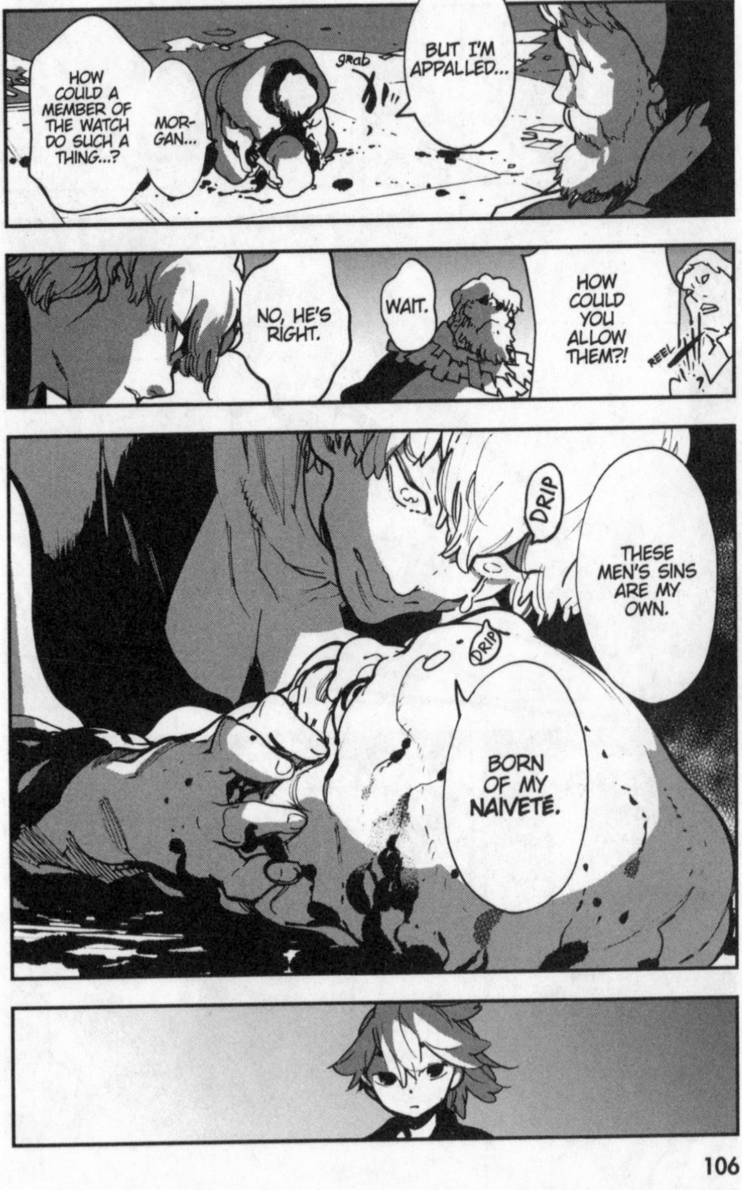
BUT I'M APPALLED...
grab
MOR-GAN...
HOW COULD A MEMBER OF THE WATCH DO SUCH A THING...?
HOW COULD YOU ALLOW THEM?!
REEL
WAIT.
NO, HE'S RIGHT.
DRIP
THESE MEN'S SINS ARE MY OWN.
DRIP
BORN OF MY NAIVETÉ.

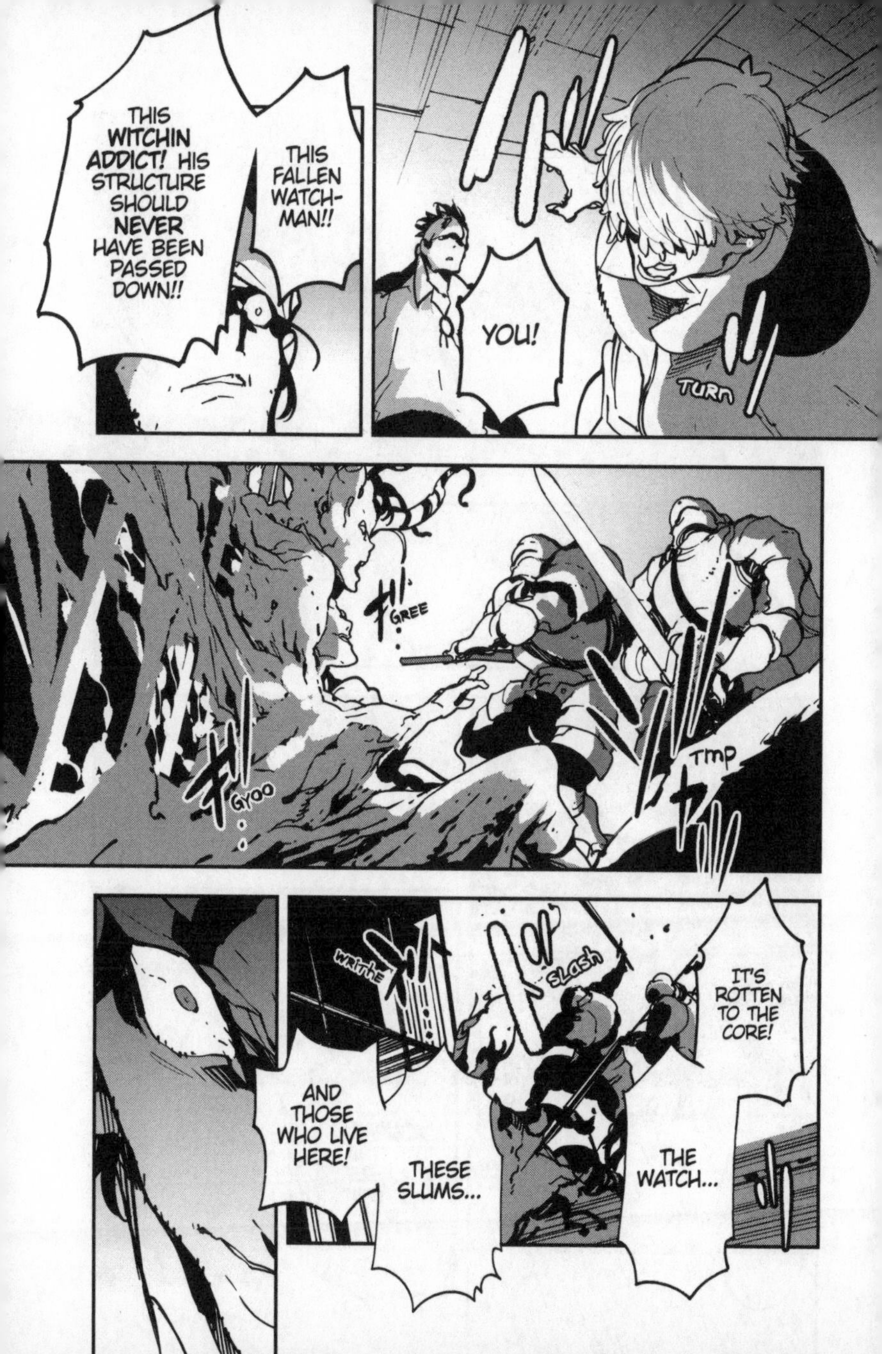
YOU!
TURN
THIS FALLEN WATCH-MAN!!
THIS WITCHIN ADDICT! HIS STRUCTURE SHOULD NEVER HAVE BEEN PASSED DOWN!!
TMP
GREE
GYOO
IT'S ROTTEN TO THE CORE!
SLASH
writhe
THE WATCH...
THESE SLUMS...
AND THOSE WHO LIVE HERE!

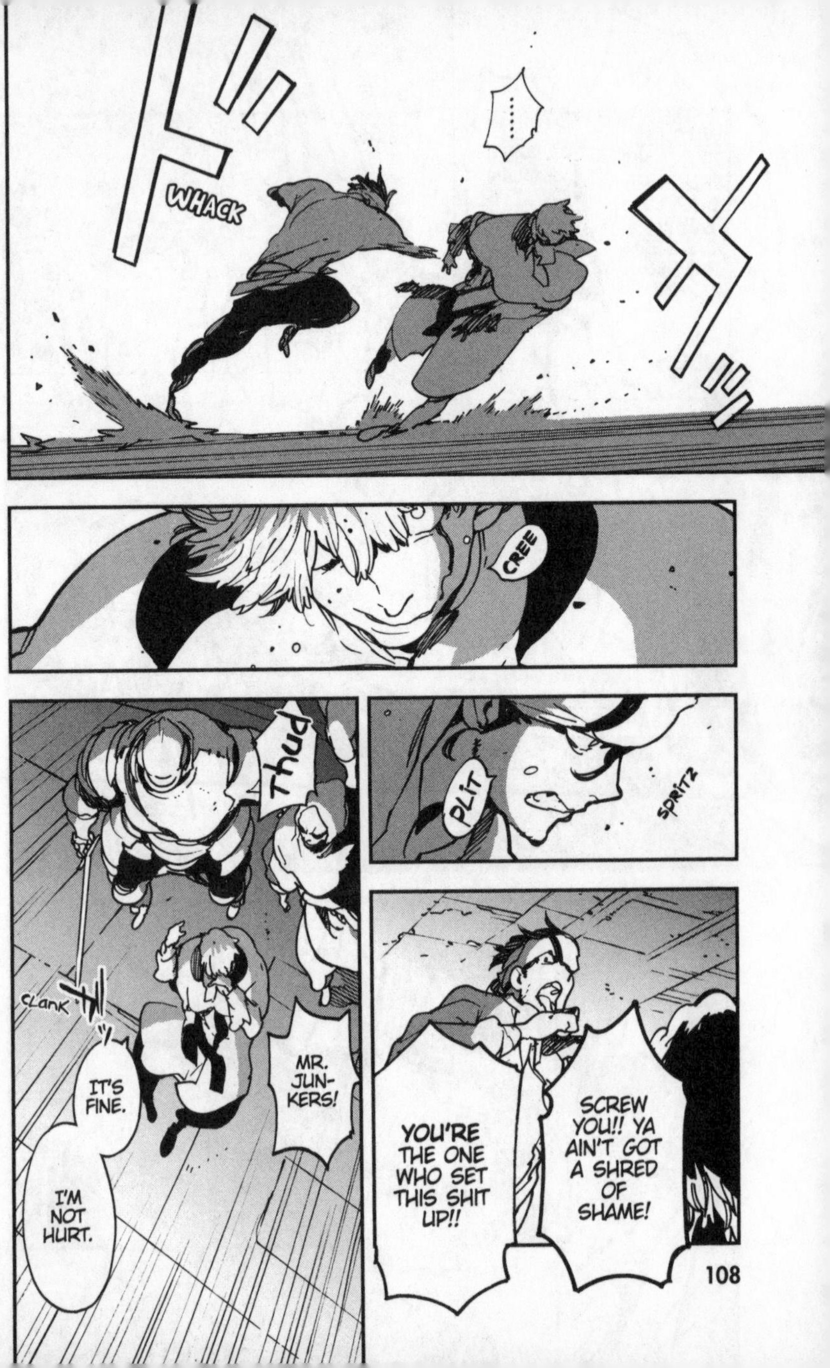
......
WHACK
CREE
PLIT
SPRITZ
SCREW YOU!! YA AIN'T GOT A SHRED OF SHAME!
YOU'RE THE ONE WHO SET THIS SHIT UP!!
THUD
MR. JUNKERS!
CLANK
IT'S FINE.
I'M NOT HURT.

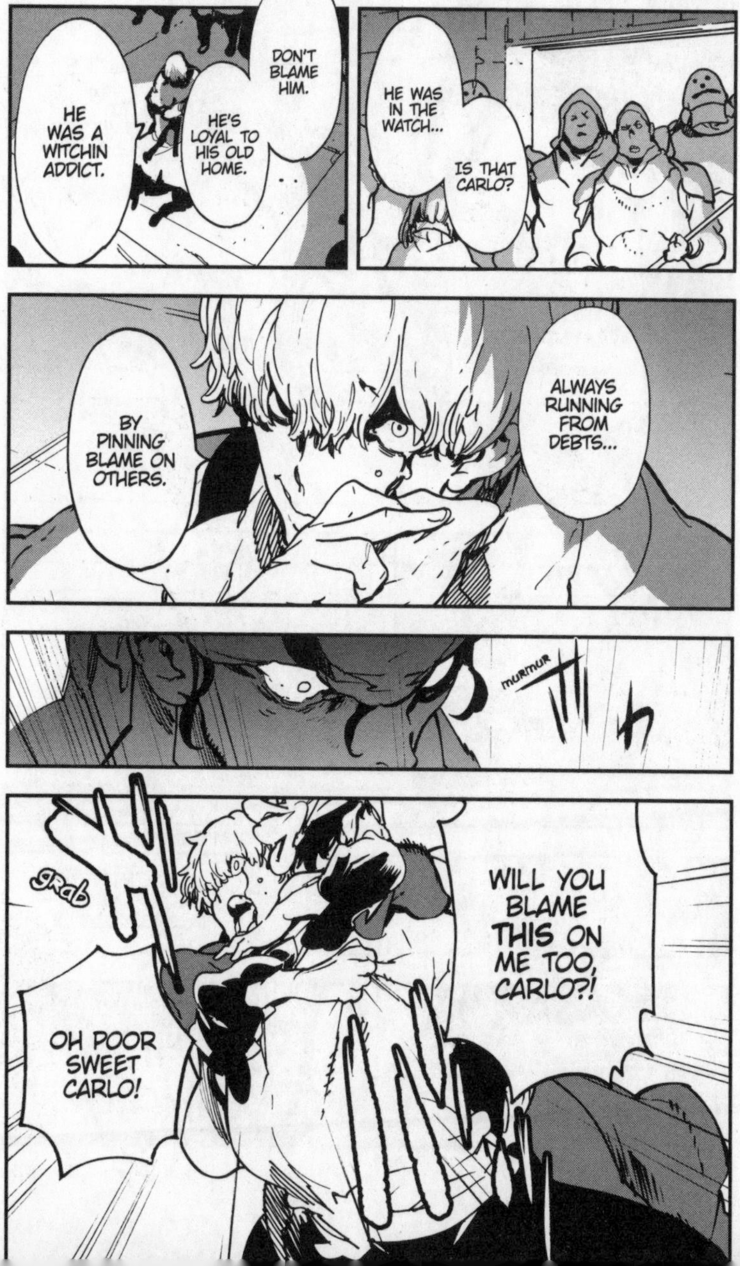
HE WAS IN THE WATCH...
IS THAT CARLO?
DON'T BLAME HIM.
HE'S LOYAL TO HIS OLD HOME.
HE WAS A WITCHIN ADDICT.
ALWAYS RUNNING FROM DEBTS...
BY PINNING BLAME ON OTHERS.
murmur
WILL YOU BLAME THIS ON ME TOO, CARLO?!
grab
OH POOR SWEET CARLO!

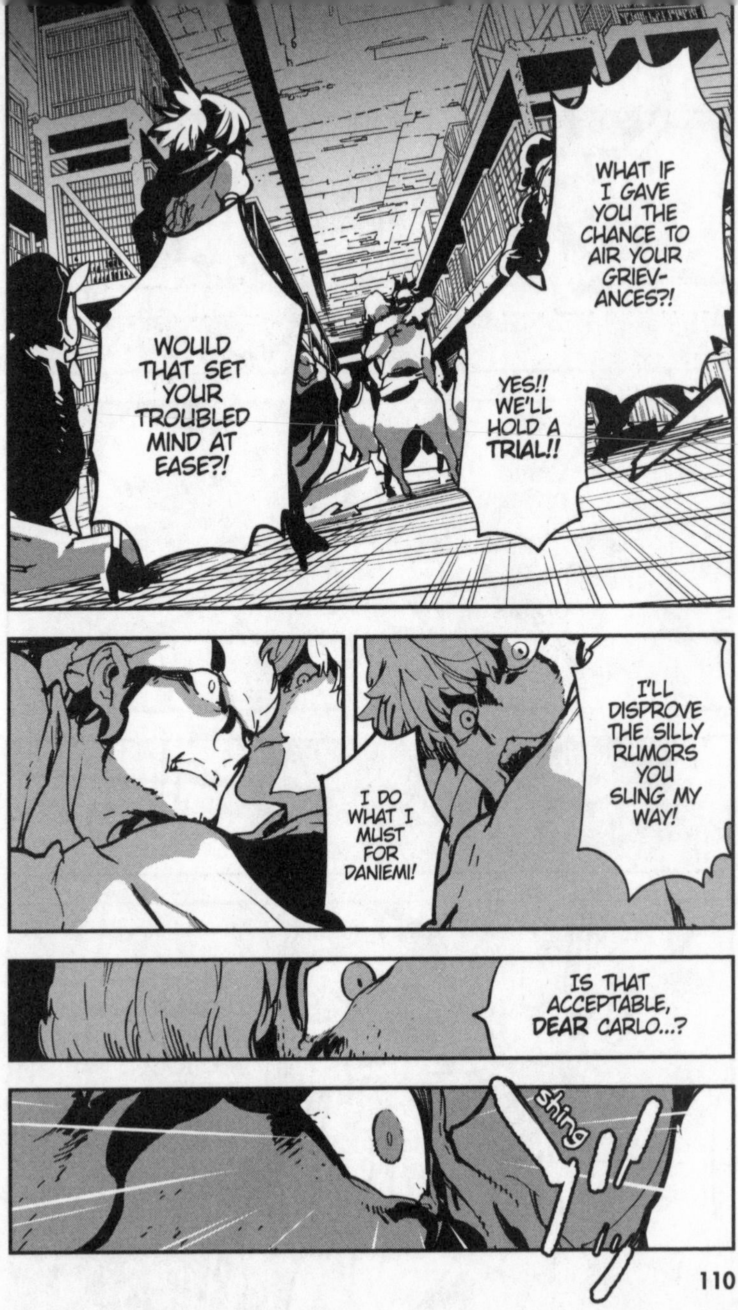
WHAT IF I GAVE YOU THE CHANCE TO AIR YOUR GRIEVANCES?!
YES!! WE'LL HOLD A TRIAL!!
WOULD THAT SET YOUR TROUBLED MIND AT EASE?!
I'LL DISPROVE THE SILLY RUMORS YOU SLING MY WAY!
I DO WHAT I MUST FOR DANIEMI!
IS THAT ACCEPTABLE, DEAR CARLO...?
shing

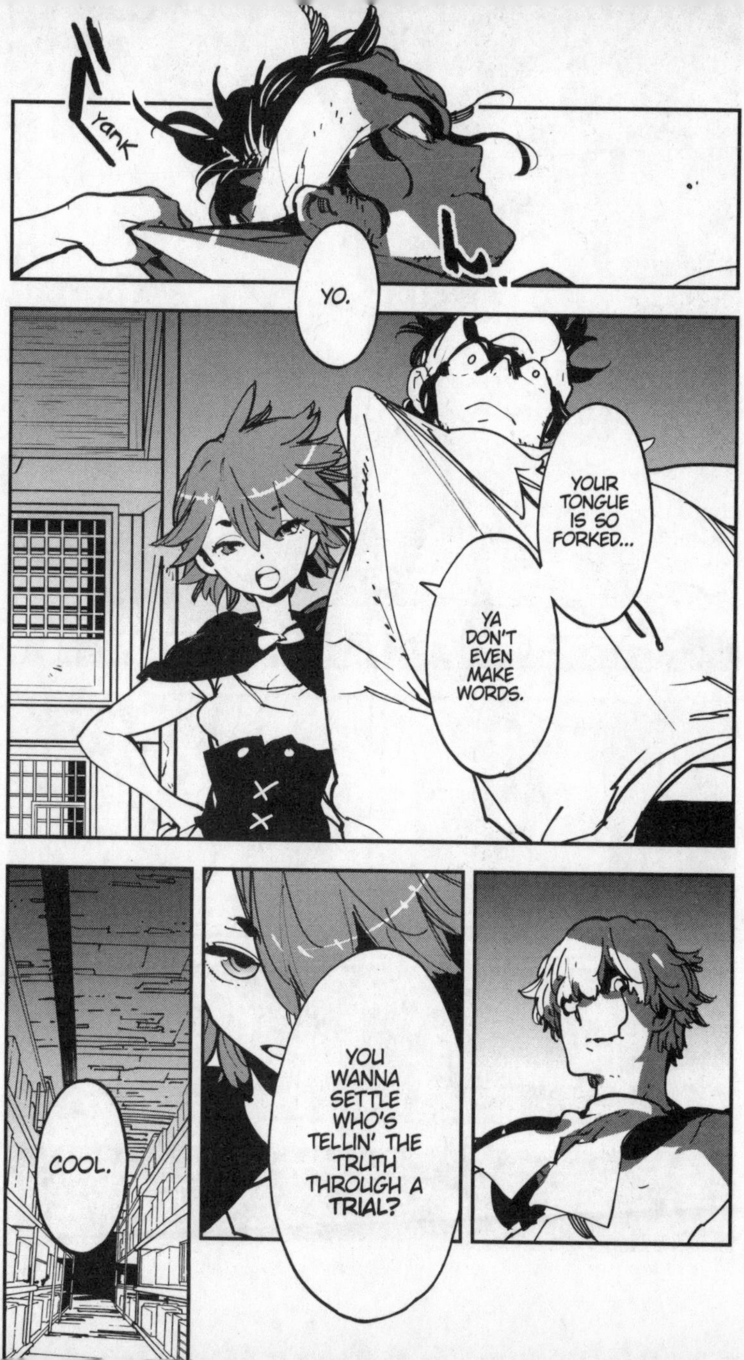
yank
YO.
YOUR TONGUE IS SO FORKED...
YA DON'T EVEN MAKE WORDS.
YOU WANNA SETTLE WHO'S TELLIN' THE TRUTH THROUGH A TRIAL?
COOL.

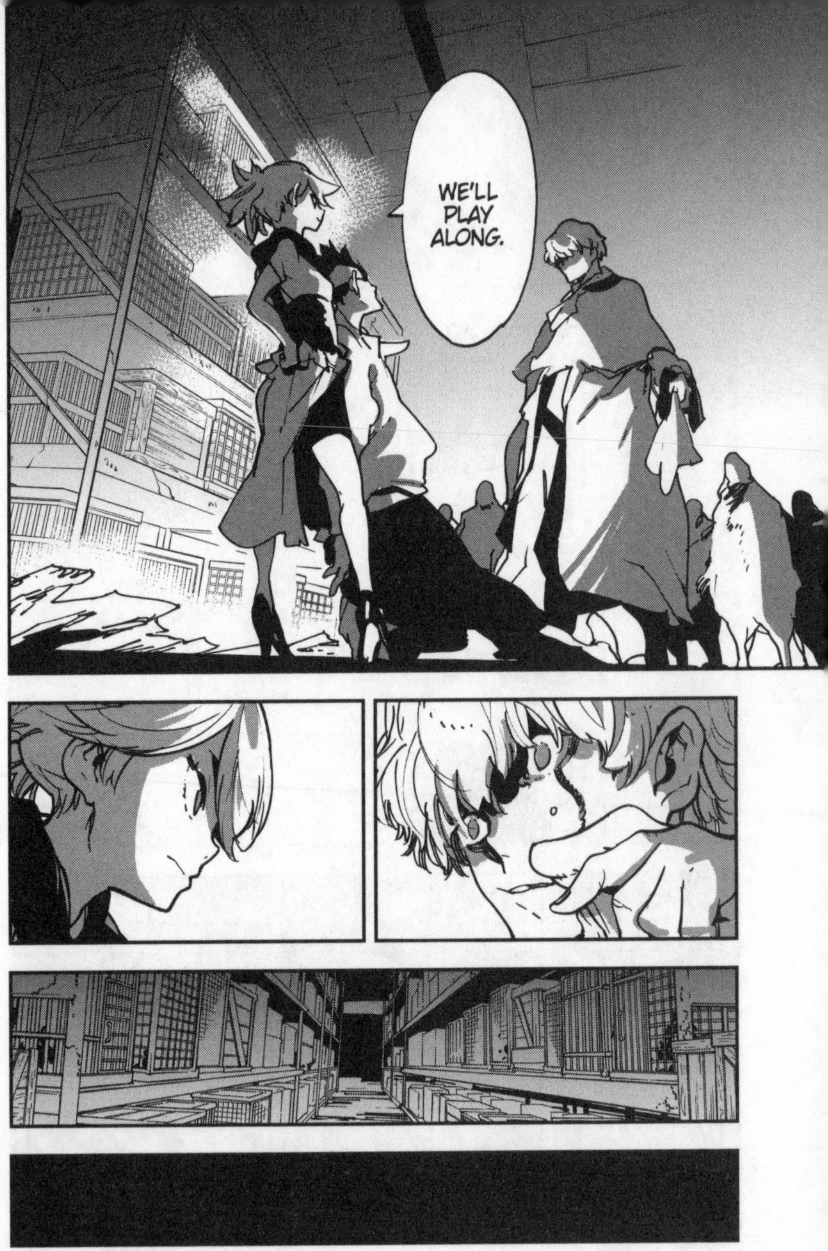
WE'LL PLAY ALONG.
...

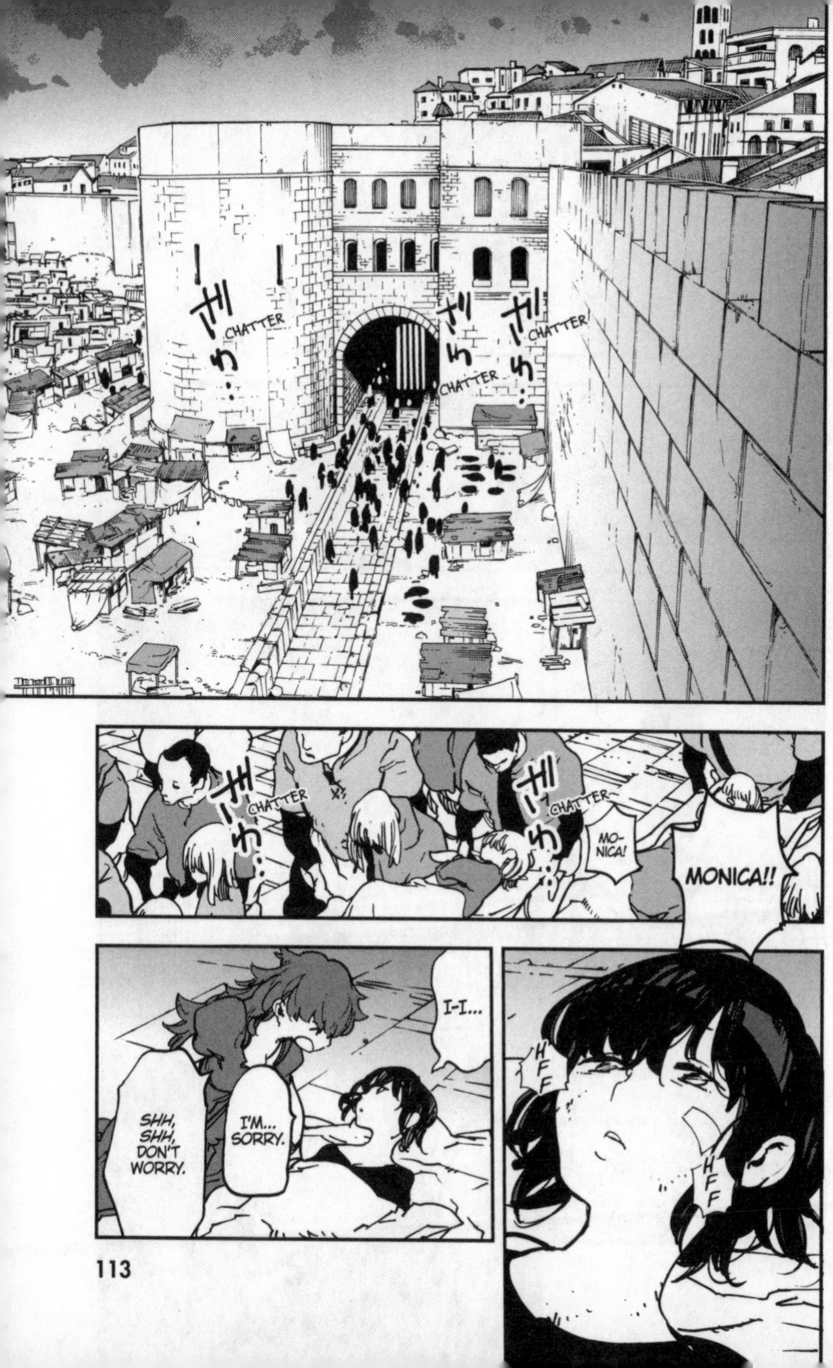
CHATTER
CHATTER
CHATTER
CHATTER
MONICA!!
MONICA!
CHATTER
CHATTER
HFF
HFF
I-I...
I'M... SORRY.
SHH, SHH, DON'T WORRY.

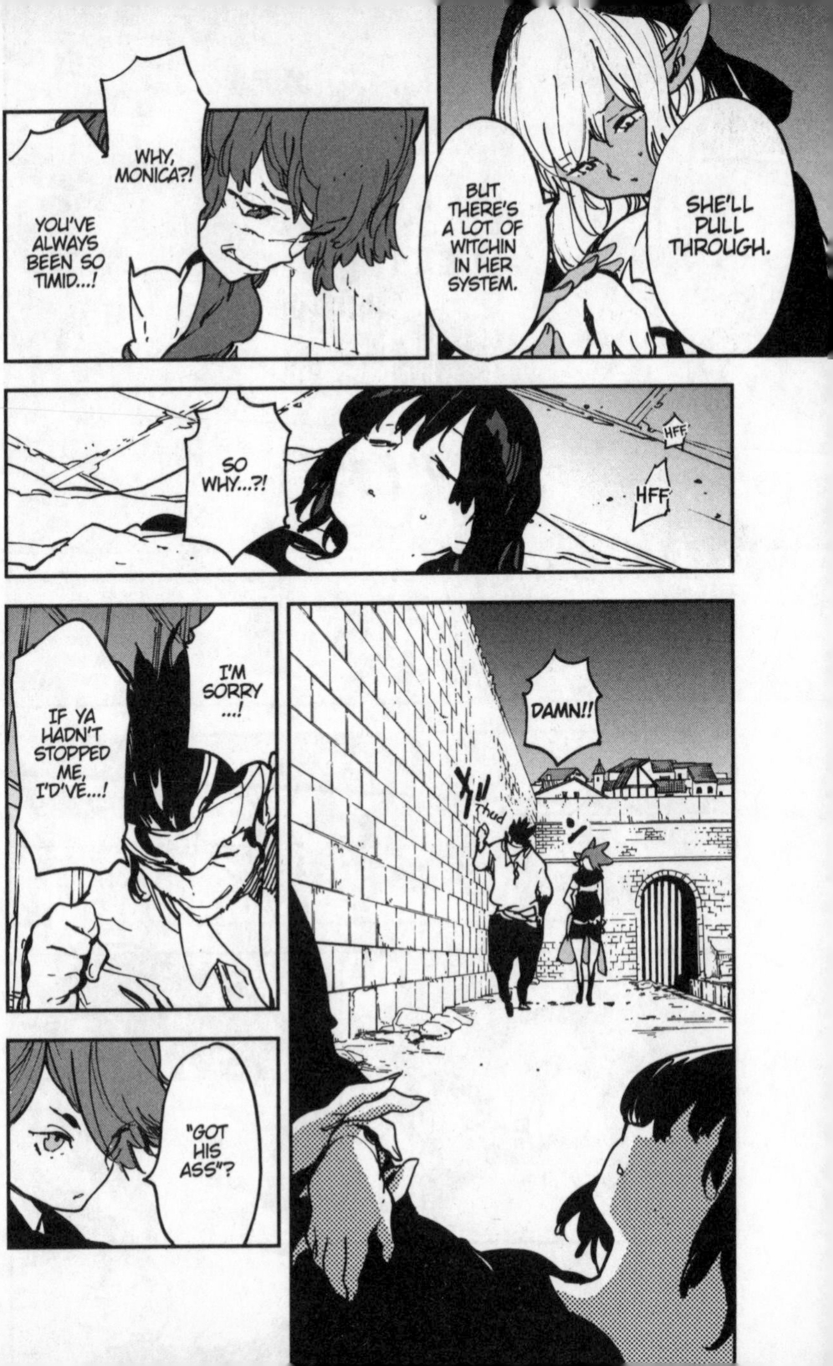
SHE'LL PULL THROUGH.
BUT THERE'S A LOT OF WITCHIN IN HER SYSTEM.
WHY, MONICA?!
YOU'VE ALWAYS BEEN SO TIMID...!
HFF
HFF
SO WHY...?!
DAMN!!
thud
I'M SORRY ...!
IF YA HADN'T STOPPED ME, I'D'VE...!
"GOT HIS ASS"?

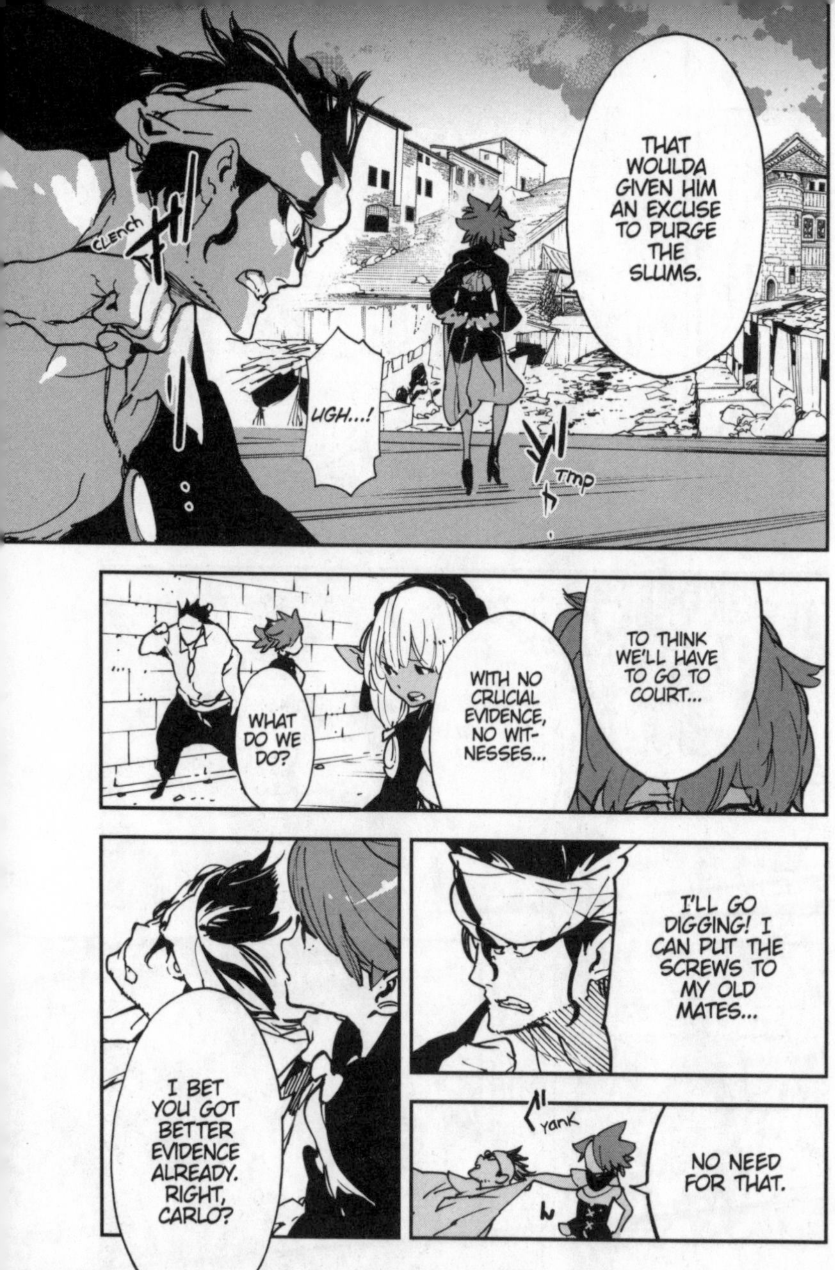
THAT WOULDA GIVEN HIM AN EXCUSE TO PURGE THE SLUMS.
Tmp
UGH...!
CLENCH
TO THINK WE'LL HAVE TO GO TO COURT...
WITH NO CRUCIAL EVIDENCE, NO WITNESSES...
WHAT DO WE DO?
I'LL GO DIGGING! I CAN PUT THE SCREWS TO MY OLD MATES...
NO NEED FOR THAT.
Yank
I BET YOU GOT BETTER EVIDENCE ALREADY. RIGHT, CARLO?

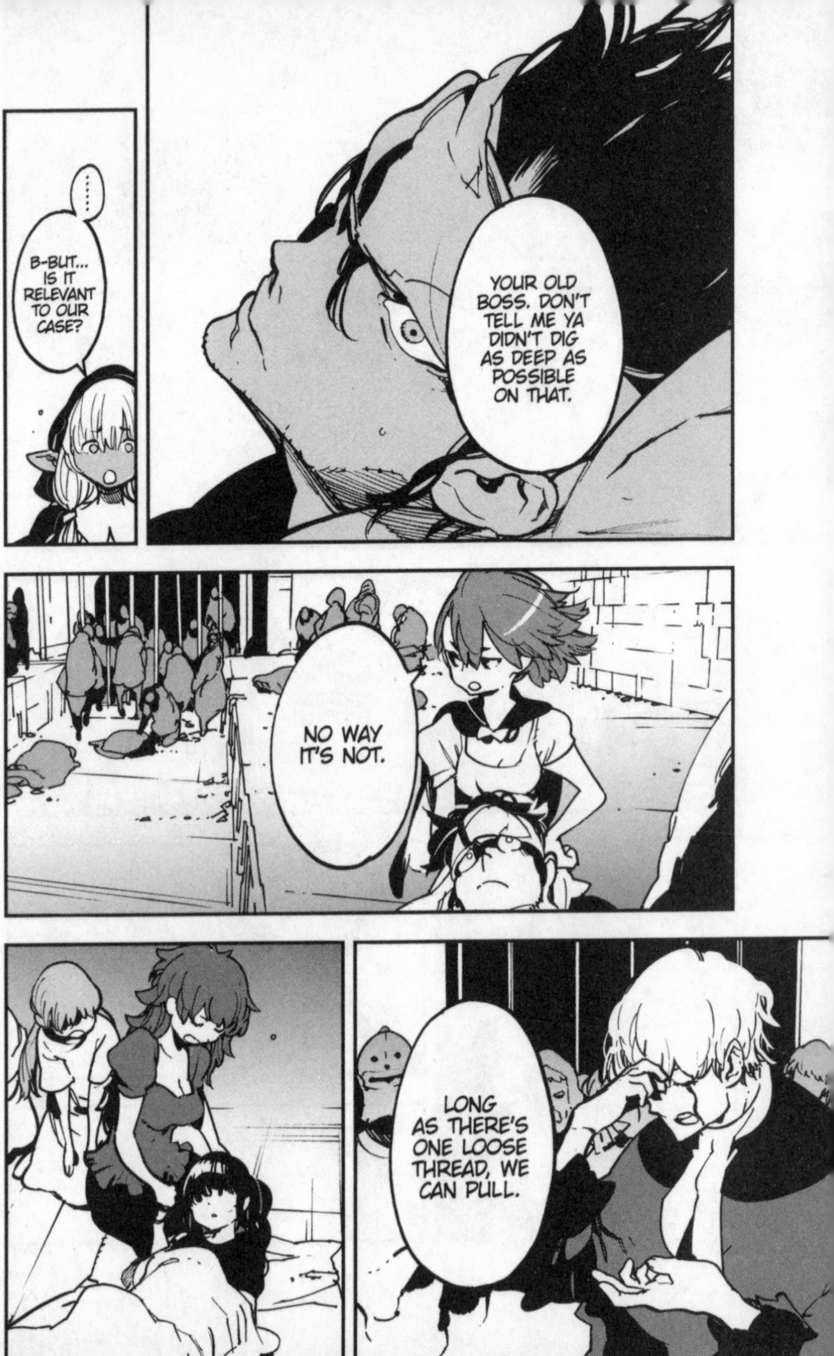
YOUR OLD BOSS. DON'T TELL ME YA DIDN'T DIG AS DEEP AS POSSIBLE ON THAT.
......
B-BUT... IS IT RELEVANT TO OUR CASE?
NO WAY IT'S NOT.
LONG AS THERE'S ONE LOOSE THREAD, WE CAN PULL.

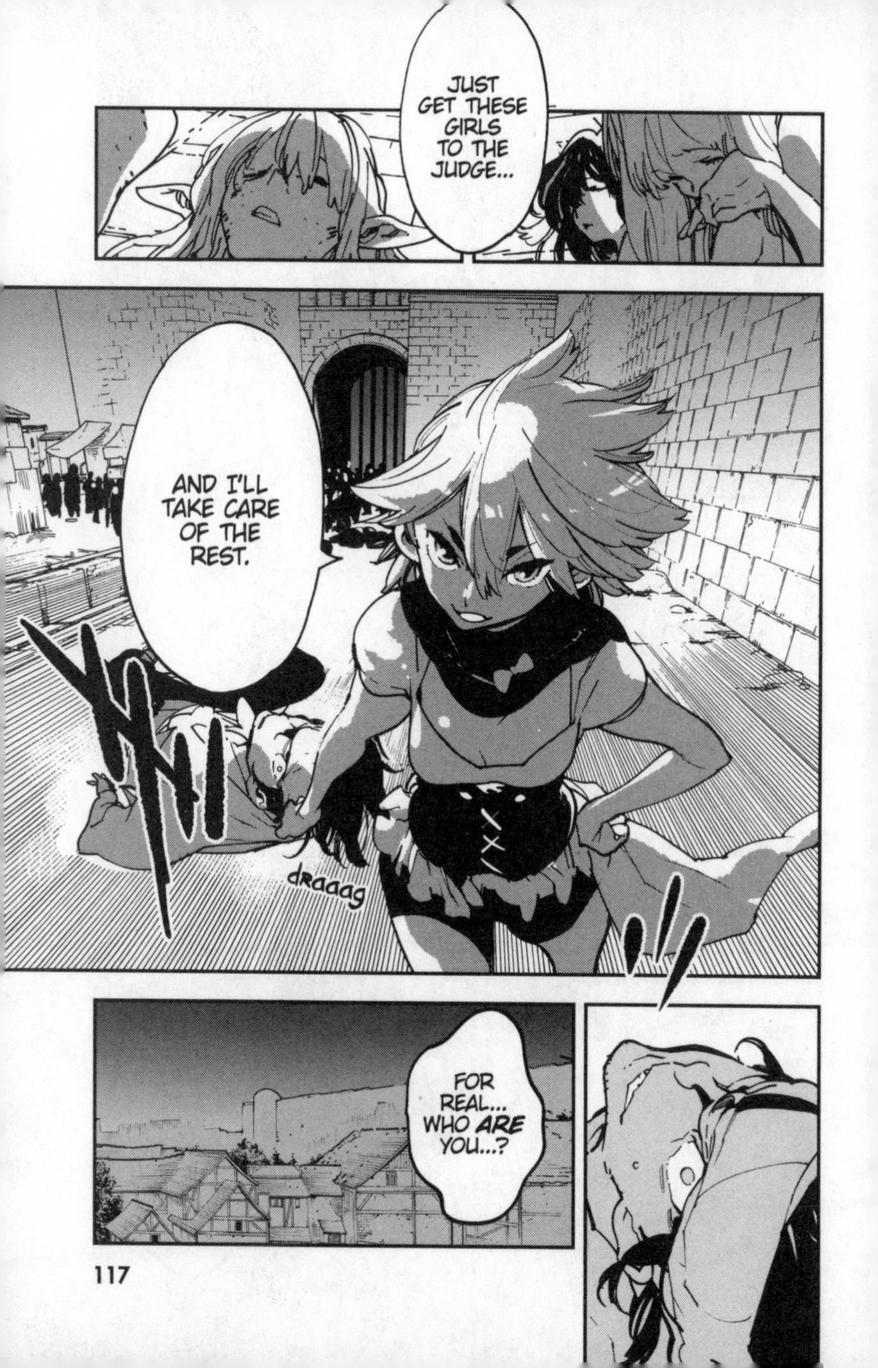
JUST GET THESE GIRLS TO THE JUDGE...
AND I'LL TAKE CARE OF THE REST.
draaag
FOR REAL... WHO *ARE* YOU...?

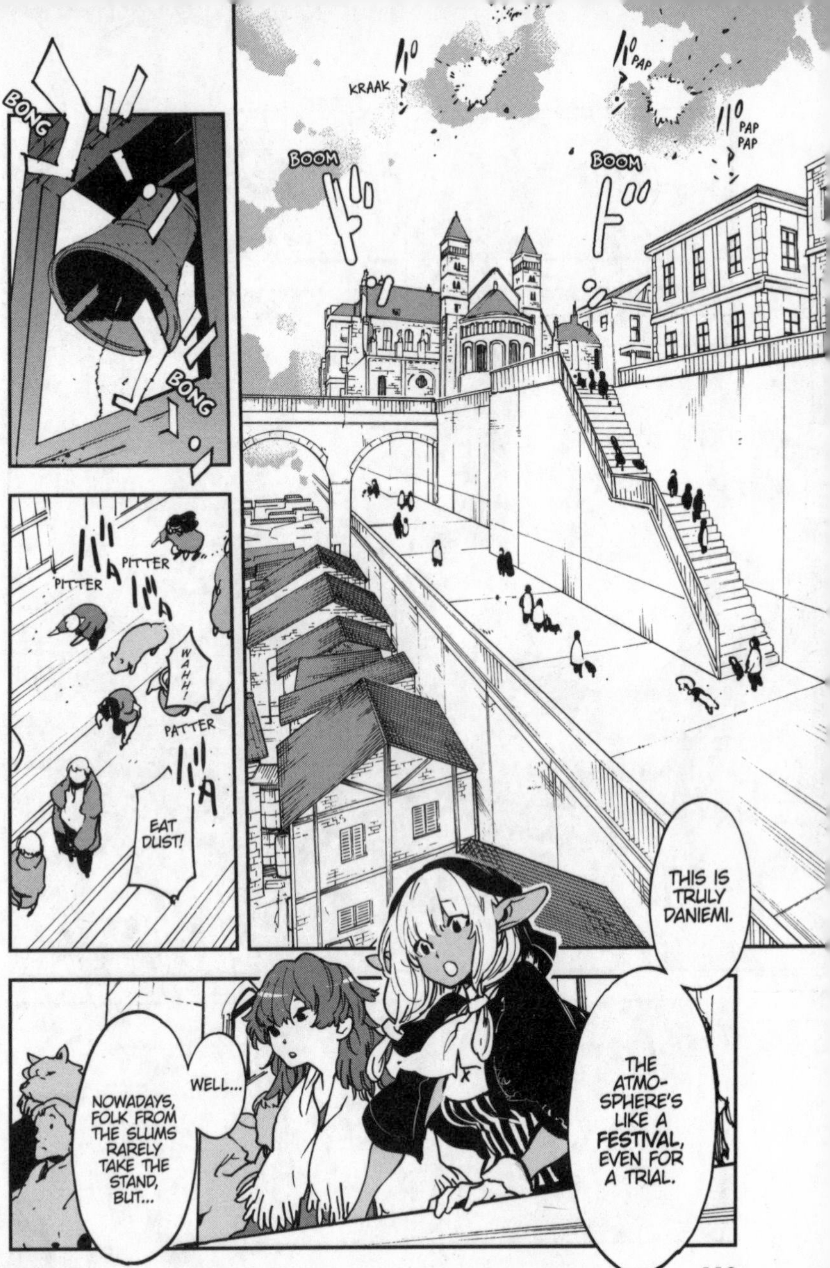
PAP
PAP
PAP
BOOM
KRAAK
BOOM
THIS IS TRULY DANIEMI.
BONG
BONG
PITTER
PITTER
WAHH!
PATTER
EAT DUST!
THE ATMOSPHERE'S LIKE A FESTIVAL, EVEN FOR A TRIAL.
WELL...
NOWADAYS, FOLK FROM THE SLUMS RARELY TAKE THE STAND, BUT...

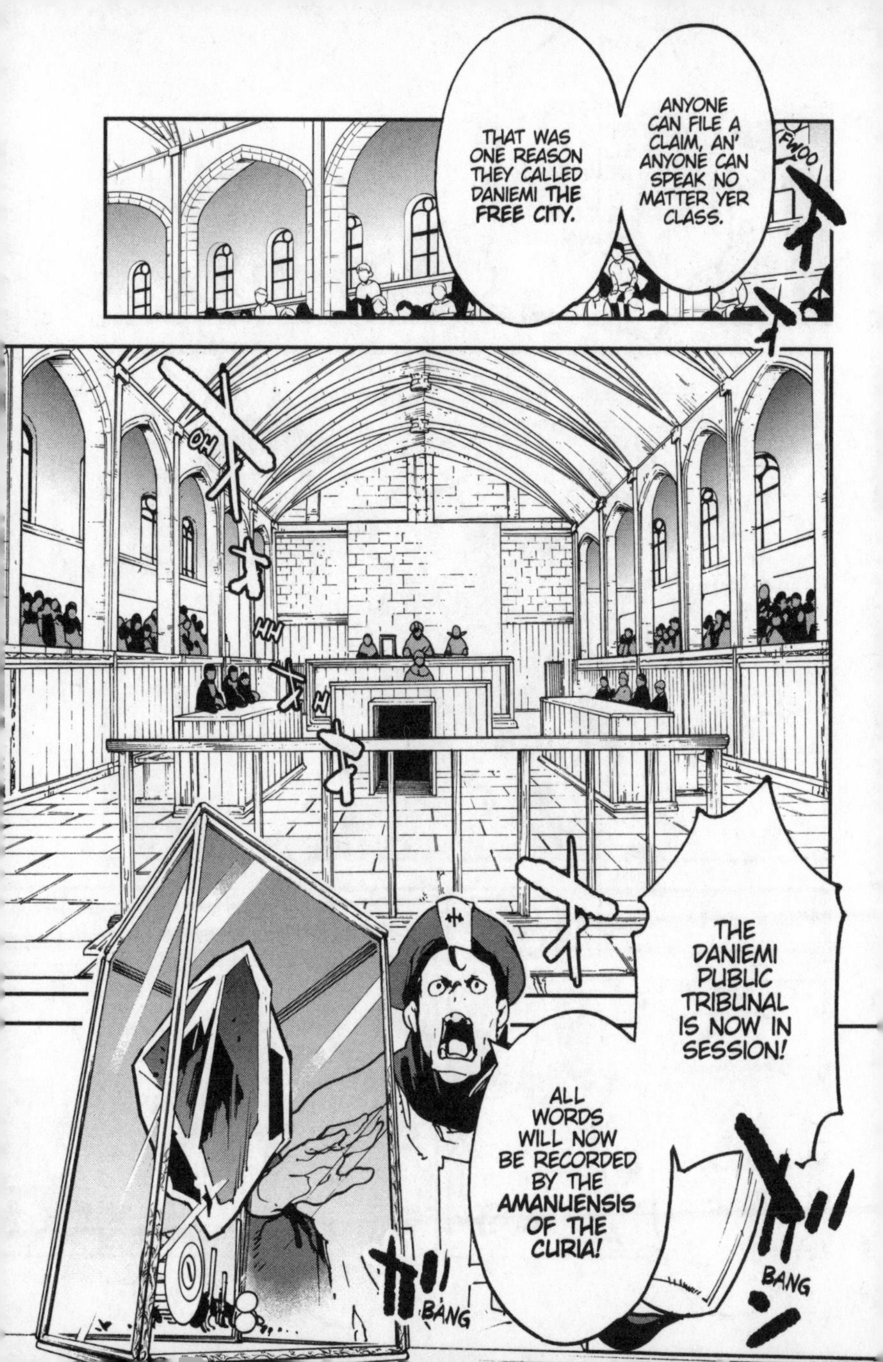

ANYONE CAN FILE A CLAIM, AN' ANYONE CAN SPEAK NO MATTER YER CLASS.
THAT WAS ONE REASON THEY CALLED DANIEMI THE FREE CITY.
FWOO
OH
HH
THE DANIEMI PUBLIC TRIBUNAL IS NOW IN SESSION!
ALL WORDS WILL NOW BE RECORDED BY THE AMANUENSIS OF THE CURIA!
BANG
BANG

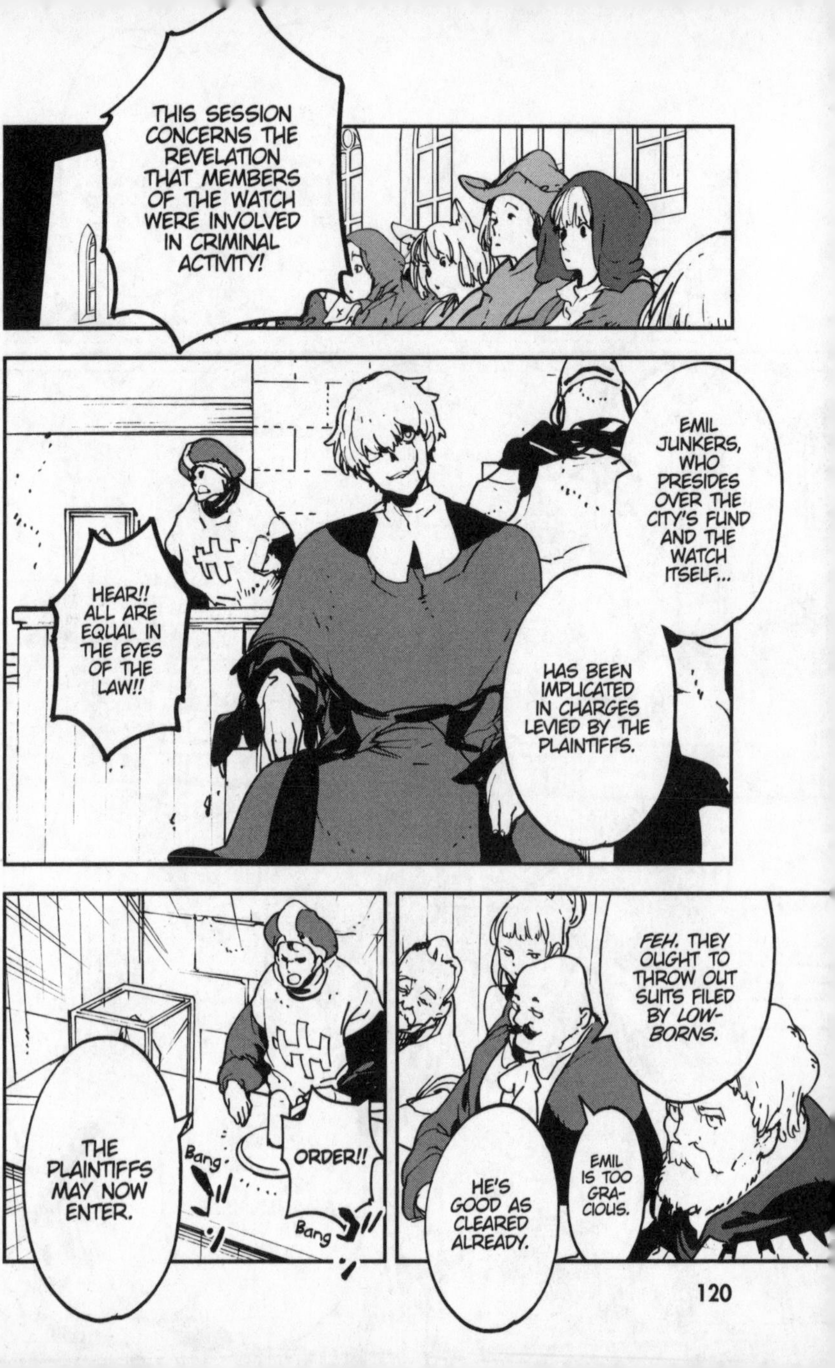
THIS SESSION CONCERNS THE REVELATION THAT MEMBERS OF THE WATCH WERE INVOLVED IN CRIMINAL ACTIVITY!
EMIL JUNKERS, WHO PRESIDES OVER THE CITY'S FUND AND THE WATCH ITSELF...
HAS BEEN IMPLICATED IN CHARGES LEVIED BY THE PLAINTIFFS.
HEAR!! ALL ARE EQUAL IN THE EYES OF THE LAW!!
FEH. THEY OUGHT TO THROW OUT SUITS FILED BY *LOW-BORNS.*
EMIL IS TOO GRA-CIOUS.
HE'S GOOD AS CLEARED ALREADY.
ORDER!!
Bang
THE PLAINTIFFS MAY NOW ENTER.
Bang

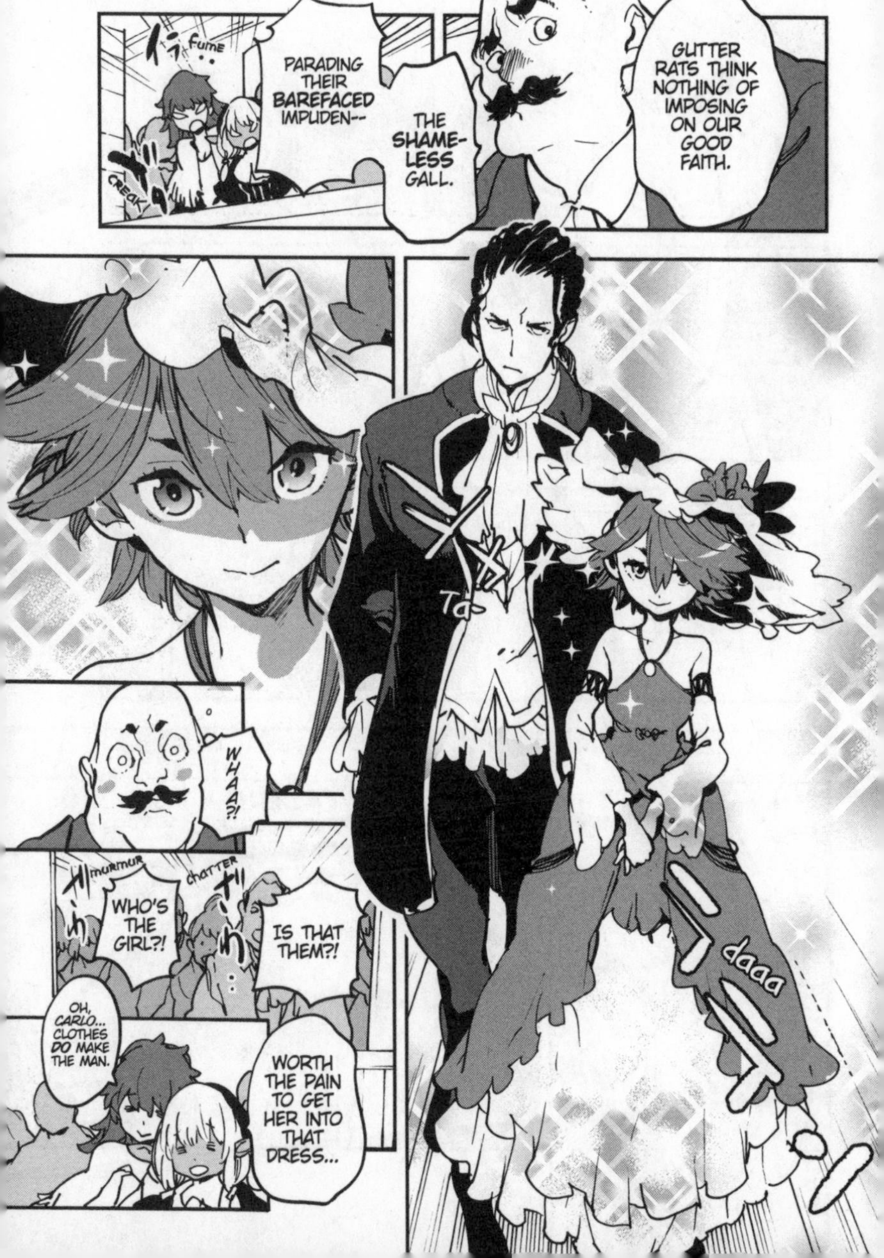
GUTTER RATS THINK NOTHING OF IMPOSING ON OUR GOOD FAITH.
THE SHAME-LESS GALL.
PARADING THEIR BAREFACED IMPUDEN--
Fume
CREAK
Ta
daaa
WHAAA?!
chatter
IS THAT THEM?!
murmur
WHO'S THE GIRL?!
WORTH THE PAIN TO GET HER INTO THAT DRESS...
OH, CARLO... CLOTHES DO MAKE THE MAN.

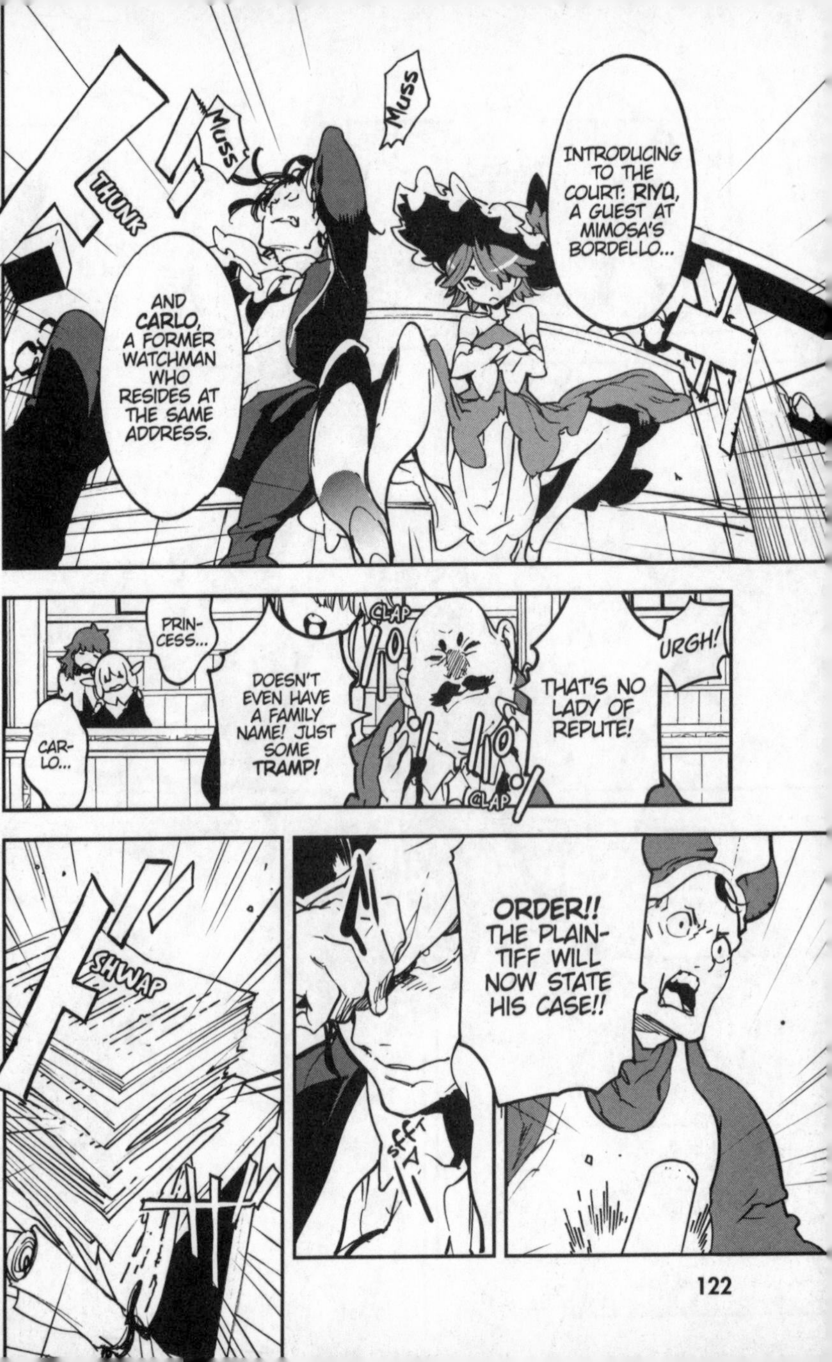
INTRODUCING TO THE COURT: RIYO, A GUEST AT MIMOSA'S BORDELLO...
MUSS
MUSS
THUNK
AND CARLO, A FORMER WATCHMAN WHO RESIDES AT THE SAME ADDRESS.
URGH!
THAT'S NO LADY OF REPUTE!
CLAP
CLAP
DOESN'T EVEN HAVE A FAMILY NAME! JUST SOME TRAMP!
PRIN-CESS...
CAR-LO...
ORDER!! THE PLAIN-TIFF WILL NOW STATE HIS CASE!!
SFFT
SHWAP

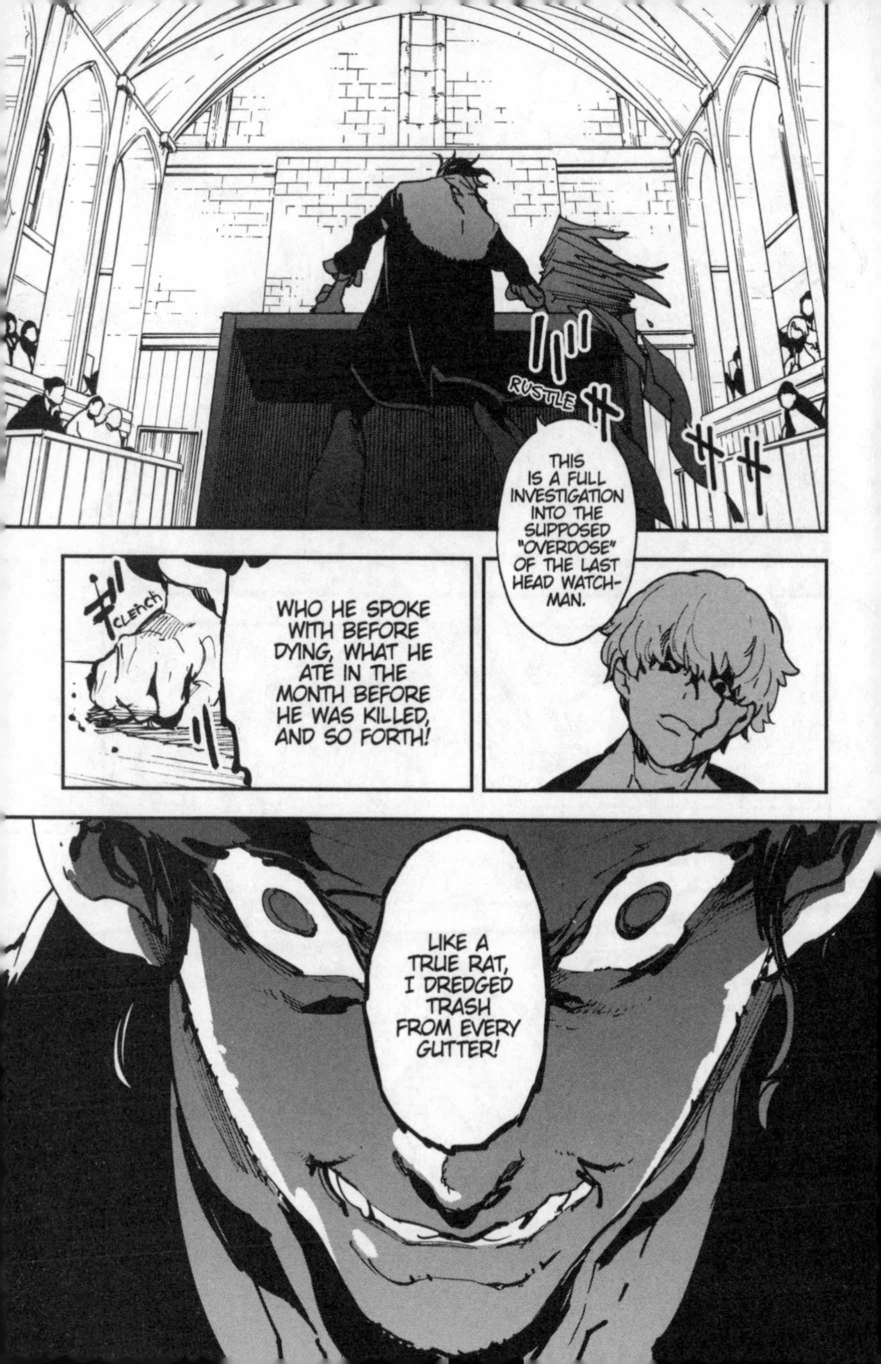
RUSTLE
THIS IS A FULL INVESTIGATION INTO THE SUPPOSED "OVERDOSE" OF THE LAST HEAD WATCH-MAN.
WHO HE SPOKE WITH BEFORE DYING, WHAT HE ATE IN THE MONTH BEFORE HE WAS KILLED, AND SO FORTH!
CLENCH
LIKE A TRUE RAT, I DREDGED TRASH FROM EVERY GUTTER!

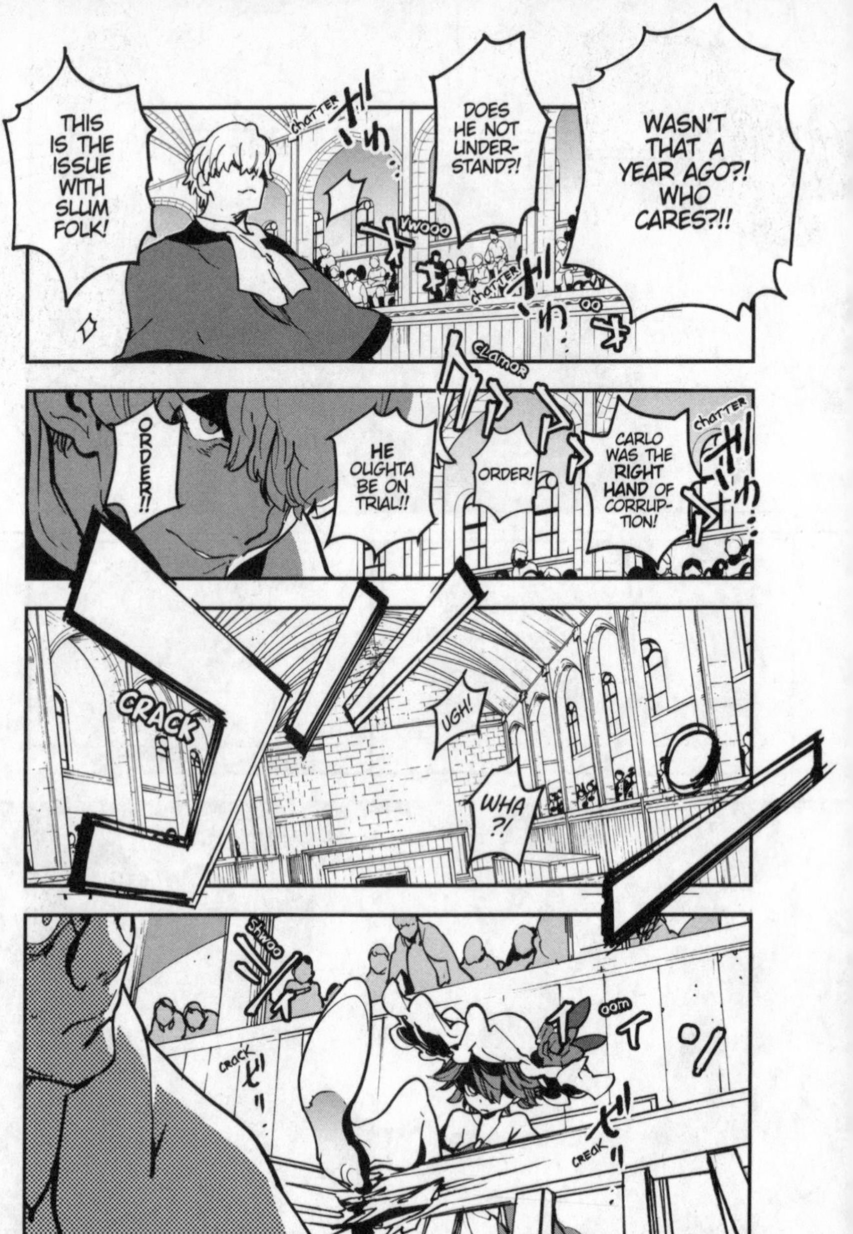
WASN'T THAT A YEAR AGO?! WHO CARES?!!
DOES HE NOT UNDERSTAND?!
CHATTER
YWOOO
CHATTER
THIS IS THE ISSUE WITH SLUM FOLK!
CLAMOR
CHATTER
CARLO WAS THE RIGHT HAND OF CORRUPTION!
ORDER!
HE OUGHTA BE ON TRIAL!!
ORDER!!
UGH!
WHA?!
CRACK
SHWOO
OOM
CREAK
CRACK

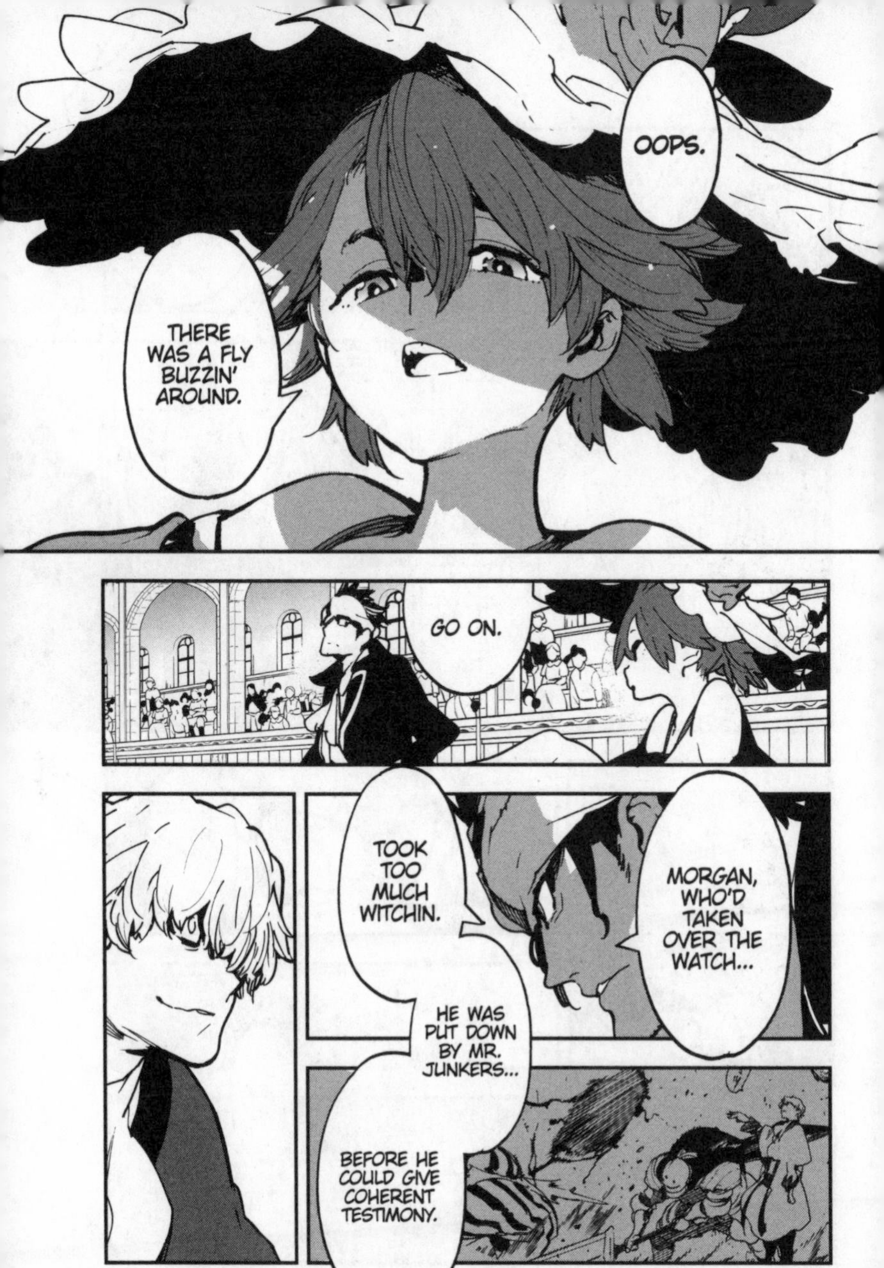
OOPS.
THERE WAS A FLY BUZZIN' AROUND.
GO ON.
MORGAN, WHO'D TAKEN OVER THE WATCH...
TOOK TOO MUCH WITCHIN.
HE WAS PUT DOWN BY MR. JUNKERS...
BEFORE HE COULD GIVE COHERENT TESTIMONY.

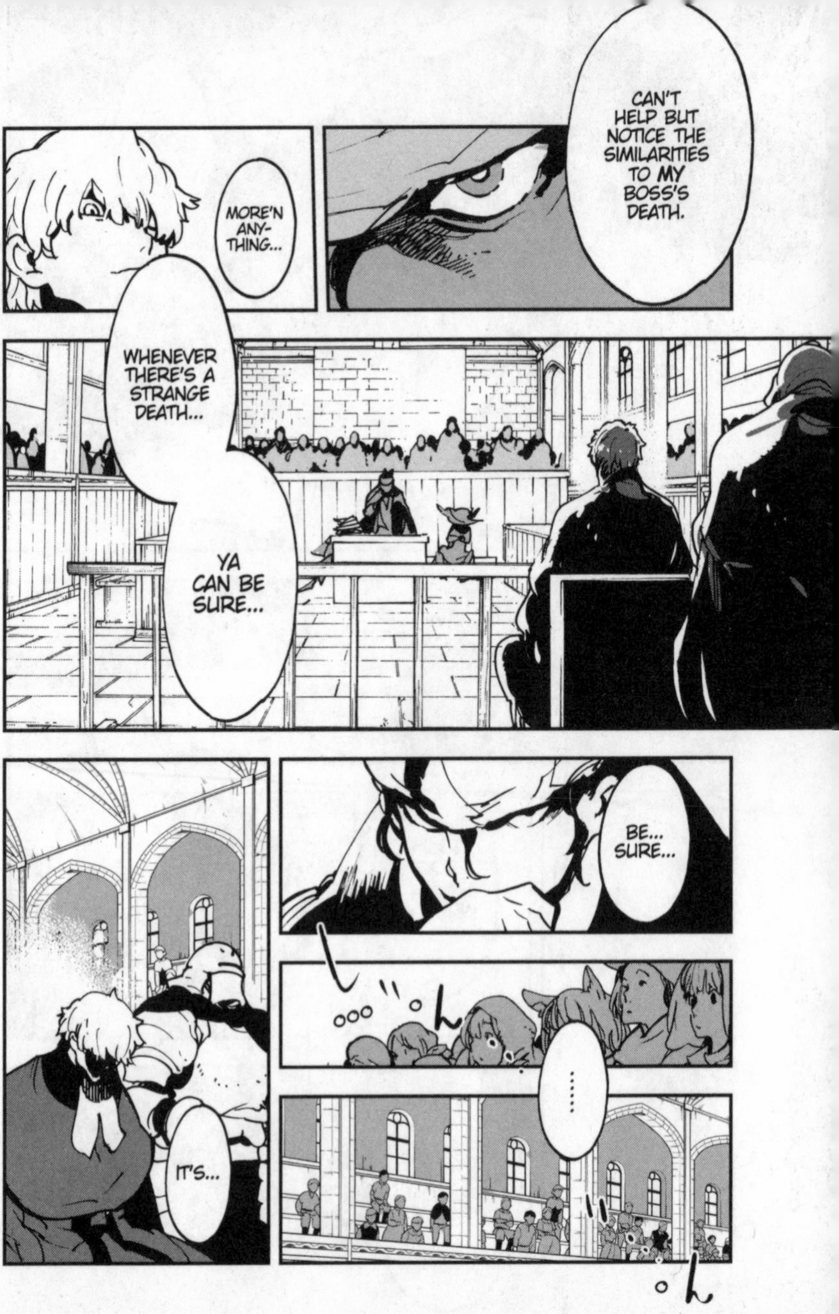
CAN'T HELP BUT NOTICE THE SIMILARITIES TO MY BOSS'S DEATH.
MORE'N ANY-THING...
WHENEVER THERE'S A STRANGE DEATH...
YA CAN BE SURE...
BE... SURE...
ooo oh
......
oh
IT'S...

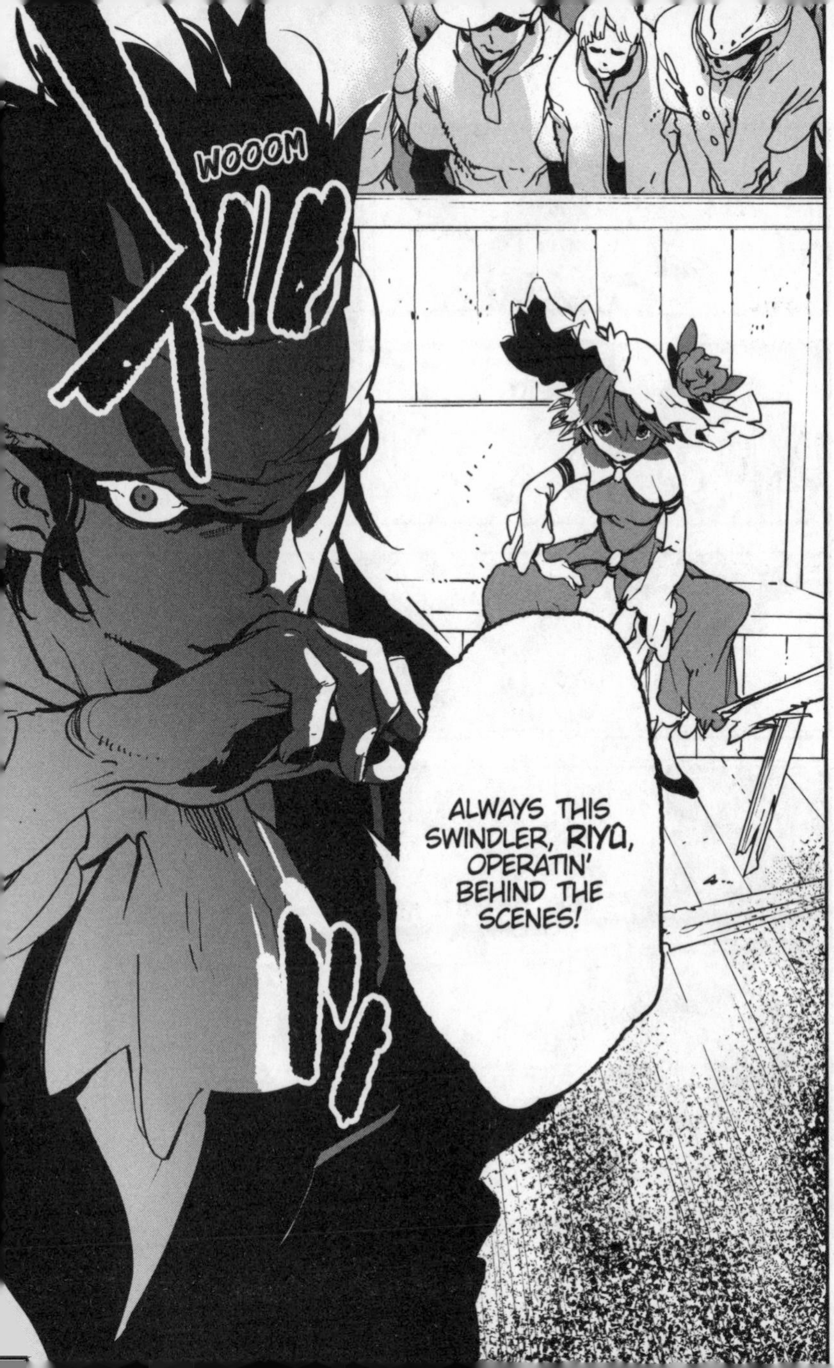
WOOOM
ALWAYS THIS SWINDLER, RIYO, OPERATIN' BEHIND THE SCENES!

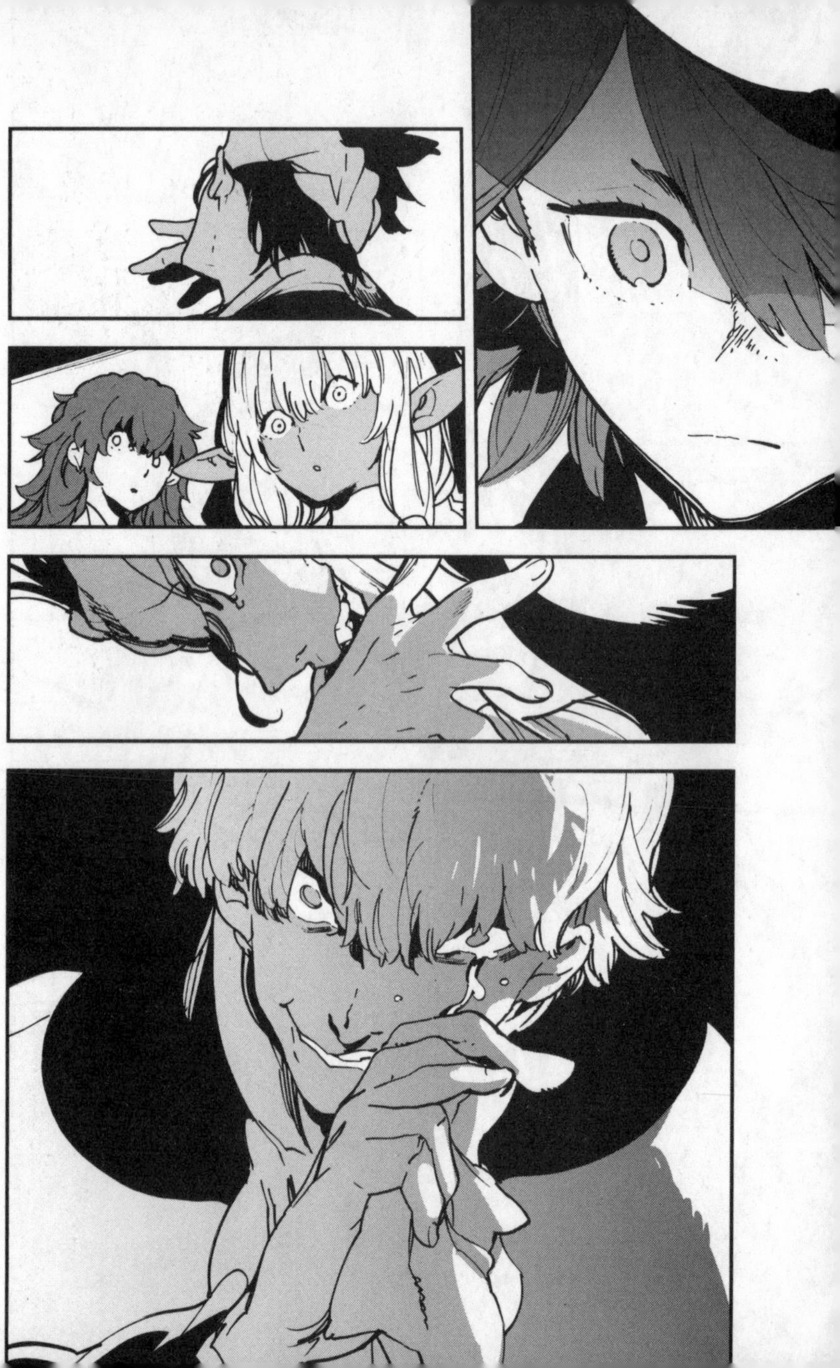

CHAPTER 12: ROLL OF THE DICE

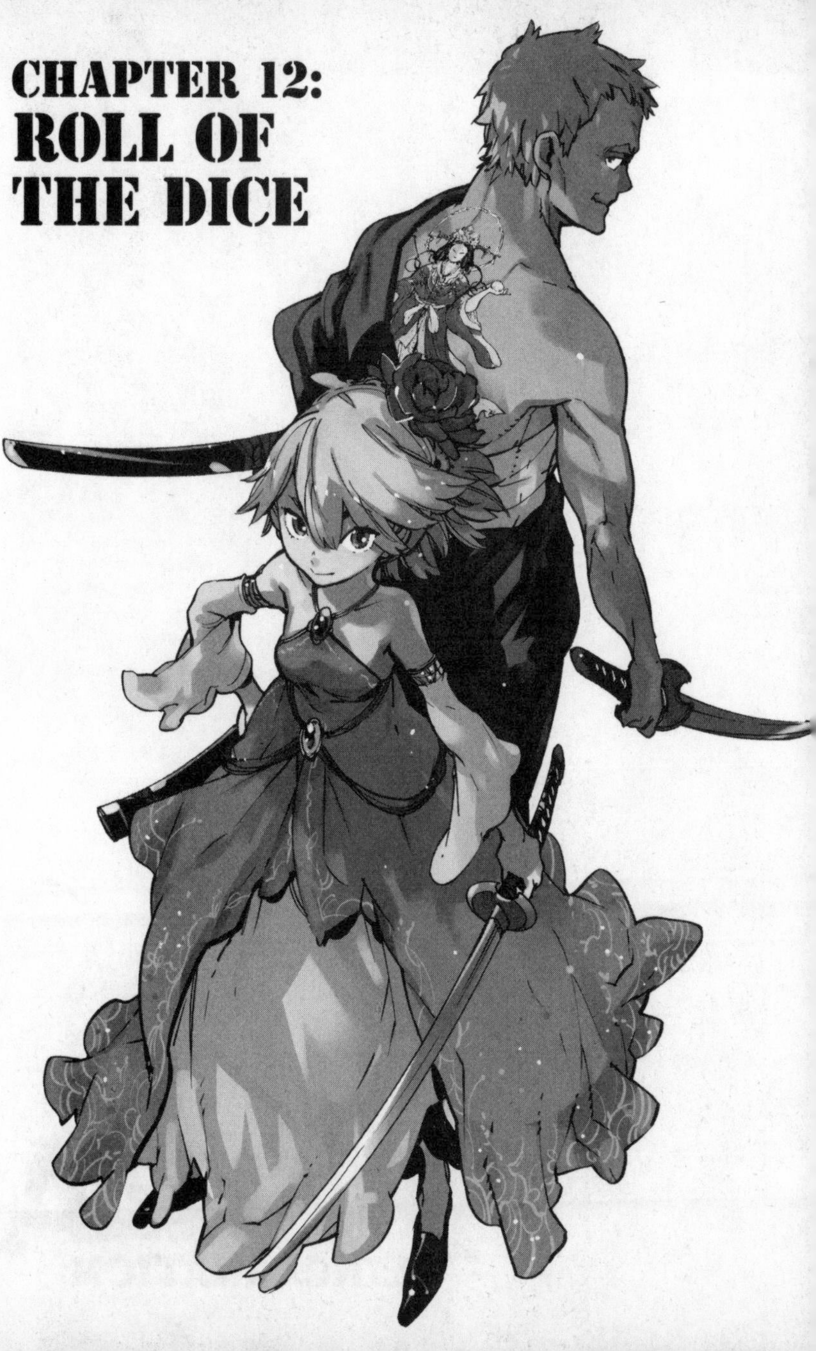

YAKUZA
REINCARNATION

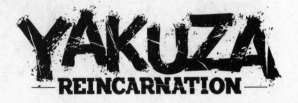

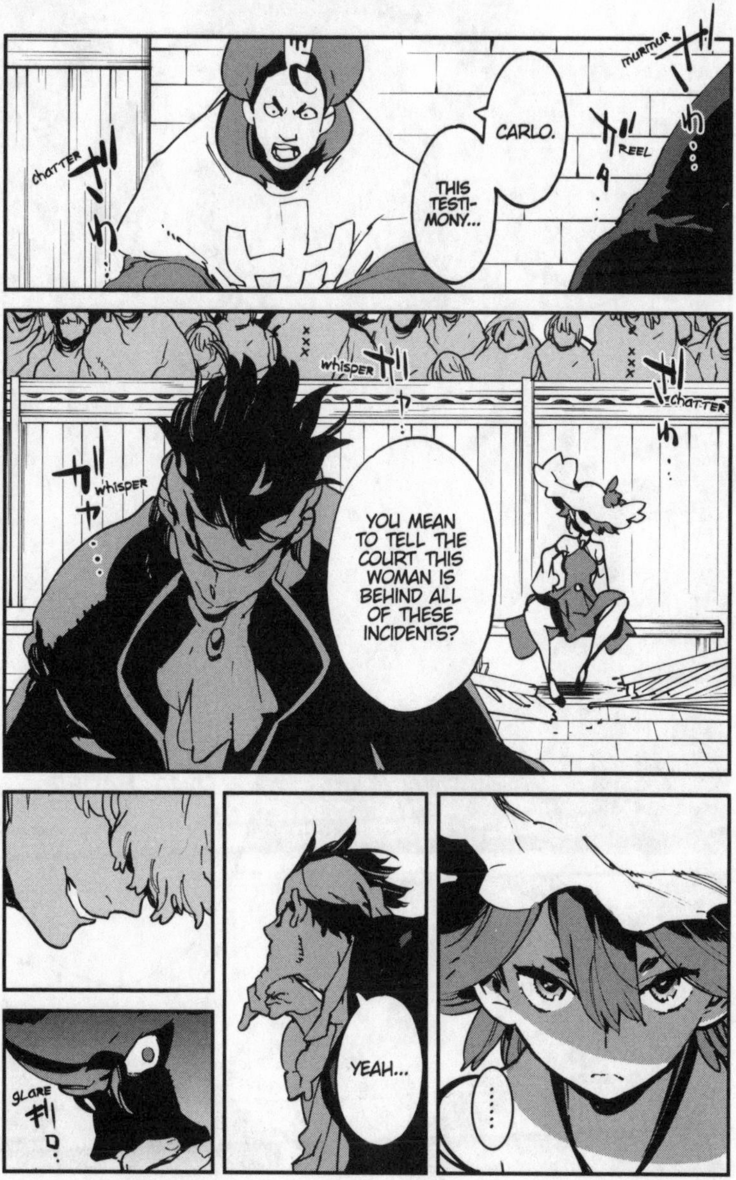
murmur
CARLO.
REEL
THIS TESTI-MONY...
chatter
chatter
whisper
YOU MEAN TO TELL THE COURT THIS WOMAN IS BEHIND ALL OF THESE INCIDENTS?
whisper
......
YEAH...
glare

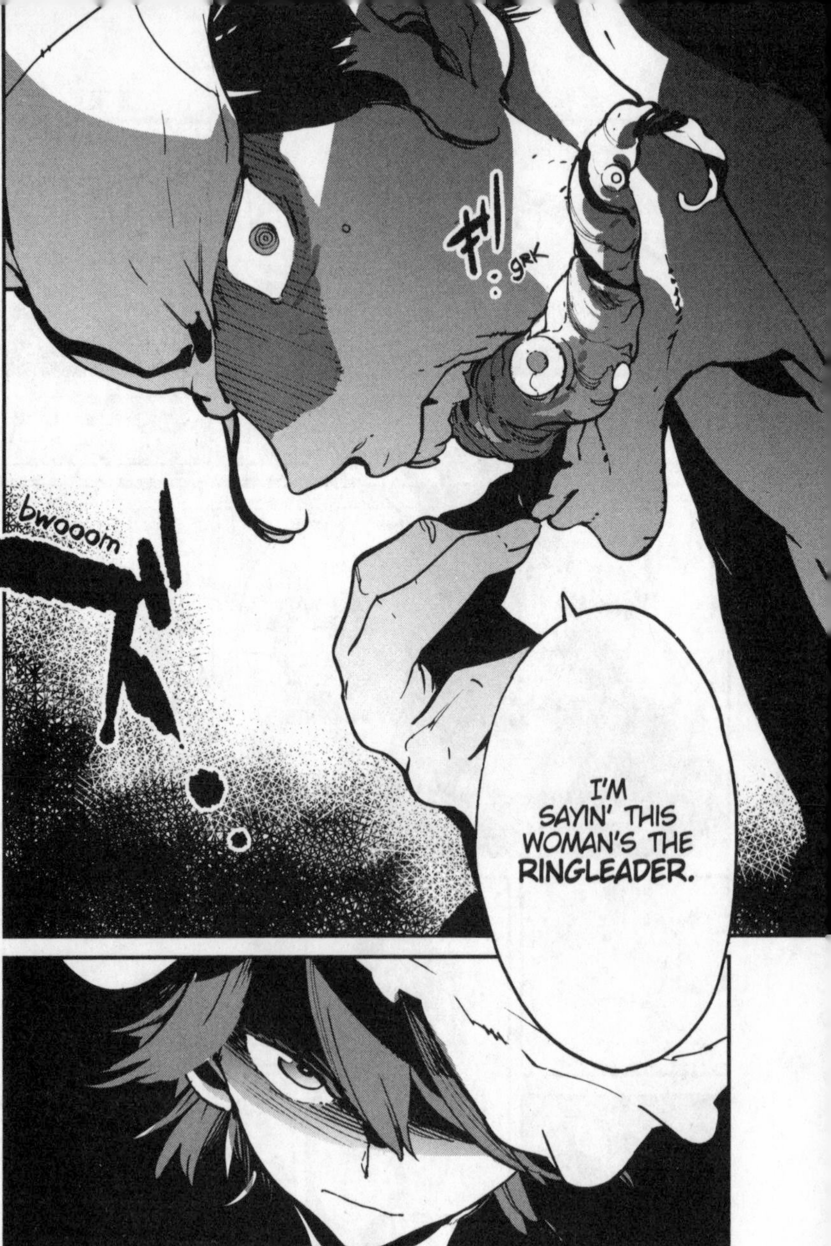
GRK
bwoooom
I'M SAYIN' THIS WOMAN'S THE RINGLEADER.

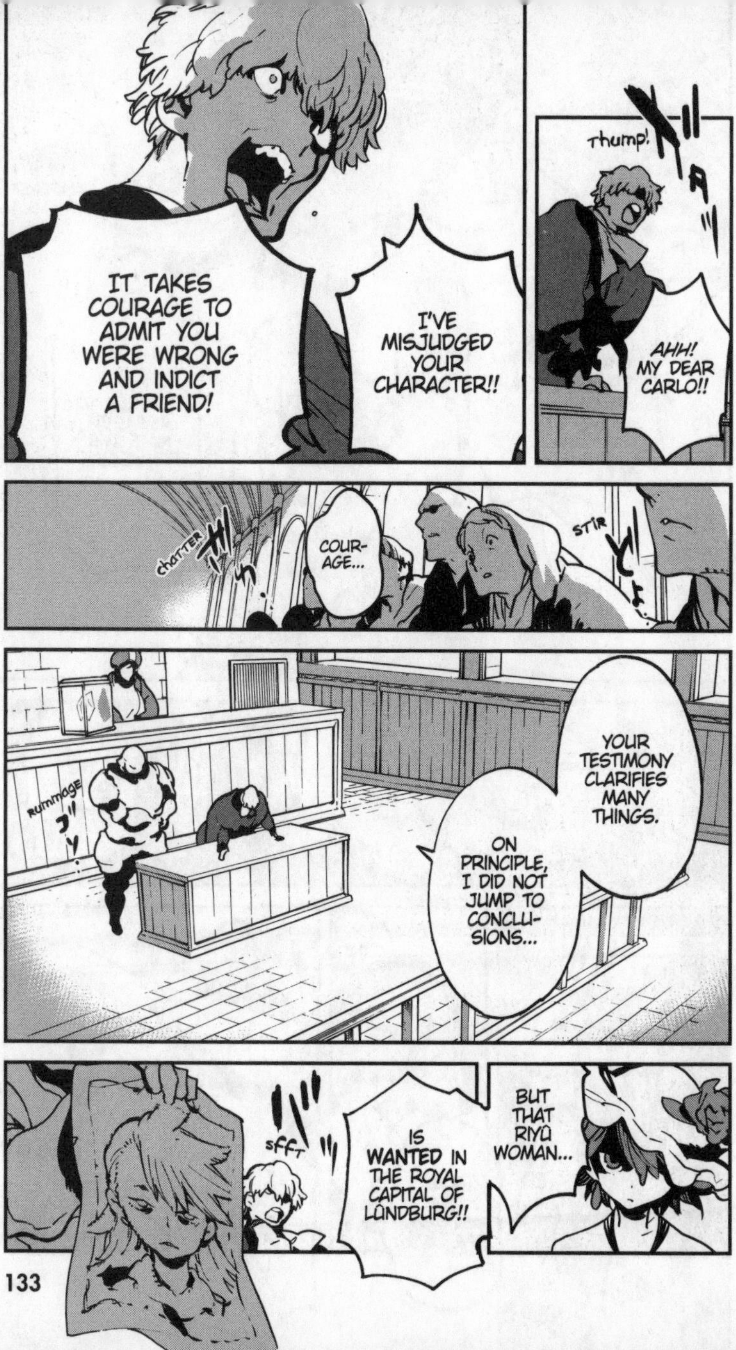
Thump!
AHH! MY DEAR CARLO!!
I'VE MISJUDGED YOUR CHARACTER!!
IT TAKES COURAGE TO ADMIT YOU WERE WRONG AND INDICT A FRIEND!
STIR
COURAGE...
chatter
YOUR TESTIMONY CLARIFIES MANY THINGS.
ON PRINCIPLE, I DID NOT JUMP TO CONCLUSIONS...
rummage
BUT THAT RIYŪ WOMAN...
IS **WANTED** IN THE ROYAL CAPITAL OF LŪNDBURG!!
sfft

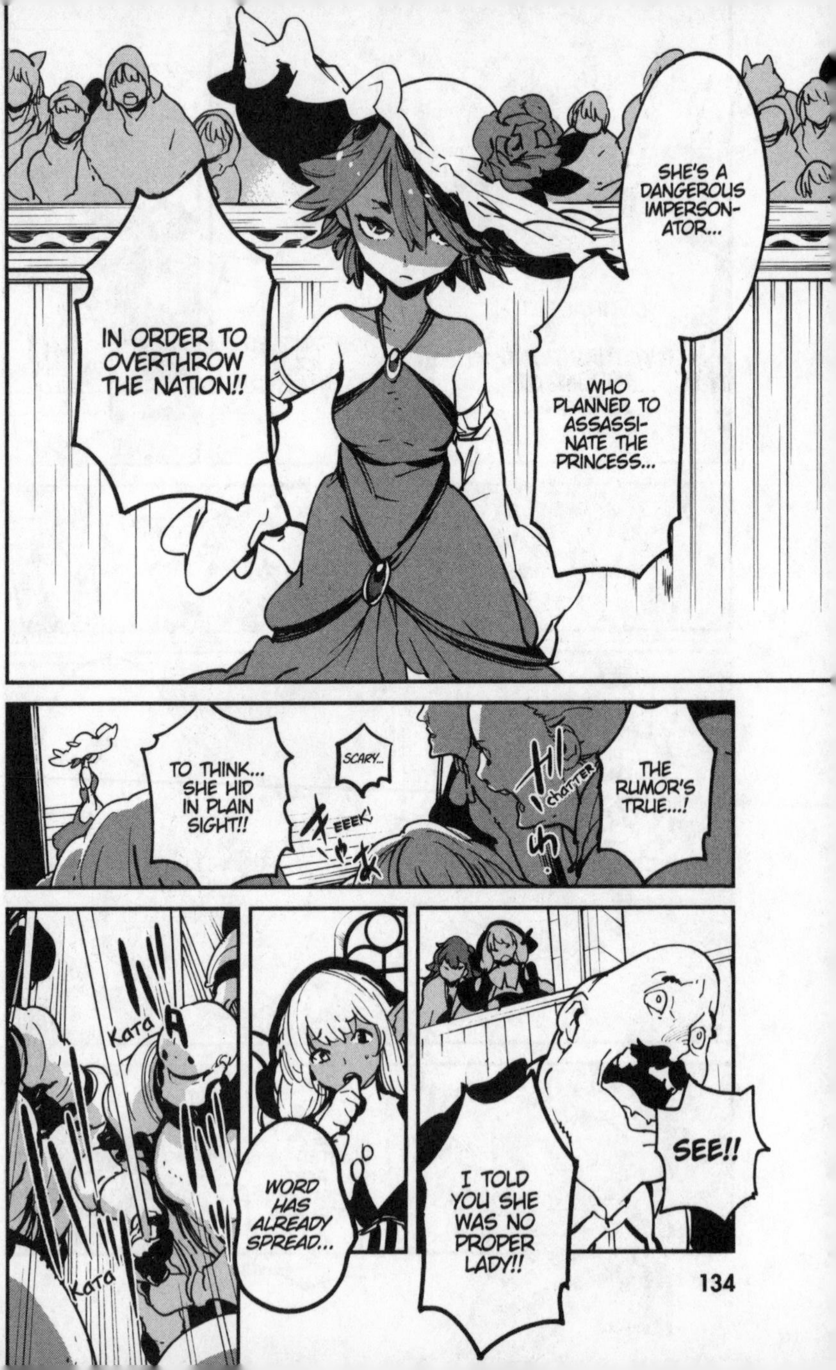
SHE'S A DANGEROUS IMPERSON-ATOR...
WHO PLANNED TO ASSASSI-NATE THE PRINCESS...
IN ORDER TO OVERTHROW THE NATION!!
THE RUMOR'S TRUE...!
chatter
SCARY...
EEEK!
TO THINK... SHE HID IN PLAIN SIGHT!!
SEE!!
I TOLD YOU SHE WAS NO PROPER LADY!!
WORD HAS ALREADY SPREAD...
Kata
Kata

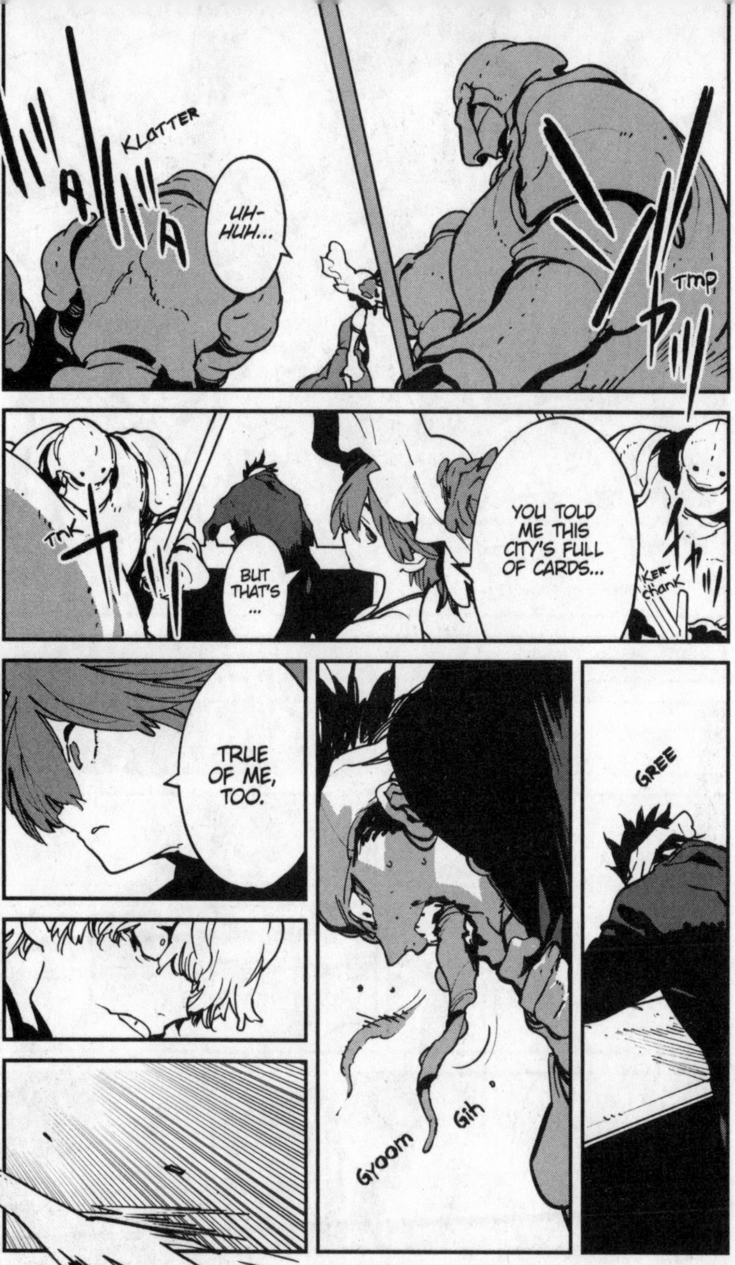
TMP
UH-HUH...
KLATTER
A
A
KER-CHANK
YOU TOLD ME THIS CITY'S FULL OF CARDS...
BUT THAT'S ...
TNK
GREE
Gih
Gyoom
TRUE OF ME, TOO.

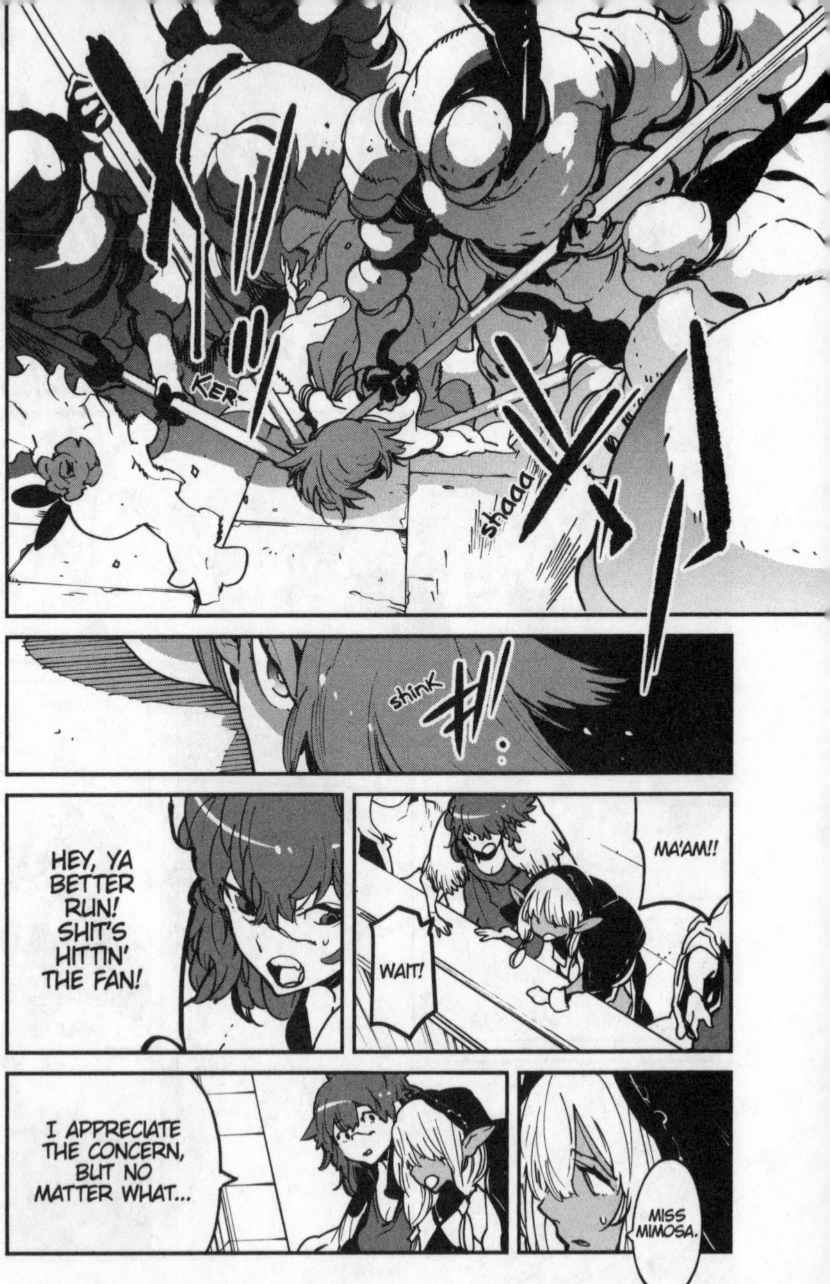
KER-
shaaa
shink
MA'AM!!
WAIT!
HEY, YA BETTER RUN! SHIT'S HITTIN' THE FAN!
MISS MIMOSA.
I APPRECIATE THE CONCERN, BUT NO MATTER WHAT...

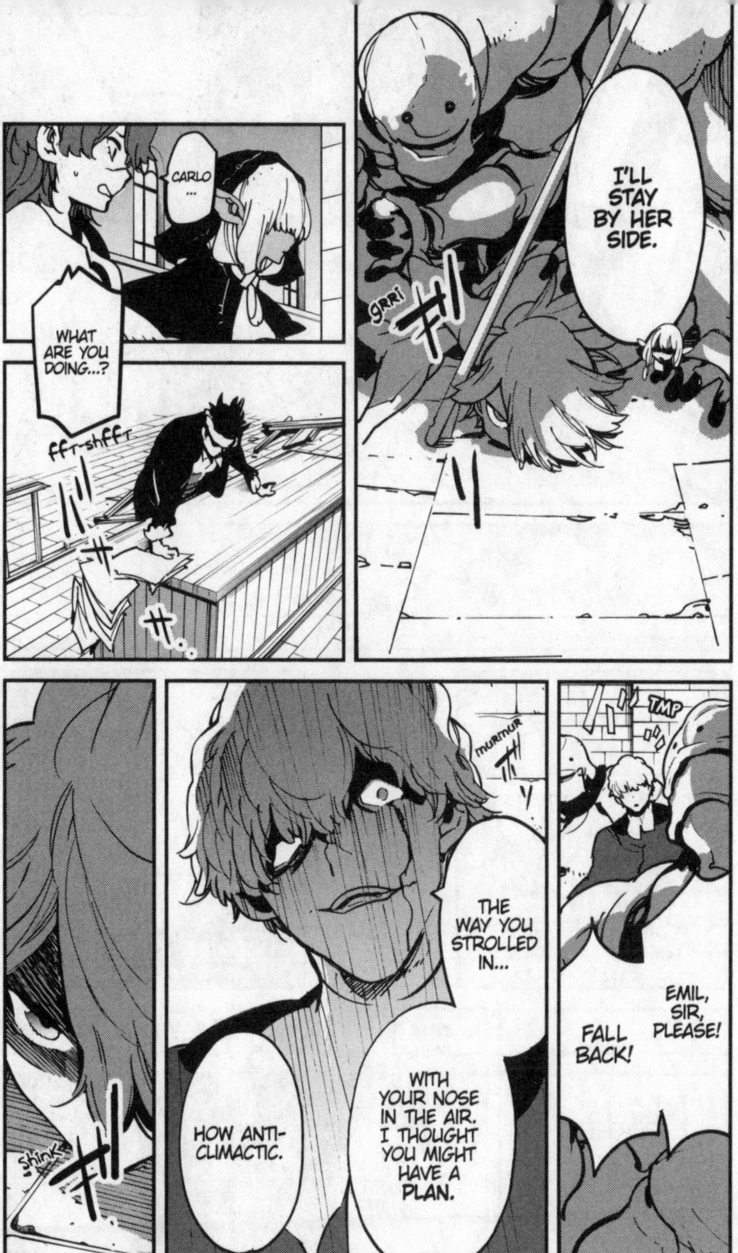

I'LL STAY BY HER SIDE.
grri
CARLO...
WHAT ARE YOU DOING...?
fft-shfft
TMP
EMIL, SIR, PLEASE!
FALL BACK!
murmur
THE WAY YOU STROLLED IN...
WITH YOUR NOSE IN THE AIR. I THOUGHT YOU MIGHT HAVE A PLAN.
HOW ANTI-CLIMACTIC.
shink

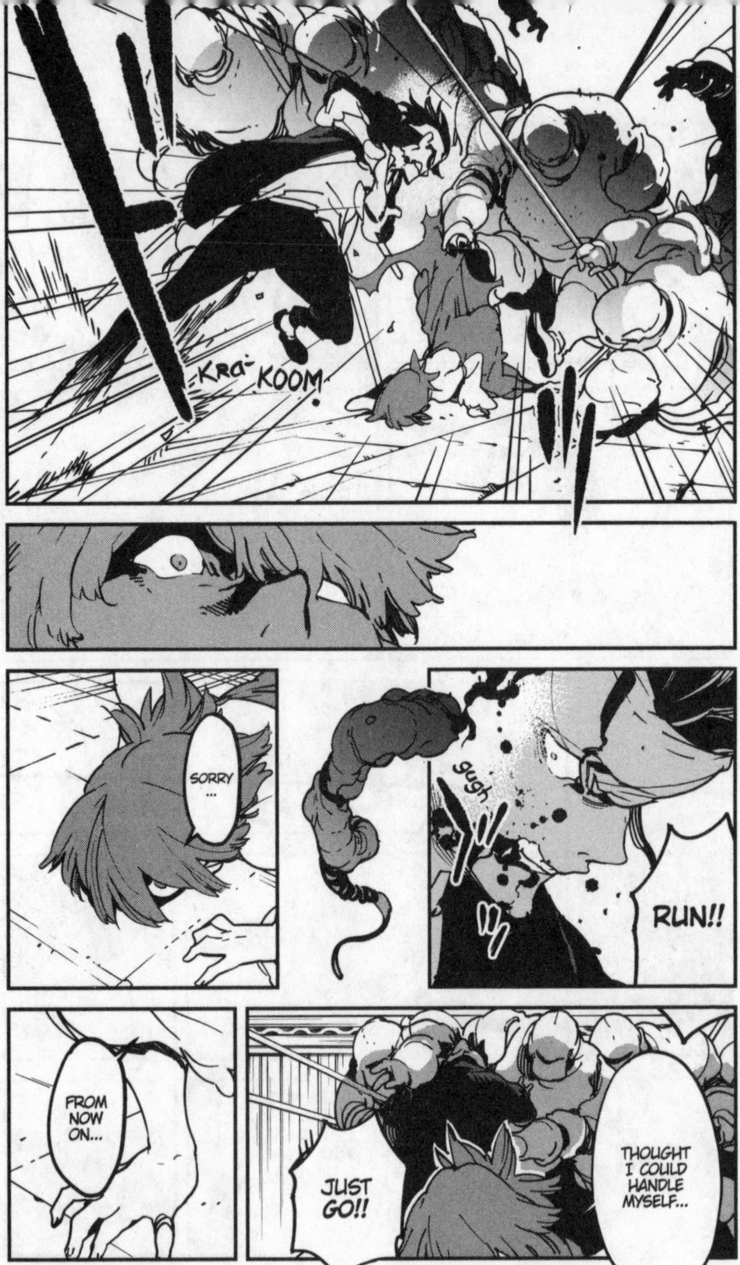
KRA-KOOM
gugh
RUN!!
SORRY...
THOUGHT I COULD HANDLE MYSELF...
JUST GO!!
FROM NOW ON...

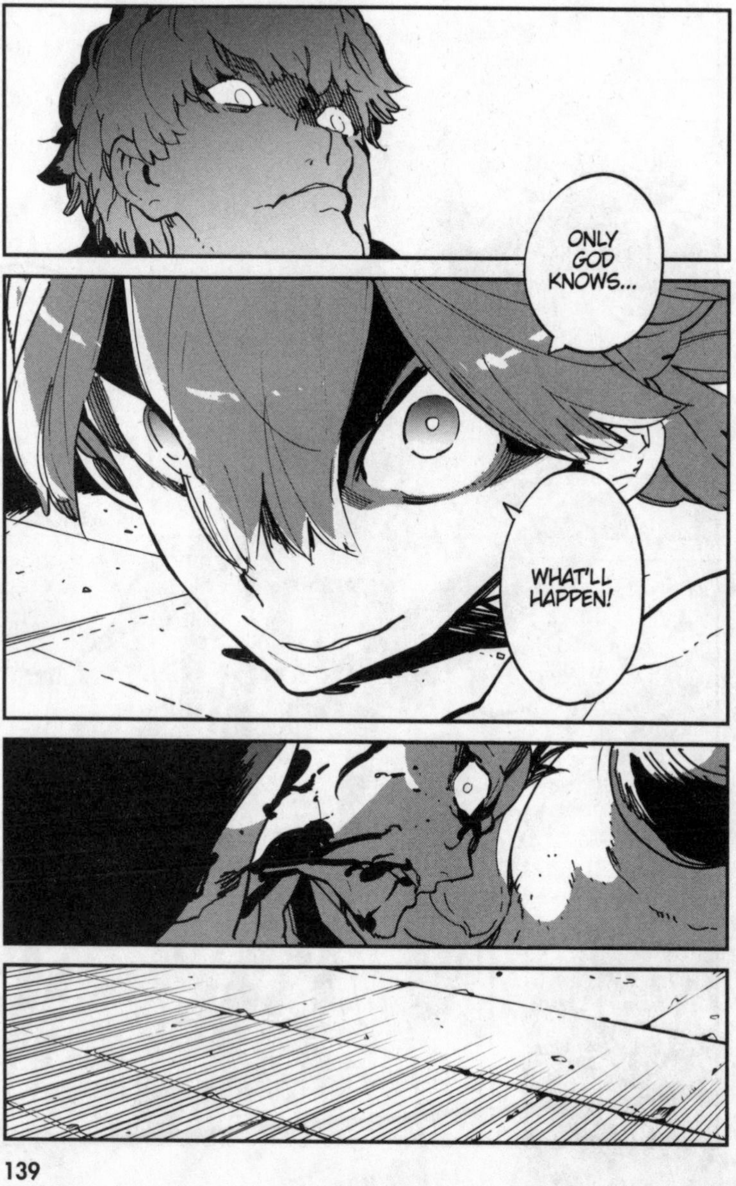
ONLY GOD KNOWS...
WHAT'LL HAPPEN!

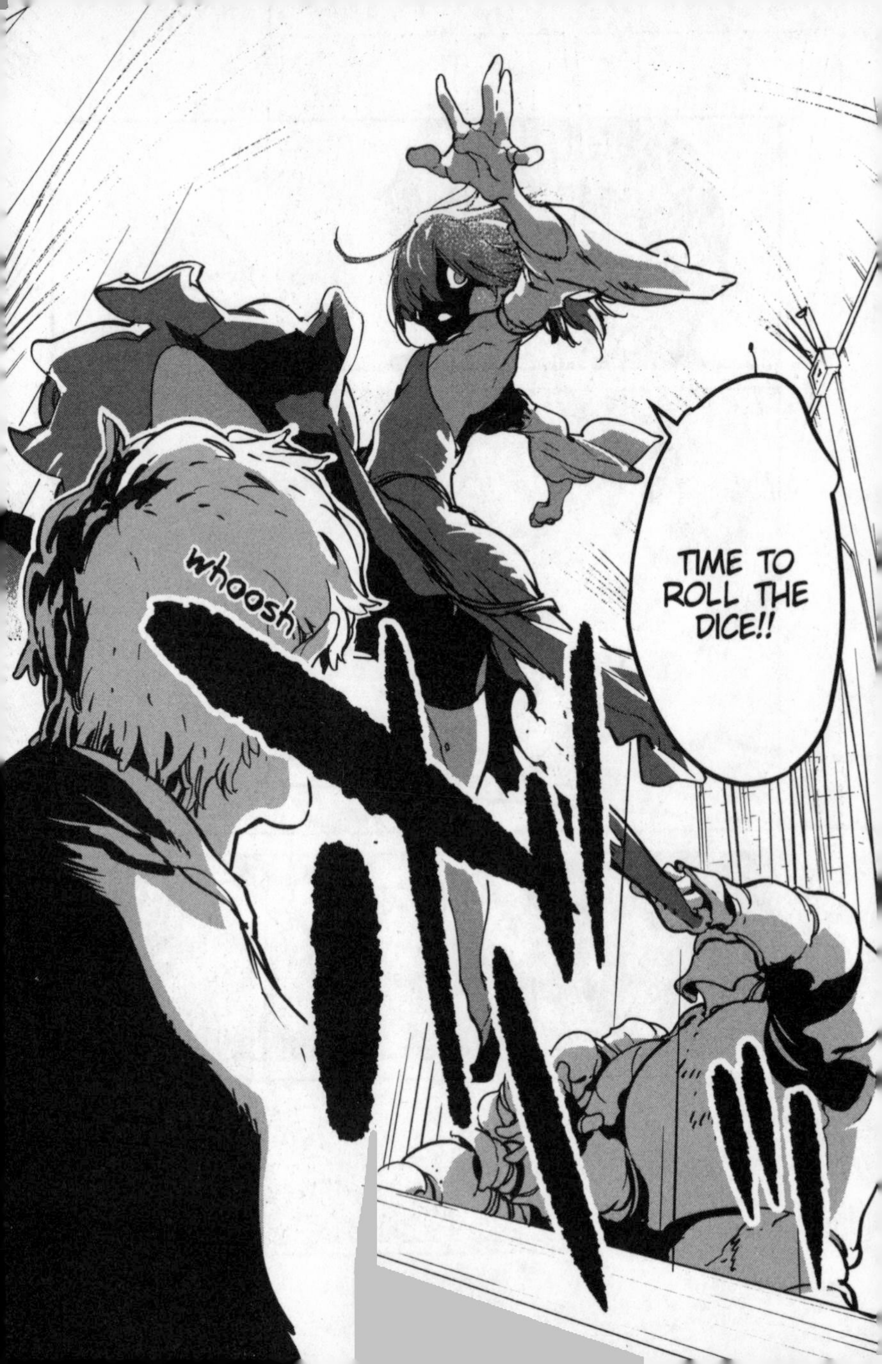
TIME TO ROLL THE DICE!!
whoosh

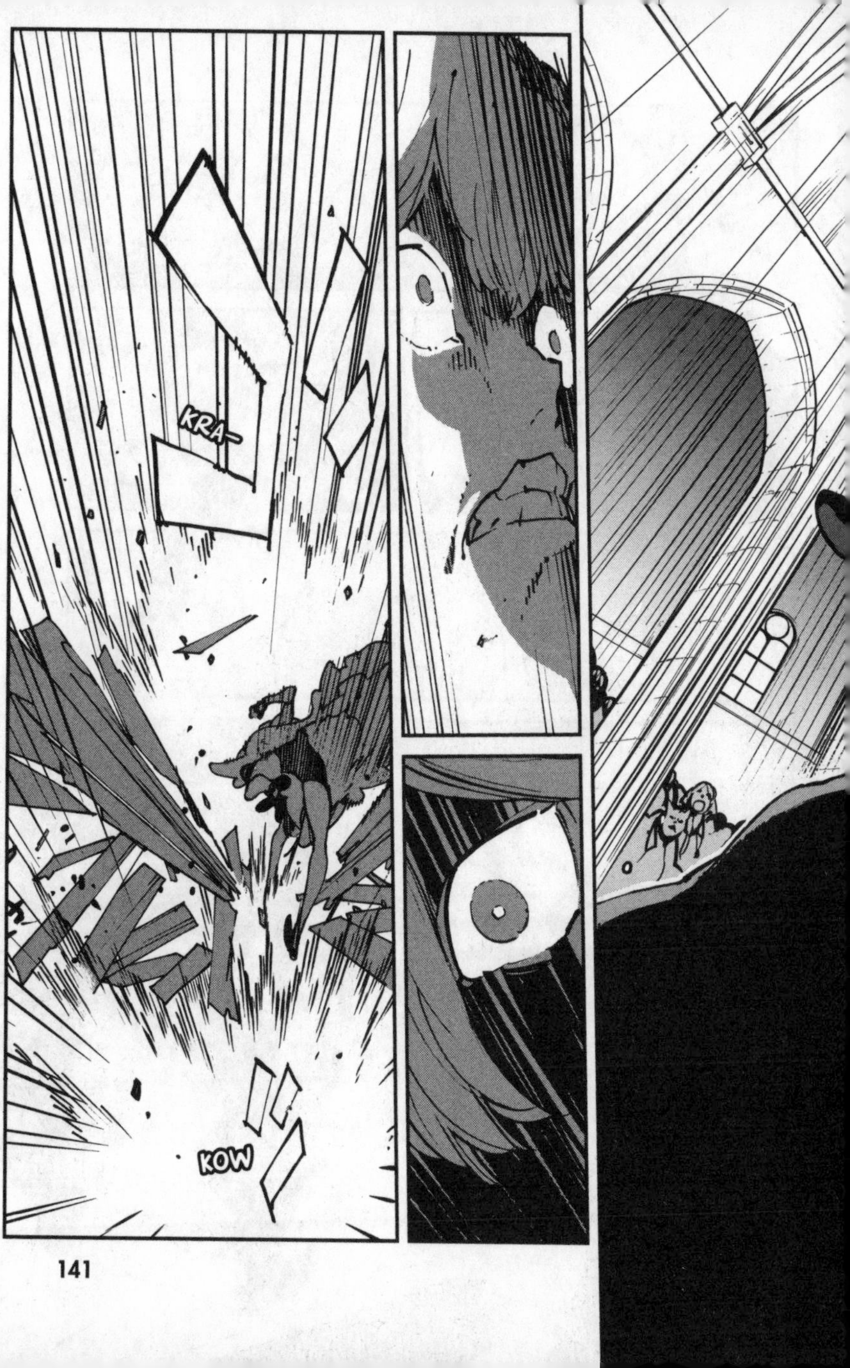
KRA-
KOW

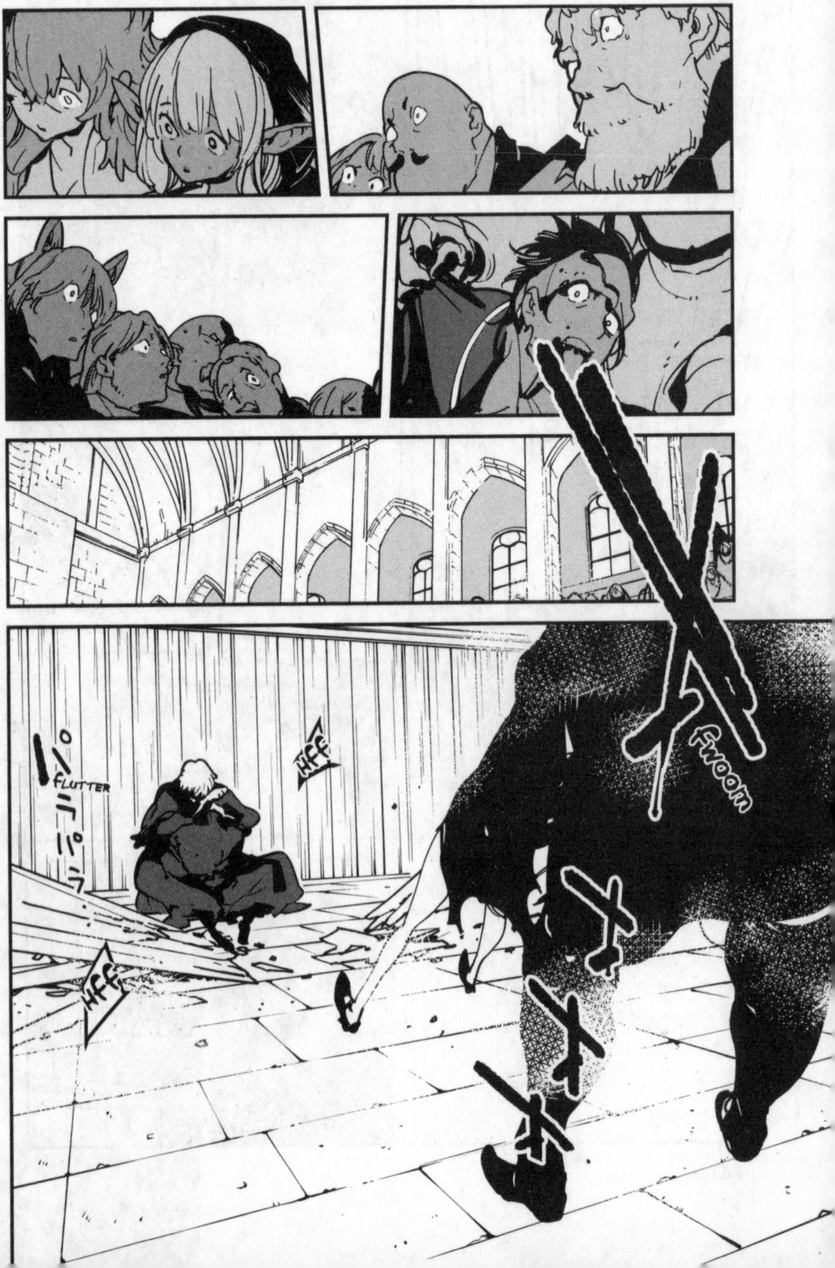
fwoom
HFF
FLUTTER
HFF

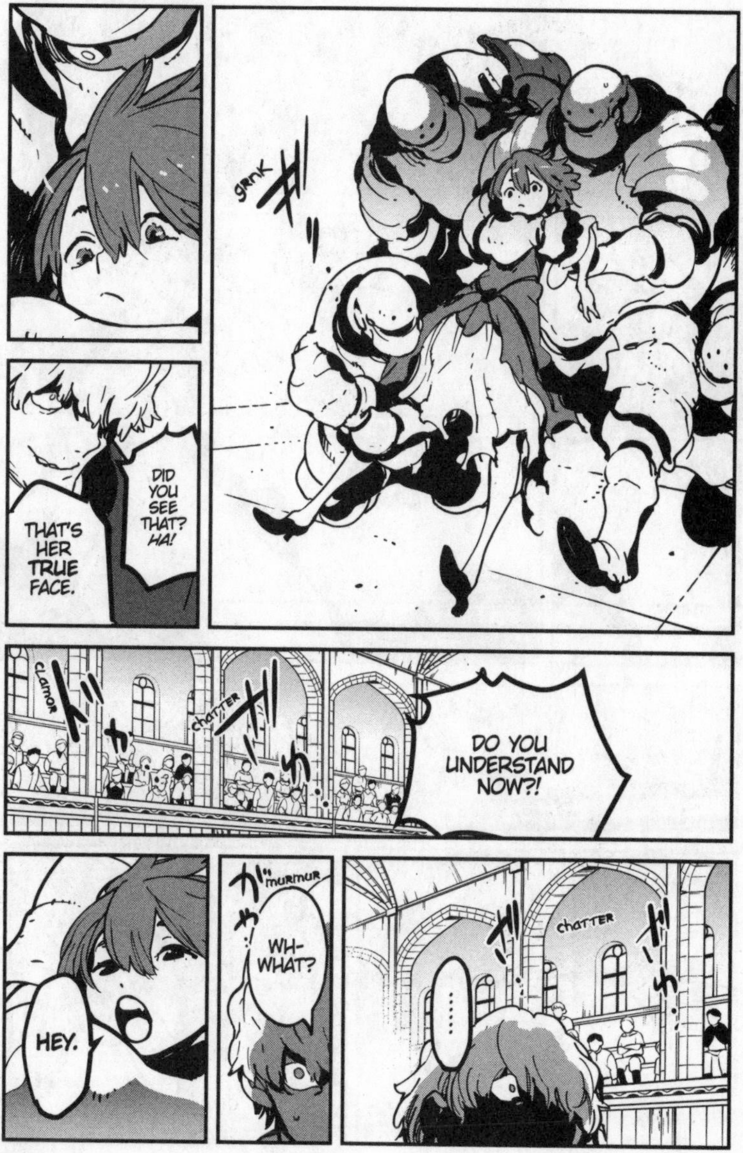
grnk
DID YOU SEE THAT? HA!
THAT'S HER TRUE FACE.
DO YOU UNDERSTAND NOW?!
chatter
clamor
chatter
......
murmur
WH-WHAT?
HEY.

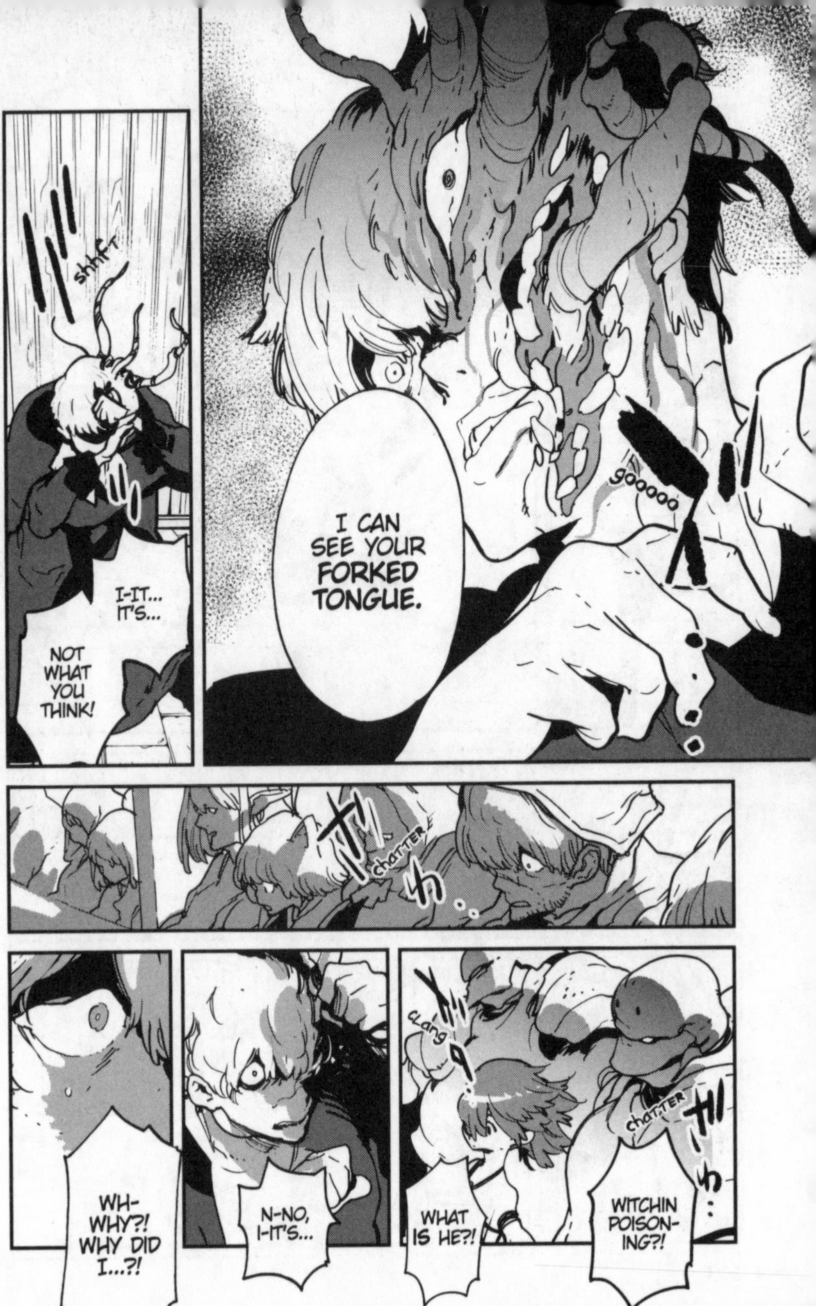
goooooo
I CAN SEE YOUR FORKED TONGUE.
shhft
I-IT... IT'S...
NOT WHAT YOU THINK!
chatter
chatter
WITCHIN POISONING?!
clang
WHAT IS HE?!
N-NO, I-IT'S...
WH- WHY?! WHY DID I...?!

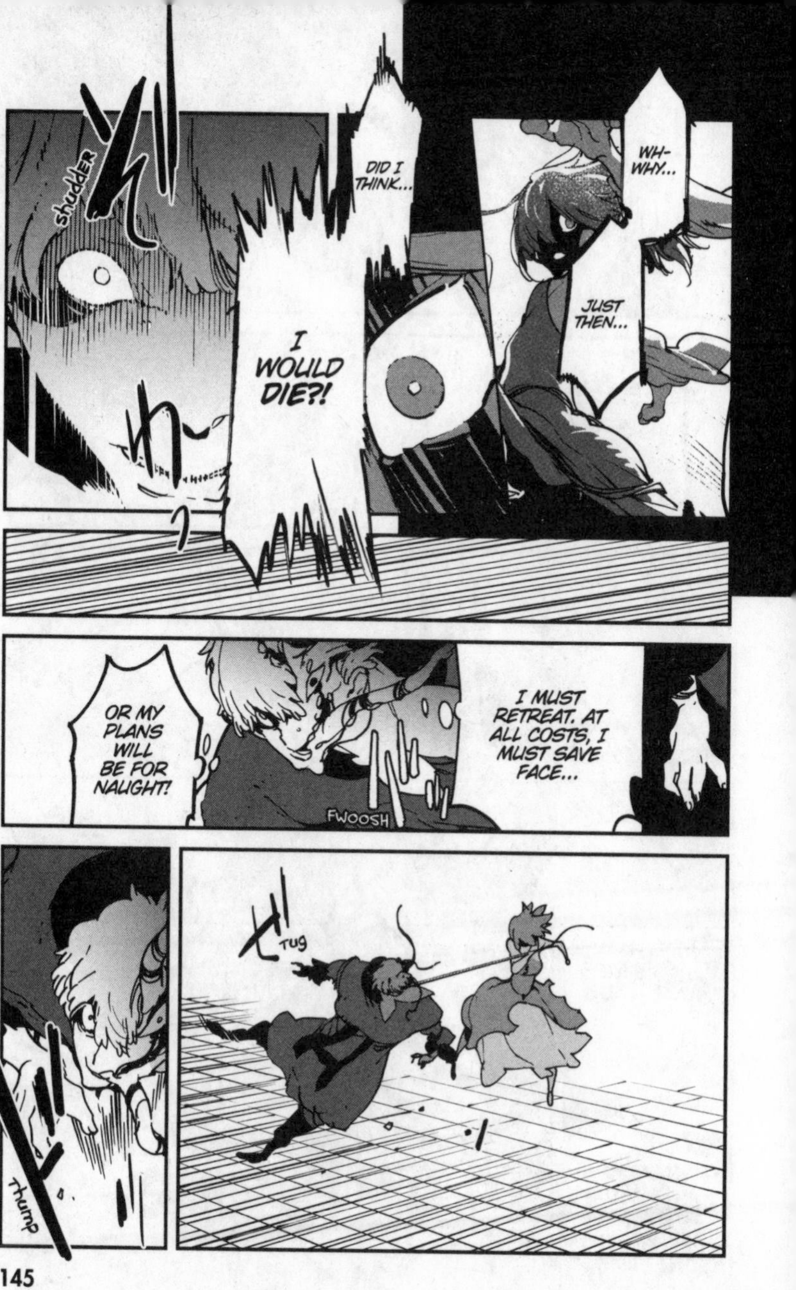
WH-WHY...
JUST THEN...
DID I THINK...
I WOULD DIE?!
shudder
I MUST RETREAT. AT ALL COSTS, I MUST SAVE FACE...
FWOOSH
OR MY PLANS WILL BE FOR NAUGHT!
TUG
thump

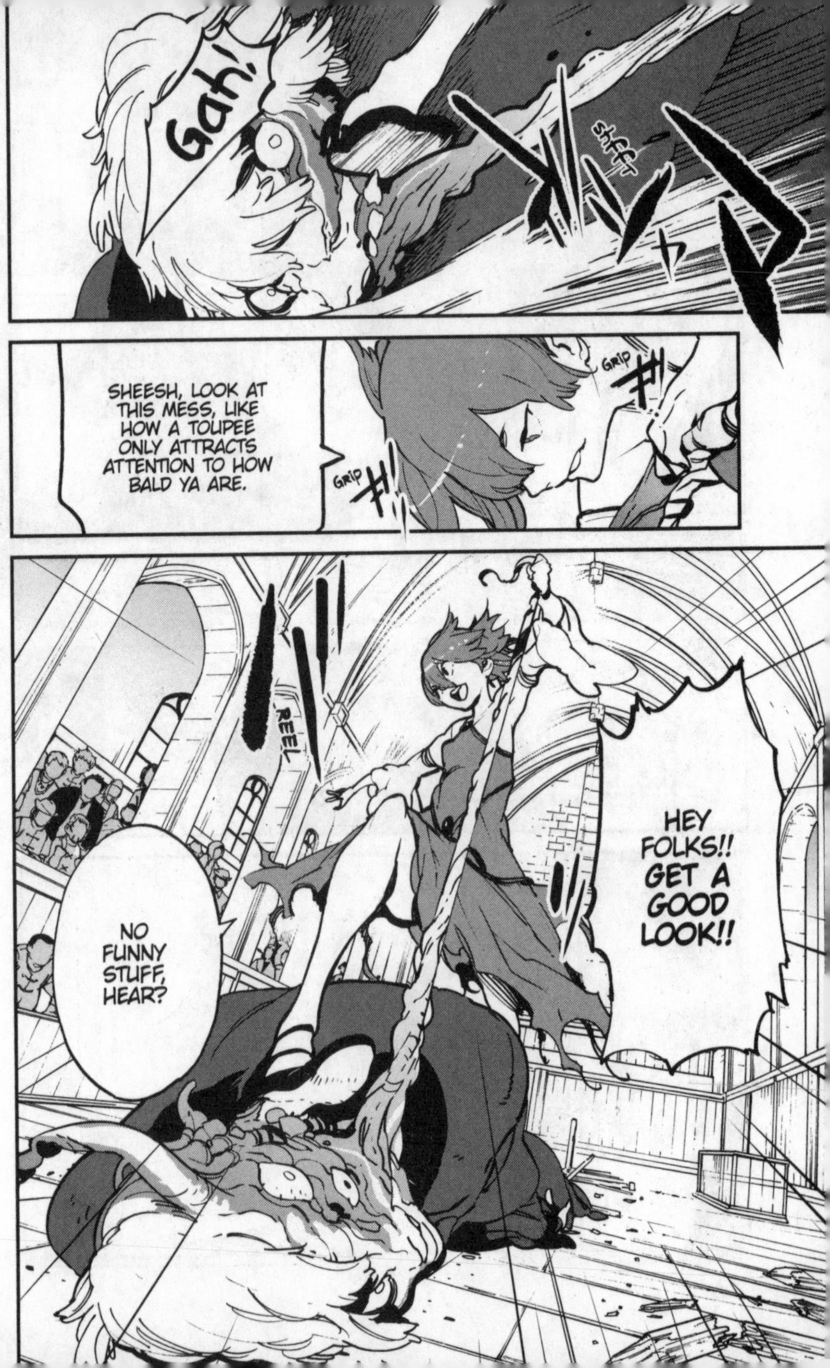
Gah!
shfff
Grip
Grip
SHEESH, LOOK AT THIS MESS, LIKE HOW A TOUPEE ONLY ATTRACTS ATTENTION TO HOW BALD YA ARE.
HEY FOLKS!! GET A GOOD LOOK!!
REEL
NO FUNNY STUFF, HEAR?

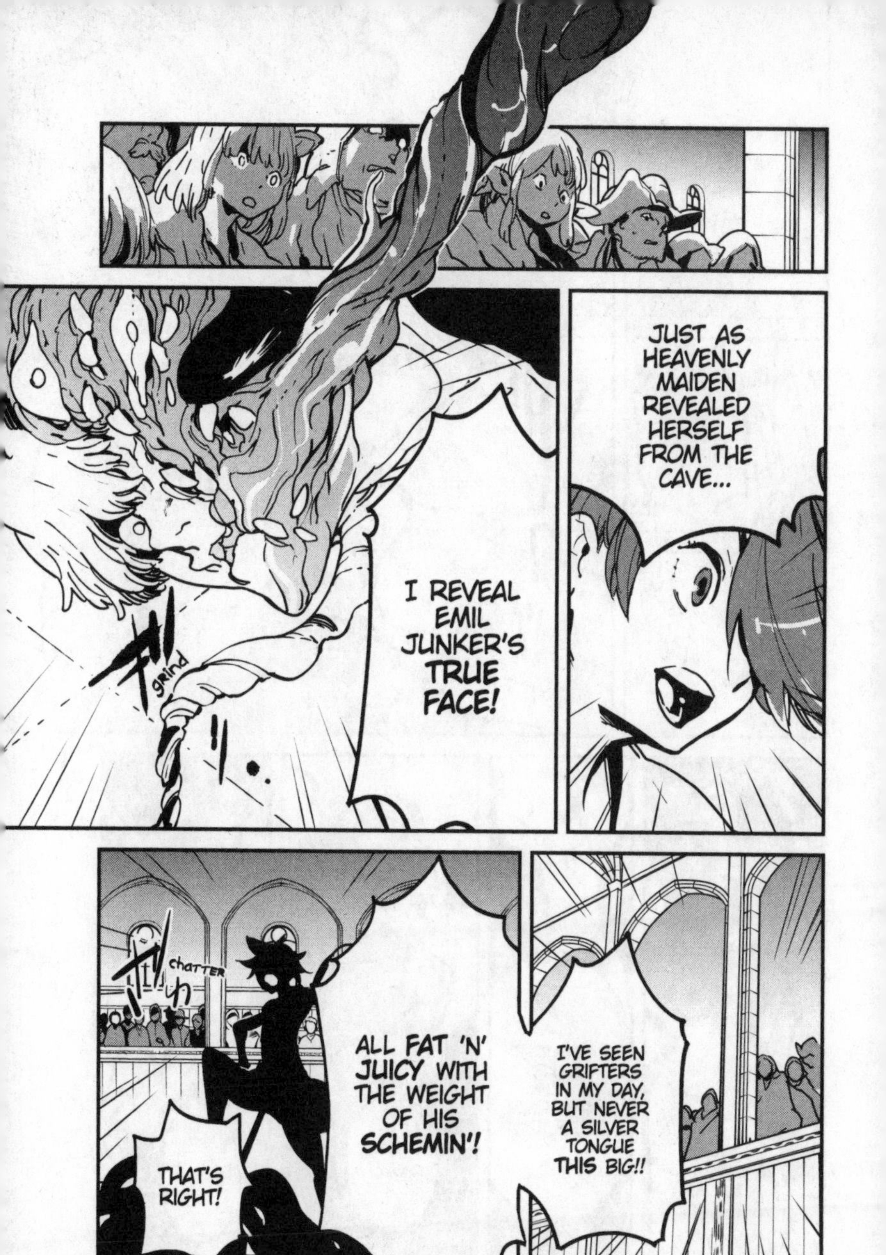
JUST AS HEAVENLY MAIDEN REVEALED HERSELF FROM THE CAVE...
I REVEAL EMIL JUNKER'S TRUE FACE!
grind
I'VE SEEN GRIFTERS IN MY DAY, BUT NEVER A SILVER TONGUE THIS BIG!!
ALL FAT 'N' JUICY WITH THE WEIGHT OF HIS SCHEMIN'!
chatter
THAT'S RIGHT!

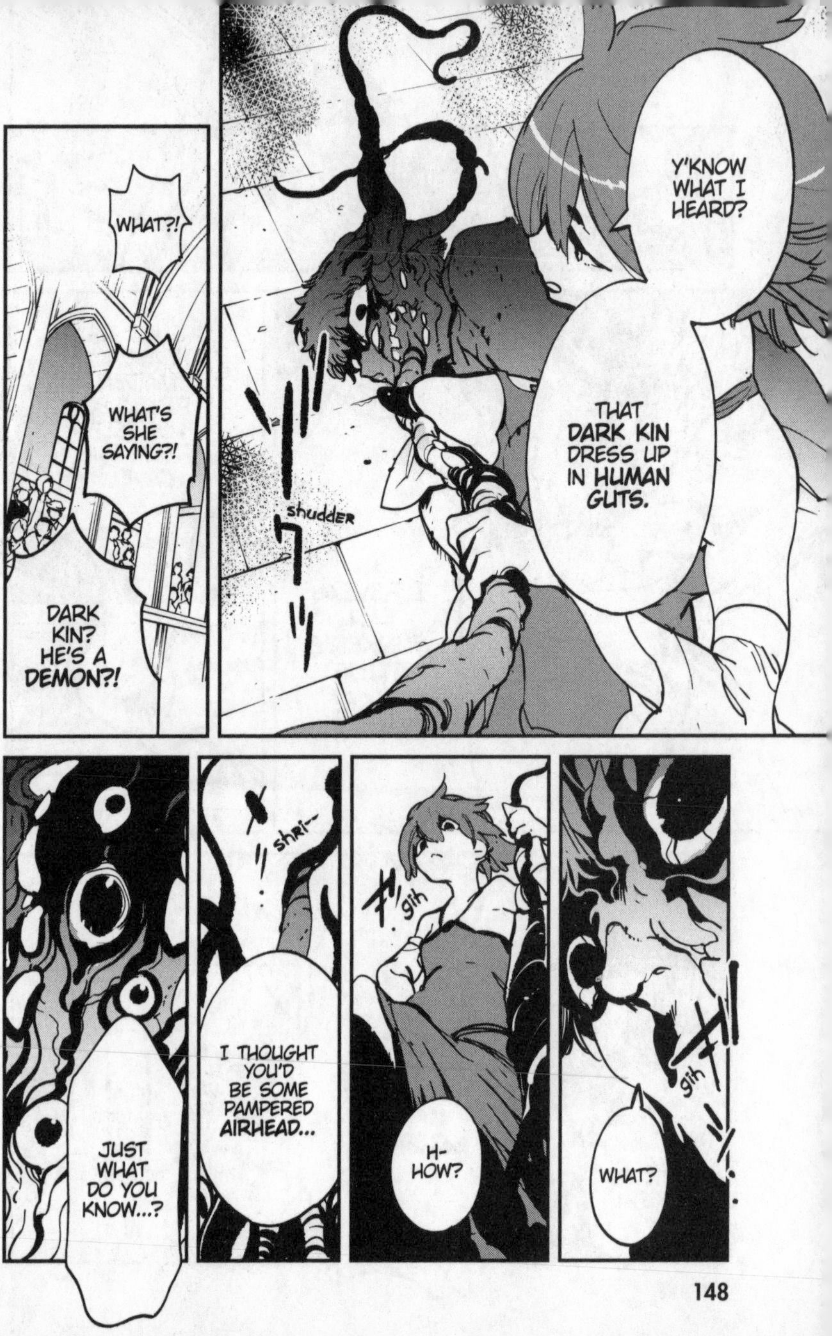
Y'KNOW WHAT I HEARD?
THAT DARK KIN DRESS UP IN HUMAN GUTS.
shudder
WHAT?!
WHAT'S SHE SAYING?!
DARK KIN? HE'S A DEMON?!
gih
WHAT?
gih
H- HOW?
shri-
I THOUGHT YOU'D BE SOME PAMPERED AIRHEAD...
JUST WHAT DO YOU KNOW...?

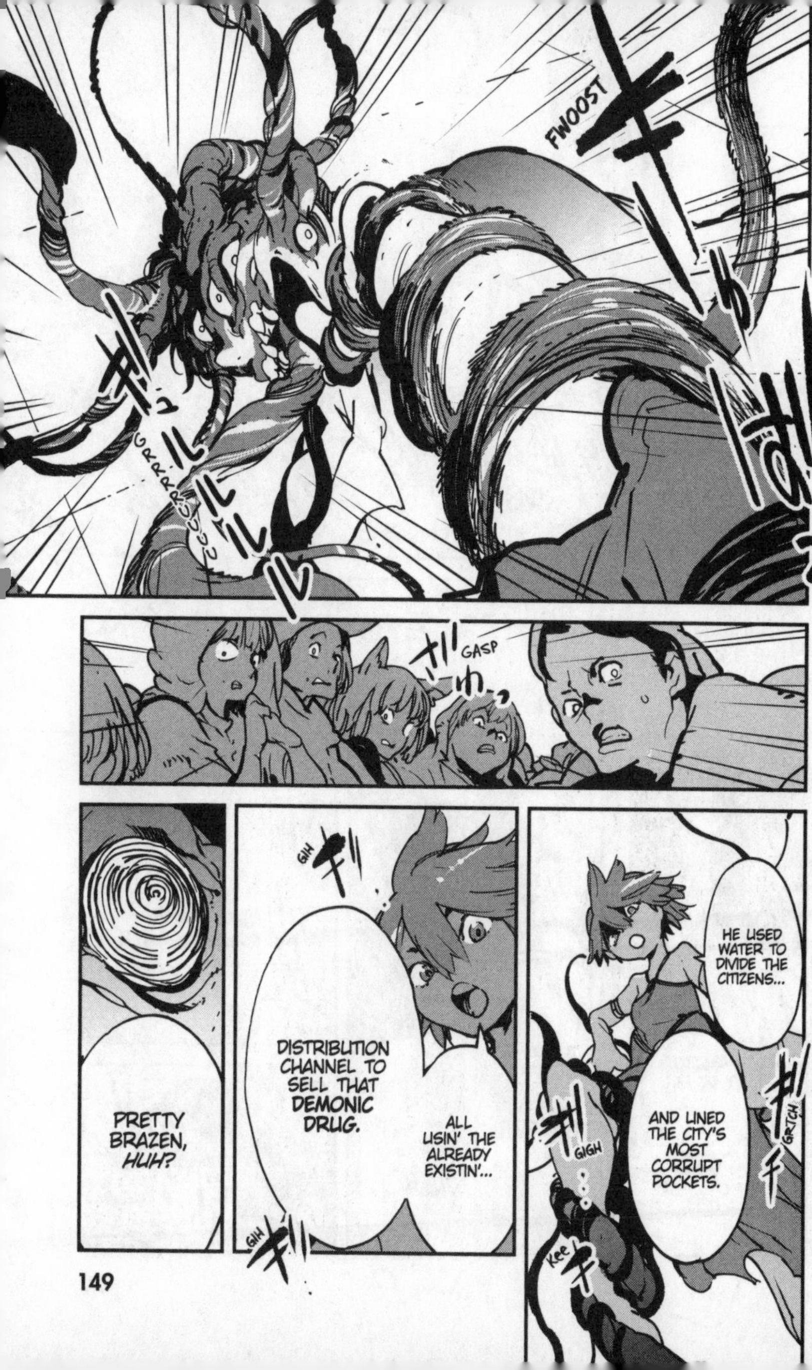
FWOOST
GRRRRUUUU
GASP
HE USED WATER TO DIVIDE THE CITIZENS...
AND LINED THE CITY'S MOST CORRUPT POCKETS.
GRITCH
GIGH
KEE
GIH
ALL USIN' THE ALREADY EXISTIN'...
DISTRIBUTION CHANNEL TO SELL THAT DEMONIC DRUG.
GIH
PRETTY BRAZEN, HUH?

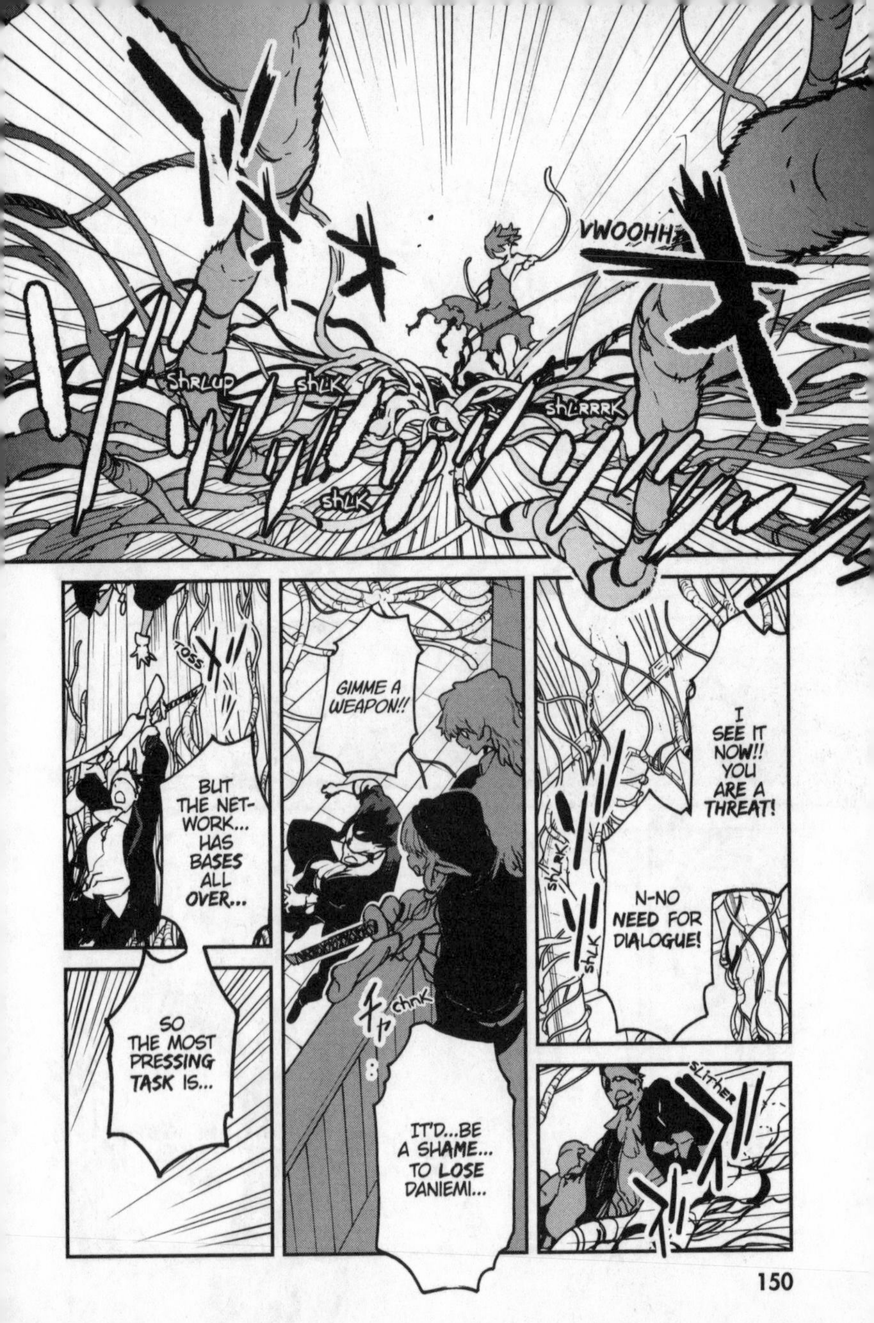
VWOOHH
shLRRRK
shLIK
shLIK
ShRLUP
I SEE IT NOW!! YOU ARE A THREAT!
shLRK
shLIK
N-NO NEED FOR DIALOGUE!
SLITHER
GIMME A WEAPON!!
chnk
IT'D...BE A SHAME... TO LOSE DANIEMI...
TOSS
BUT THE NET-WORK... HAS BASES ALL OVER...
SO THE MOST PRESSING TASK IS...

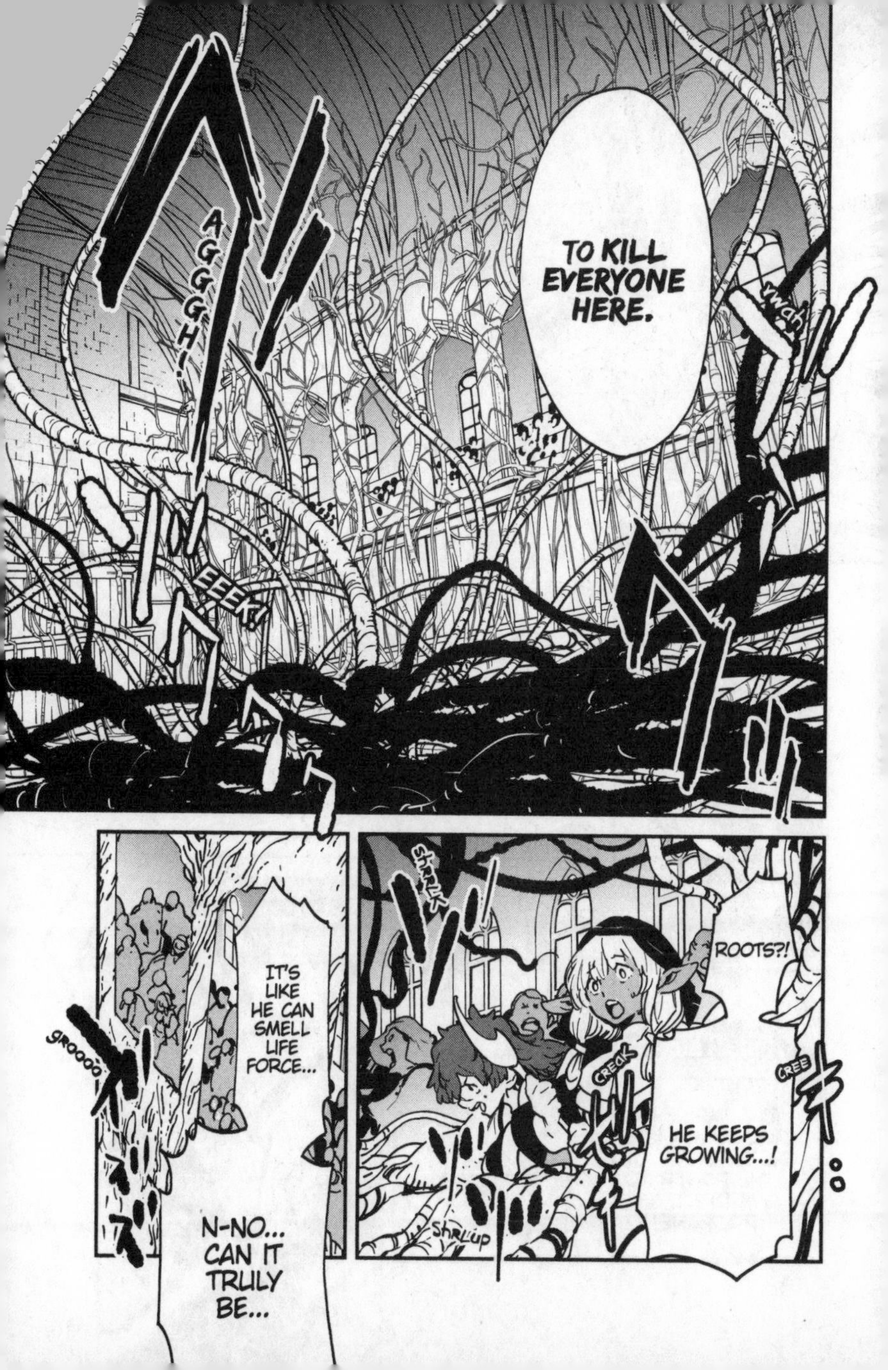
TO KILL EVERYONE HERE.
ywah
AGGGH!
EEEK!!
ROOTS?!
SHRLK
CREE
CREAK
HE KEEPS GROWING...!
shrlup
IT'S LIKE HE CAN SMELL LIFE FORCE...
grooooo
N-NO... CAN IT TRULY BE...

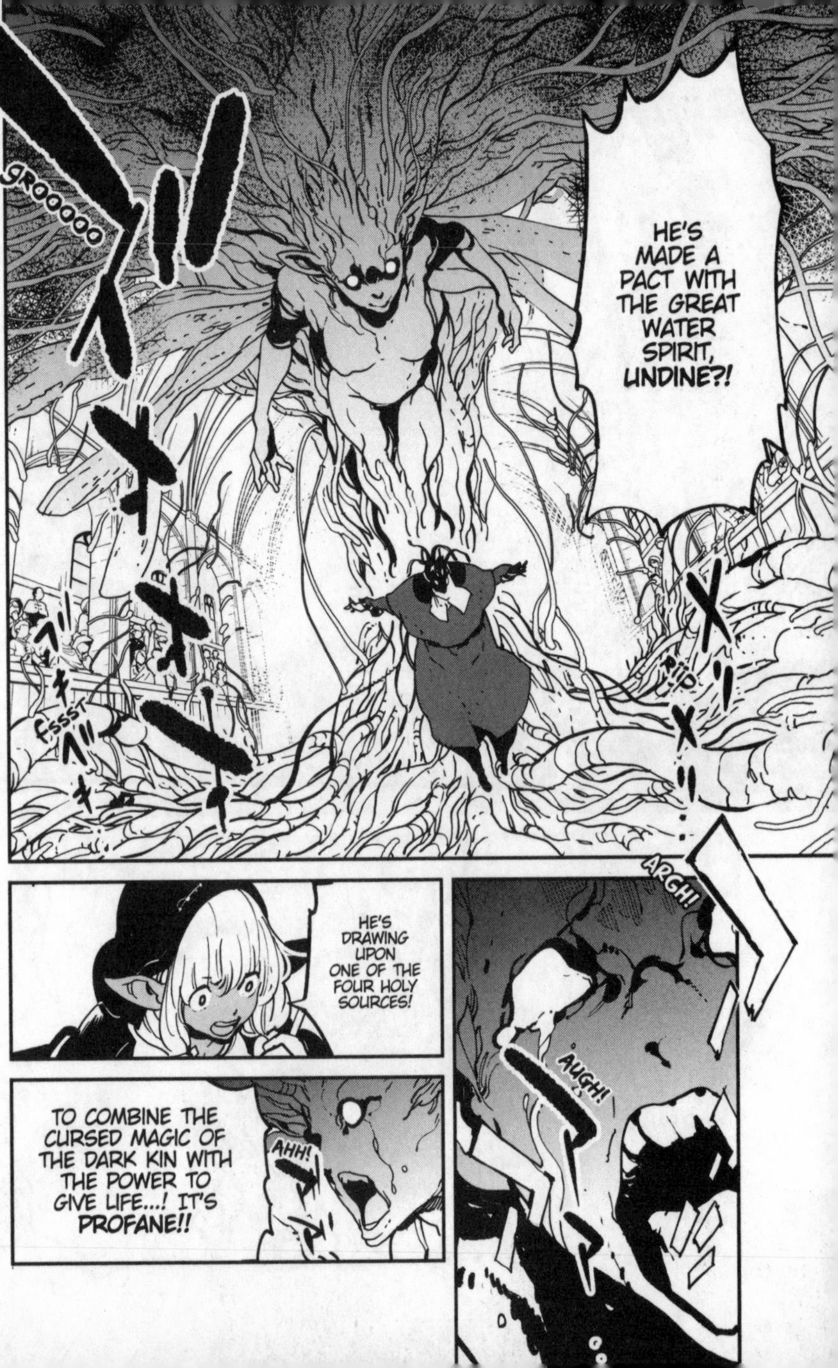
HE'S MADE A PACT WITH THE GREAT WATER SPIRIT, UNDINE?!
GROOOOOO
RIIP
FSSST
ARGH!
AUGH!
HE'S DRAWING UPON ONE OF THE FOUR HOLY SOURCES!
TO COMBINE THE CURSED MAGIC OF THE DARK KIN WITH THE POWER TO GIVE LIFE...! IT'S PROFANE!!
AHH!

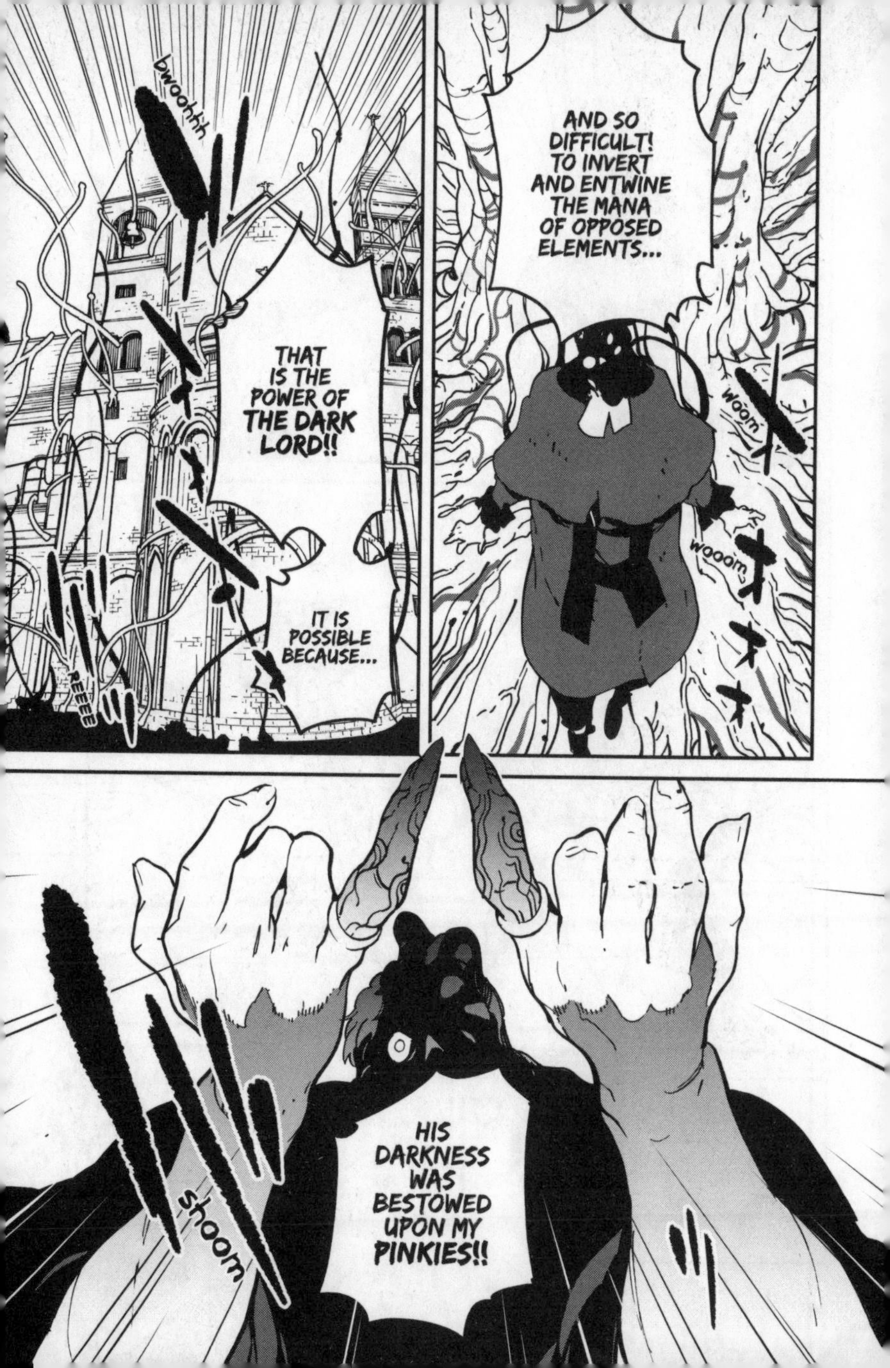
AND SO DIFFICULT! TO INVERT AND ENTWINE THE MANA OF OPPOSED ELEMENTS...
wooom
wooom
bwoohhh
THAT IS THE POWER OF THE DARK LORD!!
IT IS POSSIBLE BECAUSE...
REEEE
HIS DARKNESS WAS BESTOWED UPON MY PINKIES!!
shoom

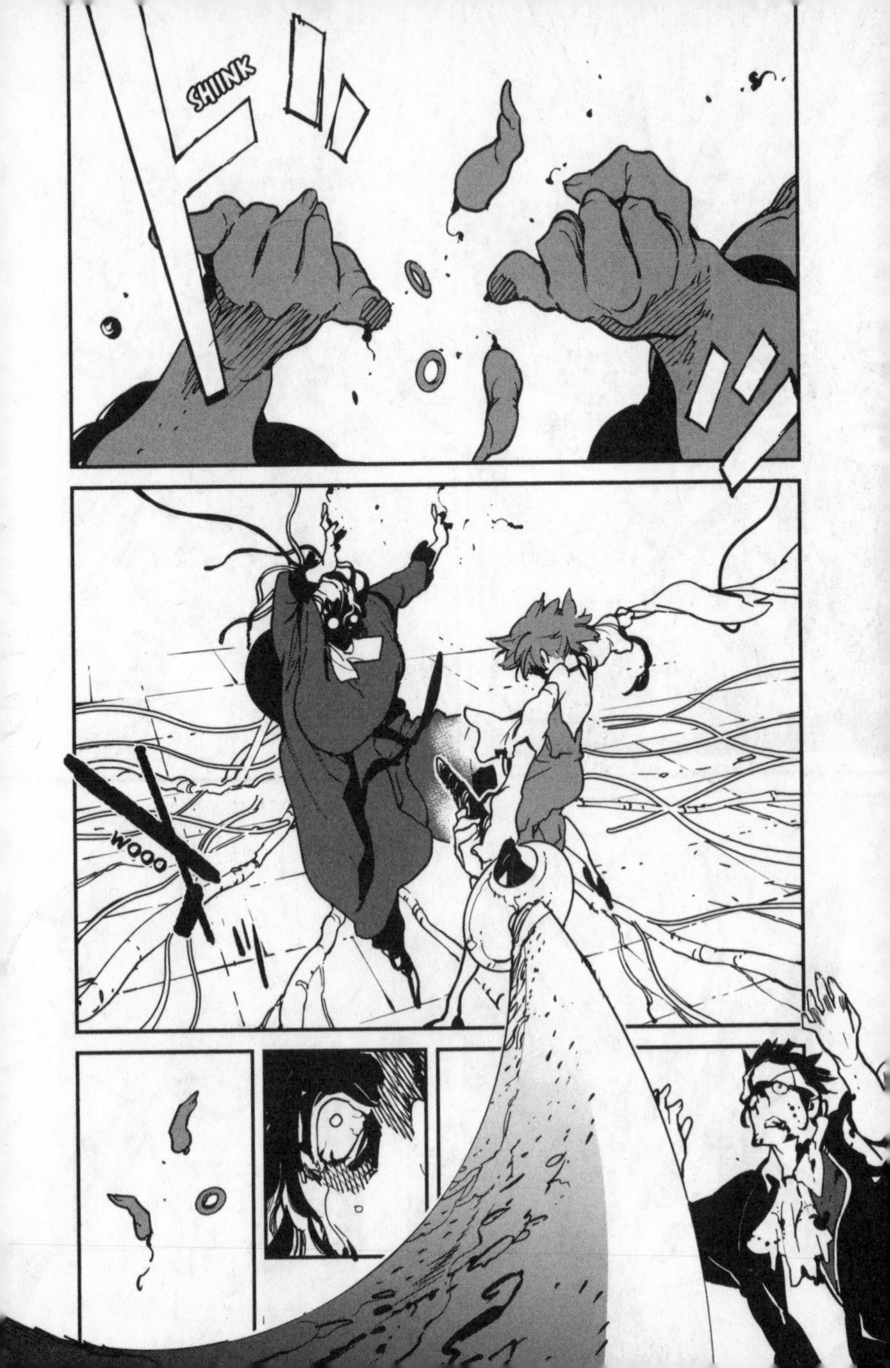
SHIINK
WOOO

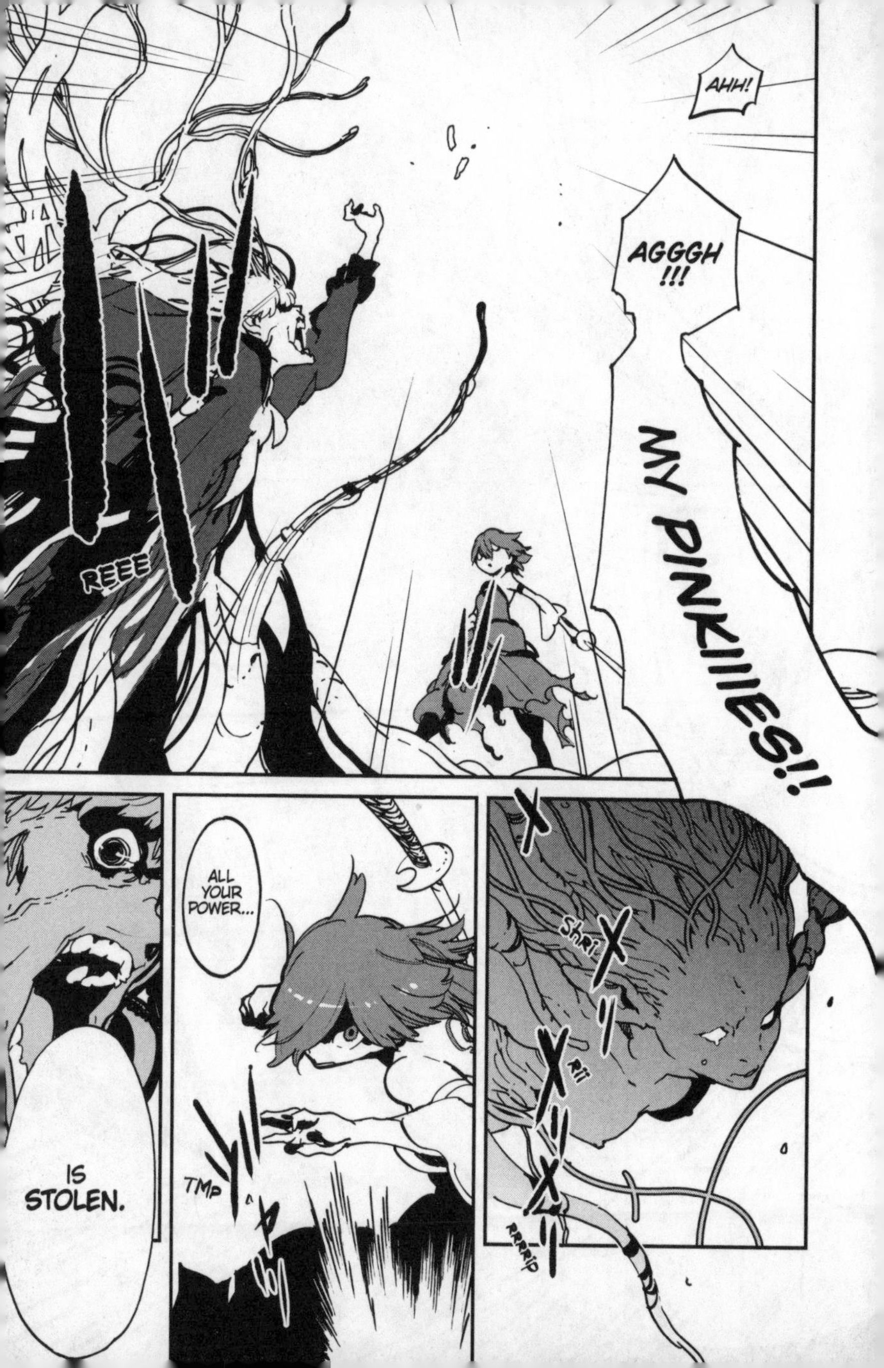

AHH!
AGGGH !!!
MY PINKIIIIES!!
REEE
Shri
Rii
RRRRIP
ALL YOUR POWER...
TMP
IS STOLEN.

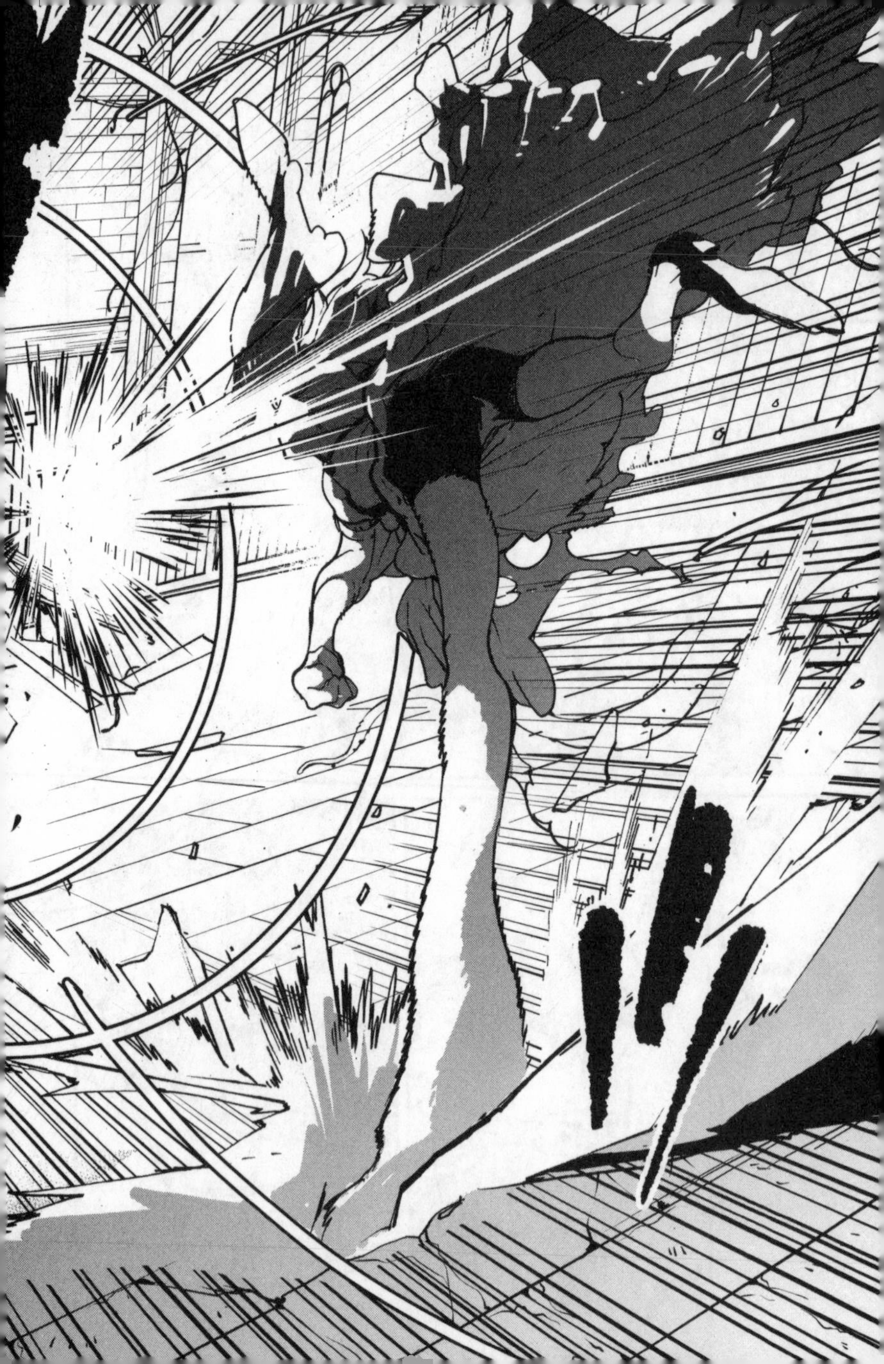

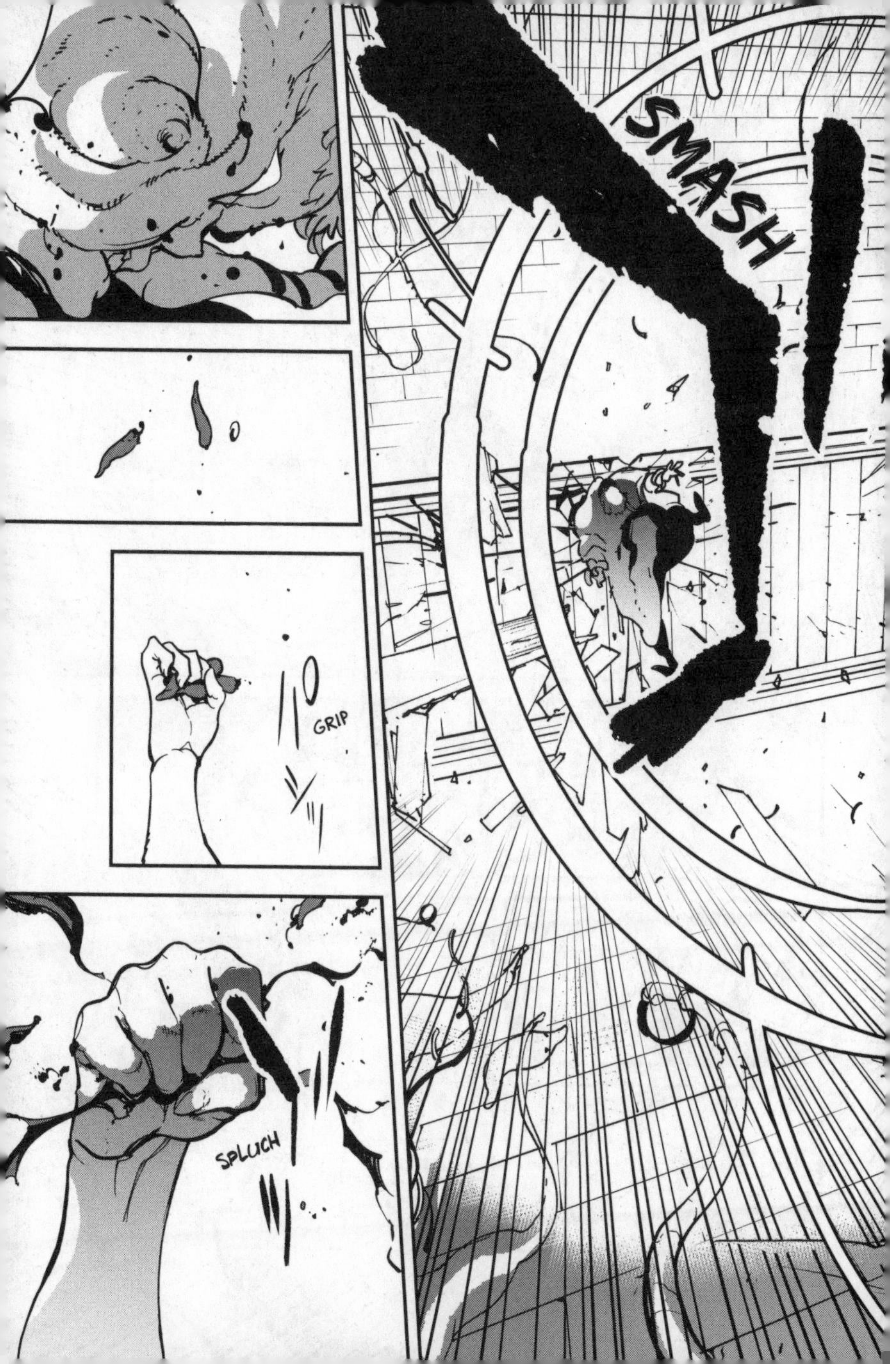
SMASH
GRIP
SPLUCH

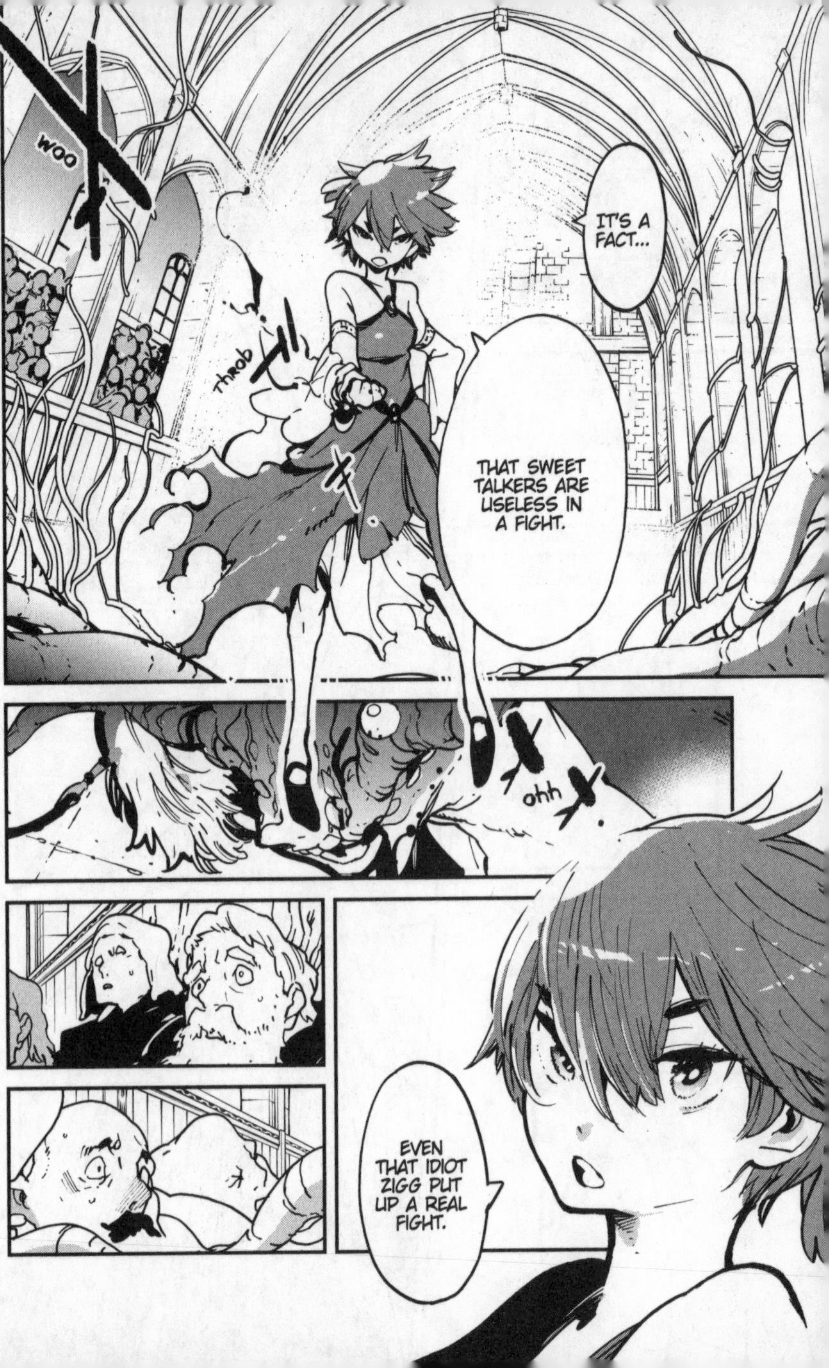
IT'S A FACT...
THAT SWEET TALKERS ARE USELESS IN A FIGHT.
woo
throb
ohh
EVEN THAT IDIOT ZIGG PUT UP A REAL FIGHT.

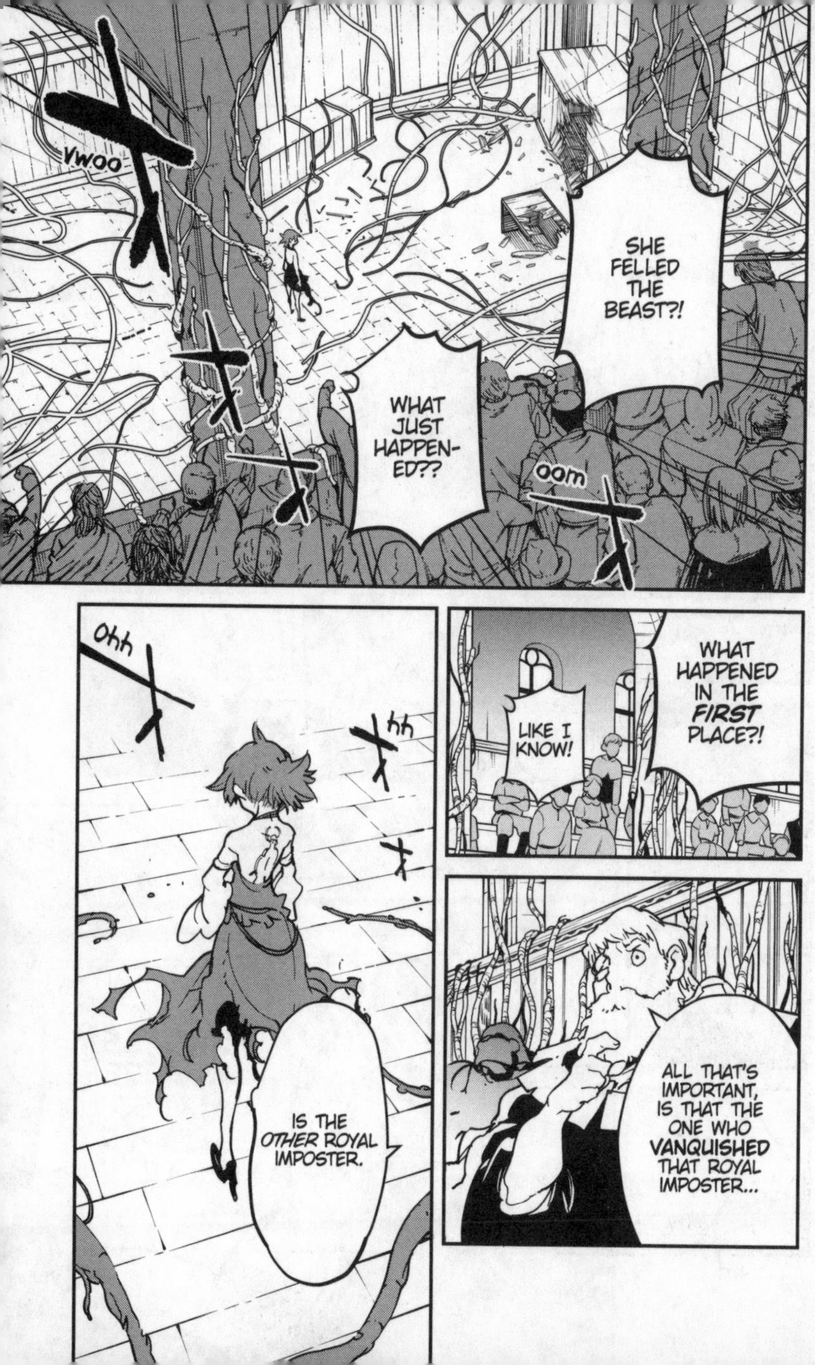
VWOO
SHE FELLED THE BEAST?!
WHAT JUST HAPPEN-ED??
oom
WHAT HAPPENED IN THE *FIRST* PLACE?!
LIKE I KNOW!
ALL THAT'S IMPORTANT, IS THAT THE ONE WHO **VANQUISHED** THAT ROYAL IMPOSTER...
Ohh
hh
IS THE *OTHER* ROYAL IMPOSTER.

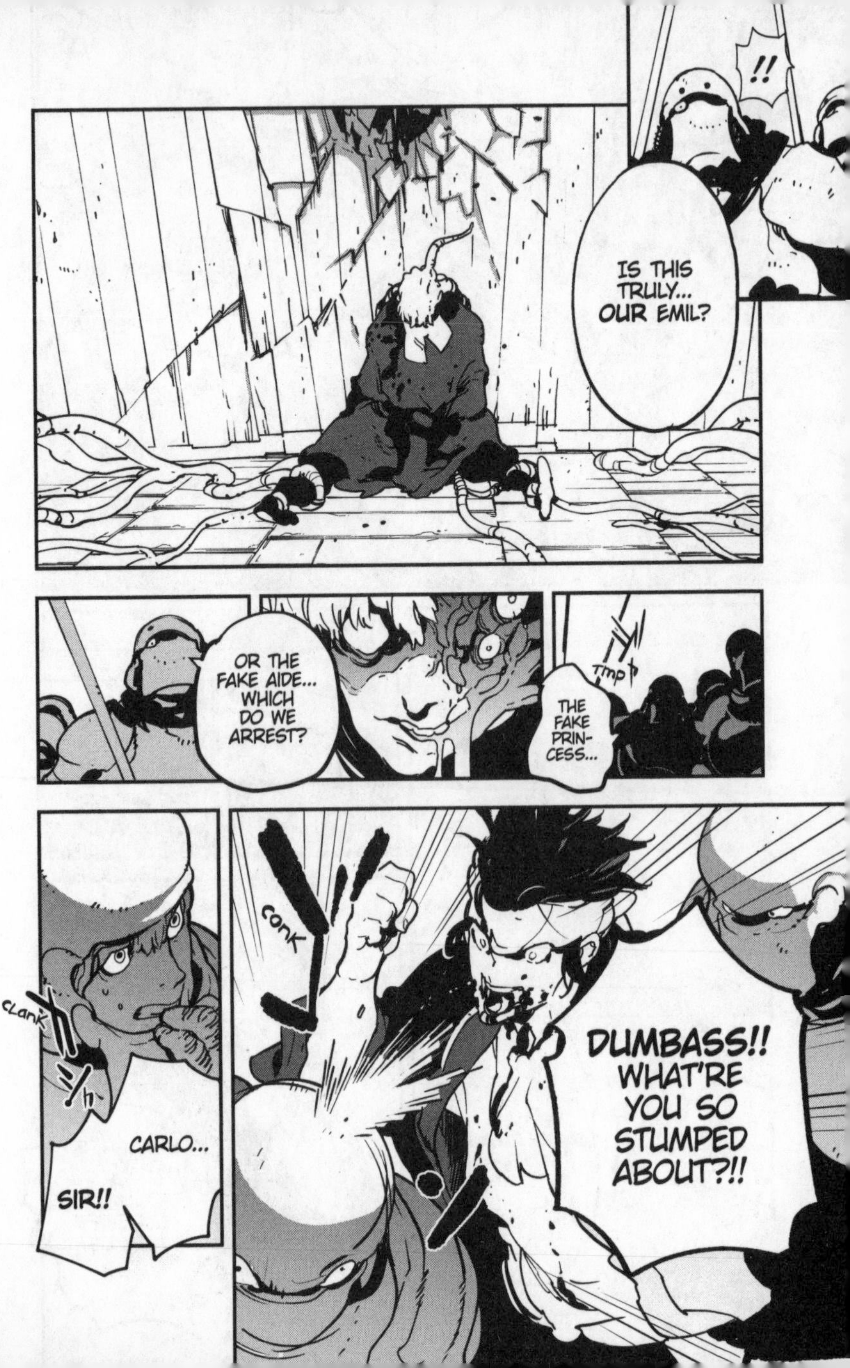
!!
IS THIS TRULY... OUR EMIL?
Tmp
THE FAKE PRINCESS...
OR THE FAKE AIDE... WHICH DO WE ARREST?
conk
DUMBASS!! WHAT'RE YOU SO STUMPED ABOUT?!!
Clank
CARLO...
SIR!!

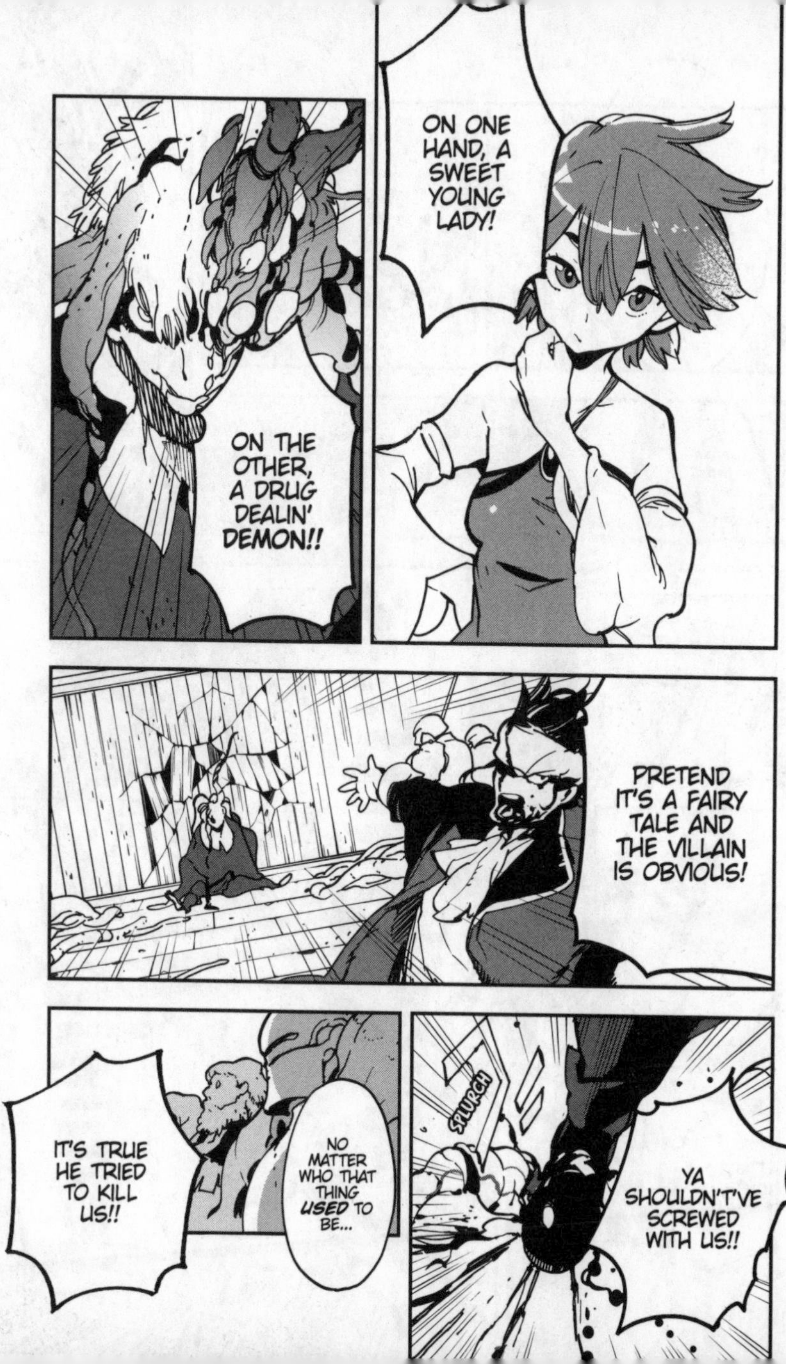
ON ONE HAND, A SWEET YOUNG LADY!
ON THE OTHER, A DRUG DEALIN' DEMON!!
PRETEND IT'S A FAIRY TALE AND THE VILLAIN IS OBVIOUS!
SPLURCH
YA SHOULDN'T'VE SCREWED WITH US!!
NO MATTER WHO THAT THING *USED* TO BE...
IT'S TRUE HE TRIED TO KILL US!!

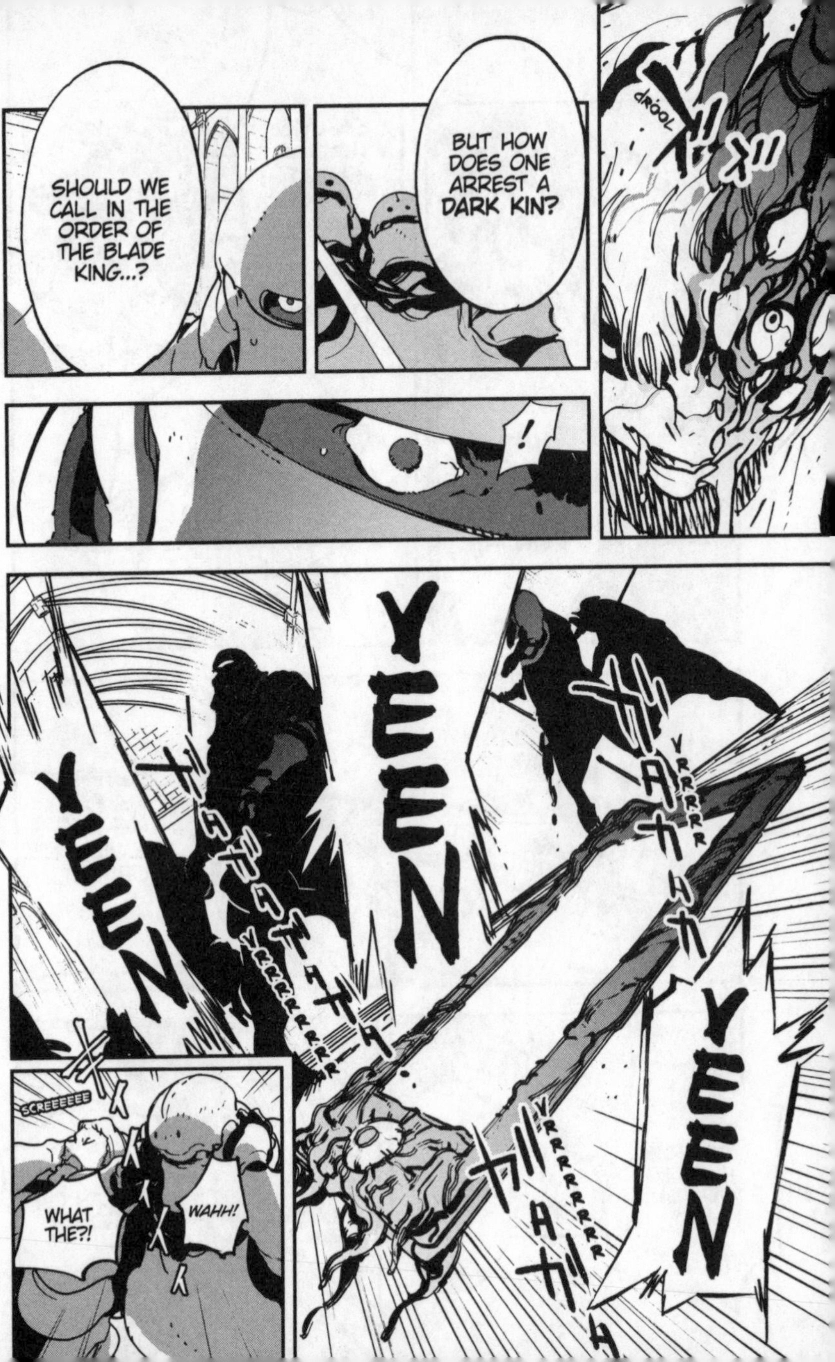
DROOL
BUT HOW DOES ONE ARREST A DARK KIN?
SHOULD WE CALL IN THE ORDER OF THE BLADE KING...?
!
YEEN
VRRRRR
YEEN
VRRRRRRRR
YEEN
VRRRRRRRRR
SCREEEEEE
WAHH!
WHAT THE?!

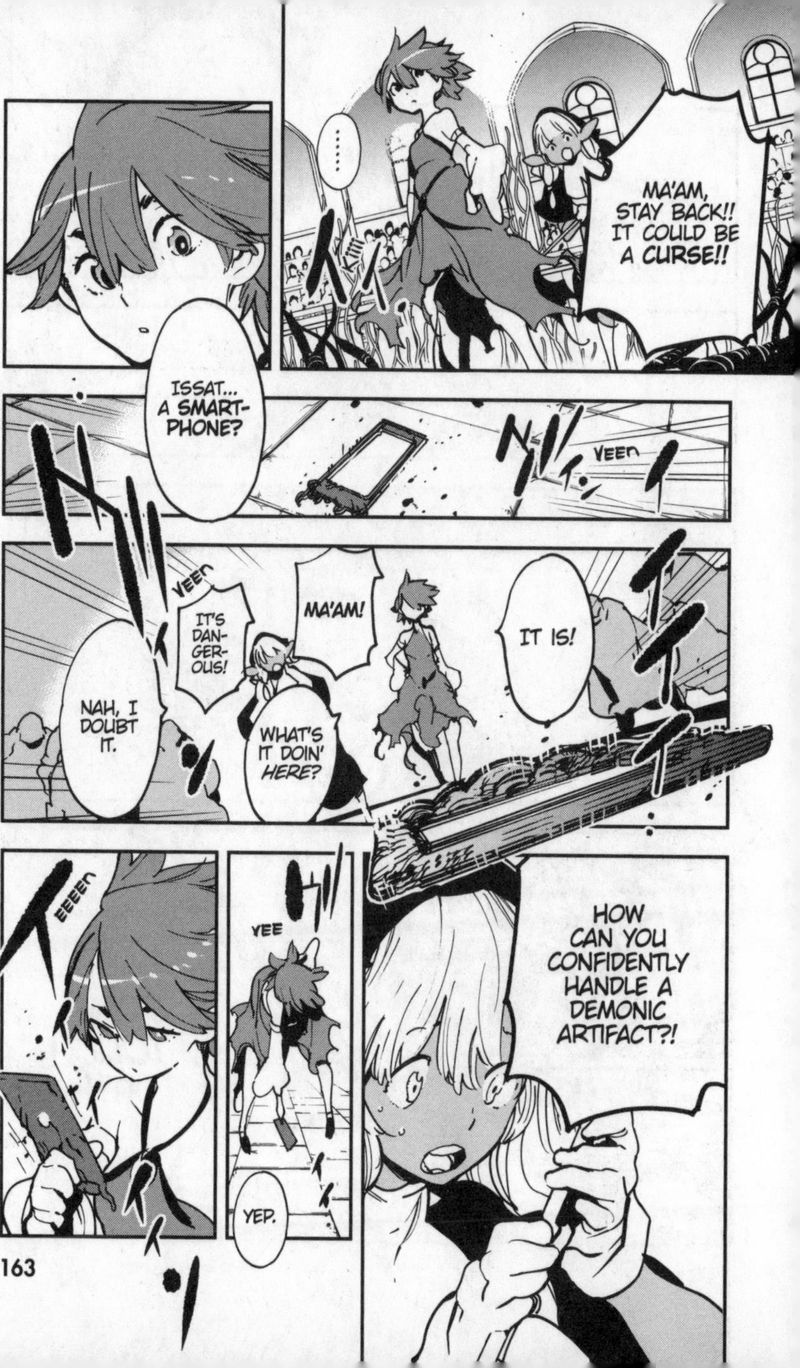
......
MA'AM, STAY BACK!! IT COULD BE A CURSE!!
ISSAT... A SMARTPHONE?
VEEN
IT IS!
MA'AM!
IT'S DANGER-OUS!
WHAT'S IT DOIN' HERE?
VEEN
NAH, I DOUBT IT.
HOW CAN YOU CONFIDENTLY HANDLE A DEMONIC ARTIFACT?!
VEE
YEP.
EEEEEN

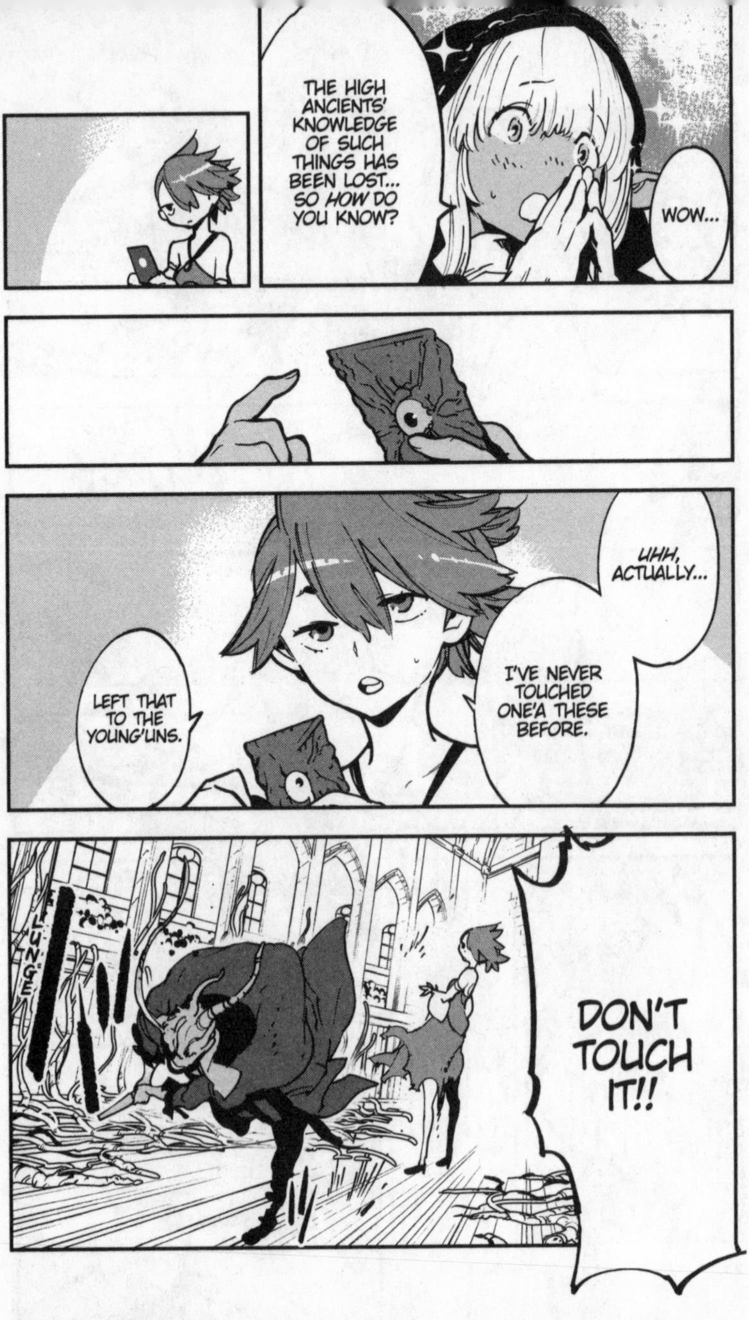
WOW...
THE HIGH ANCIENTS' KNOWLEDGE OF SUCH THINGS HAS BEEN LOST... SO *HOW* DO YOU KNOW?
UHH, ACTUALLY...
I'VE NEVER TOUCHED ONE'A THESE BEFORE.
LEFT THAT TO THE YOUNG'UNS.
DON'T TOUCH IT!!
LUNGE

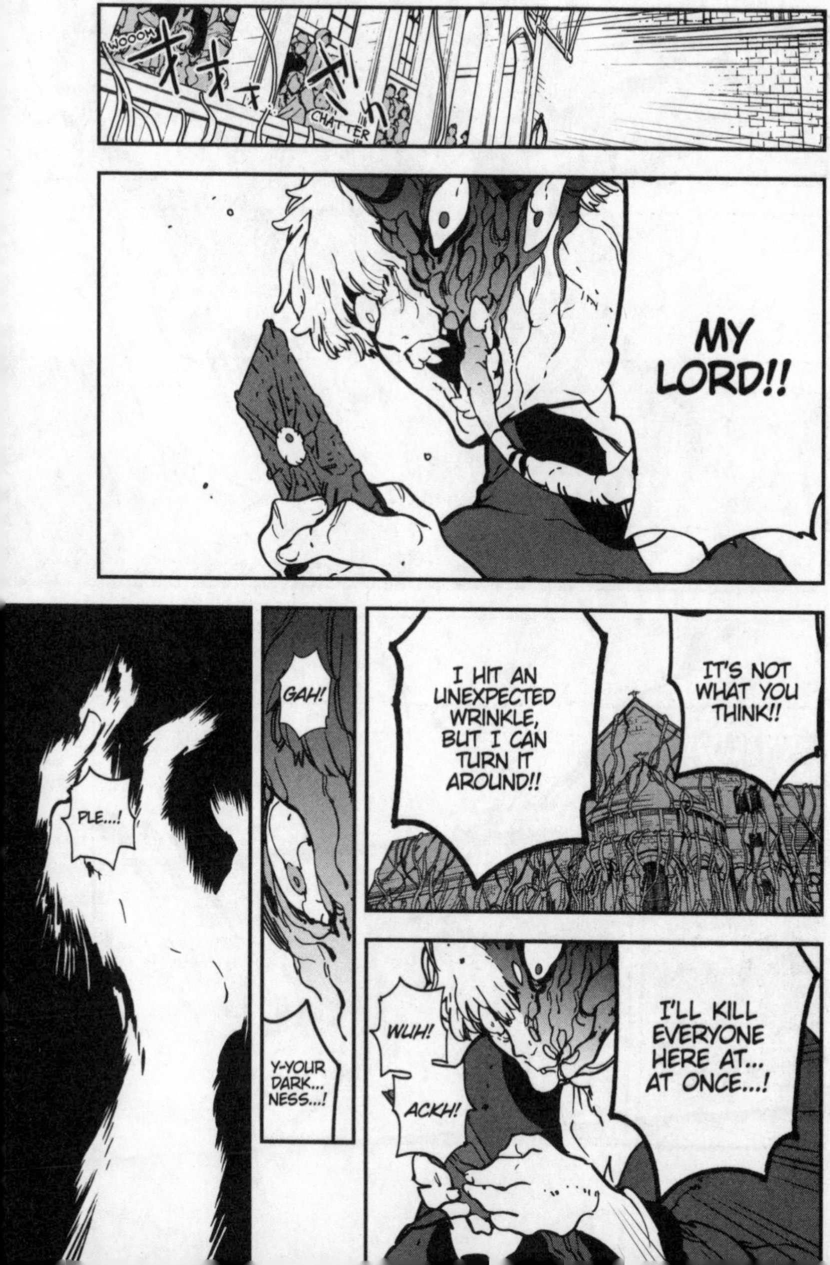
WOOOW
CHATTER
MY LORD!!
IT'S NOT WHAT YOU THINK!!
I HIT AN UNEXPECTED WRINKLE, BUT I CAN TURN IT AROUND!!
I'LL KILL EVERYONE HERE AT... AT ONCE...!
WUH!
ACKH!
GAH!
Y-YOUR DARK... NESS...!
PLE...!

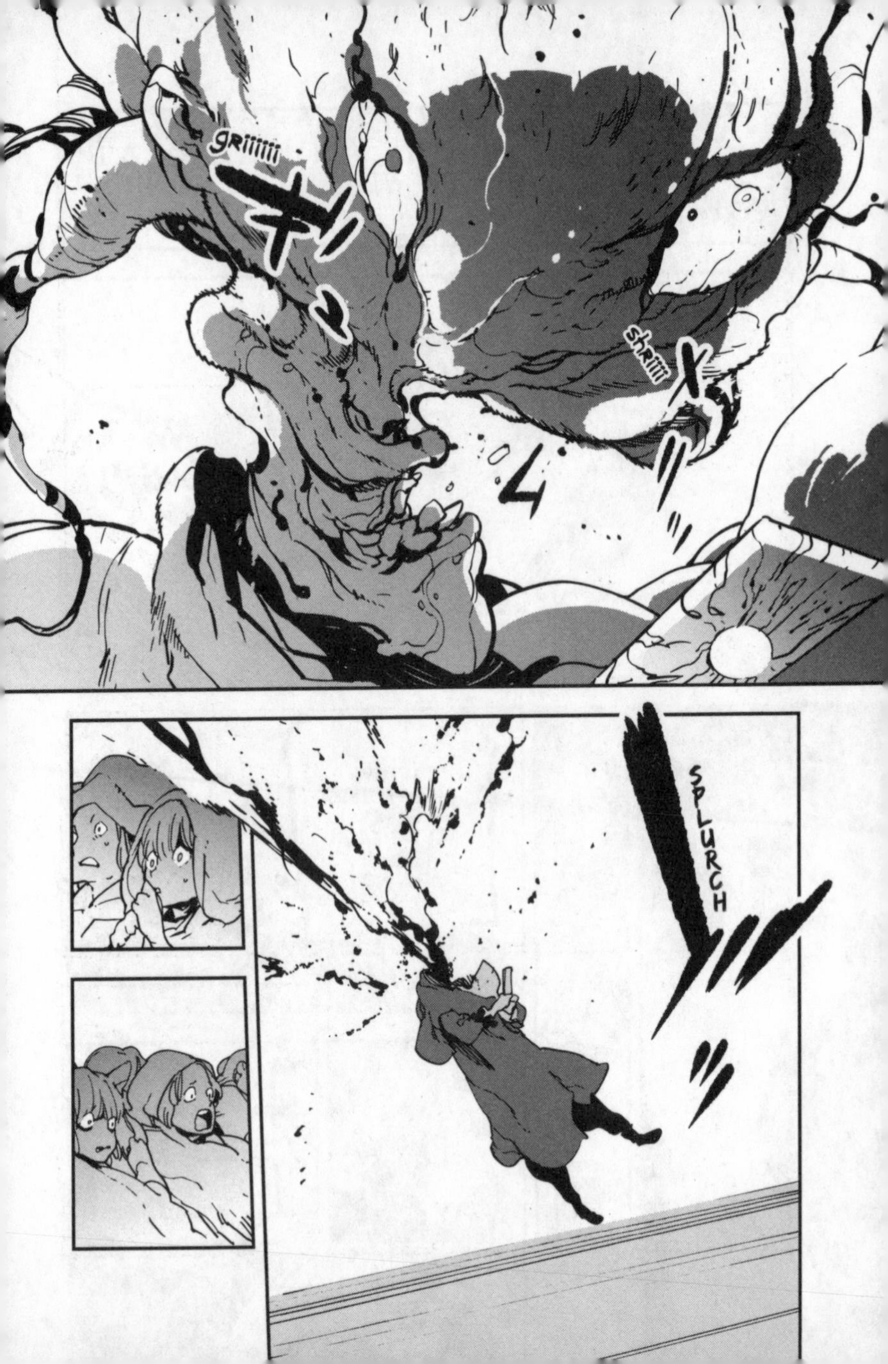
griiiiii
shriiiii
SPLURCH

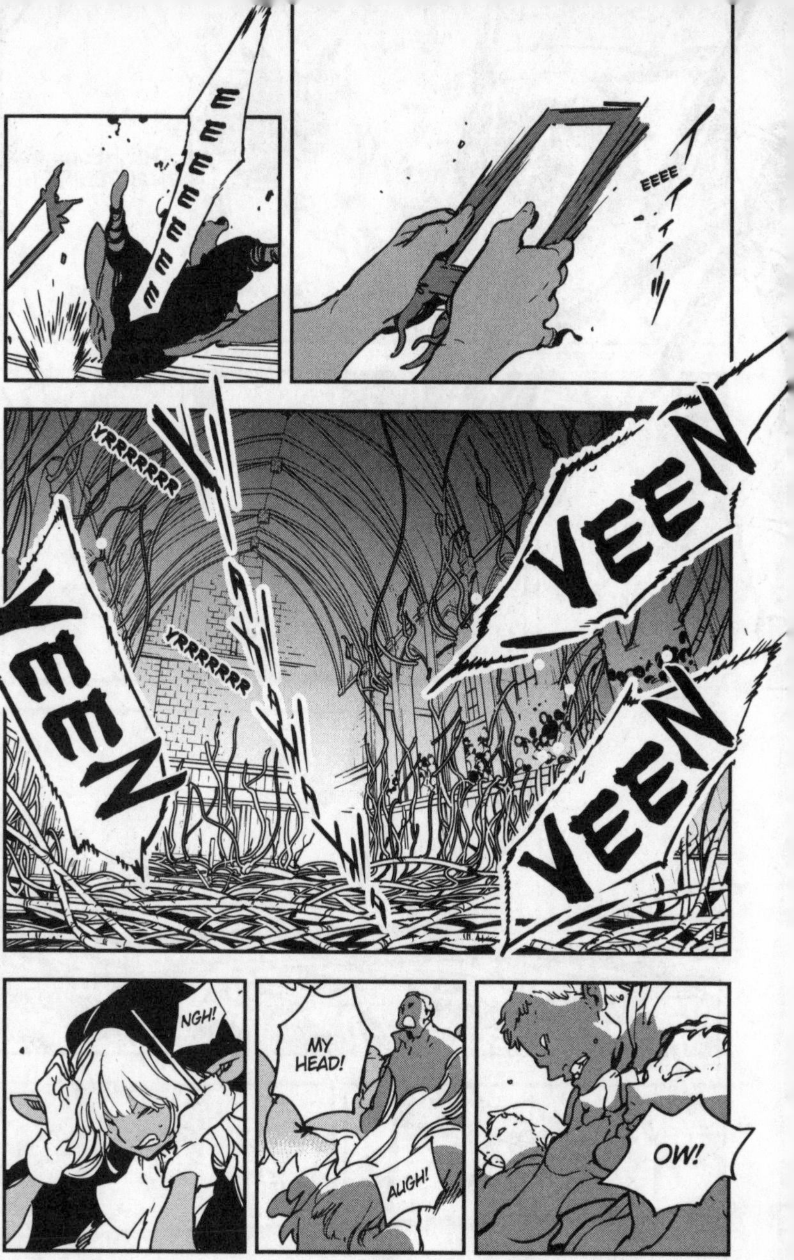
EEEE
EEEEEEE
VEEN
VEEN
YRRRRRRR
YRRRRRRR
VEEN
OW!
MY HEAD!
AUGH!
NGH!

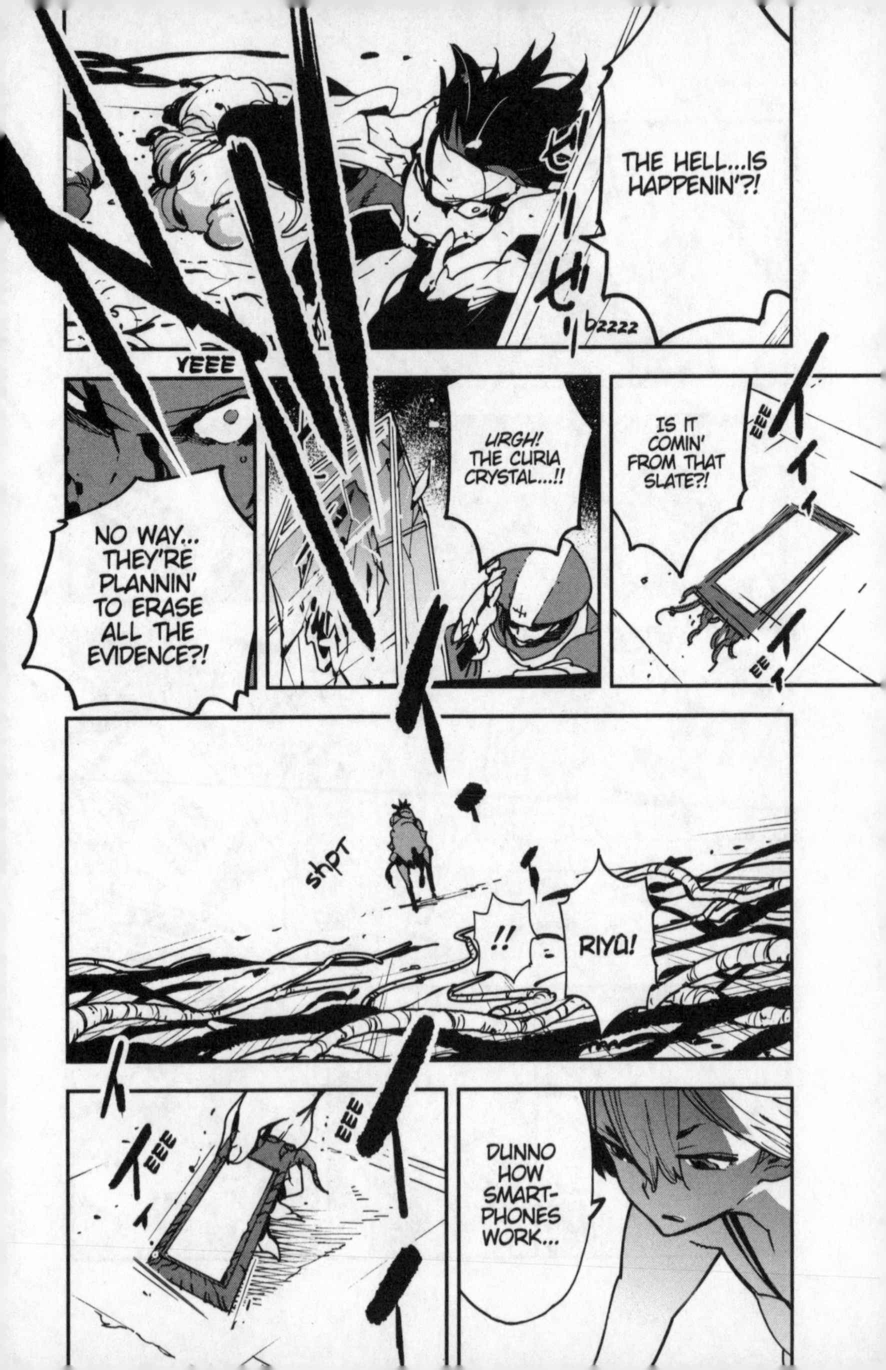
THE HELL...IS HAPPENIN'?!
bzzzz
IS IT COMIN' FROM THAT SLATE?!
EEE
EE
URGH! THE CURIA CRYSTAL...!!
YEEE
NO WAY... THEY'RE PLANNIN' TO ERASE ALL THE EVIDENCE?!
shpt
!!
RIYŪ!
DUNNO HOW SMART-PHONES WORK...
EEE
EEE

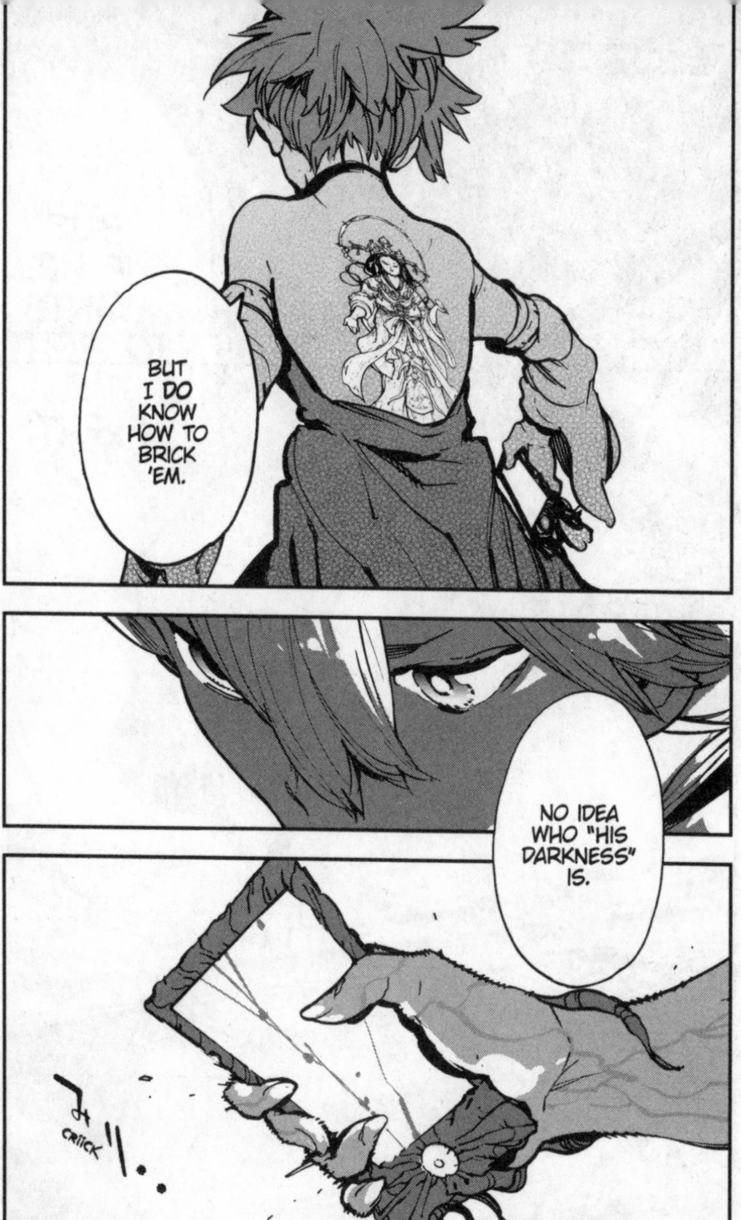
BUT I DO KNOW HOW TO BRICK 'EM.
NO IDEA WHO "HIS DARKNESS" IS.
CRIICK

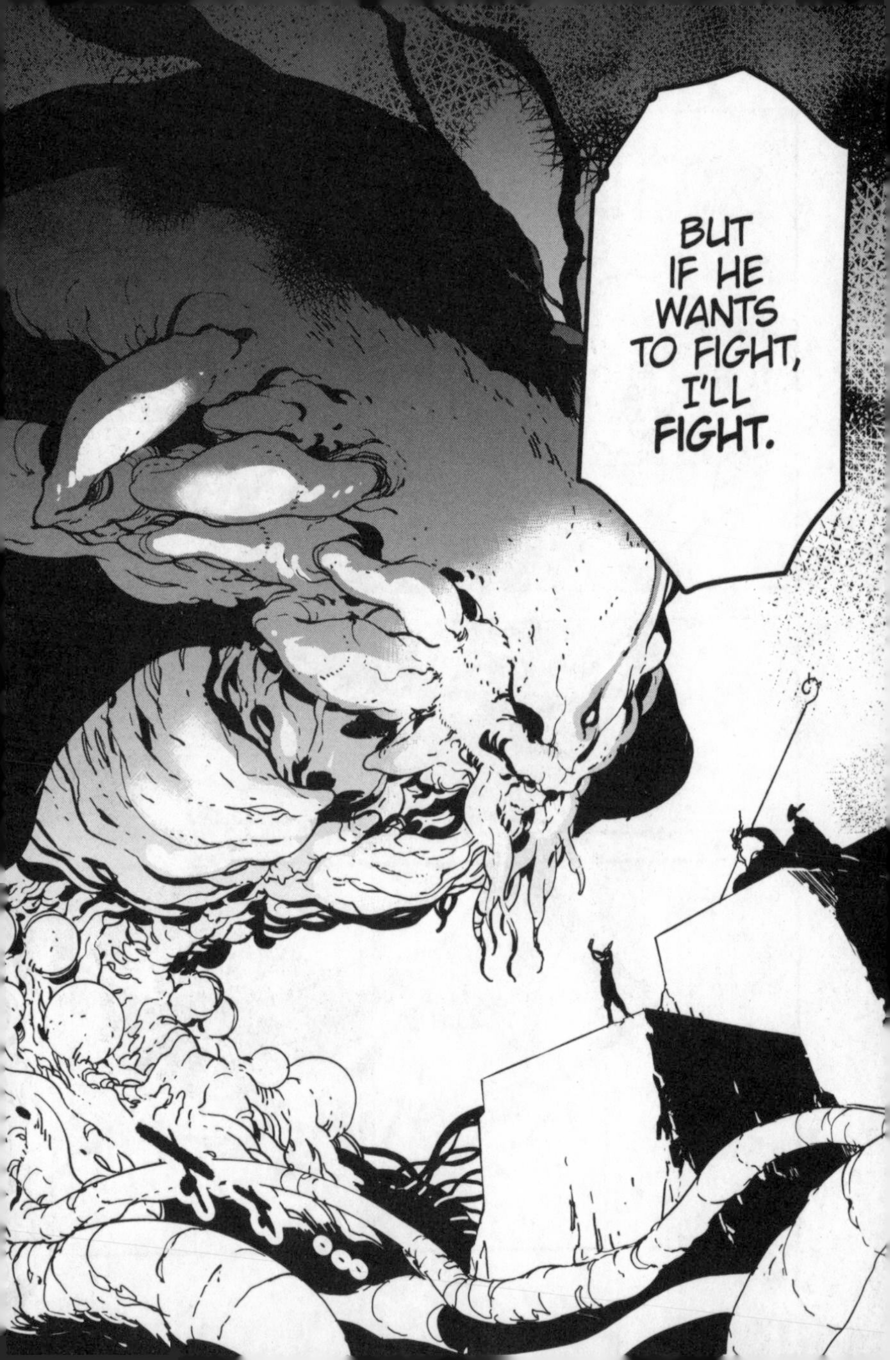
BUT IF HE WANTS TO FIGHT, I'LL FIGHT.

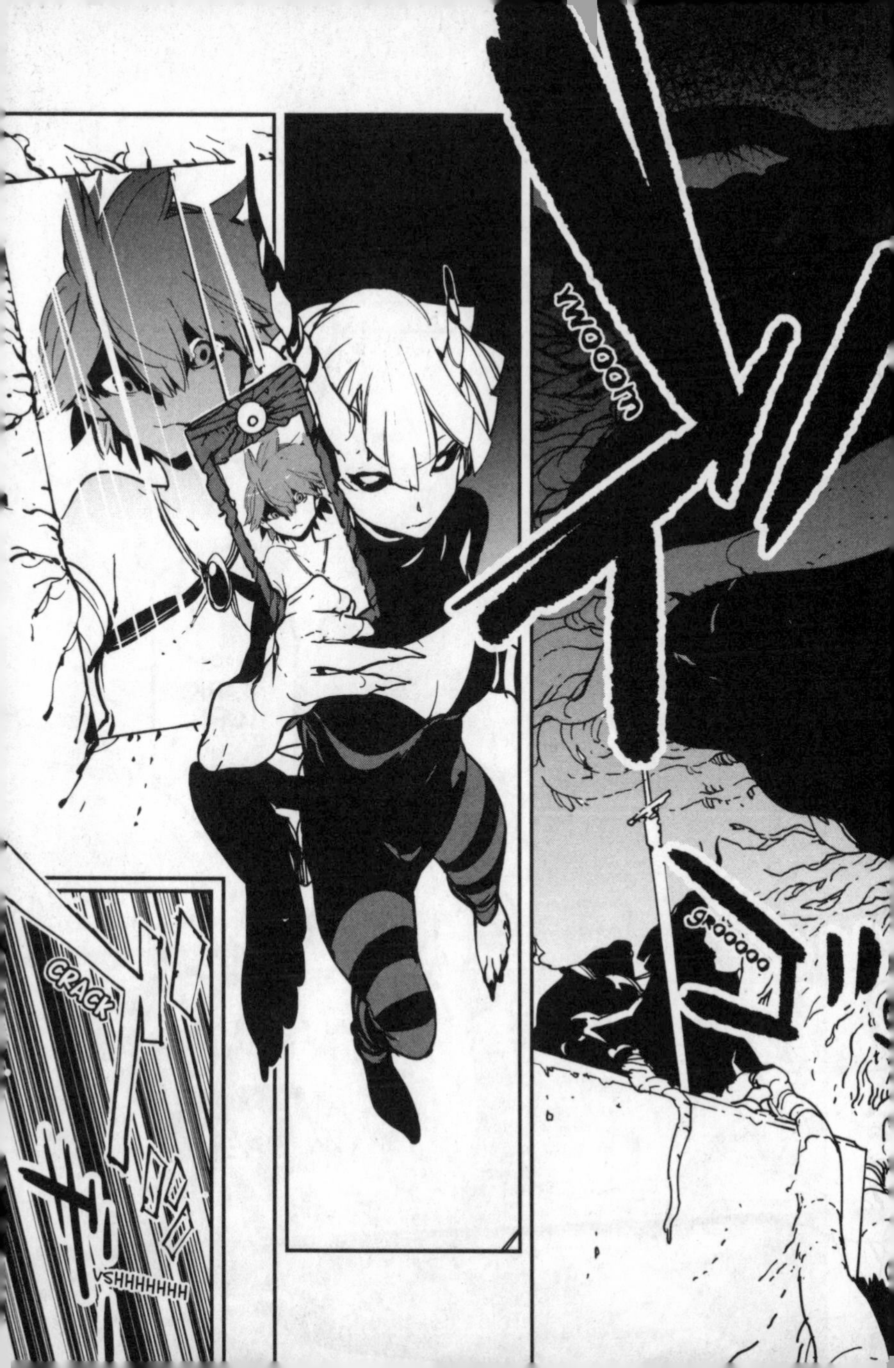
vwooom
grooooo
CRACK
vSHHHHHHH

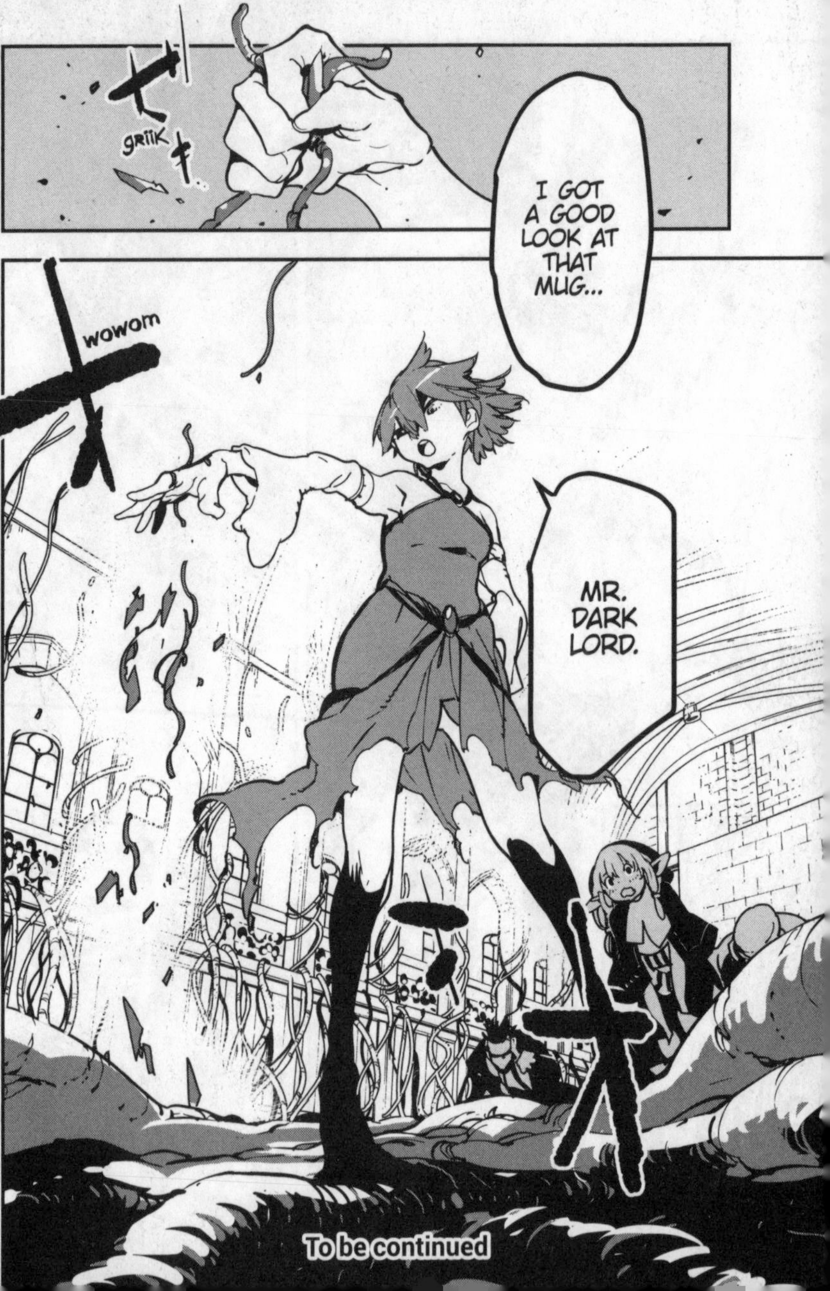
griik
I GOT A GOOD LOOK AT THAT MUG...
wowom
MR. DARK LORD.
To be continued

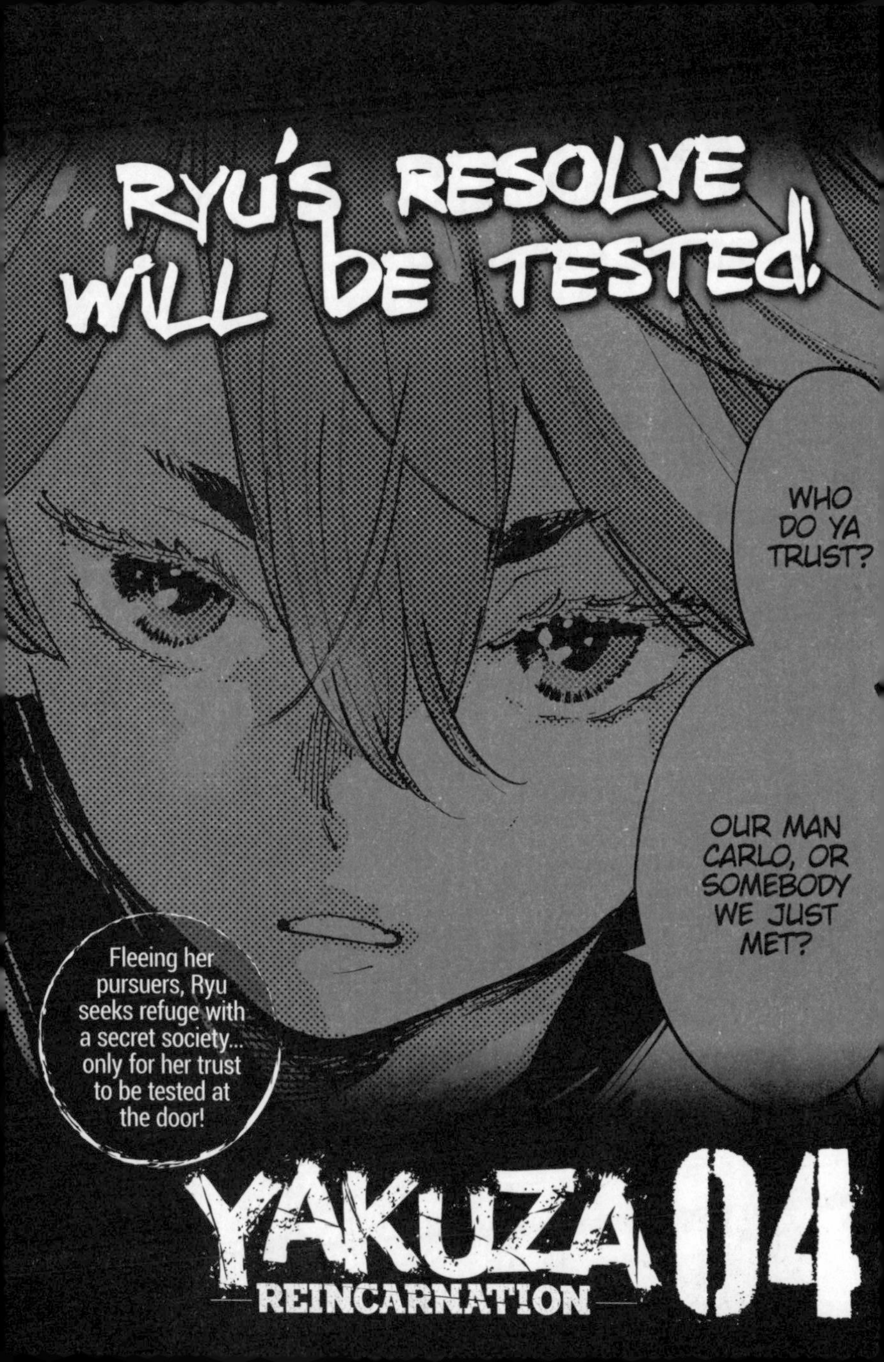
RYU'S RESOLVE WILL BE TESTED!
WHO DO YA TRUST?
OUR MAN CARLO, OR SOMEBODY WE JUST MET?
Fleeing her pursuers, Ryu seeks refuge with a secret society... only for her trust to be tested at the door!
YAKUZA REINCARNATION 04

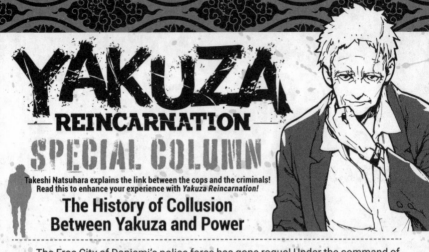

YAKUZA REINCARNATION

SPECIAL COLUMN

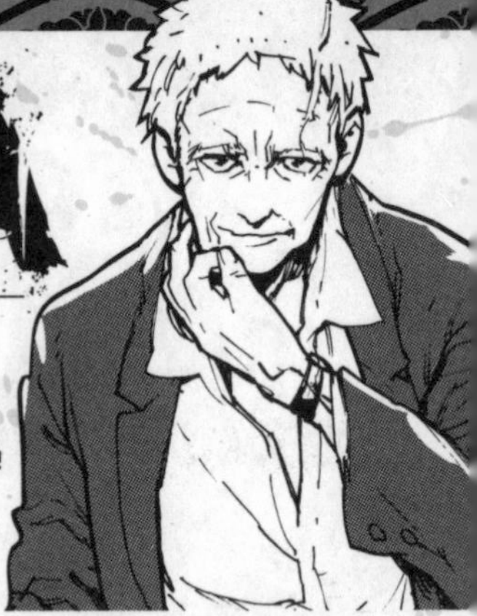

Takeshi Natsuhara explains the link between the cops and the criminals! Read this to enhance your experience with *Yakuza Reincarnation!*

The History of Collusion Between Yakuza and Power

The Free City of Daniemi's police force has gone rogue! Under the command of a corrupt leader, the Watch has become a mercenary band of thugs and enforcers for the top echelons of power. It's a sad state of affairs, but this sort of collusion is reality all over the world. In Japan, the yakuza and the government remained in bed until well after the war. The phrase "wearing two hats" (which some might be familiar with from *jidaigeki* period dramas) describes this phenomenon. Groups of *bakuto* gamblers often wielded *jitte*, a weapon synonymous with police in the Edo period (and did their dirty work too). It was even worse in the demesne, where local yakuza were under direct control of the shogunate or one of their *hatamoto* vassals. These landlords essentially used the yakuza as agents of violence and chaos to rule over the peasants.

The collusion persisted through the Meiji Restoration (1869-1889), with politicians tapping *oyabun* yakuza bosses to help beef up the fledgling modern police department. The relationship between crime and police deepened during the Showa period (1926-1989), with the rise of right-wing ethno-nationalism and military espionage. Yakuza helped keep the civilians in check, being mobilized for tasks such as supervising labor on construction sites, as depicted in the film *Shura no Mure*.

Japan went through major upheavals after World War II, but this shadowy connection didn't go along with it. The black market was a powerful force in post-war Japan, where social disorder was rampant and access to American military and consumer goods was already changing the culture. The black market itself was run by the yakuza. Police and politicians wagged their finger, but gave tacit approval behind closed doors, as they viewed the market necessary to maintaining public order. However, it's possible the government simply didn't have reach to keep the yakuza in line.

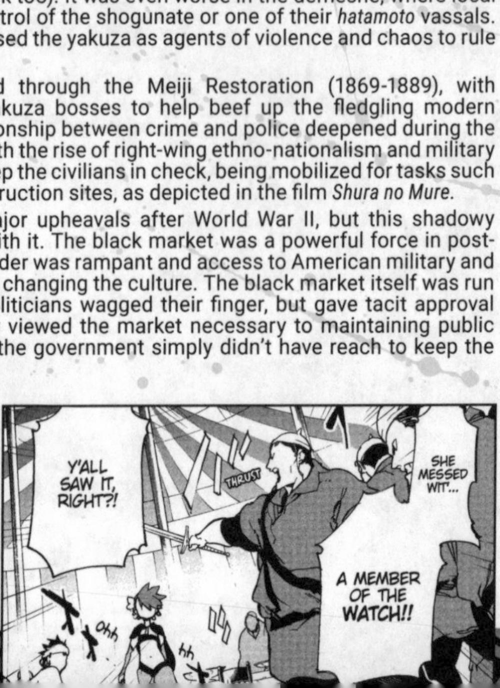
SHE MESSED WIT'...
THRUST
Y'ALL SAW IT, RIGHT?!
A MEMBER OF THE WATCH!!
Ohh
hh

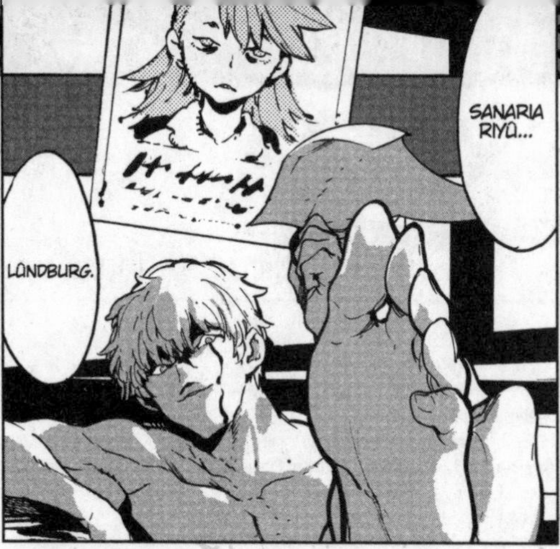
SANARIA RIYO...
LANDBURG.

Thanks to the alternative market, yakuza groups steadily grew in power and size. Yakuza even started getting elected to city or prefectural councils, like the Italian mafia. The infiltration was so intense in Italy that when they did a crackdown on mafiosos, members of parliament were arrested.

Though it never got that deep in Japan, there are a few incidents symbolic of how tight the relationship between yakuza and power was. In 1951, Minister of Justice Tokutaro Kimura proposed the formation of a 200,000-strong "Anti-Communist Drawn-Sword Regiment" composed of *bakuto, tekiya* and *gurentai* hooligans from all over the nation. Kimura was a lawyer, but he was also fiercely anti-communist and a key figure in Reverse Course remilitarization policies.

Another was when a third-generation Yamaguchi-gumi boss became honorary chief of police for a day as a token of honor from his local station. It's odd that this is so unremarked upon, considering all the drama surrounding modern yakuza involvement in the entertainment industry. It was only after the economic miracle turned Japan into an affluent modern nation that the relationship between the government and yakuza really changed. Police stations became more organized, and the parliament filled with bureaucrats. It was a man from the ministry of foreign affairs, Prime Minister Shigeru Yoshida, who shut down the Anti-Communist Drawn-Sword Regiment proposal. The yakuza still had friends amongst the self-made businessmen of the Liberal Democratic Party, but the bureaucrats wouldn't trust them.

And so the storied relationship between yakuza and law enforcement faded away. Today, there are strict laws against organized crime. Modern countermeasures even gutted operations of the Police Bureau's fourth investigation division, which once maintained a network of moles and contacts that worked closely with the yakuza. Today, it's difficult for the police to obtain information from criminal organizations.

Maybe for the best, since there's nothing scarier than an unaccountable group with links to institutional authority, like the police.

–Written by Takeshi Natsuhara

SEVEN SEAS ENTERTAINMENT PRESENTS

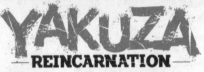

YAKUZA REINCARNATION

story by TAKESHI NATSUHARA art by HIROKI MIYASHITA VOLUME 3

TRANSLATION
Giuseppe di Martino

ADAPTATION
Jennifer Geisbrecht

LETTERING
Carl Vanstiphout

ORIGINAL COVER DESIGN
Masato Ishizawa
+ Bay Bridge Studio

COVER DESIGN
H. Qi

PROOFREADER
Kurestin Armada

SENIOR COPY EDITOR
Dawn Davis

EDITOR
K. McDonald

PRODUCTION DESIGNER
Christina McKenzie

PRODUCTION MANAGER
Lissa Pattillo

PREPRESS TECHNICIAN
Jules Valera

PRINT MANAGER
Rhiannon Rasmussen-Silverstein

EDITOR-IN-CHIEF
Julie Davis

ASSOCIATE PUBLISHER
Adam Arnold

PUBLISHER
Jason DeAngelis

Seven Seas press and purchase enquiries can be sent to Marketing Manager Lianne Sentar at press@gomanga.com. Information regarding the distribution and purchase of digital editions is available from Digital Manager CK Russell at digital@gomanga.com.

ISBN: 978-1-63858-671-5
Printed in Canada
First Printing: September 2022
10 9 8 7 6 5 4 3 2 1

READING DIRECTIONS

This book reads from ***right to left***, Japanese style. If this is your first time reading manga, you start reading from the top right panel on each page and take it from there. If you get lost, just follow the numbered diagram here. It may seem backwards at first, but you'll get the hang of it! Have fun!!

1
2
3
4
5
6
7
8
9

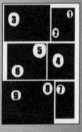

Follow us online: www.SevenSeasEntertainment.com